BIRDS

Homeopathic Remedies
from the Avian Realm

Copyright 2004 Homeopathy West. All rights reserved.

ISBN 0-975-4763-0-0

Homeopathy West
1442A Walnut Street #138
Berkeley, California 94707
USA

www.HomeopathyWest.com

Book and cover design: Sharon Skolnick Design • www.visigraf.com
Graphic arts production: Acme Graphics • www.acmegfx.com

Hawk illustration page 56 courtesy Roger Hall • www.inkart.net

BIRDS

Homeopathic Remedies from the Avian Realm

Jonathan Shore, MD

Judy Schriebman

Anneke Hogeland

HOMEOPATHY WEST

PREFACE

To capture birds in print is a task that turned out to be quite difficult. As soon as an essence of bird is put into final word form, the feeling comes up that we have lost that which makes it vital and living. Birds are about movement, fluidity and freedom. Words are black fixed images on white paper. When reading these captured images, please allow yourself the freedom to fly with the material into the wide-open skies or dive deep into the water to meet the spirit of these creatures.

Judy and Anneke

ACKNOWLEDGMENTS

We wish to acknowledge everyone who has made contributions to the knowledge gathered in this book. Specifically we thank Kara Adanalian, Greg Bedayn, Mariette Bernstein, Doug Brown, Divya Chabra, Eveline Franken, Peter Fraser, Jessica Jackson, Barbara Milisits, Roger Morrison, Eileen Nauman, Misha Norland, Marguerite Pelten, Todd Rowe, Jan Scholten, Elizabeth Schulz, Jeremy and Camilla Sherr and Alize Timmerman. Special thanks to our proofreaders: Deborah Gordon, Linda Corenthal, Harriet Gershaw and Annie Susnow. Any mistakes still remaining are wholly ours. Thanks to our layout artists Sharon Skolnick and Kara Adanalian, who made the book beautiful. Very special thanks to our indexer Kathrin Unger. ReferenceWorks has been our invaluable tool: thank you David Warkentin for this awesome software. And a very special thanks to Maribeth Thompson and to every member of the Larkspur Landing Proving Group and Michael Quinn at the Hahnemann Pharmacy of San Rafael for their participation and support of the provings.

FOREWORD

In *Clarke's Dictionary* we find 997 remedies listed. Of these, 589 are from plants, 300 are from minerals and 82 are from animals. In the 1990's, this disproportionate distribution of remedies was noticed as a potential problem by Sankaran, Herrick, Sherr and many others. Great attention began to be placed upon various groups of animals to try to elucidate where our paucity of animal provings should be corrected. Great credit belongs to Jonathan Shore and his colleagues for recognizing that of all the neglected animal groups, the birds had been the most completely ignored. In the present work, 16 bird remedies are discussed, correcting the absence of avian species from our *Materia Medica*. Even more impressive is the fact that the authors are not presenting merely preliminary data. *BIRDS: Homeopathic Remedies from the Avian Realm* takes a giant step toward elucidating the nature of this family of remedies, complete with detailed prescribing tips. The homeopathic profession will long remember this contribution.

Having witnessed first-hand Jonathan Shore's ongoing discoveries into the nature of patients who require bird remedies, I am delighted to make some opening remarks in this book. Jonathan, together with Anneke Hogeland and Judy Schriebman, has brought into being a new class of remedies. This was accomplished first through a series of preliminary provings, then later through the study of natural history and, most importantly, through carefully documented cured cases.

I am certain that every homeopath who tests without prejudice the information and guidelines given here will be satisfied with the results. Clinical results speak more eloquently than words.

In addition to bringing invaluable knowledge to the homeopathic community, the authors have created a template for future homeopathic texts. Homeopathic books should pass one simple test before being written. The prospective author should ask, "Is this a book which I would find an indispensable addition to my practice?" *BIRDS: Homeopathic Remedies from the*

Avian Realm meets and surpasses this test. What makes this book even more admirable is that the authors have aimed it directly at the needs of the practitioner. It is practical and to the point, filled with pearls based upon clinical experience. Following the injunctions of the first aphorism, the authors spend far less time discussing their methodology than in giving concrete prescribing points. The homeopathic community will reward the authors with the highest form of praise: cures of patients who, without this book, would have continued to suffer.

Roger Morrison

Dedicated to all bird beings.

FALCON FREEDOM

I'm a bird locked away,
I'm a bird who wants to play,
I want to speed among the air,
I want to be freed among the land,

Can I be free?
Can I once again soar through the air?
Can I stray again please?
Can I divide the air again?

I want to soar through the land,
I want the air to hit my face again,
I want to dive down and strike prey,
I want freedom!

> Poem written by a 10-yr-old boy
> after receiving *Falco-p*

Contents

Preface	4
Acknowledgements	4
Foreword	5
INTRODUCTION	13
BIRD CHARACTERISTICS	20
Bird Mind	21
Physiognomy and Physiology	23
Additional Notes	27
AVIAN REALM	
Bird Morphology	31
Bird Facts	31
A Quick Guide to Scientific Nomenclature	32
KEY FEATURES	
Brown Pelican	34
Scarlet Macaw	42
Ring Dove/Woodpigeon	50
Red-Tailed Hawk	56
Great Horned Owl	66
Great Blue Heron	76
Bald Eagle	88
Raven	98
Peregrine Falcon	110
Saker Falcon	110
Turkey Vulture	124
Andean Condor	134
Humboldt Penguin	140
Swan	146
Wandering Albatross	154
PROVINGS	
Introduction to Provings	163
Brown Pelican	172
Scarlet Macaw	191

Ring Dove (Woodpigeon)   199
Red-Tailed Hawk   202
Great Horned Owl   223
Great Blue Heron   227
Bald Eagle   251
Raven   253
Peregrine Falcon   277
Saker Falcon   281
Turkey Vulture   285
Andean Condor   291
Humboldt Penguin   296
Whooper Swan   298
Mute Swan   301
Wandering Albatross   303

CASES

Brown Pelican   310
Scarlet Macaw   320
Ring Dove (Woodpigeon)   337
Red-Tailed Hawk   349
Bald Eagle   368
Raven   390
Peregrine Falcon   402
Turkey Vulture   428
Andean Condor   431
Humboldt Penguin   452
Whooper Swan   458
Mute Swan   463
Wandering Albatross   464
Tuberculinum aviaire   466

About the Authors   474
Bibliography   476
Appendix   478
Index   486

BOOK OUTLINE

INTRODUCTION
An overview of the bird kingdom. This includes bird characteristics, general bird notes and a brief guide to bird nomenclature.

KEY FEATURES
The key points that emphasize the central characteristics of each bird and what makes it unique. It includes natural history and any important mythology and symbolism that shed light on the remedy. This part includes a section of prominent rubrics specific to the bird.

PROVINGS
The actual material of the provings is given; trituration, journal entries, dreams, experiences and physical sensations. This allows for more in depth study of the provers' own language so that it can be seen how core ideas and key aspects have been extracted.

CASES
A selection of edited cases to illustrate how the remedy shows up in practice.

> It is our hope that this format will permit the reader in the first instance to easily recognize when a patient needs a bird remedy, and in the second instance, to do a thorough differential analysis to find the specific bird.

INTRODUCTION

"Do you hear that bird?" asked Dan. I told him I did.
"Do you know what he is saying?"
"I don't speak 'bird'," I answered.
"You should," he twinkled. "Learn a lot. The birds are
'two-leggeds' like us. They are very close to us."
    from *Neither Wolf nor Dog: On Forgotten Roads with an Indian Elder*,
    Kent Nerburn, New World Library, Novato, CA 1994

The intent of this book is to bring together the currently available information on this group of remedies in a form which will facilitate both a good grasp of the characteristics of the group as a whole and the ability to focus down simply upon its individual members. Thus emphasis is placed not upon the small details but is rather weighted between the generals and the particular individualizing characteristics of each remedy. Although the body of knowledge in relation to these remedies is still in the early stages of development I believe we have sufficient data to paint pictures that are accurate in their broad outlines.

Why Birds?

My first bird prescription came about in this way: for some 3 or 4 years I had treated a young woman, initially with *Cann-i* and then with *Natrum phosphoricum*. Although the remedies acted well she continued to return with the same complaints. During these years she would tell me of her recurrent dreams of collecting feathers and using them to build a pair of wings. Not having any repertorial references or any satisfactory basis for homeopathic interpretation this data played no part in the choice of remedy. With the passage of time and the influence of Rajan Sankaran, the possibilities of what may or may not be useful information for prescribing took on a new life and the idea of bird entered my mind.

Certain events assume a life of their own, having a potential way beyond our immediate understanding. The next time I saw her she reported a detailed and vivid dream of an eagle. The only bird remedy available at

Introduction

that time was Eagle (*Haliaeetus leucocephalus* 30C), it having been recently proven by Jeremy Sherr. The clarity, depth and duration of the response affirmed the correctness of the choice. At this same time one of the students at the Hahnemann College needed to complete an original research project as part of the course requirement. At my suggestion she chose a bird (a red-tailed hawk) for a proving. This remedy was proven both in the classical way by her as well as in the form of seminar provings in Finland and Germany by myself. The collected data was quite extensive and reliably uniform between the American and European experience despite the diversity of methodology.

In regards to the provings, my study at that time was focused on the passage of remedy information and energies between people in groups, and only incidentally on birds.

However, for whatever reason, people began to send me bird feathers, which, somewhat like the original bird dreams, I filed away in some drawer. While struggling with another case I chanced to look at one of the feathers labeled Scarlet Macaw. It was so beautiful I looked this bird up on the Internet and realized this was the remedy for the case at hand. The non-existence of the needed remedy opened a new phase of proving experimentation. It was necessary to make it from scratch and this presented an opportunity for a different kind of proving; one in which the proving and the making of the remedy were the same event. The impact of this experiment on all the participants was profound and changed my attitude toward proving procedure in a fundamental way.

After completing these provings of two quite different birds, Hawk and Macaw, I was struck by the commonality of certain symptoms. In the first proving, the hawk, a notable symptom was stabbing, stitching pain in the eye. At the time the obvious explanation was derived from the fact that the bird was blind in one eye, most likely having been injured by a sharp twig. The appearance of these same symptoms in the second bird proving, the Macaw, threw the initial explanation into question (and in fact raised doubts about the explanations we make up for proving symptoms in general). Another common symptom in these two provings was pain in the extremities, especially the hip and shoulder. This brought to mind the Eagle proving conducted by Jeremy Sherr, wherein he had concluded that the symptoms of pain in the shoulder and upper limb were caused by the fact that that particular bird had broken its right wing. In fact all three birds had in common: stitching, stabbing pains in the eye, as well as a significant emphasis on pain in the extremities. The recurrence of these specific symptoms in completely different birds was a great surprise, which can best be explained by their being symptoms common to all birds, an explanation indeed borne out by later bird provings. (These facts, combined with an incident from the seminar proving of the hawk, where the main prover had a dream of being connected by a leather thong to a gloved hand, have brought about a much wider perspective in the interpretation of proving symptoms).

Subsequent provings of Owl, Pelican, Penguin and Heron along with a review of the work of others such as Greg Bedayn (Raven), Misha Norland (Falcon), Jeremy Sherr (Eagle), Todd Rowe (Vulture), and Elisabeth Schulz (Dove, Falcon, Condor) confirmed the idea that most of the symptoms arising in these provings were **common bird symptoms**. That is to say, they belonged to the general family of birds, and only a small number (10 – 15%) of the symptoms were directly connected to the nature of the specific remedy. Whether this applies to other groupings or not I cannot say for sure at this point (although among the snakes the evidence is pretty compelling), but within the realm of the birds it is definite.

Whatever has been conjectured in the past and whatever debate occurs in the present as to the existence or nonexistence of kingdom and family classifications, the data presented in this book sets a precedent for the reality of at least one significant family group: the birds. The individualization of a remedy can take place within a field much more limited than the totality of the known Materia Medica. The recognition of this situation allows for a much clearer extraction of the central feature or essence from proving data in addition to bringing into the consciousness of the prescriber the idea of bird long before the individual bird itself is identified.

Introduction

Statistics

Over a 10-year period from 1985 through 1995 I kept a record of all prescriptions that I considered had brought about a definite amelioration in the case. These amounted to some 1150 prescriptions. My statistics for the top 10 remedies compared almost identically to records kept by the Hahnemann Pharmacy of all prescriptions filled during the same time period. The remedies were widely spread throughout the Materia Medica; the most common being *Sulphur*, constituting just under 6% of all prescriptions. The Kali salts as a group, all taken together, formed 3% of the total. If at that time I had prescribed as many bird remedies as I have during the past 7 or 8 years, birds as a group would weigh in at a little over 1.25%, as compared to spiders at 1%. Although these are not precise statistics, they do give a sense that birds as a group should be somewhere in the median range of prescribed remedies.

Are New Remedies Needed?

While an ongoing growth of detail and complexity is the result of a creative process, it is by no means evidence of evolution or of a movement towards a unified understanding. Life around us is becoming increasingly complex. We are exposed to influences and pressures that were unimagined a few 100 years ago.

Any discipline, any practice, any living process has no choice but to fall under the influence of the age in which it lives. Thus if the science of Homeopathic Medicine is to live, it must also correspond to the world around it. Now I am not suggesting that it become other than what it is. There is no inherent demand to step outside itself and take on characteristics of another discipline, i.e., become closer or more acceptable to allopathic medicine or any other science. The only and unavoidable demand of life is for it to respond to the 'spirit' or moving force of the time.

In the realm of human life we can see clearly the multiplication of facts, of information, and the demand on our minds to grasp, sort and integrate all this new data from telephones to computers. Some resist this and call it bad, others enthusiastically embrace it as the good, and between the two camps there is ongoing struggle. In homeopathy we have experienced an immense growth of information. Much has been added to 'old' remedies and so many 'new' ones are described that computer databases are almost essential to store and organize this data. Thus we have added new information about already existing remedies and new information about new topics simply as a response to the demands of the time.

There exists another demand, simultaneous but not inevitable: a demand to unify all this data, to enfold this complexity in a movement back towards the simple underlying principles of all life, so that our perceptions and understanding may penetrate ever more deeply to the heart of things.

In this work we have attempted to document the results of these two movements; the natural outgrowth of a creative engagement with the world around us and an attempt to unify the resulting data so that it leads us back to the source, to the experience of the mystery of life.

Nature, Essence and the Vital Force

In the 1970's and 1980's, with the revival of homeopathy, George Vithoulkas reintroduced the concepts of essence and of vital force. These were, right at the outset, of great value as abstract intellectual concepts, as opposed to living experiences. That is to say, the time required between the grasping of an idea by the mind and its assimilation or transmutation into a direct experience of the organism, as a whole spans many years of effort.

We are still far from a direct experience of the essence of things, "that by which a thing is what it is," but are in fact beginning to approach a feeling for the transformation and expressions of the vital force.

The descent of undifferentiated life energy into matter is a complex process which may be crudely visualized as follows: if life is to take on the form of a tree, it must first take on the form or materiality of all trees, then enter into the form of a certain class of trees, say Conifers, then more specifically a Sequoia and finally manifesting as this or that individual Redwood. This process holds for all forms of matter: minerals, plants or animals.

Introduction

Thus any remedy must in its nature express all these levels of differentiation. This can be clearly seen in the Bird remedies, which express primarily the particular or specific characteristics of birds as a group and then in more precise and differentiated detail the uniqueness of their particular family. Thus it will be seen from the proving data that the majority of symptoms in any one proving are those which are **common to all bird provings**, and only a much smaller number are those which express the individuality or distinguishing characteristics of the family or bird.

There are two main points which arise from the above discussion. One is the importance of a careful study of the natural history of our remedies. The other is the potential value of family groupings as an aid to remedy identification.

Value of Family Grouping

When much time has passed in the use of a certain remedy it can be perceived directly.

The remedy is known and thus can be recognized when it comes before us. Prior to this stage of familiarity it can be very helpful in the analytic process to be able to identify the broad grouping of which it is a member. For example, on listening to the case we begin to sense that the vital force expresses itself first through the animal, and more specifically through the bird realm. Now when the feeling for bird is present, when the evidence or data in the case begins to take on the shape of bird, then even if the remedy is scarcely known, the number of substances to be researched and studied becomes manageable.

Jonathan Shore, MD

BIRD CHARACTERISTICS

> It cannot be emphasized strongly enough that the characteristics presented in this section are common to all bird remedies.

The following elements will be seen to a greater or lesser extent in almost every careful anamnesis. The degree to which any combination of symptoms is most prominent, the center of the case, will determine exactly which remedy is chosen. How one remedy differs from another, in the emphasis of its central characteristics, will be the focus of the later sections on the individual birds. This is simply a review of symptoms that express the picture of the family as a whole. The presence of any one or more of these common symptoms in a case must in no way be taken as an indication for any specific bird.

The second point which must be clearly understood is that while the general characteristics are derived from a large enough body of data to ensure their reliability, the individual images are still in their early stages of evolution and are thus incomplete and one sided. **This means that if the picture in the case corresponds to one of these images the remedy can be prescribed with a high degree of confidence. However, there will surely be occasions when a specific bird remedy is needed when the data of a case does not match the information we have.** It is only through continued experimentation, trial, error, success and failure that the various facets of each remedy will be revealed. It is clear that the process of sharing information from cases where newer remedies have acted in whole or in part is useful to bring the more complete remedy picture to the foreground.

BIRD MIND
CONCEPTUAL ORGANIZATION
Bird mind organizes itself around concepts, around ideas which allow for a dynamic shifting of emphasis, as opposed to classification, which

Bird Characteristics

is the hallmark of the mineral kingdom, as seen in the Periodic Table where everything has its own box, its own immutable place.

In animal mind the story comes out in an easily comprehensible sequential manner, well ordered for the sequences of events, rather than for the exact details of the event. The ability to take large amounts of apparently unrelated data and synthesize it down to its essential components has been observed in such disparate remedies as Macaw and Falcon.

A SENSE OF IMPARTIAL DETACHMENT
This may be related to a state reported in the provings as that of an observer, a 'fly on the wall,' or in the words of Sherr's Eagle proving **'the witness beyond good and bad.'**

INTUITION OR NATURAL KNOWING
The ability to stand outside the self came through in the provings in another form as well. It was as if the mind could not function in its usual way. Provers were unable to focus on and recollect information in the ordinary manner, yet their thoughts were informed by real knowledge, a knowing arising from some deeper place.

This inner clarity gives a confidence, a sense of the rightness, a sense of ease and naturalness of action.

> The negative side to this change in the function of the thought process gives rise to an inability to focus the attention, making it difficult to concentrate or to find the words needed to express or describe the inner experience.

SENSATION AS IF DRUGGED
DISORIENTED IN BOTH TIME AND SPACE
Provers made mistakes in giving and taking directions, they got lost and took wrong turns. They made mistakes in the choice of words, often calling things by the wrong names. There was a marked inability to add or calculate.

SPIRITUAL AWARENESS
A strong sense of spirituality is often present in the case, appropriate to the connection between air, breath and spirit. This search for spirituality is a unifying expression of many bird characteristics, including the need for freedom, the deeply experienced intuition and the sense of the rightness of things.

EMPATHY
This may not be the exact word but it is close. Birds are very related on an interpersonal level. They are connected through feeling to each other and to the larger group or family. They are by nature family oriented, caring, protective and helpful. This feeling sense, coupled with an impartial attitude and spiritual awareness, leads to a significant involvement in the healing professions. A high percentage of cases are to be found in therapists, social workers, massage practitioners, or simply in people whose jobs are directly concerned with public good.

RELATIONSHIP
An interesting distinction can be made here between those birds that live in large flocks such as Macaw or Pelican and those whose time is spent in a more nuclear family setting like Eagle and Hawk. The concerns of the former revolve around their relationship to the group or society while in the latter the emphasis is found in individual relationships. The central themes of Macaw and Pelican are those of connection/separation and issues around their role in the community. By contrast in Hawk we find the desire to be alone, the desire for understanding from individual family members, as well as the fear of or sense of abandonment.

FREEDOM AND TRAVEL
The gift of flight grants such freedom that birds are the world's greatest travelers. Many travel thousands of miles in their seasonal migrations. Some species migrate from North Pole to South Pole and back again every year. Thus the desire for freedom and the urge to travel constitute an integral part of bird nature. Many bird people are cosmopolitan, sophisticated and have explored a wide variety of countries and/or occu-

Bird Characteristics

pations. In clinical cases the use of the word freedom and the love of travel is often observed and should bring this class of remedies to the mind of the practitioner.

PERFECTIONISM
This trait, although more prominent in some birds than in others, appears to run through all the species. Expressed most clearly as the 'urge to get it right' rather than a true fastidiousness, it forms a network of symptoms along with pride, humiliation, guilt and shame. Thus far it is only the Dove that exhibits guilt and shame as a central feature, but all birds have it to some degree. Although pride is quite common, it is understated and does not lead to a true haughtiness.

PHYSIOGNOMY AND PHYSIOLOGY

Relative to humans, birds have **a very light bone structure, a much higher metabolic rate and a different way of handling fluid balance**. The ramifications of these features will be evident in the symptomatology outlined below. Although diathesis finds its place only among the confirmatory symptoms and should not be used to exclude a remedy, there are classical features that appear in archetypal cases. In these cases, the people are **fine featured, delicate, light boned**. The **eyes of the Eagle** are large, clear and penetrating.

Careful observation will reveal the 'claw sign.' A claw-like movement of the hand and fingers, as if grasping for something, especially at those times when the patient is expressing a feeling of 'I want.'

GENERALITIES
The feeling of the case is one of a **delicate vibration; light yet intense**. This inner vibration (possibly the result of the increased metabolic rate) may be experienced by the patient as an inner buzzing or pulsation, which, if exaggerated, gives rise to a **nervous restlessness.** This restless-

ness does not arise from the muscles or peripheral nervous system but more centrally from an excessive and disharmonious movement of the inner energies. These do not circulate smoothly through their usual channels but get stuck, accumulate and are discharged either as **trembling, aimless restlessness** or as **irritability**. This excess may result from, and is certainly compounded by, a heightened level of sensory awareness. Visual impressions, sound and touch are experienced as overwhelming. People talking, the touch of a loved one, and stimulating environments, are all too much and create the desire for solitude. ?

Relative to humans, birds consume enormous quantities of food. To keep pace with our avian brothers and sisters it would be necessary to eat some 80 hamburgers at one meal. Thus it should come as no surprise that **disturbance of appetite** is a common component of the symptom picture, and can manifest all along the spectrum from lack of desire for food to sudden hunger and voracious appetite. Likewise there can be **great thirst** and **frequent, copious urination.**

Stabbing, stitching or lancinating pains are the most characteristic physical features occurring especially in the **eye, chest and abdomen.** The abdominal pains may be intestinal or menstrual and the latter especially may be very severe. Note that although these sharp pains occur also in the joints and muscles it is more characteristic to have **stiffness, tension and cramping** in the back and extremities.

Metabolically there is a **strong desire for open air** and they can be **warm blooded** or experience heat of single parts such as the feet.

HEAD

Headaches are common. At this time no particular modality or location has been established. Sensations of **fullness, pressure and heaviness** came through strongly in the provings. These are associated with an upward movement of energy and a sense of being somewhat outside or above oneself. Although not a true vertigo as in spinning, the sense of disorientation in space and time may be characterized as **vertigo as if floating.** The top of the head may feel open or lifted up.

Bird Characteristics

FACE, JAWS AND TEETH
Sensations of **pressure and sharp pains** in the zygomatic bones reminiscent of sinusitis are common. Similar pains in the lower jaw and many symptoms around the teeth are prominent, ranging from **pulsation in the gums**, through actual **toothaches**, to **delusions of weakness in the teeth** and **delusions of teeth softening** (strongly seen in water birds).

EYES AND EARS
The eyes proved to be an outstanding area for the concentration of symptoms. Both the tissues of the eye itself with **sharp, stabbing pains, irritation** and **dryness** as well as distortions of vision ranging from enhanced visual acuity through **hazy blurred vision** to **loss of peripheral vision, central scotoma** and **fear of blindness.**

    Pelican: Fear of going blind
    Heron: Vision blurred (strongest of all birds), central scotoma, great irritation, itching and tearing
    Owl: Issues with depth perception, the eyes function separately

The ears received less attention but came in for their share of **increased sensitivity to sound** and **stabbing pain.**

    Owl: Sensitivity to the human voice, to meaningless conversation

NOSE
Not much emphasis here. **Obstruction, coryza, sneezing,** which taken along with the dryness and irritation of the eyes, is suggestive of hay fever. **Epistaxis** occurred in the provings of Hawk, Pelican and Vulture.

THROAT
A distinction may be made between the water birds, such as Pelican, Heron and Swan, which swallow their food whole and have long gullets, versus other birds in which the gullet is less emphasized. In the former group many obstructive sensations are found: of a **lump** or **plug,** as if something **stuck, difficulty swallowing, constriction** and **tension** while the latter exhibit a more **inflammatory 'sore throat'** type picture.

STOMACH AND ABDOMEN/ FEMALE ORGANS
Although digestive symptoms are scattered through the provings they do not represent a very strong focus. There are often extreme changes in appetite as well as very specific food cravings. Nausea, tension and emptiness in the stomach. **Stabbing, cutting** abdominal pains arising both in the intestines and in the uterus and ovaries. **Severe dysmenorrhea.**

CHEST
The emphasis here is on the usual **sharp, stabbing pains**. In addition there is a sense of **constriction** or **tightness** with a **desire to breathe deeply**, as if one could not get enough air.

BACK AND EXTREMITIES
This is the central pathological focus. The neck is significantly represented. Although as always the pains can be sharp, here in the musculoskeletal system the emphasis is on **tension, stiffness, drawing** and **cramping. Tension** and **stiffness in the neck**, often extending to the shoulder or arm. As with the neck, the upper back or dorsal region exhibits similar muscular tensions.

Both the upper and lower limbs have many symptoms. Generally speaking the lower limbs are more heavily represented. The one notable exception to this has been the Owl with a strong concentration of head, neck and shoulder symptoms. **Severe shoulder pain.** Pain in elbow, wrist, hand and fingers. More significant than the distal pains, however, are the sensations of **heaviness, weakness, numbness and tingling.** These sensations are even more emphasized in the lower limbs. It goes without saying that the opposite is always true as well and thus **sensations of lightness** and **increased strength** and **mobility** may also be found.

Sciatica, **pain in the hip and knee. Clumsiness** and **awkwardness** of both the upper and lower extremities. Drops things, stumbling and bumping into furniture.

Bird Characteristics

ADDITIONAL NOTES

RISING ABOVE

Although this topic has already been mentioned it is so universal in the provings that it merits further elaboration. It is reasonable that, given the physical realm in which the birds move in relation to the earth and thus to us humans, a phenomenon of this nature might be expected. What is fascinating, however, is the manner and detail of its presentation. On the simplest level it is quite usual for provers to feel outside of and slightly above themselves. For example:

> MIND: Delusions, head, open, top of is (Pelican, Falcon)
> MIND: Consciousness expanding above him (Falcon)
> HEAD: Sensation of lid on vertex lifting off (Pelican)

In those with little experience in the sensing of energy movement in the body this can give rise to lightheadedness. On a deeper level this appears as an ability to stand outside of events, both with the mind which is able to observe without being caught up in all the subjective egoistic considerations of the moment, and with the feelings which can rise above the usual negativity associated with unfortunate events in our lives.

As the highest flyer, the Eagle produced these states most obviously and directly:

> "So you try and rise above your normal life, looking with objectivity from above. Like from the eyes of a bird."
> "To rise above negative feelings within you."
> "People put me down. I rise above negative feelings inside."

However, even in the low fliers such as the Raven this phenomenon appears:

> "It is 'reality' and then something clicks and you're back to real reality, so in a way it is as if I'm floating between two dimensions."
> "I'm on the divide between two worlds with decreased attachment to the physical world… it is something like being not 'in' this world as I used to be. It's a kind of clarity about other people's feelings."

This theme is repeated in many other birds:
> ✓ MIND: Delusions; separated; world, from the; in the present and simultaneously detached (Falcon)
> MIND: Separate, myself, ability to (Macaw)
> MIND: Observe, ability to, involved without being. (Macaw)
> MIND: Accept, things as they are (Macaw)
> MIND: Dreams; fly on the wall, as if (Macaw)

"There's an awesome silence and calmness that simply feels different. There is a kind of stability and calmness that I feel. My energy was really up, felt like a lot of extraneous stuff was cleared away......feeling of clarity, clear vision, freedom from worry even in these circumstances." (Pelican)
"It made me feel very calm and wise, but very detached at the same time...
I was observing my own life rather than living it, watching the world go by." (Owl)

DREAMS OF WATER

Water is a prominent dream element even among the land birds. This was expressed several times as the ability to breathe under water. *The Complete Millenium 2 Repertory*, which by no means contains all the birds, has this rubric:
> MIND: Dreams, water; waves; high, of (8): <u>all-c.</u>, bamb-a., corv-c., falco-p., germ., haliae-lc., lim-b-c., ozone.

Bubo-v. can be added to this rubric and *Buteo-j.* can definitely be added to dreams of water. The inclusion of 4 birds in a 9-remedy rubric is even more significant, as the provings were done by completely independent proving groups.

DOGS

The number of dreams involving dogs was another unanticipated aspect. It is an historical fact that Saker falcons, when hunting big game such as gazelle, work very closely with dogs, and Ravens have been known to cooperate closely with wolves. It is worth noting that both dogs and birds are used by humans when hunting to retrieve game.

Bird Characteristics

MUSIC
At this time the authors have no experience with a proving of a songbird. Although a relationship to music and song was anticipated it has not yet arisen in any of the provings done so far. Our clinical cases, however, have shown a significant numbers of musicians. A search for the words 'sing' and 'music' in the ReferenceWorks® database reveals the following rubrics (limited to birds alone).

Sing (132): *bute-j.*, *cath-a.*, **corv-c.**, *falco-p.*, *haliae-lc.*, *lar-ar.*
Music (177):*aqui-c.*, **cath-a.**, *colum-p.*, *corv-c.*, **falco-p.**, *haliae-lc.*, *lar-ar.*, *ovi-g-p.*

An unlimited search has about 350 remedies in each category leaving the birds with a pretty insignificant weighting (2%) for a group renowned as musicians.

Birds communicate with bird sounds that humans interpret as musical, but for the birds, it is just a method of communication.

WATER BIRDS

We have noticed that the water birds as a group show a constellation of symptoms in common that sets this group apart from other birds.

One significant differential is to be found in the **throat symptoms.** In most birds, especially amongst those which eat meat, the throat is subject to irritation and inflammation, whilst in water birds, which tend towards longer necks and swallowing their food whole, the emphasis is on **constriction or a lump sensation** causing difficulty in swallowing.

The elements of **isolation, grief, the sense of being an outcast, the sense of not belonging, and self-reproach** are more intense and more central in water birds as compared to other birds. The Penguin expresses this the most strongly; being the most hopeless and self-hating (Leprosy miasm).

Another interesting phenomenon is the sensation as if the teeth are softening, becoming rubbery or weak, giving rise to the feeling that they will be unable to chew their food.

AVIAN REALM

BIRD MORPHOLOGY

The most recognizable and unique characteristic of the birds, which distinguishes them from every other animal group, are the feathers. Feathers are specialized structures confined entirely to the Aves class and take various forms, from long, stiff, wing feathers to soft, flexible, down feathers. They are thought to be phylogenetically related to reptilian scales. As well as providing insulation, feathers offer camouflage and make flight possible.

BIRD FACTS:

- 8700 living species widely distributed over the world, from the Arctic to the Antarctic, on sea as well as on land
- Reproduction via a hard shelled egg
- Endothermic, capable of producing their own heat and a fairly high body temperature
- Hollow bones. The larger bones contain pneumatic cavities connected with the respiratory system
- Horny beak variously adapted for feeding, from thin and needle-like, to broadly curved, to hooked to paddle shaped
- No teeth
- Cervical vertebra are more numerous and variable in number than in any other living group of vertebrates
- Adaptation of the forelimbs into wings
- Four-chambered heart, like the mammals
- Gizzard, an organ which collects grit with which the toothless birds grind up their food
- Cloaca, a pouch into which both feces and urine are dumped, as in the reptiles
- Highly developed muscular system that supports flight
- Highly developed respiratory system. Although the lungs are relatively small with poor expansion, birds have developed nine air sacs that serve as reservoirs as well as having air spaces in the bones. Respiration occurs in synchronous action with the wings in flight

Avian Realm

- In most birds, the right ovary and oviduct become vestigial so that only the left genital is functional
- Poor sense of smell but large optic lobes
- Annual loss and replacement of feathers (molt)
- Scaly feet ending in claws. Swimming birds have the additional modification of webbing between the toes
- Diurnal birds of prey see color, which may play an important role in food identification and reproductive behavior.
- Acute sense of taste, used to help avoid harmful foods. Sensory receptors inside the bird's mouth detect sweet, salt, sour (acid), and bitter tastes. Sensitivity to each of these tastes differs from species to species.

A QUICK GUIDE TO SCIENTIFIC NOMENCLATURE

Animals and plants, which have no respect for boundaries created by people, began collecting a number of different common names in the course of language development. For biologists it could be very confusing trying to determine if the animal you knew as a woodpigeon was the same bird as what your neighbor called the ring dove. (We're still having trouble to this day also in homeopathic circles!) Early attempts to classify and organize the living world, beginning with Aristotle, resulted in a number of different systems, based primarily on observing similarities between different plants or animals and grouping them accordingly. Thus was born the concept of *Genus*, an inclusive group of similar individuals showing a similar morphological "plan." For example, all cats, whether they be the kitty on your lap or the tiger in the jungle, belong to the same Genus, *Felis*.

In 1753, Carolus Linneaus, a Swedish naturalist, decided that it might make life even easier if these individuals were further classified within their Genera with a secondary name. The chosen term was species, defined as individuals within a genus that do not ordinarily breed with other members of the group. This 2-word (*binomial*) shorthand way of describing life was quickly adopted by the scientific community and continues today. Scientific names are all in Latin (or Latinized; e.g., *Peggykissme* for certain butterfly species), as Latin was the official language of science and had the advantage of being readily understood by all scholars of the time. It offered a reliable, consistent means for identifying any particular life form, no matter what the common names might be.

Careful analysis of the groupings reveals similar characteristics and evolutionary linkages as well. From the individual species, we go up into ever more inclusive groups: Species, Genus, Family, Order, Class, Phyllum, Kingdom.

The largest grouping is the Kingdom. Three Kindoms were recognized classically as Animal, Plant and Mineral. The Mineral Kingdom is described by the Periodic Table while three new Kingdoms have been recently added, taking members originally found in the Plant and Animal Kingdoms and identifying these members as the Fungi, Protista (protozoans, unicellular algae), and Monera (blue-green algae, bacteria) Kingdoms.

For birds, the classification structure goes as follows:

    KINGDOM: **Animalia**
        PHYLLUM: **Chordata**
            SUBPHYLLUM **Vertebrata**
                CLASS: **Aves** (Birds)
                    SUBCLASS: **Neornithes** (True birds)

Avian Realm

Order & Family: There are 6 extinct and 27 living orders of birds further broken down into over one hundred Families. The ones we will be exploring in this book are these:

    Order: **SPHENISCIFORMES** (Penguin)
        Family: **Spheniscidae** (Penguin)

    Order: **PELECANIFORMES** (Pelican)
        Family: **Pelecanidae** (Pelican)

    Order: **PROCELLARIIFORMES** (Albatross, Shearwater and Petrel)
        Family: **Diomedeidae** (Albatross)

    Order: **CICONIIFORMES** (Heron, Stork, Ibis, Flamingo and Vulture)
       Family: **Ardeidae** (Heron-like birds)
        Family: **Cathartidae** (American Vulture, Condor)

    Order: **ANSERIFORMES** (Waterfowl)
        Family: **Anatidae** (Duck, Geese & Swan)

    Order: **FALCONIFORMES** (Diurnal Birds of Prey)
        Family: **Accipitridae** (Old World Vulture, Hawk & Eagle)
        Family: **Falconidae** (Falcon)

    Order: **COLUMBIFORMES** (Sandgrouse, Dodo, Pigeon, Dove)
        Family: **Columbidae** (Pigeon & Dove)

    Order: **PSITTACIFORMES** (Parrot)
        Family: **Psittacidae** (Parrot & allies)

    Order: **STRIGIFORMES** (Owl)
        Family: **Strigidae** (Typical Owl)

    Order: **PASSERIFORMES** (Perching Bird)
      Suborder: **Passeres** (Songbird)
        Family: **Corvidae** (Raven, Crows, Jays, Magpies)

THE RELATIONSHIPS BETWEEN THE PRINCIPAL BIRD GROUPS AS SUGGESTED BY RECENT DNA STUDIES

Vertical lines represent the approximate time of evolutionary separation. For example, the lineage leading to frigate birds and penguins diverged from the the heron/ibis lineage about 48 million years ago.

from *The Cambridge Encyclopedia of Ornithology*, Michael Brook and Tim Brikhead, Ed.

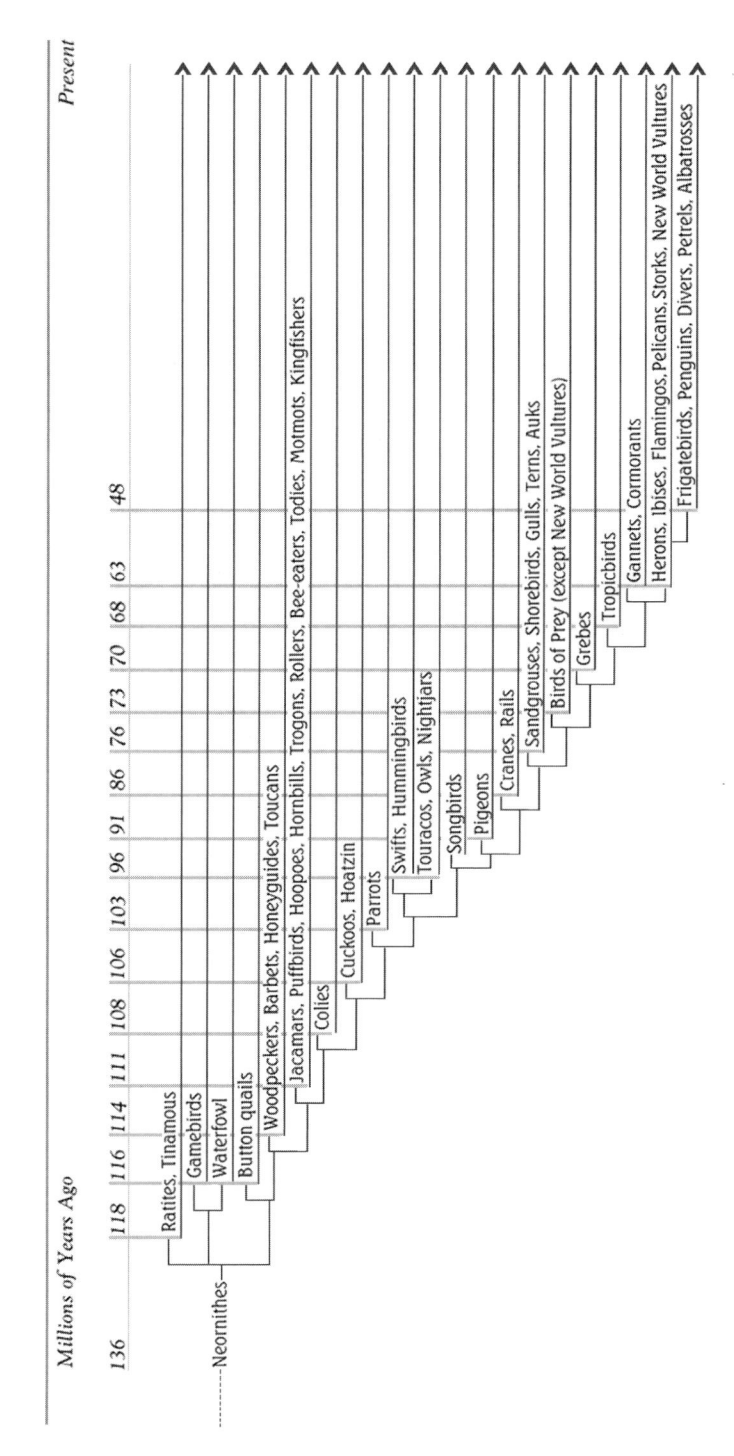

Millions of Years Ago

| 136 | 118 | 116 | 114 | 111 | 108 | 106 | 103 | 96 | 91 | 86 | 76 | 73 | 70 | 68 | 63 | 48 | Present |

Neornithes

- Ratites, Tinamous
- Gamebirds
- Waterfowl
- Button quails
- Woodpeckers, Barbets, Honeyguides, Toucans
- Jacamars, Puffbirds, Hoopoes, Hornbills, Trogons, Rollers, Bee-eaters, Todies, Motmots, Kingfishers
- Colies
- Cuckoos, Hoatzin
- Parrots
- Swifts, Hummingbirds
- Touracos, Owls, Nightjars
- Songbirds
- Pigeons
- Cranes, Rails
- Sandgrouses, Shorebirds, Gulls, Terns, Auks
- Birds of Prey (except New World Vultures)
- Grebes
- Tropicbirds
- Gannets, Cormorants
- Herons, Ibises, Flamingos, Pelicans, Storks, New World Vultures
- Frigatebirds, Penguins, Divers, Petrels, Albatrosses

B•I•R•D•S 31

32   B•I•R•D•S

Key Features

Whatever has been conjectured in the past and whatever debate occurs in the future as to the existence or non-existence of kingdom and family classifications in the realm of homeopathy, the data presented in this book sets a precedent for the existence of at least one significant family group: the birds. There is a set of symptoms and a manner of presentation that mark them distinct from other remedy groups, as well as general patterns that put them within the animal kingdom. Recognition of this family gestalt has allowed for a much clearer extraction of the core idea and key feature of each individual bird remedy.

What makes an individual stand out from the flock? In the birds, we find this differentiation most clearly at the level of Mind and Spirit.

Brown Pelican

Pelecanus occidentalis

ORDER:	Pelecaniformes (Pelicans and allies)
FAMILY:	Pelecanidae (Pelicans)
GENUS:	*Pelecanus*
SPECIES:	*occidentalis*

REMEDY NAME AND ABBREVIATION:
Pelecanus occidentalis, *Pelec-o*

CORE IDEA

FREEDOM TO BE. FREEDOM FROM JUDGMENT. THEY SUFFER FROM THE OPINIONS OF OTHERS AS TO HOW THEY <u>SHOULD</u> BE IN THE WORLD.

BROWN
PELICAN
KEY FEATURES

The central issue in the psyche of this remedy is the axis of judgment: judgment not with respect to *what I say* (Macaw) but *how I am* in the world. The pelican has to do with being in society, with freedom from judgment for one's being and one's actions, not one's verbal expression (Macaw). Ancient knowledge related to instinctual being.

A number of other themes have been elucidated. Some of them, such as issues with vision, protection of family and spirituality, Pelican shares with other bird remedies. Within these broad themes, however, this individual remedy sounds a particular note. For example, issues of perfectionism and the need to 'get it right', are part of the general bird picture. In the Pelican these issues revolve around the core idea of 'being judged': e.g., **doing right lest you be judged.** Many provers experienced this freedom from judgment and found they were frequently able to act from natural knowing.

Compounding the dilemma of the issue of judgment, is the problem of trying to do it right in the midst of being unable to figure out *how*? The need to 'figure it out' versus 'the bliss of being in the moment' featured strongly in the proving. The ability to be in the moment allows for freedom from unjustified fears, griefs and terrors, leading to the possibility that one can live with emotion but not be the prisoner *of* emotion.

KEY ASPECTS

CONNECTION VERSUS SEPARATION

In some provers who were overly interconnected or concerned with what others think and do, Pelican gave a sense of separateness, which was a relief. What others said or did was of no importance, and certain conversations that the prover found trivial were tuned out or became irritating. For some, this separation became scary, leading to a sense of isolation that was unpleasant.

Key Features

> *"There is a sense of sadness, this sense of separation between myself and the real world."*
> *"I have been in a really good realm – where I need to be, not where I should be."*
> *"Overall I felt a very deep loneliness. Felt like I needed to connect but did not know how."*
> *"It seemed like a millennium ago since I worried about what they thought."*
> *"Noticed a level of uneasy competition. Am I doing it right? Can I talk? What's the protocol? I began to relax and 'not care' about the group."*

INSTINCT VERSUS REASON

Things were known or not known. It was very difficult to mentally figure things out. Thinking either did not work well or did not matter. People would ask questions and with a bit of time, the answer would become known. But it was not a mental process at all. It was more like the information was being accessed from somewhere else, and it took a little while to get to it. There was also an intensity of focus, of being in the moment, which was a strange feeling as it lacked the mental component normally associated with intensity of focus.

> *"I felt like I was sharing some kind of secret. There was a common sort of knowledge."*
> *"When you follow your own personal integrity you find perfect freedom."*
> *"A sense of aloneness. Really powerful, wonderful, to really stand alone, to have my power, my own identity."*

MENTAL CONFUSION VERSUS CONSCIENTIOUSNESS OVER DETAILS

There was a tremendous desire to 'do things right' coupled with an utter inability to master the small details of any process. Being in the moment was blissful. Trying to put order into one's life or thinking was distasteful or impossible and made everyone irritable. The minutia of any task was completely impossible to focus on; the mind was just not going to go in that direction. Holding onto more than one idea or thought at a time was hopeless. Trivial details were incredibly irritating.

CALM VERSUS ANXIETY/FEAR

Provers experienced an emotional calmness that came from just being, without judgment. The shocking events of the terrorist attacks in New York and Washington in 2001 were met with a centered calm and objective clarity that was remarkable. Provers were affected but not devastated, pulled off center, traumatized, etc. One woman whose son lives in New York, near the scene, reported calmly calling him up, finding out he was ok and saying "fine". Normally she felt she would have insisted that he leave and come home. Another prover found that the mental judgments which normally arise for her when confronted by a group and which usually provoked her emotions were absent, leaving her very calm.

> "There is an awesome sense of silence and calmness that simply feels different."
> "Freedom from worry, even in these circumstances."
> "Just being buoyed up; a clown you would hit and it would bounce back up. This ability to land on my feet. I am not really comfortable with that feeling of safety."

BROWN PELICAN KEY FEATURES

LEADERSHIP

With the sense of separation from the group (and, more importantly, separation from the need to fit in) and the sense of emotional clarity, many provers found themselves taking positions of leadership in groups where they had previously avoided it because of fear of judgment. Like assuming a mantle, leadership became a simple, straightforward process, like stepping in line. There was no ego or agenda in this, just a sense of seeing clearly, knowing what ought to be done and being willing to do it. There was an ability to see the big picture. Details were irrelevant. Several provers experienced clear physical vision as well.

> "Went into my meeting, people talking about leadership. We signed a contract that I would teach for 6 months. I surrendered to it – before I would sabotage it. This meeting was no big deal, I just did it. I am going to teach now."
> "The unnecessary stuff was cleared away. A feeling of clarity, clear vision, freedom from worry."

SOLEMNITY, JOY, PURITY

A quiet sense of joy at taking part in something important was felt as part of the ritual of the trituration. We were serious but not heavy or guilt-ridden. There was a consciousness of purity in the trituration. (This also shows strongly as a theme in Diamond).

> "Awesome silence and calmness."
> "Quiet sense of joy. Things are and will be all right."
> "Serious and quiet but had this great desire to laugh."

Key Features

Right-sidedness
Most of the head symptoms were strongly right sided.

Hypersensitivity
Like most birds Pelican has a heightened sensitivity, specifically to noise and odors. There are many symptoms in the head, cheekbones, jaws, teeth, occiput, bridge of nose and brain. People experienced piercing, needlelike pains in various body parts, particularly the eye and chest. One prover experienced severe piercing pain in the chest, continuing over a 2-week period (One old story tells of how the pelican wounded its own breast and fed its young on the blood). Itching bumps broke out on people's bodies, sometimes feeling like blunt hairs growing in.

> "The itching continues. It is like the itching of hair growing in, but very thick non-flexible hair."
> "It felt like a bar was going through my head."
> "Felt a needlelike pain going into my eye."
> "Some chest symptoms. Almost frightening chest pain."

Teeth
Teeth and gums were painful, weak, soft and pulsating.

PROMINENT RUBRICS
*Note: Rubrics marked with an * indicate suggested new rubrics.*

MIND
*Accepting, outside issues don't affect much
Concentration; impossible; irritable when he tries
Delusions, imaginations; blind, that he is
*Delusion, elongated, neck is
Fear, cancer of
Fear, mistakes, to make
Focus intense
Irritability; concentrate, when attempting to
*Leadership (fears taking)
*Rhymes and rhythm, drumming
Wrong; doing things

HEAD:
    Lifting up of the skull, sensation of
    Removed, as if calvarium is

EYE:
    Open lids, as if; closed lids are wide open
    Dryness
    Open lids, as if; wide

FACE:
    Drawn; jaw, lower, drawn backward, as if
    Loose feeling in lower jaw
    Trembling; jaw

NOSE:
    Epistaxis

MOUTH:
    Pulsating; Gums

TEETH:
    Pain; pulsating
    Pain; pulsating; lower
    Soft, feel
    Weakness in teeth

CHEST:
    Pain, Shooting, sharp, lancinating; sternum, in between breasts, left side

BROWN PELICAN KEY FEATURES

NATURAL HISTORY

With its large bill, flat head, and enormous wingspan, the Brown Pelican is an unmistakable bird found in the coastal waters of the southern Unites States all the way south to the northern edges of Brazil and Chile in South America.

This bird was at the brink of extinction as recently as the early 1970s, largely due to DDT pesticide contamination, which caused eggshell thinning and failure of breeding. They have since rebounded with the banning of DDT. Fishermen still consider them competitors and at times deliberately kill or injure these birds.

Key Features

Pelicans organize themselves in very close groups, often to an extent that makes them vulnerable to natural phenomena such as lightning strikes or hailstorms, which have the potential to take out the entire group. The flocks fly in orderly lines and alternate several flaps with a glide, each bird taking the rhythm from the bird ahead. Lines of Pelicans scale close to the water, almost touching it with wing-tips. At times, the lead bird may drop out of formation to dive for fish or take a break. After diving, it arises from the water and rejoins the line at the rear. The whole process is repeated over and over, like a well-choreographed ballet.

Pelicans have long necks, which they hold in an "s" curve as they fly. When diving, they stretch their necks out right before striking the water. Sometimes they hit the water with such force that it can blind them. A pelican cannot survive without sight. If a pelican is alone, it is likely sick or injured. Their feeding is spectacular as they plunge headlong into the water, often from as high as 60' above. They open their bills underwater to catch their prey. The folded skin below their beaks stretches wide, acting like a great elastic pouch. They come to the surface with fish in bill, tilt the bill down to drain the water then toss the head back to swallow. They are incredibly buoyant and cannot sink because of a system of air sacs under the skin.

The male Pelican displays himself to draw the attention of the female. They build the nest together from material gathered by the male. He puts a lot of energy into nest building in order to impress the female that he is a good mate and will stay the entire 5 to 6 months it takes to raise a fledgling. The female lays two to four eggs of which generally only one will survive. The couple is monogamous for the duration of raising the young bird.

Adults tend to be silent and rarely emit a low croak; nestlings squeal. They are quiet birds, unlike seagulls, and keep to themselves, even as they fly, fish and nest in groups.

MYTHOLOGY AND SYMBOLISM

Symbolically, the Pelican is imaged as the calm bird that dips into the vastness of the ocean (emotional realm) and easily emerges. Emotions are not foreign, but they are not overwhelming either. Mythology tells of the Pelican opening her breast with her beak so that the young can feed from the blood of her heart.

BROWN
PELICAN
KEY FEATURES

REMEDIES TO CONSIDER
Carcinosin

PROVING INFORMATION
This was a Jonathan Shore trituration/proving to the C4 level done in California in September, 2001.

September 11, 2001
Everyone is aware of the events that occurred on September 11. These tragedies happened one week after we started the proving. This event had an impact on all of us and colored the proving in ways we cannot predict or separate out.

FOR FULL PROVING INFORMATION SEE PAGE 172.

FOR CASES SEE PAGE 310.

SCARLET MACAW

Ara macao

ORDER:	Psittaciformes (Parrots and their allies)
FAMILY:	Psittacidae (Parrots and their allies)
GENUS:	*Ara*
SPECIES:	*macao*

REMEDY NAME AND ABBREVIATION: Ara macao, *Ara-m*
(NOTE: This remedy may be listed as *Psitt*.)

CORE IDEA
Tension between Individuality and the Group

Expression of what is really oneself, one's own truth, versus being an integral and useful member of the group, either family or society.

Parrots live together in large groups, hundreds of them. This is their world; the world of group, of society. The central concerns of Macaw (or one might say, the area in which the pathology begins to take hold) are about fitting in with the larger group, with society. Living a life that is both true to the inner urges of individuality whilst being both acceptable and useful to others. It touches on the development of individual expression as it relates to society.

Scarlet Macaw key features

In the Macaw, the form of this expression is most characteristically verbal, as in the phrase "Speaking my Truth." The emphasis here is not on the egoistic "my," but rather "how can I really express myself without disturbing the harmony of the group around me? How can I really be myself and also contribute to the whole without being disruptive?" They need to find a way to express their individuality within the context of the group. When young, they express themselves and this creates a disturbance so they pull back. They tend to know *who* they are but the free expression of it is the difficulty. Because of the structure of society, the appearance of any real individuality is a difficult thing. It is too strong, too unusual. In most instances, there is no encouragement for children to be themselves, but rather to conform, to fit the mold.

INDIVIDUATION

The tension is between myself as a human being, as an individual, and the societal circumstances in which I find myself. A loose analogy may be drawn between this and the Jungian process of individuation, the process of becoming oneself. It is not for those who are in the world for the first time, who are in awe of everything as new and inexplicable, rather it is for those who 'have been around for a while.'

Key Features

KEY ASPECTS

Speaking one's truth
Unacceptable to speak one's truth
Feels she must hold back

Relationship with the group
Love for people in the group
Comfortable to speak in a group
Sense of connection to the group
Ease of communication

Feeling of giving, but not getting anything back

Acceptance/Impartial observation
Allowing
Accept things as they are
Accepted by the group
As if a fly on the wall
Ability to observe without being involved
Ability to separate myself

Nervousness, sensation of
Never able to relax
Feels as if split
Tense
Sensation of just being there
Nervous energy wound up inside

Bright Colors; Exotic
Will wear bright colors, especially red and blue
Exotic appearance

Loquacity
Busy talking

Awkwardness
Bumping into things
Dropping things
Lack of coordination

NATURAL HISTORY

The Scarlet Macaw is arguably the most magnificent bird of the parrot family. This bird is about 35 inches (90 cm) long. The feathers are bright red with bits of yellow, orange and blue on the wings. The bill is very curved. The feet are zygodactylous; the 2 outer toes point backwards and grip in opposition to the 2 forward-pointing toes. They are excellent climbers. Males and females are similar in appearance. With their wide strong wings, macaws can reach speeds of 35 miles per hour. They often fly in pairs or small groups and often call to each other in raucous, hoarse voices.

SCARLET MACAW KEY FEATURES

Macaws appear to prefer higher elevations and riparian (riverine) forests. They are known to have very large territories. The Scarlet Macaw is found in tropical rain forests in Central and South America. They prefer to nest in holes high up in trees and lay one or two eggs. They feed on specific fruits such as polewood, roaming large areas searching for clumps of their favorite foods.

Scarlet Macaws eat fruit, seeds, and nuts. Like other parrots, they are seed predators. They destroy the seeds that they eat and do not disperse them. Some macaws are sometimes seen eating clay from river banks. No one is sure why they do this, but the clay seems to be important to them. One hypothesis is that the clay helps the parrots to digest or detoxify the poisonous chemicals found in the unripe fruit they eat.

Parrots mate for life. Females lay two plain white eggs in each clutch (a set of eggs laid at one time). Both parents incubate the eggs for about 24 days. The young stay with the parents for up to two years. The adult parrots will not rear another clutch until the young leave the nest.

MYTHOLOGY AND SYMBOLISM

Birds figured prominently in the Mayan conception of the world. Near the Copán Valley, for example, the people named their most sacred area "Macaw Mountain." One month of the year (*Muan*) is indicated by the sign of a bird's head. And the founder of a dynasty of kings was called Yax-Kuk-Mo, which means, "Blue-quetzal-macaw." (The quetzal is a scarlet

Key Features

and gold bird with tail plumes two feet long.) In pictograms, this king has the head of a bird.

The word "Macaw" comes from the proto-Mayan word "*wok*" designating the mythical bird that descends from the sky. This is the same root word that is used to identify the originating spirits from which the South American people descended ("*waka*") as well as the spirits of the honored dead that were said to exist with the *wakas* in the "world above." The root "*wok*" is also widespread in the many names for god throughout the Americas, North and South, further evidence of the divine nature of the macaw.

The macaws were messengers of the gods, being uniquely suited by being able to speak two distinct languages, human and animal, as well as having the ability to travel to and from the abode of gods in the sky. Andean peoples mimicked this ability when praying to the *wakas* by wailing and using non-human vocalizations, imitating the speech of animals, crying out with sounds instead of words to the spirit world, whose inhabitants would understand this emotional language completely.

This linguistic ability of the macaw also made them important intercessionaries between native peoples and god. They were called upon for ceremonies honoring the ancestors. Headdresses decorated with feathers or whole wings of Macaws were used. They are found carved in prominent places at many sacred sites, frequently at the tops of columns.

One macaw myth involves twin brothers hiding in a hut high upon a mountain, starving to death after narrowly escaping from a severe flood. They forage and try to plant but are unsuccessful. One day they return to their hut to find an abundance of food and beer laid out for them. This goes on for many days until they decided to find out who's bringing this to them. They hide and soon see two macaws, richly dressed, entering the hut and preparing the food. After a short time, the birds remove their head coverings and are found to be two beautiful women, or macaws with the heads of women. The men are crude and try to rape them, at which point they fly off and do not come back for many days. The brothers repent and pray to the gods to pardon their actions. At last the women return. The brothers are genuinely sorry and speak kindly to them and ask why they have been so generous. The women tell them that the god had instructed them to render assistance so that the two would not die of hunger. The four are married and become the ancestors of the Canari people.

PROMINENT RUBRICS
*Note: Rubrics marked with an * indicate suggested new rubrics.*

MIND:
    *Accept, things as they are
    *Accepted, group, by the
    Colors, charmed by blue, green, red
    *Colors, desires blue
    *Colors, desires red
    Communicative, expansive
    *Confrontation, avoids, no longer
    *Connection, sense of, to the group
    *Delusions, bubbles, blood in, as if
    *Delusions, drug, taken a love drug
    Extravagance
    *Give, feeling, but does not get
    *Hold back, feels he must
    *Individuality, sense of
    *Interesting, desires to be
    *Love, people in the group, for
    Love, falling in love easily
    *Mask, absence of
    Passionate
    *Passionate, desires to be wildly
    *Relax, unable to
    Responsibility
    *Speak, unacceptable to, one's truth
    *Speak, feels comfortable to, in a group
    *Touched, pleasure in being
    *Truth, speak one's own

SCARLET MACAW KEY FEATURES

Key Features

DREAMS:
    *Good and evil
    *Extravagant, feels too
    *Observer, an
    *Observe; ability to, involved without being
    *Passive, change, unable to the situation
    *Tropical places

FACE:
    Swelling, general, lips

EXTREMITIES:
    Awkwardness, hands, drops things
    Awkwardness, lower extremities, knocks against things
    Awkwardness, lower extremities, stumbling when walking

GENERALITIES:
    Clumsiness
    Coordination affected, disturbed
    *Coordinated, very
    Food and drink; fruit, desires
    Nuts, desires
    *Sunflower seeds, desires

REMEDIES TO CONSIDER
Corv-c (Raven): The issue in Raven is more connected to the protection of individuality rather than the expression of it. There is much more aggression, more a sense of violation of the inner life, more cunning and more deceit. Raven has this inner life that has to be looked after and protected from invasion and violence. Raven uses his cunning ways to gain an edge.

CONDITIONS TO CONSIDER
Peripheral neuropathy

PROVING INFORMATION
This was a Jonathan Shore trituration/proving done in California in 2000.

SCARLET MACAW KEY FEATURES

FOR FULL PROVING INFORMATION SEE PAGE 191.

FOR CASES SEE PAGE 320.

RING DOVE (WOODPIGEON)

Columba palumbus

ORDER:	Columbiformes (Sandgrouse, Dodos, Pigeons and Doves)
FAMILY:	Columbidae (Pigeons and Doves). Plump, fast-flying birds with small heads and low cooing voices. The family Columbidae includes the domestic pigeon (Columba and Columbina) and the Mourning dove (Zenaida, Scardafella, Streptopelia, *et al*).
GENUS:	*Columba*
SPECIES:	*palumbus*

REMEDY NAME AND ABBREVIATION: Columba palumbus, Colum-p

CORE IDEA

SUFFERING ABUSE

The core theme is the idea of suffering abuse, a passive and longstanding suffering. The world is a harsh place for the dove, full of violence and personal injury; people are cruel. Dove is very sensitive, filled with guilt and shame. They are too gentle for this world and may appear as delayed or even retarded, but in reality they are not. Unlike *Baryta*, Dove has merely withdrawn from the harshness of this world.

KEY ASPECTS

JUDGMENT AND CRITICISM

They feel judged, criticized, and are filled with grief and shame.

SEX AND SEXUAL ABUSE

There are issues with sex, sexuality and sexual abuse. Urinary problems are common.

GENTLENESS AND SADNESS

Grief and suppression of grief. Ability to console and love even the aggressor. Complete suppression of anger.

RELIGION

The only bird mentioned in the Bible is the dove. It is a messenger from God to man, often depicted with an olive branch of peace. The dove is a passive messenger, serving the community and God within the realm of established religions. The higher-flying birds tend to be more spiritual, having or seeking an active and direct personal connection with divinity in a much broader arena.

SERVICE

'I always have to serve.' Strong feeling of community. The dove only serves; it is a long-suffering martyr to do the bidding of others. The wings are clipped. Homing and messenger pigeons do the bidding of their owners. (NOTE: One pigeon was awarded a Purple Heart. While delivering a message in World War II, it continued its mission even after a leg had been shot off).

RING DOVE
KEY FEATURES

Key Features

PROMINENT RUBRICS

MIND:
- Ailments from; abuse
- Ailments from; abuse; childhood, in
- Ailments from; domination by others, a long history of
- Anxiety; conscience, of
- Delusions, imaginations; crime; committed, he had
- Delusions, imaginations; criticized, that she is
- Delusions, imaginations; neglected; duty, his
- Delusions, imaginations; reproach, has neglected duty and deserves
- Delusions, imaginations; wrong; he has done
- Grief; general
- Introspection
- Introverted
- Mildness
- Mortification
- Religious; affections, general
- Remorse; general
- Reproaches; himself
- Sadness, despondency, depression, melancholy
- Sensitive, oversensitive; general
- Sensitive, oversensitive; general; cruelties, when hearing of
- Timidity
- Will, loss of
- Will, none of his own, has
- Yielding disposition

URETHRA:
- Inflammation
- Inflammation; children (1)

FEMALE:
- Constriction; vagina (10)
- Inflammation vagina, vaginitis (62)
- Sexual; desire; wanting (19)
- Sexual; desire; suppressed (8)

NATURAL HISTORY

The words 'dove' and 'pigeon' are often used interchangeably. Pigeons are generally larger and doves smaller. There are many different varieties of pigeons and doves found everywhere in the world.

With a wingspan of about 40 centimeters, the blue-gray ring dove is one of the largest doves in western and northern Europe. Doves can be easily recognized by the white on the neck and on the wings set against the darker body color. The loose fit of body feathers is typical for this group. The feathers detach quite easily, which might be a protective mechanism against enemies. They live mainly in open landscapes with clumps of trees, but can also be found brooding in parks and gardens, since they have lost their shyness towards humans to a great extent. Ring doves can be found in temperate and tropical zones of the world.

They can be recognized by their famous calling "coo-coo-roo-coo-coo" and also by their clapping take-off. The mating flight of the cock pigeon during the spring season is conspicuous. With very loud clapping of his wings, he rises high and straight into the sky, then comes to a sudden stop, and in a very slow circular pattern, glides towards the ground before soaring up again.

RING DOVE
KEY FEATURES

Ring doves can breed two or three times per year. Their nest, mostly built on top of trees, is made out of grass and straw mixed with brushwood and put together loosely. A clutch consists of one to two white eggs. Both parents brood for sixteen to eighteen days. The little ones are fed by both partners first with crop milk, a fatty milky secretion from the dove's crop wall, then with some seeds. The hormone prolactin controls the production of the crop milk just as it does in mammals. Within five weeks the young birds are fully able to fly. Their food consists mainly of seeds but also of fruits, leaves, different buds, vegetables and clover. At the end of the mating season, ring doves flock together for either migration or spending the winter together.

In contrast to all other birds, doves drink by sucking the water through their beak. They don't have to lift their heads every time because they can close their nasal openings.

Key Features

People around the world keep pigeons or doves for a variety of purposes. Some raise homing pigeons to race. There are fancy types for competitive showing. There are rollers and tipplers who do aerial acrobatics. Doves fly within their group in a beautiful formation, covering great distances to return to their master.

MYTHOLOGY AND SYMBOLISM

In Greek mythology, the dove belongs to the love goddess Aphrodite (Venus) as a symbol for peace, purity, innocent love, and spiritual connection. It refers to peaceful marriage and family life. White doves are still a popular love symbol often found on wedding cakes.

In Judeo-Christian tradition, the dove is a symbol of the Holy Spirit and of divine inspiration. The dove brings Noah the message that the danger of the Flood is over. A dove hovers over Jesus during his baptism in the Jordan River and comes down to Mary at the Annunciation.

When a martyr dies, the spirit, in the form of a white dove, leaves the body. After a life of sacrifices, the soul of the martyr finds release.

Doves are symbols for femininity, nurturing and peace. Ambiguity with this holy symbol becomes obvious when we hear the words "my little dove" as an erotic name for the lover but also as a nickname for prostitutes.

Dove meat and eggs were known as aphrodisiacs. Meat, inner organs, and blood were supposed to have therapeutic effects. Even dove's dung was used for preparing bandages.

REMEDIES TO CONSIDER

Staphysagria: Dove looks like the animal analog to Staphysagria.
Carcinosin: The overlap with Carc. is in the sensitivity to reprimand. Also, since Carc. is an animal product, it has certain animal qualities in common with Dove, i.e., abuse and sensitivity (to the state of the world).

Baryta: The timidity in Baryta comes from a feeling of not knowing enough rather than a need to withdraw from the violence of the world.
Lac caninum: It also has sensitivity to reprimand but it comes from the need to please. The compensation in Lac caninum is in a perfectionistic way, there is aggression in it. In Doves there is not the anxiety about health or the thinking that they have a disease. Rather, there is more shame and guilt. In Dove the compensation is a withdrawal into one's own world.

PROVING INFORMATION
Elisabeth Schulz did a trituration/proving to C4 in Germany.

FOR FULL PROVING INFORMATION SEE PAGE 199.

FOR CASES SEE PAGE 337.

**RING DOVE
KEY FEATURES**

Red-tailed Hawk

Buteo jamaicensis

ORDER: Falconiformes (diurnal birds of prey; includes Vultures, Hawks, Eagles, Osprey and Falcons)

FAMILY: Accipitridae (Old World Vultures, Hawks and Eagles)

GENUS: *Buteo*

SPECIES: *jamaicensis*

REMEDY NAME AND ABBREVIATION: Buteo jamaicensis, Bute-j

CORE IDEA
Freedom and obligation

They feel a very strong sense of responsibility to family. More than a duty, they naturally want to care for and support members of their families. This tends to be in a material way, not so much spiritual. This caring and responsibility was expressed very clearly in the provings. In one proving, a man dreamt he had cared for a disabled person for five years in complete freedom, voluntarily and happily. In another proving, the primary prover wished she could be like her sister. The sister has two retarded kids she spends all her time caring for without any complaining. The prover wanted to be free like her sister, free to be a caretaker.

Notice here the emphasis is on individual rather than group relations, coupled with the strong yearning for freedom. The hawk is a strong individual, always having to struggle between following his personal will versus taking care of dependents. These birds spend more time looking for food for their young than any other bird.

In hawking, as in falconry, the hawk is attached to the gloved hand of the birder by a strong leather leash. The image prevails of the strong-willed powerful bird returning loyally to the leash on the glove. Yet every once in a while the hawk disappears for no reason and never returns.

KEY ASPECTS

Feeling exploited, especially by family
People take more from them than they want to give. There is a desire for understanding from their mate or their family. People have difficulty relating to others. They can feel neglected, abandoned, defensive and injured.

Aversion to company
A desire to be alone, even though it causes sadness.
> "Feeling relieved and relaxed to be in a space where no one could interfere."
> "I did not want to be around anyone. I wanted to be in my own little state."

Not wanting to deal with people.

Red-tailed Hawk
KEY FEATURES

Key Features

> "Aloof from people. I did not want to get involved. I didn't really care that much."
>
> "I felt like I did not want them to be around. I wanted to be alone and not bothered by them… I don't think I would seek people out if I had a choice."
>
> "I had a kind of detachment and yet at the same time I seemed more sensitive. It was like I could feel the energies of people more intensely."
>
> "On the other side of a glass wall there was a group of Plains Indians and I thought, 'That is where I want to be.' I could not get through that glass to the other side."
>
> "Husband talking with people in a pool. I felt left out."
>
> "Blue all day. Couldn't get anything accomplished. Overwhelmed feeling."

In particular the sensitivity here is to family members.

FREEDOM

They have a great desire for freedom and being carefree.

They are unable to be carefree because they feel a strong sense of responsibility.

ENERGY/POWER/WILL

They have a feeling of power, an increased sense of athletic prowess. This came up in several ways. One person went climbing and said they felt *"strong like an Amazon woman and could climb forever."*

Another had dreams of athletic prowess, being able to do things not normally able to do. Another prover dreamed she could

> "carry a giant thick plate-glass table top like it was a tray. I felt strong, purposeful, able to do anything, totally in control, confident. It was a great feeling."

A more obscure dream:

> "Of a bull crashing through a window. I wasn't hurt, but I could feel the force of it…a huge bull. The feeling was the power of it."

Anger/Irritability
Can be very irritable, more so than other birds. Nine provers felt some aspect of this. Some felt it only slightly, so that for them it was a matter of speaking up more. Another described it as irritable and antisocial. Others were more affected:

> "I was ready to honk my horn I was so angry. I was ready to kill her and I was definitely more aggressive than I usually am and more willing to show it, be more vocal about it."
>
> "More aggressive and anger at the defeat of not being able to put my bird back in the cage. I was angry not at the bird but at the defeat and not being in control of the situation."
>
> "I was extremely irritable and angry because I felt left out."
>
> Feeling really put out because a family member asked the person to do something for them.
>
> "My fuse was short."
>
> "I was irritable almost beyond my control."

Periodicity
Three provers mentioned that they felt well one day and poorly the next, a 'one day on, one day off' phenomenon.

Sadness and Depression
This varied from *"nothing seems right and I can hardly get myself to do things"* in reality to a dream of one prover which produced a feeling of *"sadness, futility, emptiness."* Another prover:

> "It was that sinking feeling of depression like you are in a hole. Dismal like there is nothing to look forward to. There is no hope"....the sense of a black cloud and yet the entire thing cleared when she was out with people.
>
> "Low again today. I just sat on the porch where the sun came in and did not move for hours, just sat there. I did not talk to anybody. I just let things pass through my mind."

Another got very upset when someone made a rude gesture in traffic. She became really sad and cried.

Red-tailed Hawk
KEY FEATURES

Key Features

PROMINENT RUBRICS
*Note: Rubrics marked with an * indicate suggested new rubrics.*

MIND:
    Anger, general, kill, with impulse to
    *Athletic, prowess, increased
    *Carefree, desires to be
    *Control, desires to
    *Control, able to, be in
    Delusions, imaginations; injured, is being
    Delusions, imaginations; injury; receive, will
    Delusions, imaginations; neglected; he is
    Dictatorial, domineering, dogmatic, despotic; control others, wants to
    *Dreams, caretaking; family member, legs paralyzed, with
    *Dreams, divorced, of getting, because husband abusive
    *Dreams, excelling of
    Dreams, family, own
    Dreams, people, handicapped
    *Dreams, leash, connected by, gloved hand to
    *Dreams, group, not fitting in with
    Dreams, scolding
    *Dreams, scolding someone for not being a good citizen
    *Exploited being, feels as if
    *Interference, aversion to
    Interruption, aversion to
    Irritability
    *Power, feeling of
    Power, love of
    *Understanding, desire for, mate from
    *Understanding, desire for, family from

HEAD:
    Pain, general, forehead, middle
    *Pain, in third eye, nail, like a

FACE:
    *Pain, general, eyebrows, between
    Pain, general, forehead

THROAT:
> Inflammation

ABDOMEN:
> Pain, general, hypogastrium
> Pain, general, hypogastrium, extending to, upward

FEMALE:
> Pain, cramping
> Pain, cramping, menses, before
> Pain, cramping, menses, during
> Pain, cramping, uterus
> Pain, general, menses

EXTREMITIES:
> *Pain, pulling sensation, lower limbs, legs, thigh
> *Thigh, tendons of, pulling

LOWER LIMBS:
> Tension, lower limbs, tendons
> Tension, lower limbs, thighs, tendons, hamstrings

NATURAL HISTORY

There are over 250 species of hawks around the world. From its abundance, wide distribution, and striking appearance the Red-tailed Hawk is probably the best known of all the larger Hawks. Most birds are dark brown colored on top and light underneath. They show dark marks on the stomach and have a rust colored tail.

RED-TAILED HAWK KEY FEATURES

The red-tailed hawk lives in North and Central America and in the Caribbean. Being about 50-60 cm tall, the red-tailed hawk is a big bird of prey. It lives in a wide variety of biological habitats ranging from grazing lands to prairies to mountain meadows. Mammals, birds, reptiles, insects are its food. If hard pressed by hunger, however, it will eat any form of life, and will not even reject offal and carrion: dead crows, poultry which has been thrown on the compost heap, and flesh from the carcasses of goats, sheep and the larger domesticated animals are eaten at such times. The larger insects, such as grasshoppers, crickets, and beetles, are sometimes used as food. The bird catches sight of its prey from a vantage point in a

Key Features

low searching or shaking flight. It kills with its claws and strangles its victim. The claws have a lot of power and are as sharp and pointed as daggers.

Because of its size, the Red Tailed Hawk spends much if its time looking for food. In general, male and female birds share the territory. They mate for life. If one of them dies, a new partner is chosen. Usually, one stays in the aerie, the other one wanders and looks for food. They spend more time searching for food for their young than any other bird.

The nest is a large and bulky structure generally placed well up in the forks of a large tree from 40 to 30 feet above ground, constructed of quite large sticks and lined with smaller twigs, bits of bark, and usually with the tips of hemlock branches, fern leaves or moss. The same nest is occupied year after year and the annual addition of material adds to the bulk. 2 to 4 eggs are laid per year.

MYTHOLOGY AND SYMBOLISM

As a high-flying raptor, the hawk shares much of the symbolism of the eagle. It is associated with light, royalty, power, the sun, watchfulness, and the heavens. Many solar gods have the hawk as an attribute or messenger. Gods portrayed in the form of hawks or as being hawk-headed are almost always sun gods. Like the eagle, the true hawk was thought capable of staring directly into the sun.

In ancient Egypt, the hawk was considered a royal bird and a symbol of the soul (ba). Egyptians believed that the ba of a mummy walked the earth, visiting the body from time to time, until eventually being reunited with the resurrected body. The Egyptian sphinx is sometimes hawk-headed. According to Egyptian mythology Isis, in the shape of a hawk, fluttered above the body of her dead husband while she conceived Horus (the son who would avenge his death). The remarkable rapidity of their flight caused the Egyptians to make hawks the hieroglyphic emblem of the wind.

In Greco-Roman mythology, the hawk is the 'swift messenger of Apollo,' and is associated with the sorceress, Circe. Aztecs also considered the hawk a messenger of the gods. Gayatri is the Hindu hawk who brought an intoxicating drink of immortality known as 'soma' from heaven. The Hawk is also a vehicle of Indra. Polynesians endowed the hawk with the powers of prophecy and healing. The Chinese associated this bird with war.

Because of the hawk's swiftness in darting down and grasping its prey, this raptor is a symbol of death, injustice, violence, and those people who prey upon the weak. Their tendency to seize prey with their sharp claws has caused them to be named after the Middle English word "hafoc," meaning "to grasp," from which we get the word 'havoc.'

In Christian symbolism this bird is the antithesis of the dove, a symbolism that continues today in the common phrase 'hawks versus doves,' for pro and anti-war factions. In early Christian symbolism, the wild hawk represented evil; the tamed hawk signified the convert; and the hooded hawk symbolized the Christian believing in the Light of Christ even though surrounded by the darkness of this earth.

The Lakota admire the hawk (Cetan) for its speed, endurance, perseverance, and sharp eyesight. Kawaiisu legend tells of a fierce hawk-like creature, known as Nihniknoovi, who carries people to his mountain home and eats them. The Shawnee tell the story of a man named Waupee or White Hawk who captured and married the youngest daughter of a Star. They had a son together but the Star Maiden missed her family and, taking her son with her, ran back to her home in the sky. As he grew, the boy missed his father so much that Star told his daughter to take the child to visit Waupee and invite him to live with them in the heavens. Being a great hunter, Waupee took a claw, foot, tail, or feather of each animal that he hunted with him to make a great feast in the sky. The guests who took claws or feet turned into mammals; those choosing feathers or wings turned into birds. Waupee, the Star Maiden and their son each chose a white hawk's feather whereupon they turned into white hawks and flew to earth.

Aesop taught people to avoid remedies that are worse than the disease by telling the story of 'The Hawk, the Kite, and the Pigeons.' A group of

RED-TAILED HAWK KEY FEATURES

Key Features

pigeons hired a hawk to defend them from a kite. Unfortunately, within a day of being admitted into the coop, the hawk had eaten more pigeons than a kite could take off within a year. Another of Aesop's fables features a nightingale, which, being swept up by a hawk, tried to persuade his attacker to release him and seek out a larger and more desirable meal. Being no fool, the hawk replied that a bird in the hand was better than birds yet unseen.

REMEDIES TO CONSIDER
Falco-p or *Falco-c*

> Note: The hawk (Bute-j) is related to the family, to the restrictions involved in the care of others; to struggles within the family arena. Thus the axis lies between freedom and obligation. Although the will is often strong, it is a secondary characteristic for hawk. The falcon, although also connected strongly to the family, is more about will, about the expression of one's own individual force in the world.

CONDITIONS TO CONSIDER
Severe abdominal, menstrual cramping

PROVING INFORMATION
Jonathan Shore seminar provings. One proving used scrapings from the beak, talons and feather. Another was made from blood. **Despite the difference in materials, the two provings showed no difference at all.** Virginia Baker did a comprehensive proving in Arizona.

FOR FULL PROVING INFORMATION SEE PAGE 202.

FOR CASES SEE PAGE 349.

RED-TAILED
HAWK
KEY FEATURES

Great Horned Owl

Bubo virginianus

ORDER:	Strigiformes (Owls)
FAMILY:	Strigidae (Typical owls; includes about 140 owls except for barn owls and bay owls.)
GENUS:	*Bubo* (BEW-boh is from the Latin word meaning "owl" or from the Greek word for "eagle owl" used by the great 1st century Roman naturalist Pliny. Great horned owls are related to the eagle owl of Eurasia.)
SPECIES:	*virginianus* (meaning "of Virginia" where the first specimen of great horned owl was collected. The common name "horned owl" comes from the large ear tufts.)

REMEDY NAME AND ABBREVIATION: Bubo virginianus, Bubo-v.

CORE IDEA

TEACHING, KNOWLEDGE AND WISDOM

The owl looks everything over from above and has wisdom and knowledge; it is a penetrating wisdom. The whole being is about knowing and teaching. Owl is a wise old soul who teaches whenever necessary. There is not an inner drive to teach for the sake of teaching, rather the knowledge of the owl makes him the holder of the moral compass. He gives support with his teaching to enable his charges to pass through difficult situations or times, to help them gain a true understanding and deeper wisdom.

"I had a dream with symbol, a circle with a square inside of it. It represents the teacher to me."

"It made me feel very calm and wise, but very detached at the same time."

"Being guided by an inner wisdom, giving me all the answers I needed, giving me all the knowledge and answers I needed."

"Needing to know the truth and needing to know what was going on."

KEY ASPECTS

FAIRNESS

"I caused the entire seating arrangement at a seminar to be re-arranged to allow people sitting in the back to sit in the front. Another time someone in clinic did not get a turn to speak and I called this to the attention of the teacher."

UNRUFFLED

"I felt very unruffled. Work was hectic, but I was not affected by it. I was the calm spot in the center of the hurricane."

"Feeling of calmness stayed with me."

"It made me feel very calm and wise but very detached at the same time."

"I had to accept that I was going to die, then I woke up and I was OK with it."

"I have a fear of dogs, but in the dream I had no fear."

HEARING

"Hearing would come and go — I was hearing things on a completely different level than I had before."

GREAT HORNED OWL
KEY FEATURES

Key Features

"I didn't want to have conversation, and I really did not want to have MEANINGLESS conversations."
"I would hear a voice calling my name."
"Very much in tune with different sounds, like a clock ticking."
"The hum of my computer was unacceptable. It was so loud, and I could not deal with it."
"All the talking in my life, there was no place I could go to be quiet."

VISION
Visual strangeness
"I have issues with vision and I totally gave that up — I completely surrendered to having no sight."
"It was a depth perception issue."
Blurry – when driving, losing three dimensional orientation, had to be careful, changing lanes on freeway
"I almost could not read, the words would get blurry."
"I was aware of eyes functioning separately — am I seeing with my right eye or my left eye?"
"Every room in my house seemed too dark."
"I would get a headache; in general I could not focus on specific things."

HEAD AND NECK
"That day, and every day after, felt a tightness in the jaw and my ears hurt."
"More on the left. My teeth really bothered me, like they were too big for my face. Bothered me all day the day after we made it. Same thing happened when I took the pellets." (The dry remedy in 30C potency was given one week later.)
"Thought I had gum disease. It was funny; it was all teeth and ears."
"Left ear, gummy like rubber cement, something new, it was the color and consistency of rubber cement."
"Tremendous amount of neck pain."
"I felt like I was losing my neck, like it was fusing onto my head."
"Tremendous pain in the back of my neck."

EXTREMITIES AND BACK
Extremities, especially upper limbs
Right shoulder pain, bursitis
   "Tingling and circulation stuff in arms."

PROMINENT RUBRICS
Note: Rubrics marked with an * indicate suggested new rubrics.

MIND:
   Company; aversion to, aggravates; solitude, fond of
   Company; aversion to, aggravates; walk alone, wants to
   *Conversation; meaningless prattle; averse to (Pelican)
   Delusions, imaginations; blind, he is
   *Delusions, imaginations; neck fused to head
   *Delusions, imaginations; voices, hears, name, his own
   Detached
   Dreams, animals, dogs
   *Dreams, animals, dogs jumping
   Dreams; flying
   Injustice, cannot support
   Intellectual
   Intelligent
   *Nature; love of, and the outdoors
   *Observing; life own
   Quiet, disposition
   Quiet, wants to be
   *Teacher; feels like a
   Tranquility, general
   *Truth; desire for
   Wander; desires to; home, from, and ranges in woods
   *Wilderness, desires
   *Wisdom
   *Wisdom; inner; guided by

VISION:
   Accommodation; defective
   Acute
   Acute, see even in darkness, seems to

GREAT
HORNED OWL
KEY FEATURES

Key Features

      Blindness; sensation of
      Blurred
      *Depth perception; impaired
      *Distorted; eyes function independently
      Field of vision; sees objects beside
      Focal; distance changes; reading while
      *Impaired, intermittent
      *Impaired, intermittent, blindness with
      Stereoscopic, hyper-acute

EARS:

      Discharges; general; glutinous, sticky
      Foreign body sensation; internal
      Stopped sensation; alternating with clearing

HEARING:

      Acute; noises to, slight
      Acute; noises to, ticking of watch
      Acute; voices and talking
      Illusions; voices

FACE:

      *Jaw; tightness
      Pain; general; jaws; muscles, masseter
      Pain; general; jaws; articulation

TEETH:

      Distended, sensation
      Large and swollen, sensation
      Soft, sensation
      Spongy, sensation

Soft and spongy sensations in teeth and gums are very unusual in a meat-eating bird.

STOMACH:

      Appetite; ravenous; canine, excessive
      Thirst; extreme

      Thirst; large quantities for
      Thirst; unquenchable, constant

BACK:
      Contractions; general; cervical region; muscles of
      Contractions; sensation of; cervical tendons feel too short
      *Neck; sensation of disappearing
      Pain, cervical region
      Pain, dorsal region, scapulae between
      Pain, dorsal region, right

EXTREMITIES:
      Perspiration; general; upper limbs; arms
      Perspiration; general; upper limbs; hands
      Tingling, prickling, upper limbs

GENERALITIES:
      Food and drinks; meat, desires
      *Food and drinks; meat desires, chicken and
      Food and drinks; water; desires

NATURAL HISTORY

Great horned owls live throughout the United States and most of Canada, extending southward to Central and South America to the Straits of Magellan. They are one of the most widespread species of owls. They are found in woods, mountain forests, desert canyons, marshes, city parks, and urban forests. The owls prefer open areas to dense woodlands or nest sites close to the edge of a forest where they can hunt.

Great horned owls are big and bulky (3-4 pounds), standing 18-25" tall with a wingspan of 36-60" long. Males and females are similar in appearance, except the female is the larger of the two. In general, they have brown body plumage covered with darker brown spots and white throat feathers that contrast with the dark cross-barred underparts. The white feathers stand out like a collar against the darker underside feathers. They have feathered tufts that stick up above their ears, giving them a horned appearance and hence their name. This is their most distinctive feature.

GREAT HORNED OWL KEY FEATURES

Key Features

Throughout the winter, courting great horned owls will mark their nesting territory with night-time hooting. They are one of the earliest spring nesting birds, laying eggs as early as January or February through April. They may use abandoned stick nests of a hawk or heron or crow, but also nest in rock alcoves, hollows of trees, abandoned buildings, or sometimes on the ground. Generally 2-3 white eggs are laid, although they may lay up to 6 eggs. Both the male and female incubate the eggs for 30-35 days. Both parents also feed the young, and the parents fiercely defend their nest site against intruders. If young owls fall out of the nest prematurely, the adults will feed the bird on the ground. The young fledge from the nest at 45-55 days old. Great horned owls can live long lives. Some captive birds have lived up to 29 years.

Great horned owls tend to perch during the daylight hours in a protected rocky alcove or on a tree limb. They mainly hunt at night. From a quiet perch, the owl listens for sounds that betray a creature's presence. Once they pinpoint the sound, the owl silently swoops in, spreads its talons wide and pounces on its prey. Smaller prey is swallowed whole, but larger prey is torn into pieces. They eat a wide variety of prey, including mammals, insects and birds. Several hours after an owl has eaten, its stomach forms a pellet of fur, feathers, exoskeletons, and bones, the indigestible parts of its meal. The owl then "upchucks" this pellet.

They can rotate their heads 270 degrees, thanks to extra vertebrae in their necks. Because their eyes are fixed in their sockets - they can't move their eyes up or down or side to side - the owl has to move its whole head to compensate for the fixed eyes.

When owls are awake, they use their hearing and eyesight to alert them to danger or possible prey. Great horned owl eyes, which are almost as large as a human's, allow a great amount of light to pass through the pupil, so the owl can see in dark conditions. (If a great horned owl were as big as a human, its eyes would then be the size of oranges!) Owls have an incredible sense of hearing, a trait that allows them to hunt at night. Their ears are located on the sides of the head, but are off-set, not symmetrical like human ears. The openings of the ears are slightly tilted in different directions - often the right ear is longer and set higher up on the skull. Plus, owls have soft feathers that surround the openings which they can spread to make a funnel for sound to enter the ear. This enables the owl to use triangulation to pinpoint the source of a sound, when the prey cannot be seen. By tilting or moving their head until the sound is of equal volume in each ear, the owl can pinpoint the direction and distance of the sound. The owl's facial disk is shaped like a shallow bowl. This shape acts like a parabolic dish, to help funnel sound into the ear openings.

> Their ear tufts are large and set far apart on the head. Just like a dog, great horned owls use these ear tufts to convey body language. When the owl is irritated, the tufts lie flat and when it is inquisitive they stand upright.

Owl feathers are soft, almost like polar fleece to the touch. This helps to deaden the sound of air rushing over the feathers while the bird is in flight. Also the front edge of the first primary or wing feather is toothed like a hand saw. This helps wind pass over the wings and keep the bird's flight noiseless.

MYTHOLOGY AND SYMBOLISM

Throughout history and across many cultures, people have regarded owls with fascination and awe. Few other creatures have so many different and contradictory beliefs about them. Owls have been both feared and venerated, despised and admired, considered wise and foolish, and associated with witchcraft and medicine, the weather, birth and death.

In early folklore, owls represent wisdom and helpfulness, and have powers of prophecy. This theme recurs in Aesop's fables and in Greek myths and beliefs. In the mythology of ancient Greece, Athena, the Goddess of Wisdom, was so impressed by the great eyes and solemn appearance of the owl that, having banished the mischievous crow, she honored the night bird by making him her favorite among feathered creatures. Athena's bird was a Little Owl (*Athene noctua*). This owl was protected and inhabited the Acropolis in great numbers. It was believed that a magical "inner

GREAT HORNED OWL KEY FEATURES

Key Features

light" gave owls night vision. As the symbol of Athena, the owl was a protector, accompanying Greek armies to war, and providing ornamental inspiration for their daily lives. If an owl flew over Greek Soldiers before a battle, they took it as a sign of victory. The little owl also kept a watchful eye on Athenian trade and commerce from the reverse side of their coins.

By the Middle Ages in Europe, the owl had become the associate of witches and the inhabitant of dark, lonely and profane places, a feared specter. An owl's appearance at night, when people are helpless and blind, linked them with the unknown. Its eerie call filled people with foreboding and apprehension: a death was imminent or some evil was at hand. More specifically, to hear the owl call your name meant your death was near.

Roman myths: In early Rome a dead owl nailed to the door of a house averted all evil that it supposedly had earlier caused. To hear the hoot of an owl presaged imminent death. The deaths of Julius Caesar, Augustus, Commodus Aurelius, and Agrippa were apparently all predicted by an owl.

> "...*yesterday, the bird of night did sit*
> *Even at noonday, upon the market place,*
> *Hooting and shrieking*"
> from Shakespeare's *Julius Caesar*

REMEDIES TO CONSIDER

Trillium pendulum (Tril.): Strong association with owl. Sensation of eyes enlarged. Calm resolution of conflict. Dislikes quarrels. Quiet disposition. Thoughtful, systematic, conscientious, intellectual people. *Trillium* has more difficulties with labor and childbirth, focus is on pelvis and lower extremities.

Anhalonium: Mystical. Delusions, illusions, distortions of hearing and sight. Qualities of being a teacher. Calm, quiet. *Anhalonium* guides you and teaches you to live.

PROVING INFORMATION

This is a Jonathan Shore trituration/proving done in California in 2000.

FOR FULL PROVING INFORMATION SEE PAGE 223.

GREAT HORNED OWL
KEY FEATURES

Great Blue Heron

Ardea herodias

ORDER:	Ciconiiformes (Herons, Storks and allies)
FAMILY:	Ardeidae (Heronlike birds)
GENUS:	*Ardea*
SPECIES:	*herodias*

REMEDY NAME AND ABBREVIATION: Ardea herodias, Ard-h

CORE IDEA

Detachment and Independence

All provers experienced detachment, from friends and family as well as the rest of the world. They did not classify this as negative. They wanted and needed the freedom to go their own way and felt a great inner calm if allowed to do so. They were protective of their own ideas about achieving a task and became frustrated and irritable when hindered. They disregarded what others might think of them and did not feel the need to communicate; they just knew and acted. Although provers had pages and pages of notes describing their experiences, when asked what changes they had experienced, they answered with 'not much.' They did not monitor the environment to know what needed to be done, rather they initiated and acted from intuition and inner direction; they were completely self-contained.

> The image of the Great Blue Heron calmly wading in shallow water without stirring up any mud is a beautiful metaphor for the theme of following one's own instinctive, independent path.

Great Blue Heron key features

KEY ASPECTS

Connection versus Detachment

The provers experienced both connection and detachment. By far the majority of experiences were in the realm of detachment, separation and isolation

"More concern over U.S. politics and view of America globally, more connected."

"More spiritual connection and the need to help."

"I went out of my way to tell my friend how much I appreciated her as my friend."

"Dreams, about the closeness of others, affectionate."

"I think this remedy is about being detached."

"Feels like I'm separated from the flock."

"Detached, I don't seem to care how this turns out."

"Feeling detached, calm, life taking on a different rhythm."

Key Features

"Sense of isolation, want to get away."
"Shopping, I was very distant from people, less friendly, shut down."
"Want to move, leave partner, live alone."
"Feel I need to go somewhere, fly off."
"I'm not feeling, this is okay for now but I need to feel grief, sadness and fear or I'll be stuck in my body."

INDIVIDUALITY AND INDEPENDENCE

The heron follows its instinctive path, disregarding what is common usage or habit, or what others think.

GOAL-ORIENTED FOCUS, PATIENCE, WAITING

Provers had no problem waiting to get what they needed. They focused on the goal, disregarding hurdles. The Great Blue Heron is very patient when fishing or hunting.

Numerous provers experienced what was referred to as "waiting" in a patient self-possessed way. These experiences were in various situations such as dreams, traffic, and social situations. One prover was waiting to hear about a job he had applied for and was very excited about. He found himself extremely tolerant of the waiting period.

"I had to go to the Social Security Office. I waited there an hour and a half, while he helped the same person, by the way. Then I went to the Dept. of Motor Vehicles, and I waited there for 40 min. and I found myself waiting and I didn't mind. People were having a fit, and I was sitting there, no problem. It was unbelievable that it didn't bother me."
"This would happen to me at a red light. People would start honking behind me until it would turn green, but I could have waited all day long. The waiting was no problem, and I usually don't like it when people honk, but I did not mind."

CALM VERSUS EMOTIONAL OVERWHELM

All provers experienced an emotional calmness in their everyday lives. There were also numerous references to a state of euphoria.

"There is a calmness over me."
"Take things in stride, not bothered, calm."
"I feel gentle, sensitive and fragile."

"Dreamy feeling."
"Emotional clearing, my dreams have been about honoring my integrity."
"Less bothered by others' emotions."
"Euphoric sensations, mood-lifting, more joyful."
"Conflicting sense of calmness and agitation."

One prover experienced overwhelming emotional feelings on her first day of the proving, moving to sadness at the end of the proving.

"Emotionally overwhelming, raging outbursts, intense hopelessness."
"Hysteria upon hearing bad news."
"Emotions sensitive, sadness."
"Awareness of sadness quite strong, unsettledness, deep."

GREAT BLUE HERON KEY FEATURES

SOMETHING HIDDEN/ACTIVITY BELOW THE SURFACE

Some provers had the feeling of something hidden deep inside them, of something being missed.

"Like one of those deep undercurrent things that you did not see was coming, but then when it comes you say, 'I've been working on that for a week.' It was all very clear when it exploded, but it was like I had no warning, it did not relate to my life."

"I have the feeling I am missing something, like something going on, sort of under the surface and I am not in that place to contact it.

SEEING VERSUS NOT BEING SEEN

"I parked right in the middle of the driveway, and still felt stealth, and felt I would not be seen."

"I could sneak out and sure enough, they were right there, but I got out without them seeing me."

"She could not see me and I could see her."

"It was his studio, in the house. He had been living with us for five years, but I'd never seen him or his rooms."

"We moved down to the front, to a private area where we could see dancers and performers no one else could see."

HEAD AND NECK

"Constriction in the throat, tight, hard to swallow."
"Heat rising up to face and neck."
"Sound awareness, breezes, computer clicks, wind in the trees."

Key Features

PROMINENT RUBRICS
*Note: Rubrics marked with an * indicate suggested new rubrics.*

MIND:
    Absorbed; buried in thought, general
    *Alone; sensation of being alone
    Colors; desire for, green
    Company; aversion to, agg.; solitude, fond of
    Delusions, imaginations; abused, being
    Delusions, imaginations; body, body parts; enlarged
    Delusions, imaginations; body, body parts; expanded is
    Delusions, imaginations; suffocated, she will be
    Delusions, imaginations; watched, that she is being
    Dreams; affectionate
    Dreams; animals, of; cats, felines
    Dreams; indecent behavior of men and women
    Dreams; lewd, lascivious, voluptuous
    Expectation, sensation of
    Fear; general; suffocation, of
    Fear; general; opinion of others, of
    Handle things anymore, cannot, overwhelmed by stress
    Industrious, mania for work
    Introspection
    Irritability; general
    Irritability; general; driving a car, while
    Patience
    Rage, fury
    Rage, fury; paroxysmal
    Rage, fury; uncontrollable, can scarcely be restrained
    Sensitive, oversensitive; general; certain persons, to
    Separate, feels
    Suicidal disposition
    Talk, talking, talks; indisposed to, desire to be silent, taciturn

HEAD:
    Heat

EYES:
    Heat, general
    Inflammation; lids, blepharitis
    Pain; burning, smarting, biting
    Pain; stinging
    Lachrymation; constant
    Tears; acrid
    Tears; salty

VISION:
    Field of vision; sees objects beside
    Large; field of vision

TASTE:
    Bitter
    Bitter, putrid

TEETH:
    *Rubbery, sensation of
    *Folded in, on themselves, sensation of
    Displaced, as if
    Location of teeth has changed, as if

THROAT:
    Choking, constricting
    Constriction; uvula
    Constriction; tonsils
    Constriction; throat-pit
    Pain; sore, bruised

ABDOMEN:
    Constriction
    Liver and region of, ailments of

RECTUM:
    Constipation; general

FEMALE:
    *Energy, uterus in, sensation of

GREAT BLUE HERON
KEY FEATURES

Key Features

MALE:
    Sexual; desire; increased
    Sexual; desire; excitement of, easy
    Erections, troublesome; strong, morning

BLADDER:
    *Urination; dysuria, erection with
    Urination; incomplete; obliged to urinate five or six times before the bladder is empty

CHEST:
    Constriction; tension, tightness; sternum

BACK:
    Spine, complaints of
    Stiffness; cervical region

EXTREMITIES:
    Constriction; lower limbs; thighs

SLEEP:
    Short; general, catnaps in
    Waking; frequent

GENERALITIES:
    Clumsiness, unwieldiness
    Food and drinks; fish; desires
    Food and drinks; nuts, desires
    Food and drinks; olives, olive oil; desires; olive oil
    Food and drinks; spices, condiments, piquant, highly seasoned food; desires
    Food and drinks; vegetables; aversion
    Heat; extending; upward

NATURAL HISTORY

Herons and their ancestors have been around between 40-70 million years. The Great Blue Heron is native to North America and Canada, migrating from Alaska in summer to Middle and South America in the winter months. This lean, long-legged bird is the largest water bird in North America. The males are indistinguishable from the females, except for being slightly larger.

▸ The Great Blue's huge golden eyes are a most striking feature. There is an intense piercing quality to their gaze that is quite hypnotic.

GREAT BLUE
HERON
KEY FEATURES

Herons can be found in a variety of habitats, such as edges of salt-water bays and estuaries, lakes and ponds, fresh-water rivers and small streams, marshes, meadows and at times dry, upland fields where they engage in catching small rodents. They stand like silent sentinels, gazing into the water in search of food. They are solitary birds during the day when they hunt, but they live together in a 'family' in the rookery at day's end.

They stab their prey with their rapier bills and then struggle to swallow their catch.

The long beak serves multiple functions. Not only does it spear and gather food, it is a also a vicious weapon, nest-building tool, and is crucial for grooming. While fish are the primary food, herons are truly omnivorous, eating almost anything that will fit in their gullets. One of the threats to herons is the problem of trying to swallow something too large and choking to death. The heron does not like eating living food and will play with the catch until it dies. Its favorite time to feed is just before dawn and dusk.

Herons have long legs and can get into some deeper water than most, perhaps four feet. When it hunts, it moves very, very slowly if it moves at all. It is like someone has put the bird into slow motion, frame by frame. And at all times, the bird is in **balance** and harmony. When it walks, it very slowly pulls its foot up and out of the water.

▸ As the Great Blue Heron places its foot down in the mud of the bottom of the creek, river or lake, it NEVER stirs up the mud. The Great Blue has perfected this ability. It is **in perfect harmony** with the water element at all times.

The Great Blue will "freeze" when a victim swims by. Even in mid-stride, one leg up, and balancing only the other, it never loses its balance.

With a minimal body weight of 5 - 8 lbs., a 6- to 7-foot wingspan, an 18" neck and a lanky 4-foot frame, they are physically perfect for long

Key Features

distance flight. They fly about 25 miles an hour. Their enormous wingspan seems too big for their skinny bodies, but is perfect for the long distances they cover.

Their wing movement is unusual. When you watch a Great Blue fly you will immediately notice it never unfurls or uplifts its wings like an eagle, condor or buzzard will do. They do not have what we call "finger feathers" like these other birds. Instead, they fly with their wings in a U-shape, up and down. **Because they never EXTEND or STRETCH out the full length of their wings,** they chug along in the sky like an overweight boxer that needs to lose fifty pounds before the match. If they don't keep pumping those wings, they will drop like a rock! They never soar and they can't glide, with the curvature of the wing and the wing tips always pointing down toward the earth.

Great Blues will migrate when necessary from north to south and back. However, whenever possible, they will stay put, even when temperatures dip around twenty degrees in the winter, and prefer to hang around in their "summer headquarters" instead of flying south. If they must, then they do short migrations, not long ones. They know every mud hole, creek, river and lake along their migratory path.

Great Blues are wary. They have acute hearing and their eyesight is excellent. At the slightest different sound, they bolt into the air.

At the rookery, just as night falls, they chatter and squawk a lot. Otherwise they are silent all day long. You never hear a Great Blue chattering when in the water. They know sound travels and can scare off their food.

Every male heron has its own dance of seduction during courtship, involving feather spreads and bobbing and weaving, and sometimes fights between competing males. Courtship is an audition process after which the female selects the father for her clutch. At the end, the female receives a twig from the male to improve the nest, the "stick transfer ceremony."

Herons nest in large colonies, called rookeries. The nesting trees are repeatedly used throughout dozens of generations of birds. They become so coated with guano over the years that they turn nearly luminescent, white and leafless. The nests can be 4 feet wide and several feet deep, with a soft bed of moss inside.

A clutch contains 3 to 7 bluish eggs. At the end of the first year, approximately 30 percent survive. Both parents gather food. At about 6-8 weeks of age, the young birds find their own food.

Great Blues live approximately 20 years. A hundred years ago they nearly became extinct when the plumage of these birds became a popular fashion for hats. Estimates are that as many as 20 million birds were sacrificed for this fashion. The British Royal Society for the Protection of Birds and the U.S. Audubon Society were formed specifically as a result of the movement to stop the slaughter of herons.

MYTHOLOGY AND SYMBOLISM

Eileen Nauman gives us the following Native American perspective on the Great Blue Heron:

> The Great Blue Heron moves in sync with its intuition, its inner knowing and flows with a grace that many will envy when it comes to "knowing without knowing."

> Native Americans who work with this "medicine" are usually introverted, quiet, deep thinkers, philosophers, metaphysical, psychic, super sensitive and sensitized, intuitive and are like a 360 degree revolving radar that picks up everything around them.

> Blue Heron people are "loners", who live alone and hate the thought of being in a busy, fractious city setting, which tears them apart, internally.

> The Great Blue Heron represents the balance between our male and female energy.

Key Features

CONDITIONS TO CONSIDER
Autism

In many bird provings issues of working with autistic, retarded, handicapped or abused children arose. Consider bird remedies if you see a strong interest in this area.

Hyper sensitivity – Hyper acuity of senses
Hay fever/Allergies

PROVING INFORMATION
This is a Jonathan Shore trituration/proving up to C3.

FOR FULL PROVING INFORMATION SEE PAGE 227.

**GREAT BLUE
HERON**
KEY FEATURES

B•I•R•D•S 87

Bald Eagle

Haliaeetus leucocephalus

ORDER:	Falconiformes (Diurnal birds of prey)
FAMILY:	Accipitridae (Old world vultures, hawks and eagles)
GENUS:	*Haliaeetus*
SPECIES:	*leucocephalus* (white head)

REMEDY NAME AND ABBREVIATION: *Haliaeetus leucocephalus, Haliae-lc*

CORE IDEA
Trapped in one world
They move between two worlds: the world of daily life and the world of the dream. The one informs the other and the ability to participate freely in both is essential to their well-being. Excessive difficulty in either of these worlds hinders this process and they feel stuck and trapped.

Two Worlds
    Clairvoyance
    Confusion of mind; identity, as to his
    Delusions, imaginations; crack in his soul, or in universe
    Delusions, imaginations; double; he is
    Delusions, imaginations; separated; world, from the, that he is
    Delusions, imaginations; sun; two suns
    Dreams; twins, about
    Dreams; watching herself from above
    Reality, flight from
    Schizophrenia
    Thoughts; persistent; two trains of thoughts

Trapped
    Delusions, imaginations; prisoner, she is a
    Delusions, imaginations; trapped, he is
    Dreams; prisoner; being taken a

BALD EAGLE KEY FEATURES

KEY ASPECTS
Dream life.
Must move freely between the world of dream and daily life.
> "Dream of meeting other beings, not of this planet: while I had spiritual practices, awake in dreams: gave practice up for 15 years, then went into cannabis: it snapped my natural ability to go (into Dreams), then lower states; dreams changed: nightmarish dreams now."

> "Because in an aircraft one can have three dimensional movement. Flying has always fascinated me. The spirit of freedom. On earth you are

Key Features

stuck to two-dimensional movements. You have to walk on one plane." "I wish I were dreaming right now. Just thinking about dreams feels good. I dream about being in different places."

RISING ABOVE DIFFICULTIES
This idea presents itself as a significant adjunct to the core idea and in certain instances may indeed represent the central them of the case. There is a harshness and cruelty of the everyday world and a need to escape to a better place. This escape takes the form of rising up; to be higher; to be above.

"Rise above. To fly away. To rise high above your fears. Be free of obligations in the world. To rise above the negative feeling within you."

DUALITY
The split here is on a vertical rather than a horizontal axis.
>Delusions, imaginations; double, he is
>Delusions, imaginations; sun, two suns
>*Split; seeing two sides to everything

PROMINENT RUBRICS
*Note: Rubrics marked with an * indicate suggested new rubrics.*

MIND:
>Activity; general; restless
>Ailments from; mortification, humiliation, chagrin
>*Animals; spiders, aversion to
>Clairvoyance
>Colors; desires, white, white hair
>Country, desire for, to go into the; mountains
>*Death; fascinated with animal carcasses
>Delusions, imaginations; animals, of; birds; sees
>Delusions, imaginations; animals, of; birds; sees; eagles
>Delusions, imaginations; crack in his soul, or in the universe
>Delusions, imaginations; danger; of
>Delusions, imaginations; flying; he or she is
>Delusions, imaginations; prisoner, she is a
>Delusions, imaginations; trapped, he is

Delusions, imaginations; visions, has, of rainbows
Delusions; imaginations; separated; world, from the, that he is
Detached
Dreams; animals, of, attacking him
Dreams; blind, that he was
Dreams; flying
Dreams; fragmented
Dreams; journey
Dreams; twins about
Dreams; watching herself from above
Dreams; water; waves; high, of
Dreams; witness, she is a
Driving a car, desires; fast
Euphoria; driving a car fast, while.
Excitement, excitable; nervous
Fear; insanity, of losing his reason
Meditation; general
Mistakes, makes; time, in
Objective, reasonable
Reality, flight from
Reproaches; himself
Restlessness, nervousness; anxious
Senses; acute
Sensitive, oversensitive; noise, to
Sensitive, oversensitive; touch, to
Shrieking, screaming, shouting; must, feels as though she
Spaced-out feeling
Sympathetic, compassionate
Thoughts; vacancy of
Time; loss of conception of
Time; passes too slowly, appearing longer; ages, a few seconds seem

EYES:

Agglutinated; general
Consciousness of
Pain; light agg., fluorescent
Sensitive; motion, to

BALD EAGLE
KEY FEATURES

Key Features

VISION:
    Accommodation; diminished
    Acute
    Acute; depth, for.
    Blurred
    Colors before the right eye; Rainbow, all colors of the
    Myopia, nearsightedness
    *Split: different in left and right

EARS:
    Noises; ringing

NOSE:
    Fullness, bridge
    Obstruction; sinuses, frontal

MOUTH:
    Dryness; anxious
    Pain; sore, bruised, palate, right
    Pain: sore, bruised, gums, upper posterior
    Pain; general; gums; chewing; while

TASTE:
    Bad; chocolate tastes
    Dry; food tastes
    Salty; bread tastes

THROAT:
    Inflammation, sore throat
    Irritation

STOMACH:
    *Appetite; constant
    Lump sensation; bending forward agg.
    Lump sensation; painful

FEMALE:
    Vulva holds; sleep, on falling asleep
    Masturbation; disposition to, sleep during

SPEECH AND VOICE:
    Speech; finish sentence; cannot

BACK:
    Pain; broken as if; lumbosacral articulation

EXTREMITIES:
- Awkwardness
- Awkwardness; hands; drops things
- Cramps; upper limbs
- Electrical current, sensation of
- Electrical current; sensation of, ankles, extending to first toe
- Eruptions; blisters, blood blisters; finger
- Numbness, insensibility
- Numbness, insensibility; upper limbs; hands
- Stiffness; general
- Tingling, prickling; lower limbs
- Tingling, prickling; upper limbs
- Weakness
- Weakness; lower limbs; feet

EXTREMITY PAIN:
- General; upper limbs; wrists
- General; upper limbs; hands; joints
- General; lower limbs; hips
- General; lower limbs; knees
- General; lower limbs; ankles
- Cramping; upper limbs, hands, writing while
- Cramping; lower limbs, feet, back
- Cutting; lower limbs, feet, heels, left
- Cutting; lower limbs, feet, heels, walking agg.

SLEEP:
- Disturbed; thoughts, by activity of
- Sleeplessness; general; excitement, from

GENERALITIES:
- Air; mountain air, desires
- Food and drinks; oranges; desires, sweet
- Food and drinks; stimulants; aversion to
- Sides; right
- Split sensations
- Time; noon
- Time; midnight
- Weather; sun; desire for

BALD EAGLE
KEY FEATURES

Key Features

NATURAL HISTORY

The bald eagle is in the family of sea eagles (*Haliaeetus*) found only in North America. It is one of only three white-headed species (*leucocephalus*), and is the largest eagle in the world. Primarily a scavenger, the bald eagle hunts only when there is no easier available source of food. The favorite prey among coastal eagles is fish, especially salmon.

The bald eagle is not strictly a migratory species. Some individuals stay in the same area year round, or migrate towards seasonal food sources. They don't necessarily migrate in groups. These large birds (females weigh 10-12 lbs., males 8-10 lbs.) are not the strongest of flyers, and have to rely on updrafts of warming air to gain altitude and speed. We think of them primarily as majestic soaring birds, but it is only when the sun warms the air that they can climb to the heights.

To this day, people wrongly believe that eagles carry off lambs, calves and babies, yet bald eagles can at best carry their own body weight. Their reputation as hunters, rather than as the scavengers they are, may come from the fact that they are dominant among carrion-eaters, and are often the first to be found feeding on the carcass of a dead animal. The eagle is often the big, slow and clumsy target of harrying attacks by other smaller, faster birds, including hawks, crows and even smaller birds working in flocks.

The decimation of the bald eagle population over the last two hundred years has been caused primarily by shooting and poisoning. The main toxic enemy to the eagle was DDT, which caused eggshells to grow thin and soft with the result that few chicks survived. Today, though they are protected by law, bald eagles are still shot. More frequently, they are victims of accidental poisoning, environmental toxicity, loss of habitat and a diminishing source of food as other species upon which they rely are being destroyed, in particular the many species of salmon. Currently, the most deadly problems caused by environmental toxins are deformation of the beak, **inability to line up the left and right sides of the vision**, and deformity of the claws. Common natural diseases in bald eagles are parasites and a blistering and peeling of the skin on the claws.

Bald eagles are a quiet species of bird, rarely making any cry unless they are aggravated. They have one tree for their nest, and a **different tree for perching-and-staring**, an activity at which they spend a lot of time. The perching tree will usually be one snag that stands out above the others and offers a good view. They use the same nests and add to them year after year, so the nests become huge. Males and females share the task of hatching and feeding the single chick. Although the female may lay more than one egg, usually only the first chick survives; the later ones starve and eventually become food for the survivor.

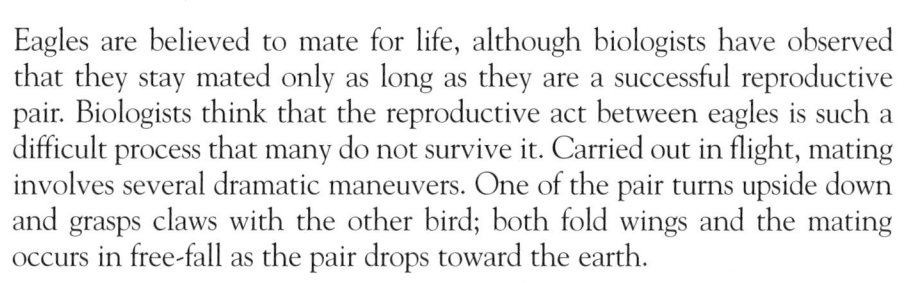

BALD EAGLE
KEY FEATURES

Eagles are believed to mate for life, although biologists have observed that they stay mated only as long as they are a successful reproductive pair. Biologists think that the reproductive act between eagles is such a difficult process that many do not survive it. Carried out in flight, mating involves several dramatic maneuvers. One of the pair turns upside down and grasps claws with the other bird; both fold wings and the mating occurs in free-fall as the pair drops toward the earth.

During their nesting cycle they are extremely sensitive to disruption and will abandon their nests and their young if they are disturbed. In recent years, a small but growing number of bald eagles have been successful in adapting to nesting in urban environments. During the summer of 1996, right after the proving was conducted, for the first time in over two decades, a pair nested and raised a chick at a suburban reservoir in the San Francisco Bay area.

MYTHOLOGY AND SYMBOLISM

The most majestic of all the birds is the eagle. Universally seen as symbols of strength, swiftness and majesty, eagles have earned their place as the icons of some of the most powerful dynasties of the world, including the Roman Empire and Nazi Germany. The United States has the eagle as its national symbol and the US Postal Service uses the Eagle to signify its messenger services.

In Native American belief, the eagle is a spirit of great vision, wisdom and power; one who sees clearly and travels high; **one who opens the**

Key Features

magic door and can carry you to the place of vision and communication with Great Spirit.

In going through various mythological sources regarding the eagle, a number of points are prominent. In the Greek legend of Prometheus, the titan Prometheus steals fire from the Gods to give to humans. Prometheus is then punished by Zeus by being chained to a rock and Zeus sets an eagle by his side to devour his liver. Prometheus' liver regenerates every night only to be torn out again every day by the eagle. Eventually Hercules, upon seeing how harshly Zeus has punished the titan, kills the eagle with an arrow and frees Prometheus. (In some versions Zeus himself regrets the severity of his punishment and, moved by the suffering of Prometheus, sends the Goddess Iris to call on Hercules to rescue the titan.)

Another myth relates an ancient king killed with an arrow and we begin to see a pattern: Eagle is always shot with an arrow. Many of the myths dealing with eagles have them shot with an arrow or killed with a sharp striking weapon. In a Native American legend, a girl is kidnapped by an eagle to be his mate. She escapes and her human rescuer shoots the eagle with an arrow. In Norse legends, Eagle tricks the Gods and steals the ox they are having for dinner, but then Loki's staff pierces Eagle as he flies off. The eagle on the United States seal has a bundle of arrows in his left claw and an olive branch in his right.

REMEDIES TO CONSIDER
Bute-j: More pragmatic than Eagle.
Helium: Alone. No noise, no company. Rise above the world. I feel like an eagle. Fly strong. Alone. Same as an eagle.
Cannabis indica: Dreamworld

PROVING INFORMATION
This is a Jeremy Sherr proving done in California and published in *Dynamic Provings Volume I*.

FOR FULL PROVING INFORMATION SEE PAGE 251.

FOR CASES SEE PAGE 368.

BALD EAGLE
KEY FEATURES

B•I•R•D•S 97

Raven

Corvus corax principalis

ORDER:	Passeriformes (perching birds)
SUBORDER:	Passeres (song birds)
FAMILY:	Corvidae (crows, jays, magpies, ravens)
GENUS:	*Corvus*
SPECIES:	*corax*

REMEDY NAME AND ABBREVIATION: Corvus corax, Corv-c

CORE IDEA

PROTECTION OF INDIVIDUALITY

The inner experience is beautifully expressed in this proving dream:

> "A woman had taken a section from my own personal journal and read it... she had given it to other people to read ... I felt humiliated, trespassed upon, ignored, disregarded, my privacy totally invaded which created anger and violence in me."

Raven is not valued by others so there is a fierce need to protect the core self at all times. This is the primary motivation for all their behavior. They are not recognized, validated or respected for what they say or do or who they are. Their reality and truth are denied by the outside world. There is nothing of their own that is private and it makes them MAD! They are not quiet about this invasion.

There is a danger from those closest to them. **There is no respect for boundaries that affirm a being as an individual entity**, as a being with value and a right to a private existence. "We were her property and she could do whatever she wanted...my mother used to call me her plaything." This is usually the product of an abusive situation and the attendant feelings of **shame and worthlessness** are an integral part of the package. What separates the Raven from the other birds, especially in this context the Dove, is the **external reaction of anger, violence and outrage.**

A consequence of the loss of sense of self and the pathologically chaotic situation which brings this about gives rise to **self-doubt.** Not only in terms of worthlessness but in the inability to correctly evaluate what is going on around one. **Doubt about what is real,** about the reality of both one's own inner experience and the experience of the surrounding world. Nothing can be trusted, relied upon. What really happened? What is the truth of the situation?

IDENTITY AND LOSS OF IDENTITY

The raven in many aspects resembles other birds. In flight it resembles a hawk. In mating ritual it has behavior similar to the eagle. It looks like a

RAVEN KEY FEATURES

Key Features

crow. It eats everything, including carrion, like vultures and condors. In social structures they resemble people, using whatever means necessary to survive in their niche, having the ability to survive in many different environments. Raven resembles Coyote in being considered a trickster in Native American myth. Raven, like many other birds, also acts as messenger, bringing news to Norse Gods, and conveying messages from the spirit world to Native Americans. Raven has even physically lost his voice, the instrument for expression of self, able to manage only a harsh 'gronk.'

> In having the ability to resemble and mimic so many other creatures, whether for purposes of deception or necessity, Raven has lost its own unique identity. Whatever core identity it has left must be fiercely guarded.

Unreality

They have a sense of unreality. What people tell them is completely different from their own reality. The outrageous behavior of others causes self-doubt: doubt about what is real, doubt even about what one has experienced. An air of **unreality** comes into life because of outrageous behavior of others.

KEY ASPECTS

Theft, Deception, Trespassing and Invasion

"In a dream, a woman had taken a section from my own personal journal and read it. How she got it I don't know and she would not tell me. I asked her where she found my journal. She would not tell. I became very angry and threatening toward her. She was quite indifferent to my feelings. The angrier I became the more she ignored me. The next scene was a crowd of people. She was there. I went and confronted her. She tried to ignore me. I pushed her, yelling, threatening. A woman came to me and said something mean. I pushed her away. The woman who took my journal said she didn't know where the journal was because she had given it to other people to read. I began to scream at her that I was going to kill myself and she'll be sorry. She'll see, I'll show her. I felt humiliated, trespassed upon, ignored, disregarded, my privacy totally invaded which created anger and violence in me."

Death, Dying, Suicide, and Killing, Damage, Destruction and Injury

"Dreamed of looking for the comet. On the horizon I saw something, it looked like an explosion, white spray, etc. I looked to my left and saw another explosion. This one had a dark cloud and it grew and grew, black, huge, it grew vertically into the atmosphere and to my utmost horror I began to see it mushroom out… People looked up to see the deadly shape of a huge nuclear blast. Then the sound and the heat of the blast hit us. Everyone had already run into the sanctuary of a church. I was the last, transfixed in horror by what I saw. The blast was beyond anything I'd ever experienced and as I dived through the door, the flesh of my legs, the last part of me exposed to the bomb, was seared off my bones. A real nightmare. On waking I felt a sense of impotent anger and despair about the savagery and utter stupidity of humans, and a fear for the life of the planet. A kind of hopelessness I sometimes feel in my waking life."

"In the dream I began to scream at her that I was going to kill myself and she'll be sorry… I felt using the threat of killing myself would get a response from her, or at least make her feel bad for her action."

Prison, Torture, Protection and Escape

"Dream of my husband or brother, sister and I are in prison. I can't remember why but we are being beaten and tortured. It is a prison infamous for this. We keep trying to escape but our attempts are foiled over and over again. There's a dark staircase that we use in several of these attempts, running up and down stairs or down and down. We are the only prisoners and there is one warden, the "baddie" who keeps catching us. We finally make it to freedom and immediately go to the prison authority to complain but my brother has been talked into denying that there was any torture by the warden **so it makes the claim of my sister and myself look like lies.** It's the usual bureaucratic bullshit, forms to fill out, skeptical paper-pushers. A nightmare until **both of us are even doubting that the torture happened.** Then I find big bumps and bruises on my left arm and elbow and both of us know that there's

Raven
Key Features

Key Features

only one way I could have received those... There was a feeling of being constantly chased in the dream and a desperation to escape the prison, the poor conditions, the lack of light, the warden. It wasn't a terrifying dream, just painful, immense frustration and always this being chased up and down many flights of stairs."

Screaming, Yelling, Outrage

She feels like screaming and she feels impotent. There's nothing she feels she can do about these idiots doing things to our planet. A rage feeling, not as in anger, but she would like to rage.

"It's so global, so big, injustices, ugliness and death."

Trickery

"The Deal Dream: Everybody is sitting in a row. A woman on my right side, a man on my left. We are discussing business, it feels like a plot, a conspiracy. All of a sudden the man on my left flips, in one hop, to in front of the woman on my right. He has a yellowish mouth. He tells her he gave all his money to her, both are laughing, tricky, mischievous laughter."

Black and White, Light and Dark, Clean and Dirty

"A skunk walked by my window three times. It gave off its scent. I had pity for this poor creature, going through the world, being smelly and everyone reacting to him negatively. Wouldn't want to trade places with him."

"Dream of someone playing the part of me. She was a young Caucasian woman (I am an African American).

"I dreamed there were people who wanted me to join their church which was out of town but I would commute when they had services. I would pack a bag of clothing that was simple, neat and clean. In a house watching a lady change a lampshade: the old one was dusty and dirty. When the new lampshade was put on everything was light and bright and there was a dark gray dirty rock floor. There was a pile of dirt with a dirty diaper on it. 'What should I do with this pile of dirt?' The woman said to spread it out. I did not feel right doing that. But I did it and felt as dark and dirty as the floor. I was in a room with a broom. There was a lady sitting in a chair across the room. She

looked like she didn't care, 'just spread it out.' Everything was light on the top and dark on the bottom."

Anxiety, Fear, Panic, Pain and Sadness
"Anxiety dreams of being in a hotel room, trying to pack to go home with lots of people in the room. We were going to miss the plane. Finally on the plane, there were problems with the seats."
"Financial and business world fell apart. Waiting, waiting, waiting, this is when the waiting began. Fretful, anxious."
"I feel like I'm spinning out of control. It's a bit scary. In the shower I couldn't get the water out of my ear. I felt deaf and therefore defenseless. I need to be able to hear what's going on around me but this was on the verge of panic."

Powerful, Proud, Queen-like and Beautiful
"My chest in the breast area feels enlarged tremendously, like the ribs are bowing out...Feeling very good, clean, strong, proud, unwoundable, like 'shoulders back, chest out.' Generally feeling really good energy, feeling strong, proud, queen-like. Firmer, straighter, walking, talking. Feeling free and powerful."

RAVEN KEY FEATURES

PROMINENT RUBRICS
*Note: Rubrics marked with an * indicate suggested new rubrics.*

MIND

    *Absorbed; in her own closed world
    Anxiety; anger; during
    *Anxiety; defend, when she needed to, herself
    *Delusions; body; enlarged; in chest area, as if ribs bowed out
    *Delusions; dark; things looked, as if less light in the world
    *Delusions; defenseless, feels she is, with panic and anxiety
    Delusions; protection, defense, has no
    Delusions; protect, she must, herself
    Delusions; queen, she is a
    Delusions; space; empty space, between brain and skull, that there is

Key Features

Despair; of the beauty and life destroyed by humans
*Discontented, displeased, dissatisfied, frustrated; efforts with, sadness and agitation
Dreams; anger, family, towards
Dreams; crimes; committing
Dreams; conspiracies
*Dreams; dark and dirty, feels she is
Dreams; dirty, she is
Dreams; dogs
Dreams; killing
*Dreams, killing, black parrot, a
*Dreams; lying, not telling the truth
Dreams; magic
*Dreams; magician's apprentice, she is a
*Dreams; nature, of pristine, ruined by man
*Dreams; people, of, in mobs, furious and looting
Dreams; pollution, of, environmental
*Dreams; poisonous smoke, an oil refinery belching out clouds of
Dreams; prisoner; being taken of
Dreams: rape
Dreams; stealing, of
Fear; poisoned, of being
Rage, fury; cursing, with
Sensitive, oversensitive; general, odors to menses during, blood, of menstrual
Shrieking, screaming, shouting; anger during
*Shrieking, screaming, shouting; rage, with; at injustices, ugliness and death
*Sympathetic, compassionate; animals; skunks

THROAT:
Choking, constricting

STOMACH:
> Appetite; ravenous, canine, excessive
> Nausea; beer; amel.

COUGH:
> *Echo, like an; over and over

CHEST:
> *Enlarged; sensation as if
> *Lungs; sponge, as if lungs were a, water would run out

SLEEP:
> Sleeplessness; thought, from, revenge

GENERALITIES:
> *Food and drinks; green foods, desire for

NATURAL HISTORY

The raven is a large bird, 24" tall, much larger than the crow, all black with a massive bill. It is the largest of all the corvidae. Long shaggy feathers on the chin and throat give it a distinctive 'goiter' like appearance. In flight it resembles the hawk, alternating flapping with soaring. They are very skillful flyers, with the ability to fly upside down and turn somersaults. It is omnivorous, feeding on practically anything, including carrion, shellfish, and rodents. They hide their food in secret caches.

Males have elaborate courtship flight maneuvers, including steep dives, tumbles and barrel rolls. The nest is a bulky mass of twigs, earth and dirt, lined with roots, moss and hairs. The female lays 4 to 8 eggs, which are light blue and spotted. Both parents feed the nestlings until they are big enough to walk around in the tree tops. Pairs mate for life, returning annually to the same nest.

Ravens have large communal roosts in fall and winter, generally consisting of non-breeding birds. Breeding pairs tend to stay in their own territories year around. Their range is widespread in North America, from the Arctic to Nicaragua, Eurasia and Africa.

RAVEN KEY FEATURES

Key Features

To some, ravens are the apotheosis of avian form and a spirit worthy of the highest artistic tribute. Others consider them competitors, more to be destroyed than admired. It's hard to imagine that anyone professing sensitivity would not recognize these birds as a most remarkable consolidation of highly evolved animal social systems, physical apparatus, skills, and beauty. They also demonstrate directly that often-elusive capability to sustain healthy populations within the carrying capacities of their chosen environments. To some degree, perhaps greater than most of us would admit, we find this intelligent family of birds not too unlike ourselves.

Their foibles are ours. They squabble within their families and wage battle with those clans that would impinge upon their home ground. Their lives involve a struggle for identity in their social hierarchy and survival in the biologic community of their choosing. Like us, they seem to have fleeting moments of joy when the mate is won, the game is played, the belly is full, and the sun shines on our backs. There is also that intriguing element about corvids that is of the unknown. These birds are more than descriptions by weight, measure, color and distribution, for behind their amber eyes are answers to questions we may never learn to ask.

Tony Angell, *Ravens, Crows, Magpies and Jays*

MYTHOLOGY AND SYMBOLISM

Few creatures have been elevated to the status of Deity by the human race as the raven, whose profound and seemingly divine influence has encircled the globe since the beginnings of time. Considered by ornithologists to be the most intelligent of all birds, the raven's mischievous exploits are prolific, even legendary.

Many Native American of the Pacific Northwest coast have countless legends about the Raven ranging from subjects about his being responsible for creating the world, to many accounts of Raven's behavior involving every aspect of tribal life. Raven was, for the North American Indian a God-like creature, and their ancient folklore reflects a rich devotion both to Raven's colorful personality and to his idiosyncratic behavior.

The afterbirth of a male newborn was given to ravens to peck so that when the boy became a man, he would understand their various cries, and could interpret changes in weather, the possibilities of attack from enemies, an imminent death, or hunting prospects.

Every day the Norse God Odin sent a pair of Ravens out at dawn to fly worldwide. They returned at noon to perch on his shoulders and whisper in his ears the secrets they had learned. Other Norse Gods heeded Raven's advice and Viking soldiers followed his banners into battle.

Raven's character is very similar to that of Coyote, indeed, the two appear in stories carrying out very similar roles, the former in the North, the latter in the South. Both Coyote and Raven are driven by greed: Raven's for food, Coyote's for more carnal pleasures.

His creative nature usually shows itself through circumstance rather than intent, through the desire to satisfy his own needs, rather than any altruistic principles. He is the great shape shifter, creative magic personified.

RAVEN KEY FEATURES

In another guise Raven is at his most devious and tricky: he can be also cruel, with little thought for anyone or anything other than his own stomach. He will go to great efforts to satisfy his appetite, from tricking his cousin Crow out of his entire winter's food supply, to tricking Deer into leaping onto some rocks so that he may be devoured, to even tricking an entire tribe into being killed by an avalanche so that he might eat their eyes.

It is the Raven at whom the young Haida men are allowed to laugh, but is also the Raven of whom to be most wary. He can be much more cruel than his heroic self. This Raven will have you in fits of laughter while he distracts you from the fact he is tricking you into doing something for him you may not actually want to do, and which may cost you dearly.

Ravens are particularly important in the lore of Britain where they hold a place of superstitious honor in the famous Tower of London. In fact, it is considered such bad luck for the ravens to leave that **their wings have been clipped to prevent their escape.**

B•I•R•D•S 107

Key Features

The Raven and related birds (Crow, Magpie) manifest closely the energy of night. Ravens have jet black feathers with a green, blue or purple shine. The Raven often represents the upset in life necessary to create something new, something transformed from darkness into light, something from the unconscious made visible, real. Raven brings out the light that was lying in darkness; they can be taught to speak. Nightshades represent messages from the spirit realm brought into daily life. They give form to what is concealed in darkness.

The only thing you can be sure of with this character is that he is to be found at the extremities. The constancy of Raven is his quest to fulfill an appetite, whether this be food, news, the sight of the slain on the battlefield, spirits of the dead for the Underworld, healing or prophecies of the future. The appetite is sometimes Raven's, sometimes that of the deity he signifies, but the appetite is always there. He is a creature of need, of want, of greed and gluttony, and can also demonstrate a possessive and jealous nature. Yet from that need and want, from the satisfaction of that appetite, great acts of creativity arise.

Raven can do almost anything, and will, but only if he gains by it. His smaller cousin, Crow, is a much more merciful and fair character. His concern is with justice, albeit oft times extreme justice, and he tempers Raven's greed in the European myths. Raven, in particular, is a creature of paradox, and to take him at face value is to ignore his devious nature.

REMEDIES TO CONSIDER
Spider remedies: note the differential with these remedies because of the anger and "everyone else is wrong and out to get them."
Opium
Medorrhinum
Bell, Stram

CONDITIONS TO CONSIDER
Borderline personality disorders
Opiate addiction

PROVING INFORMATION

Greg Bedayn organized and directed the proving on Raven's blood (*Corvus corax principalis sanguis*) during Lou Klein's Master Clinician course in Berkeley in 1996. Kim Baker assisted in the proving and Jessica Jackson extracted the rubrics.

FOR FULL PROVING INFORMATION SEE PAGE 253.

FOR CASES SEE PAGE 390.

**RAVEN
KEY FEATURES**

Peregrine Falcon
Falco peregrinus

ORDER: Falconiformes (diurnal birds of prey)

FAMILY: Falconidae (Forest Falcons, Pygmy Falcons, Caracaras, Falcons)

GENUS: *Falco* (Falcons, Gyrfalcons, Kestrels)

SPECIES: *peregrinus*

REMEDY NAME AND ABBREVIATION: Peregrine falcon, *Falco-p*

Saker Falcon
Falco cherug

ORDER: Falconiformes (diurnal birds of prey)

FAMILY: Falconidae

GENUS: *Falco*

SPECIES: *cherug*

REMEDY NAME AND ABBREVIATION: Falco-cherug, *Falco-c*

Note: There are two provings of falcon available, the Peregrine and the Saker. The Peregrine Falcon proving was done by Peter Fraser and The School of Homeopathy under the direction of Misha Norland in England. The Saker falcon proving was conducted by Elizabeth Schulz in Germany. The exact differences between them appear to be minor; thus, elements from both provings which affirm each other, in combination with clinical experience, have been taken to form the core idea and key aspects. The proving of Peregrine is much more complete and thus shows up more frequently in the repertories.

CORE IDEA
Will, Power, and Domination

"I wanted nothing but to try to live that which wanted to come out of myself."
from Demian by Herman Hesse

The powerful will is the feature which distinguishes this bird. The will is intense, strong and direct. Falcon needs to exert his personal will in the world. Issues of **pride, humiliation and domination** are prominent. Although the urge for freedom is characteristic of birds in general, it finds its most intense expression in the Falcon in the form of resistance to subjugation or domination by another.

> Delusions; horse, she is a reined-in wild stallion that desires to be free.

Falcon Key Features

KEY ASPECTS
Protecting Children

> "I take a child that is in danger to calmer waters and protect him. It was as if I had spread my protecting wings so that the waves couldn't harm the child."

Note: Horus the Egyptian falcon god protects children.

Family
The relationship to Hawk is striking. Whereas hawk submerges his will to care for family, Falcon's will comes first and his concern for family is sec-

Key Features

ondary. Both anxiety about children in the family and desire to escape from family came out in the provings.

Speed
"I hunt with them, but I remain a free hunter. Speed. Sailing above the desolate land. I wear the crown of freedom. I tremendously enjoy plunging myself into the depth."

- Driving; fast; with recklessness and indifference to consequences
- Driving; speed; desire for

Anger
Anger is very strong. A cold, hard anger, especially at anything perceived as restraint.

"The sense for these provers was of being humiliated, scorned, undervalued, even menaced. The coldness of unfeeling anger especially towards their own children, and, indeed, anything, perceived as posing a restraint." (School of Homeopathy proving)

- Anger; cold; detached
- Rage; fury; biting, with
- Rage; fury; cursing, with
- Indignation; rage, with

Coldness, Indifference, Lack of Feeling
A coldness, an unfeeling anger
— *"Death or life, I want the prey."*
Delusions, imaginations; queen, ice queen, she is

Resignation and Paralysis
It is notable that these symptoms appear in two independent provings and two of the clinical cases suffered from degenerative disorders of the nervous system leading to paralysis.

Sensations of paralysis in hands and arms.

Despair, no prospects for the future.
A horrifying image: all land and water is desolate or polluted.
Feelings of loneliness and being captured
Being institutionalized.
Having no family, no support, no work.
A handicapped child.
> Indifference, apathy; conscience, to the dictates of
> Indifference, apathy; joy, to
> Delusions; paralyzed; he is

Opinion of Others
Despite the strong will of the falcon, the provings brought out a strong desire for the good opinion of others. Falcon gives up its freedom for acceptance. The image of the Falcon on the gloved hand of the falconer, tethered, yet free, is a striking metaphor for this aspect.

> *"I think about giving up my freedom, giving up freedom in exchange for admiration, acceptance, and love."*
>
> *"Wish for acceptance. Being trained. A wild animal only does what it feels. It doesn't want acceptance or to be fed. It enjoys the hunt."*
>
> *"A feeling of being embedded and forced into a restrictive society."*
>
> *"Am I a bird or am I a soul? Feelings of infinite freedom. I allow people to capture me because I want to feel as they do."*

Stretching one's neck to be equal with the others.
Wanting to be faultless.

Colors
Desire for yellow

Addiction
Addictions in all forms showed up.
Desire for alcohol

Childhood abuse
There is a theme of abuse and abandonment.
Deepest childhood wounds surface

Falcon key features

Key Features

PROMINENT RUBRICS
*Note: Rubrics marked with an * indicate suggested new rubrics.*

MIND:
    Ailments from domination
    Ailments from domination; others, by, a long history of
    Ailments from humiliation
    Ailments from scorn
    Anger; cold, detached
    Anxiety; children - about his
    Anxiety; family; about his
    Anxiety; others, for
    Anxiety, compelled, when, to do something
    Artistic aptitude
    Audacity
    *Biting; impulse to bite
    Children; desire to be with
    Colors, charmed by
    Colors; yellow, desire for
    Company; aversion to, aggr.; alternating with; desire for company
    Concentration; difficult; fixing attention impossible
    Concentration; difficult: conversation, during
    Confidence, increased
    Confidence; self, in
    Confidence; want of self-confidence
    Confidence; want of self-confidence, talking amel.
    Confident; alternating with timidity
    Confusion; driving while
    Confusion; identity, as to his: own, as if it were not his
    Confusion; loses his way in well-known streets
    Contemptuous
    Courageous; danger, in spite of
    Cursing; contradiction from
    Danger; no sense of, has
    Delusions; shield around him, has an iron
    *Delusions; horses, reined in wild stallion that desires to be free, she is a

Delusions; horse, horses; she is, desires to be free
Delusions; duty; he has neglected his
Delusions; Queen, she is; ice-queen
Delusions; paralyzed; he is
Delusions; prison, is in a
Delusions; prostitute, is a
Delusions; repudiated; relatives, he is repudiated by
*Delusions; secure, feels, even with chaos
Delusions: separated; world, from the, that he is
Delusions; spirals
*Despair; others, about; poverty and ugliness in
Dictatorial
Dictatorial; command, talking with air of
*Disgust; deceit of others, at the
Driving a car, desires, fast
*Driving; recklessness and indifference to consequences
*Driving; speed, desire for
Duty; aversion to; domestic duty
Escape, attempts to; family and children, from her
Estranged; flies from her own children
Estranged; family, from her
Estranged; wife, from his
Estranged; partner, from
Fastidious; appearance, to personal
Hatred; revenge, and
*Hatred; vengeful and detached
*Ideas; abundant; ability to communicate them, and
Indignation; rage, with
*Indifference; danger, to
Indifference, apathy; conscience, to the dictates of
Indifference, apathy; joy, to
Indifference, apathy; opinion of others, to
*Industrious; alternating with lassitude
Injustice; cannot support
*Injustice; cannot support, cool in the face of anger

Falcon
key features

Key Features

- ✓ Longing for; good opinion of others
- ✓ *Pleasing; desire to please others
- ✓ *Pleasing; desire to please others, puts on make up
-   Rage, fury, biting, with
- ✓ Rage, fury, cursing, with
- ✓ *Speed; desires
- ✓ *Will, clearness of purpose
- ✓ Will, loss of will power
-   *Will, strong will power

NATURAL HISTORY

THE PEREGRINE FALCON

The Peregrine Falcon is one of 38 species of the genus Falco, the true falcons, which includes the Kestrel and the Merlin. There are several features that distinguish the falcons from other raptors. They do not build nests but lay their eggs in "scrapes", depressions made on cliff ledges, in holes in trees or even on the ground. They have proportionally longer and narrower wings than the eagles and hawks which makes them stronger and faster in the air but less maneuverable close to the ground. They have a "tomial tooth" a projection on the upper beak with a corresponding notch on the lower one. This serration allows them to kill their prey immediately with a bite to the back of the neck and they do not generally have to contend with a struggling victim as the hawks do.

The name Falcon comes from the Latin falx, a sickle, and alludes to the sharp beak that, like the grim reaper, brings sudden death. Falcon is actually a term for the female, the male being called tercel meaning "one-third." The male is actually 1/3 smaller than the female. The falcon, the larger, more powerful hunter, is the bird of choice for falconry.

The adult bird is black/brown on top with a yellowish-white breast with rust-red streaks. The tail has horizontal black stripes. It has distinctive facial markings with a black mask or "moustache" around the eyes. The female weighs up to a kilogram and is up to 50cm in length. The falcon (female) is more powerful but the tercel is often more agile. The feet and talons are disproportionately large and colored bright yellow, as is the fleshy area around the beak. This yellow becomes even brighter around the breeding season.

The falcon's flight takes the form of a series of rapid strokes of the wings followed by a short glide. It usually climbs above its prey and then dives on to it. This dive is called the "stoop." It is variously estimated from a hundred to two hundred miles an hour. The Peregrine Falcon is the fastest creature on earth.

Courtship starts at the beginning of February, with impressive aerial displays. A clutch of 2-4 eggs is laid in April and the female incubates them for 28-33 days. The chicks take about six weeks to develop and for the first few weeks the female stays with them in the nest.

Falcons have bony tubercles in their nostrils that may act like air baffles, slowing airflow through the nasal passages during high-speed stoops.

In the making of jet airplanes, engineers encountered a problem. As planes got faster engines started choking out at a certain speed. The air, instead of going into the cowl of the engine, encountered resistance from a wall of still air from the engine cowl and so split and went around the engine instead of into it. Puzzled, the researchers wondered how falcons could still breathe at such incredible speeds. Looking at the falcon's nostrils, they found the answer. In the opening of the nostril is a small cone that protrudes a bit. Fashioning a similar cone in the opening of the jet engine, they discovered that the air could pass into the engine even at great speed. Once again a human invention is inspired by an animal adaptation.

FALCON KEY FEATURES

Key Features

The Peregrine Falcon is one of the most cosmopolitan of birds. It was found worldwide except in the arid tropical deserts, though due to pesticide poisoning they have almost completely disappeared from the Americas east of the Rockies and the Andes.

The establishment of nest and roost sites on city high-rise buildings has had the effect of increasing falcon populations in close proximity to humans, with ensuing human gratitude because of the pigeon control that followed.

THE SAKER FALCON

The Saker falcon is a hunter. This falcon was imported from the orient during the time of the Crusades for purposes of falconry. In falconer's terminology the female bird is called Saker and the smaller male bird, Sakret. A sprinter, the Saker falcon reaches a top speed of 90 miles per hour.

The Saker falcon is a very specialized hunter adapted to specific environmental conditions for hawking in open areas close to the ground. The Saker falcon's nutrition is dependent on medium sized birds and small mammals, which are active during the daytime.

Falcons don't build their own nests. They use the nests of other birds and have to be satisfied with what they find. The breeding period lasts about five months.

The Saker falcon has several natural enemies: the eagle owl, the hawk and the stone marten. The Saker falcon is vulnerable to infections. In captivity, the birds can reach the age of twenty.

The Saker falcon can catch flying as well as running prey. For ages, she has been known as one of the best hawking birds. The Saker was especially appreciated because she could be used to hunt prey that would normally be physically superior to her: gazelles, fully-grown rabbits, cranes. The hunt for gazelles always takes place with a dog. It is especially recommended that the hunter create a very close relationship with the Saker falcon, based on trust, so that she doesn't turn herself out (to turn herself out means that a hawking bird does not come back to the falconer).

Falconry

The art of hunting with birds of prey has almost certainly been practiced for more than four thousand years. The earliest record of the practice is a Hittite carving of the 13th Century, B.C.E. in which a child is holding the leash of a jessed Falcon. There is evidence that the Assyrians were keen falconers. The Egyptians, perhaps because of their devotion to Horus, never took up falconry in spite of their close contact with the Assyrians. The Greeks and Romans were also never particularly taken by the sport, though it was popular among the Germanic peoples, the Gauls and the Celts. The sport, as it still is today, was important in the Middle East. During the early Middle Ages the Moorish invasion of Spain met with the Franks who were already interested in Falconry and the art found a new importance that lasted through the Middle Ages and the Renaissance and reached its apogee in the reign of Louis XIII.

In the Orient Falconry has a similar history. It was part of the Samurai world in Japan and was widespread in India and Central Asia. Today only some of the Arabian princes have the resources and the will to carry it on as a Royal Art, but in many countries there remain small numbers of committed falconers and hawkers.

There are two distinct branches of hunting with birds of prey. Hawking uses short winged birds of prey, the hawks, which are launched from the fist when the quarry is sighted. Their power and maneuverability allow them to catch up with their prey and to capture them on, or close to, the ground. Hawks are used to hunt hares, small animals and game birds. Falconry uses long winged birds, the true falcons, which are let go and then climb to a great height before the quarry is flushed from cover. They stoop at great speed, taking their prey in mid-air. The stoop is so fast that to take the prey on or close to the ground would be very dangerous. They are therefore only used in the hunting of airborne prey.

Falconry takes advantage of the natural instincts of the birds. In Falconry a dog is used to "point" the position of the quarry. The dog stays absolute-

Falcon Key Features

Key Features

ly still while the falcon is let slip and given time to climb in a circling motion. When the falcon is in position, the dog flushes the quarry and the bird stoops on it at great speed, killing or stunning it. The falcon brings its prey to the ground and 'mantling' (spreading its wings tent-like over its prey), it begins to pluck its feathers out. The falconer must approach quickly while the bird is engrossed. Then he offers a lure of fresh meat, which the falcon will instinctively take, giving the falconer a chance to snatch the quarry and catch the falcon by its jesses (leather straps attached to the legs). The falcon is given a small part of the kill, the "faire courtoisie".

The training of the falcon is necessary partly to accustom the bird to people and the accoutrements of the hunt, but most importantly to give the falconer a way of calling the bird back to him.

The bird, if a young one or captive bred, is kept in "hack," a state of semi-freedom, until its wings are fully grown. It is always fed by the falconer and wears large hacking bells to prevent it from taking its own prey. Jesses, lengths of supple but hard-wearing leather, are attached to each of the bird's legs. The jesses can be attached by a leash, a long strong cord, to hold the bird or prevent it from flying away. Jesses are worn all the time, even when the bird is in flight.

The bird is left tethered in semi-darkness without food. After a substantial time, when the bird is exhausted and starving, it is offered a morsel of meat on the gloved fist. When it is driven by hunger to eat, it will step on to the glove to take the meat. Gradually the bird gets used to coming to the fist to feed and to being carried around. Hawks are always fed on the fist and are called by being shown the gloved hand. Falcons are fed from, and called to, the "lure". This is a horseshoe-shaped piece of padded leather with birds' wings on either side and a ring, to which meat is tied, in the center. The lure is swung in a circle on a piece of cord. Whenever the bird is offered food a distinctive whistle is sounded.

When the bird is familiar to people and dogs and to being fed, it is introduced to the hood. This is a padded leather hood, which fits over the falcon's head and is tied on with laces. It is kept on the bird when transporting it and during the hunt to prevent the bird from being distracted or becoming over-excited.

A bird of prey is never domesticated. The learned response to the lure and the sound of the whistle will usually call back the bird but if it were to fly out of sight or hearing it would be free. These days miniature radio trackers are fitted to the trained birds so they can be traced.

Although the falcon is not the largest or the rarest of the birds of prey, it has always been regarded by falconers as "The Noble Bird" or "The Gentle Bird" and has always been the favorite of the true cognoscenti. The Saker is the fastest and most acrobatic of the falcons, and the one most willing to take on something bigger than itself, but it is also the bird with the most character, the one that seems to be the most human. It is often tame and quite easy to train but it can also be the most obstreperous and difficult.

MYTHOLOGY & SYMBOLISM

The Peregrine Falcon has been regarded as a mystic bird and often as a messenger from another world, a stranger in ours. The North American Indians believe it to be a messenger that brings us guidance from the spirit world. The Ancient Egyptians believed the Falcon brought the Sun in the morning and dragged it away in the evening.

FALCON KEY FEATURES

In Egyptian mythology the Falcon found its most powerful expression. Horus, which means "the distant one" or "that which is above", was the most important of the many Falcon Gods. Horus, the child of Osiris and Isis, was hidden in the papyrus marshes of the Nile Delta and brought up in secret by his mother. Horus is often depicted as a vulnerable child, either sucking at Isis' breast or sitting on her lap sucking his fingers. He is sometimes referred to as 'Horus, the child with his finger in his mouth'

Patients will often place a finger at the corner of or in the mouth.

Key Features

The secrecy and danger of Horus' upbringing meant that his mother was continually concerned for his welfare. Spells and cures for ill or injured children called on Isis by comparing the sick child with Horus.

On coming of age, Horus, guided by his mother's guile and forensic skills, set about persuading the Court of the Gods that the Kingdom of Egypt had been usurped by his Uncle and was rightfully his. As a sky god, his right eye was said to represent the Sun and his left the Moon. In one of the numerous contests and incidents between Horus and Seth, the left eye of Horus was shattered.

Through the magic of Thoth the eye was restored to perfection and became the Udjat, a human eye surrounded by the Falcon's facial markings. The Udjat became a symbol of soundness and perfection and of protection and purification. It was one of the most potent amulets of protection and is still an immensely powerful icon. The phases of the Moon reflect this shattering into small pieces and healing to wholeness. After a trial that consumed the gods and their rivalries for more than eighty years, Horus won his case against Seth and was awarded the Kingship of Egypt. As such, he and the Pharaoh, as God and Ruler of Egypt, were one and the same. The Hieroglyph of the Falcon therefore meant kingship and is always found preceding the name of a Pharoah.

REMEDIES TO CONSIDER
Anacardium orientale: Poor self-image, internalized anger, feeling trapped or restricted, and outbursts of anger.
Bute-j: Can also have the sensation of being trapped. It is the only hawk which is used as a hunting bird like the falcons.
Nux vomica

CONDITIONS TO CONSIDER
- Degenerative disorders of the nervous system leading to paralysis
- Peripheral neuropathy
- Severe abdominal menstrual cramping
- Claustrophobia

PROVING INFORMATION
Falco-p was proved by Misha Norland and the School of Homeopathy in England. *Falco-c* was proved by Elisabeth Schulz in Germany.

FOR FULL PROVING INFORMATION SEE PAGES 277 AND 281.

FOR CASES SEE PAGE 402.

FALCON
KEY FEATURES

Turkey Vulture

Cathartes aura

ORDER:	Ciconiiformes (Heron, Stork, Ibis, Flamingo and Vulture)
FAMILY:	Cathartidae (American Vultures)
GENUS:	*Cathartes*
SPECIES:	*aura*

REMEDY NAME AND ABBREVIATION: Cathartes aura, *Cath-a*

CORE IDEAS

Catharsis

Discharges on physical and emotional levels
"Felt like an exorcism inside. Much less struggle. Overall it feels like a cleaning healing; a lot of emotional residue that needed to be gotten rid of."

Letting go of old relationships/emotional residue

Draining Pus
Sudden drainage of sebaceous cyst just below left knee, which I'd had for 10 years. Oatmeal-like discharge smelling like bad cheese and vomit.
Pus pockets in tonsils.
Zit on back; enormous and full of pus.
Grey pus on incision.

Purification/Detoxification

Returning to retrieve possessions/Returning to things forgotten

Flashbacks

KEY ASPECTS

Communication/Messages
Frustration and blocked communication. (The Vulture has no syrinx and can only hiss.)
Messages and dreams.
Ability to communicate with animals.

Throat and Skin
Every prover experienced a sore throat.
Septic inflammations.

Dry scratchy throat. Sore throat. Pus pockets in tonsils. Difficulty breathing at night due to swelling in throat. Doctors said it was the worst looking throat they'd ever seen in prover with no prior history of sore throats.
"Itching feelings all night–something crawling all over my skin. Felt like I had bedbugs in my bed."

Itching, discharging cysts, acne, pus, wens.

TURKEY VULTURE KEY FEATURES

Key Features

SENSITIVITY/HYPERSENSITIVITY
Sensitivity to alcohol.
Hypersensitivity of body scars.
Joints less sensitive to storms.
Painful pimples.

FRUSTRATION/THINGS BREAKING
Car battery died; hood latch broken; washer broke; dryer wouldn't take coins.
Frustration and anger. Irritability. Tremendous frustration with uncompleted tasks.
Forced to take the lead; to be in charge; to drive on a trip.

SECRECY
Covert operations.
Sneaking.
Breaking the rules, rules do not apply to them.
Getting away with things.

PAIRING
Yellow and black. Red and white. Red and green. Green and white.
Color always shows up in pairs.
The number four.
Pairing of 2 numbers or people in pairs.

PROMINENT RUBRICS

MIND:
    Artistic; aptitude
    Biting; nails
    Conscientious about trifles
    *Delusions, imaginations; animals, of; bedbugs
    Delusions, imaginations; animals, of; insects; creeping on face
    Delusions, imaginations; animals, of; insects; head, on back of, has
    *Delusions imaginations; invisible
    Desires; beautiful things, finery
    Dreams; animals; snakes, bugs, cats
    *Dreams: animals; phoenix, of
    *Dreams; animals of; pooping and peeing on new things

Dreams; buildings
Dreams; buildings; big and beautiful
Dreams; buildings; hospitals and clinics
Dreams; clairvoyant; solving important questions of the day
*Dreams; communication
*Dreams; furniture
Dreams; falling, confidence with
Dreams; falling; high places from
Dreams; journeys; difficulties with
Dreams; lewd, lascivious and voluptuous
Dreams; money
*Dreams; Phoenix rising from ashes
*Dreams; possessions, must run back and retrieve them
Dreams; trips, journeys; by car and bus.
*Flashbacks
Forgetfulness; purchases, of, goes off and leaves them
Rest; cannot, when things are not in proper place
Somnambulism

FACE:
Eruptions; acne
Eruptions; pustules; cheeks

MOUTH:
Gums; tender

TEETH:
Pain; bottom, left
Pain; front

THROAT:
Inflammation; sore throat; septic
Inflammation; sore throat; tonsils
*Inflammation; sore throat; tonsils, pus in pockets
Pain; general
Suppuration; general; tonsils
*Swelling; breathing difficult at night
Swelling; tonsils

TURKEY VULTURE KEY FEATURES

Key Features

RECTUM:
    Constipation; urging absent
STOOL:
    Loose
SPEECH AND VOICE:
    Hoarseness
RESPIRATION:
    *Difficult; throat swelling, from
CHEST:
    Pain; burning; sternum
    *Pain; piercing; sternum
    Swelling; lymphatic tissue; axillary
BACK:
    Eruptions; pustules
SLEEP:
    Somnambulism
SKIN:
    *Desquamating; fingers
    Eruptions; pustules
    Itching; bedbugs, as if
    Itching; crawling sensation
    *Peeling
    Rash
GENERALITIES:
    Food and drink; salty, desires

NATURAL HISTORY

Cathartes is from the Greek and means 'to cleanse.' Turkey vultures are often called buzzards, which is a British term for a large hawk. New world (i.e. Americas) vultures are thought to be different than old world (i.e. European) vultures. Old world vultures are more related to the Falconiformes. New research, including DNA studies, suggest that turkey vultures are much more closely related to storks and ibises.

The turkey vulture is one of America's largest birds of prey; they are nearly eagle-sized. The wingspan averages 60-72 inches. Adult turkey vultures are brown black over most of their body and have an unfeathered red head. The bird's bill is ivory white and the feet are also red although the color can be obscured by yellow urates that build up from urination. Younger birds are all black and it takes 12-15 months for them to develop the characteristic red head and white bill.

In flight, the turkey vultures have very long narrow wings that appear two-toned with the bird's dark gray flight feathers looking lighter than the black wing linings. The silvery undersides of the primaries and secondaries contrast with the dark leading edges of the wings and body. They are quite short necked in flight and have a narrow tail. Unlike eagles which hold their wings straight out, turkey vultures hold their wings in a 'V' pattern when soaring.

Thermal updrafts are a key to turkey vulture flight. The relatively narrow wings and tail of the species are optimized for soaring. They seek and circle through strong updrafts, especially those found along ridges, to avoid flapping and to conserve energy. They are most active between 10AM and 4PM with **peak activity around noon** when the thermals are the strongest. The turkey vulture is sometimes called the "wind master."

Their bald heads possibly help them slide into carcasses without having to spend much time cleaning their heads afterwards. The necks become increasingly wrinkled as they age. Reports suggest these birds have weak feet and a very strong odor.

Turkey vultures have a wide distribution throughout the Americas. Their habitat is diverse including riparian, agricultural, desert, grassland, scrubland and woodland habitats. Turkey vultures can be migratory.

The Turkey Vulture is family oriented. A roost is a group of vultures living together and sleeping at night in a tall tree. This is different from a nest where a mating pair will go off by themselves and lay two eggs and raise their young. Vultures do not build a nest as such, but simply lay two eggs on the bare ground. Nests are located on a rock ledge on the face of a cliff, in a cave, a hollow tree, or even in an abandoned shed or barn.

TURKEY VULTURE KEY FEATURES

Key Features

Some roosts are known to be more than 100 years old. That is, the same family of vultures has used the same tree or trees for home for many generations. They may move for the season (for some unknown reason) to a different tree in the immediate neighborhood. The following year they may adopt the new tree, or they may decide to go back to the original tree.

Individual birds will live in the same communal roost most of their life, and will usually sleep in the same roost in the same tree on their selected branch every night. However, some vultures may wander up to 200 miles, visiting different roosts each night, and then return to their home roost a week or two later.

In a roost the birds have a pecking order and use body language and eye contact in a manner which is clearly comprehensible to people who have learned to observe them.

Many of the roosts are located near human habitation. There can be the same kind of trees a half mile away in a field, but for their home the birds will pick a tree near people.

Turkey Vultures live and work together in cooperation and friendliness. They communicate with friends and neighbors when they find something to eat. They let the others know where the food is. When there is a big feast they communicate with neighboring flocks in distant roosts. Also, when they find food they will go to the California Condors and lead them to it. One roost was observed when they had a dead cow in their neighborhood. They somehow contacted a roost of 100 vultures about 30 miles away to come join them. Several days later, before they finished their feast, two more cows died. Within a day the vultures had contacted another roost to join them. At night all the birds visited together in the same or neighboring trees. At this point there were three different roosts living together. When the cow had been cleaned up, the several visiting roosts went home.

The turkey vulture is considered very intelligent and social. They prefer open country and roost in large congregations, often in large trees such as cottonwoods or tamarisks. They also often roost communally in elevated rock outcrops or cliffs. Observations of courtship, mating, and family life are rare. Mating usually begins early in March and involves elaborate courtship rituals, similar to cranes. Their breeding cycle ends midsummer and many vultures may not breed at all in a given year. There is no attempt at building a nest. Females typically lay two, two-to-three inch-long spotted eggs on the sandy floor of a cavity. Both parents attend to the eggs and incubation typically lasts for about 40 days. Hatchlings weigh only two ounces and are covered with pure white down. The adults regurgitate the food for the young. The young fledge in 6-8 weeks, although they may hang around the nest for up to 6 months.

> The turkey vulture has no voice box or syrinx making them anatomically unable to make vocal sounds, although they can give a soft hiss or groan. They may stomp one foot rapidly when approached or hiss when frightened or angry. They make a grunting sound when begging for food or during courting.

Their diet is carrion. They use olfactory senses and keen vision to discover animals that are already dead. They circle first in one direction and then the other, then land a short distance from the prey and approach cautiously on foot as they are quite vulnerable on the ground. They feed most often on animals within a day of their death and eat in groups on large items. Despite their powerful bills, turkey vultures have difficulty penetrating the hides of larger mammals and often must wait for some decomposition to take place or the activities of other scavengers to break the skin. They do not prefer putrid food and rather go for the freshest morsels, and will often refuse tainted or rotten meat. They lack the ability to close their toes or claws and are unable to grasp and capture live prey. They have been described as nature's "garbage collector" and can eat plant material when no carcasses are available. They will regurgitate their last meal as a defense mechanism and when handled, they hiss and vomit their foul smelling crop contents.

TURKEY VULTURE KEY FEATURES

Key Features

> These birds perform an important service by cleaning up the environment and preventing the spread of disease. Their excrement is sanitized and the bird has the ability to disinfect (destroy the bacteria and viruses present in the carcass). Studies have shown that they have the capacity to even wipe out anthrax in their stomachs. Currently, there are studies to explore this with hopes of applications in medical research.

MYTHOLOGY AND SYMBOLISM

The vulture is the subject of numerous myths and legends. Old world vultures are described as harbingers of death and are associated with graveyards. The most ancient images of the vulture in western culture relate to the harpy. In Greek mythology, a harpy was a monster with the head of a woman and the body of a vulture. Three harpies, daughters of Electra (a daughter of Oceanus), often called Aello, Podarge, and Ocypete, were described as filthy, hungry creatures and were sent by Zeus to snatch the food of Phineus, the king of Thrace. This was his punishment for predicting the future too accurately. Another version of the story says they were sent because Phineus had mistreated his children.

In Native American tradition, the Turkey Vulture is the bird of purification. Purification is necessary to bring back into the living world a harmony that has been broken. The Turkey Vulture presides over the dangerous transition from life to death. It has the power to dispel evil, dispel sickness, and break contact with the dead. In Hopi legend, the Turkey Vulture helps to raise the sun in the sky, although he loses his feathers in the process. He is described as a very powerful medicine man.

REMEDIES TO CONSIDER
Condor, *Vultur gryphus*

CONDITIONS TO CONSIDER
Parasites
Acne

Itching conditions of the face and head
People who are blocked or stuck

PROVING INFORMATION

This is a Todd Rowe proving, performed in Phoenix, Arizona, in the fall of 1999. The entire proving is available in ReferenceWorks.

> FOR FULL PROVING INFORMATION SEE PAGE 285.

> FOR CASES SEE PAGE 428.

TURKEY
VULTURE
KEY FEATURES

Andean Condor

Vultur gryphus

ORDER:	Ciconiiformes (Diurnal Birds of Prey)
FAMILY:	Cathartidae
GENUS:	*Vultur*
SPECIES:	*gryphus*

REMEDY NAME AND ABBREVIATION: Vultur gryphus, Vult-g

> The Andean Condor proving was conducted by Elizabeth Schulz and E. Rimmler. The findings have a lot in common with the proving of the Turkey Vulture.

ANDEAN CONDOR KEY FEATURES

CORE IDEA

THE WORLD OF THE LIVING AND THE WORLD OF THE DEAD

Like the Eagle, which forms a bridge between the everyday world and the world of the dream, the Condor navigates between the world of the living and the world of the dead.

Images of death and rebirth, of the passage from the realm of life to that of death. A new life after death.

KEY ASPECTS

REBIRTH AND RENEWAL
The image of the Phoenix showed prominently in the proving.

CHOICE
The necessity to have choices or options in one's life.
No choice = death. Stagnation. Trapped in a small space, unable to move.

CONTROL

RESPONSIBILITY
Hard working and responsible.

ALONE
Alone with no help or support.

PUTTING THINGS IN ORDER
"The vulture creates order! Death is cleaning up."

FALLING FAST WITH CONFIDENCE AND PLEASURE
"I felt secure and protected during the free fall. Nothing could harm me. I felt deep trust in letting go. I fell with an incredible speed. The speed was so fast I couldn't perceive anything about my surroundings. I relaxed and trusted the free fall. I fell and fell and had let go completely. Very quickly I experienced the fall as relaxing and joyful instead of frightening."

ITCHING

B•I•R•D•S

Key Features

PROMINENT RUBRICS
*Note: Rubrics marked with an * indicate suggested new rubrics.*

MIND:
    Biting; nails
    Conscientious about trifles
    Death; talks about
    *Delusions, Imaginations; Burning, everything is burning
    Delusions, Imaginations; dead; persons, sees
    *Delusions, Imaginations; parasites
    *Distractions; upsetting

SKIN:
    Itching
    Itching; distressing
    Itching; formicating and crawling
    Itching; intolerable
    Itching; parasites, as from
    Itching; scratch, must

NATURAL HISTORY

The condor is inseparably connected to South America and the Andes. The huge birds are seen as the rulers of their home, the Andes, the earth's longest mountain chain. The condors can be found on the whole East side of the Andes up to the Peruvian shore, from Venezuela to the Strait of Magellan. These giant vultures are habitual long distance travelers, and often they fly hundreds of miles in one day. Condors are true kings among the birds. They are unique and amazing in many ways. Their size alone is gigantic: with a height of 4 feet, a wingspread of 10.5 feet and a weight of up to 31 pounds they are among the earth's biggest flying birds.

The condor feeds almost entirely on carrion. Occasionally the condor kills sick or dying animals or feeds on eggs in seabird colonies along the Peruvian shore. Penguins and dead fish are also part of his nutrition. A strong beak and a nude head with the signature fluffy white ruff that encircles the lower neck is the perfect outfit to avoid getting soiled with blood while feeding. Condors have excellent eyesight, which they use to find their food.

Condors have a slow reproductive rhythm. The female lays a single white egg on rock ledges hundreds of feet above sea level every two or more years. Both parents brood the egg for 7-9 weeks. After 54 to 58 days the brown chick hatches. Although it is already fully-fledged after six months, it is fed until it is over two years old. The condor's life expectancy is about fifty years. The young bird reaches sexual maturity only after six to seven years. Condors engage in lasting partnerships. They seem calm and noble, sociable while feeding, and rather shy in the wild. They fly for hours at great heights looking at everything beneath them. Since condors feed on carrion they prevent the creation and expansion of epidemics and sickness in the animal kingdom by removing the carcasses.

The condor's flight is a majestic gliding on the air currents that carry him. By opening and closing his wings and using his broad tail as a rudder, the condor in flight in unsurpassed in beauty and elegance.

Condors and old world vultures belong to the same family, unlike turkey vultures which are more closely related to storks and ibises.

MYTHOLOGY AND SYMBOLISM

The current symbolism of our culture does not differentiate among the various kinds of vultures and the condor. They all perform the same task: eating the carcass. There is however an inherently different quality to how we perceive the Condor as a regal solitary king of the sky and the Turkey Vulture (Buzzard) as a pack animal scavenging whatever it can find.

The Condor brings death but also the light that releases all pain. He does not hunt like other birds of prey; he kills to set free. He eats the carrion and with it feeds his offspring. This makes him a symbol of renewal, a symbol of cosmic order: the old must die so that the new can live.

In Old Egypt, Nechbet, the Goddess of upper Egypt, was portrayed as a vulture or with vulture's skin. In the new kingdom she was worshipped as the Goddess of birth and motherhood. Vultures also appeared as the

Key Features

Goddess Mut. Egyptian queens wore a vulture's hood and therefore became symbolically the guardians of the cosmic order. In Egyptian paintings the vulture was shown frequently hovering above the pharaoh. In ancient Egypt the vulture was neither banned nor an outcast. He was depicted on precious burial jewelry because the Egyptians did not fear death. They had transformed the fear of being transitory visitors.

> "Death is not a terrible ending, but a function reaching into and surviving time created by God to renew the being, just as the sun God as an old man rejuvenates during nighttime to begin the morning of the new day as a child." (*The Egyptian Book of the Dead*)

The Vulture Goddess knows when you are truly ready for a change, because she can patiently observe and wait. **When the time is ripe, she sees the death of the old and eats it so that it can be reborn.**

In Tibet it is still the custom to offer dead people's bodies to the vultures. For us this might seem like an eerie practice, but it is supposed to signify that the body is only an empty shell, the temple of the soul.

Vultures are thought to have prophetic talents, because they often gathered at battlefields three days before the battles began. Iberians and Persians left the corpses of the fallen warriors for the vultures. The Roman War God Ares regarded the vulture as holy and therefore its killing was a crime.

> Elizabeth Schulz: "I found an unexpectedly high number of companies in Hamburg's and Berlin's phonebooks that chose the word 'condor' as their name: a construction and a scaffolding company, a trust company for builders, an insurance company, an import and export business, a shipping company, a publishing group, an airline, a tax consultant, a meat company, and offices for personal leasing and technical advice. The name condor is used in diverse business sectors to represent security, stability, quality, and international competence. I couldn't find any other bird name or animal name that was used in this way so frequently!

"I checked the use of the 'eagle' name and found it in very different sectors: the eagle is popular for pharmacies, restaurants, typewriting machines, airplanes used for hunting, coat of arms, and coins."

"In Germany, he is an established part of our subconscious, even if he lives in South America. The condor represents grandeur, expansion, success, stability, freedom, royal pride and dignity, overview, far reaching connections, and is a bridge to the hereafter."

ANDEAN CONDOR KEY FEATURES

REMEDIES TO CONSIDER
Cath-a, Turkey Vulture

CONDITIONS TO CONSIDER
People with a preoccupation with death.

PROVING INFORMATION
This is a proving conducted by Elisabeth Schulz in Germany.

FOR FULL PROVING INFORMATION SEE PAGE 291.

FOR CASES SEE PAGE 431.

Humboldt Penguin

Spheniscus humboldti

ORDER:	Sphenisciformes (Penguins)
FAMILY:	Spheniscidae (Penguins)
GENUS:	*Spheniscus*
SPECIES:	*humboldti*

REMEDY NAME AND ABBREVIATION: Spheniscus humboldti, *Sphen-h*

> NOTE: The proving was conducted in Munich, Germany by Peter Mohr. Jonathan Shore participated in this proving and took some notes. The details from the proving have been very difficult to come by. Our impression of this bird is based on Jonathan's notes. This is very preliminary and must not be taken too literally. On the other hand the feeling state of the proving experience and that of the clinical experience correspond rather well.

HUMBOLDT PENGUIN KEY FEATURES

CORE IDEA

FEELING OF BEING PUSHED ASIDE AND EXCLUDED FROM SOCIETY.
I will not get my turn; will not receive what is rightfully mine (even though I do something special to deserve it). The overall feeling is one of a heavy and intense negativity

> Being included or excluded from a group is a common theme in those animals whose lives are played out in packs, flocks, schools, etc. The emphasis in Penguin is on being pushed aside, actively excluded and deprived from the benefits of membership whilst simultaneously being denigrated and persecuted.

KEY ASPECTS

DOING IT RIGHT/WRONG
I must get it right or else I will be damned and excluded.
Nobody does it right. I will do it wrong. I have been wronged.

PRECISION, ISSUES OF BLACK AND WHITE

CLIQUES
Social groups from which I am excluded.
Secretive. Closed.
Feeling left out. Extreme isolation.
Wants to be special. I'm going to do this special thing but I will still be left out.
Anger at people with no reason.
Social restraint.

Key Features

MISTRUST/PARANOIA
    Severe mistrust of others to the point of paranoia. Anger at people with no reason.
    Never believed anyone liked him.
    Doesn't like to give; enough has been taken from me.
    Angry at the world.

CLEAN AND DIRTY
    Self-hatred and hatred of others.
    Loathing of life.

This is a smoldering anger at having been left out and excluded.

NATURAL HISTORY

Standing about 27 inches (69 cm) tall, the Humboldt penguin lives along the Pacific coastlines of Chile and Peru. Total population of the Humboldt penguin was estimated at 20,000 in the early 1980s, and in the 1990s may number around 10,000 individuals.

Like all penguins, the Humboldt is a flightless marine bird, superbly adapted to its environment. These flightless birds can survive in some of the coldest and most inhospitable places on Earth. Fossil records suggest that penguins once could fly but gave it up for life in the sea about 60 to 70 million years ago. Their wings have evolved into narrow bony flippers, which make them extremely maneuverable and fast swimmers. Early explorers thought penguins were fish, not fowl, because they are so superbly adapted to life in water.

Penguins are covered by a dense layer of small, scale-like feathers for protection against water and wind. An undercoat of downy feathers traps an insulating layer of air, which keeps them dry and warm. Beneath the skin, a layer of blubber also acts to retain the birds' body heat even in frigid waters and freezing air. In fact, for some penguins, keeping cool is more of problem than keeping warm. Humboldt penguins have a streamlined, torpedo-shaped body covered with short, waterproof, black-and-white feathers, giving them the classic tuxedoed look. They have stiff, narrow flippers, bare face and feet and eyebrow and chest stripes. There is no sexual dimorphism, so males and females look alike.

While their body is ideally suited for swimming, it is not so ideal for land. Consequently, penguins have a waddling walk. However, they are amazingly good hoppers and runners. They are capable of jumping up to almost their full height. The sounds penguins produce are not at all song-like. They are much more like donkey braying, trumpeting, and grunting. They also communicate with head and flipper waving.

HUMBOLDT PENGUIN KEY FEATURES

The Humboldt penguin nests on islands or rocky stretches of mainland coast and feeds on fish and squid in near-shore waters. They breed year round in small colonies. Humboldts dig underground burrows to protect themselves, their eggs, and chicks from the hot sun and predators. Nonbreeding penguins spend most of their time at sea, rarely coming back to land.

Males and females begin to breed at about three years. They often pair with the same mate for many years. A male arrives at the nesting area a few days before the female to prepare the nesting site. Once the nest is ready and the female arrives, a courtship dance begins and includes lots of bowing and head bobbing. The female lays two white eggs that take 39 days to hatch. Both parents alternate caring for the eggs. The two eggs hatch at different times. The chicks are born covered with very thin gray down and with their eyes shut. Both parents care for the chicks. By six weeks, the chicks begin to develop adult feathers, and have full adult plumage at about a year. They remain dependent on the parents until they are about three months old.

Penguins were heavily hunted for their meat, oil, and skins. Adult penguins and chicks were captured for zoos and private collectors. People also collected penguin eggs. Sailors on the southern seas regarded penguins as a welcome, easy meal. Penguin eggs were so prized in the Falkland Islands that the country declared National Penguin Day, a holiday when even school children were given the day off to collect eggs.

Key Features

Penguins also are vulnerable to climate variations. The occurrence of El Nino from 1982 to 1983 is thought to have caused the loss of some 65 percent of the Peruvian population of Humboldt penguins. The arrival of this unusually warm ocean current may have killed or driven away the penguins' prey species. Leopard seals and sharks prey on the penguins as they swim. Chicks are eaten by gulls, larger seabirds, and desert foxes.

REMEDIES TO CONSIDER
Remedies in the Leprosy miasm

CONDITIONS TO CONSIDER
Patients with obsessive qualities

PROVING INFORMATION
The proving was conducted in Munich, Germany by Peter Mohr.

FOR FULL PROVING INFORMATION SEE PAGE 296.

FOR CASES SEE PAGE 452.

**HUMBOLDT
PENGUIN
KEY FEATURES**

Whooper Swan
Cygnus cygnus

ORDER: Anseriformes (Waterfowls)
FAMILY: Anatidae (Ducks, Geese, Swans)
GENUS: *Cygnus*
SPECIES: cygnus

REMEDY NAME AND ABBREVIATION: Cygnus cygnus, Cygn-cy

Mute Swan
Cygnus olor

ORDER: Anseriformes (Waterfowls)
FAMILY: Anatidae (Ducks, Geese, Swans)
GENUS: *Cygnus*
SPECIES: *olor*

REMEDY NAME AND ABBREVIATION: Cygnus olor, Cygn-o

> NOTE: *Cygnus cygnus* is a proving by Jeremy and Camilla Sherr. *Cygnus olor* is a proving by Elizabeth Schulz. Helios Pharmacy also carries a remedy for *Cygnus columbianus* (Tundra Swan), *Cygnus-co*. The two swans we looked at appear very similar, so we do not differentiate them in the key aspects.

CORE IDEA

LIVING GRIEF

Actively experiencing the suffering even if it happened years prior. Overwhelmed with massive sadness and grief. As if the intervening years have collapsed into nothing. Anguish. Unresolved grief and disappointment.

> "The grief is there all the time. It's like it all happened five minutes ago… I can't escape it."
>
> "Feel very sad. Feel as if there is a big hole in my chest. Feel as if I have lost all hope of ever finding my life partner."
>
> "For me, childbirth feels like it just happened, whereas other people say you forget about it; I haven't forgotten a thing!"
>
> "Since my brother died, there is no hope, no purpose. I will never love again or feel happy."

SWAN
KEY FEATURES

KEY ASPECTS

AGGRESSION/SEXUAL AGGRESSION

> "At the age of 17, I was raped."
>
> "My husband didn't find me sexually attractive."
>
> "A recent shock happened when my ex-husband attacked me out of the blue."

THE COLOR WHITE

CHEST AND THROAT CONSTRICTION/BREATHING CONSTRICTION

> "The tiredness is accompanied by shortness of breath."
>
> "My chest is restricted, I can't breathe deeply, everything is caught in my throat."

BIRDS 147

Key Features

NATURAL HISTORY

Swans are the largest, and generally considered the most beautiful, of the waterfowl. A male is known as a cob, a female is a pen, and the young are called cygnets. Swans live in lakes, estuaries, marshes and flooded fields.

The diet of the swan consists of aquatic vegetation, and small percentages of aquatic insects, fish and frogs. Swans do not dive, but plunge their head and neck below the water's surface instead. They feed in deeper waters than the ducks and other waterfowl that share their habitat, and thus do not compete with them for food. Rather, food is made more readily available to other birds by swans because parts of the plants they consume float to the surface while the swans are feeding.

Adults are not paired for life, contrary to the stereotype of the 'pining swan' which has lost its mate. In fact, some have been observed to have as many as four mates, or even 'divorce' one mate in favor of another. However, established pairs are more successful breeders than non-established pairs.

MUTE SWAN:

The Mute Swan is one of 7 species of swans worldwide. Adult females weigh around 9kg, with males around 11kg. They are found in low lying wetland areas of the British Isles, north central Europe and north central Asia, the northeastern Atlantic coast, and around Lake Michigan in the US. These beautiful long necked birds will breed at 3 years of age, having a clutch of 3 to 8 eggs, although larger clutches have been recorded. The gestation period is 35 days from the date of the last egg. During the incubation period the male becomes very territorial and will aggressively protect his mate. He will normally use his strong wings as a weapon instead of biting.

The cygnets are born with a gray downy plumage that eventually turns to white. They can fly within 3 to 4 months and generally stay with the parents until the next breeding season when they are made to leave. Mute Swans have been known to live for over 25 years, but most only survive to 5 or 6 years old. Many cygnets die in their first 12 months, often due to flying accidents.

The nest site is selected in March or early April. The swans either build a nest from scratch, or use a previously constructed mound, such as a muskrat house. The nest is large, made of aquatic vegetation, and lined with feathers and down. It is built well above the normal water level in swampy places near a pond or lake. It is possible for clutches of 5-12 to occur, but 5-7 is most common. The eggs are pale gray to pale blue-green. The sexes share incubation, though the female spends the majority of time sitting, and the male usually stands guard. During the breeding season the male becomes very territorial and aggressive to any intruders. This behavior has been known to extend to swans fighting to the death. They often threaten humans who venture too close to their nests while issuing a warning call. The male may often take the first-hatched cygnet to the water while the female continues to incubate the remaining eggs. Cygnets are able to fly at about 60 days. Chicks can ride on the backs of their parents or under their wings. By the following breeding season, the parents drive the young away. The cygnets then join flocks of other non-breeding swans, and during this time molt their feathers, becoming flightless for a short period of time. In the next two years, the cygnets begin to bond with a mate and to look for a suitable breeding territory. Swans do not breed until about the third year.

SWAN KEY FEATURES

Mute Swans are usually silent, as the name suggests. But adults sometimes snort and make hissing noises or puppy-like barking notes, though the sounds are not far-reaching due to their straight trachea. Also, the sound of the wings during flight—which has been described as a musical throbbing or humming—is very audible. Mute Swans set up large territories of 4-10 acres, which can include an entire small lake or pond. **Even in semi-domestication, the nest is strongly defended; swans have been known to attack other waterfowl and even people.** Blows from their powerful wings can be especially painful. They can be dangerous to children, and are capable of killing or maiming some of the larger predators. Mute Swans very rarely nest in a colony. There is no mass migration, though in

Key Features

winter there may be gatherings numbering more than 100 individuals at nearby open salt water.

> When swimming, a mute swan holds its neck in a graceful curve with the bill pointing downward, as opposed to other swans, which carry their bills level and necks erect. In an aggressive posture, the male often arches his secondary wing feathers over his back.

Mute Swans were domesticated for food in Britain. Markings on their feet indicated ownership. Eventual domestication saved the bird from becoming hunted to extinction there. Feathers were also used as quills for writing, the leathery web used for purses, and the wing bones for making whistles.

The successful introduction and consequent expansion of the Mute Swan into North America has begun to pose significant concerns to native wildlife. This bird is very aggressive, and has been known to drive off such stubborn and similarly sized species as the Canada Goose and Trumpeter Swan.

WHOOPER SWAN:

Whooper Swans breed in Iceland and the north of Europe and Asia. They migrate south in the winter to west and central Europe, to around the Black, Aral and Caspian Seas, and to China and Japan. The yellow markings on the bill of the Whooper Swan are like a human fingerprint; they are all different and individual birds can be recognized by their bill pattern. From a distance they can be separated from Mute Swan (*Cygnus olor*) by the straighter neck and the flatter profile of the body.

MYTHOLOGY AND SYMBOLISM

The species name *Cygnus* originates in Greek mythology. Kygnus was a friend of Phaeton, son of Helios, the sun God. On an excursion in the sun chariot, Phaeton came too close to Earth and Helios' anger caused him to crash. Kygnus in his grief transformed into a swan. His plaintive cry became famous as the swan-song, a lament upon dying or leaving. He is eternalized in the night sky as the constellation Cygnus, the Great Swan, which has served sailors as well as astrologers over the millennia. In another Greek myth, Zeus seduced Leda by taking the form of a swan. She later gave birth to Apollo, God of light, and Artemis. White swans are often seen pulling Apollo's carriage and in some paintings, Aphrodite and Artemis are accompanied by swans.

According to ancient Greek beliefs the Swan possessed the ability to predict the future. German mythology also places a close connection between the Swan and the gods. "Es schwant mir" means "I sense something" (swan is Schwan in German). This idiom is still used in the German language when intuition and a power to see the future come through.

Since earliest times, the Swan has been a symbol of light, purity, and grace. The Swan guides the boat of death that brings the souls into another world, being in contact with the kingdom of the dark goddess of death, Hel. Yet on the island of Rügen, the Swan takes the role of the Stork and brings babies, demonstrating the Swan's ability to guide beings into life as well as into death. Hans-Christian Andersen's fairy tale *The Ugly Duckling* is a modern example of swan mythology where the poor bird is ruthlessly tormented until she finally finds her proper place among others of her kind.

SWAN KEY FEATURES

In the middle ages, the image of the Swan served as a heraldic beast on coats of arms. Considering the prevailing poverty and famine then, the swan's meat was a tasty complement on poor people's menu (swans belong to the duck family). Later, at the English and Prussian royal courts, white swans that had become rare enjoyed the status of a protected inviolable species. Swan breeding was a privilege of the nobility.

Strongly associated with the Swan is the color white, standing for purity, perfection, and light. White is a symbol of innocence and virginity. Angels and holy beings are depicted dressed in white like the swan, as are

Key Features

the gowns of brides and children at their first communion. The color white also represents the absolute, the beginning and end as well as their union, which is why it is used so frequently for birth, marriage, initiation, and death rites of passage. White in other cultures holds the place of black in ours, being the color of grief and funerals.

REMEDIES TO CONSIDER
Natrum muriaticum
Ignatia

CONDITIONS TO CONSIDER
Long-standing grief
Victims of sexual abuse, rape

PROVING INFORMATION
Cygn-o is a proving by Elizabeth Schulz and can be found in ReferenceWorks. *Cygn-cy* is a proving by Jeremy and Camilla Sherr as yet unpublished. Excerpts from their article are used with kind permission from Nick Hewes, editor of *The Homeopath*, (October 2002, No. 87).

> FOR FULL PROVING INFORMATION SEE PAGES 298 AND 301.

> FOR CASES SEE PAGES 458 AND 463.

**SWAN
KEY FEATURES**

Wandering Albatross

Diomedea exulans

ORDER:	Procellariiformes (Albatrosses, Shearwaters and Petrels)
FAMILY:	Diomedeidae
GENUS:	*Diomedea*
SPECIES:	*epomophora*

REMEDY NAME AND ABBREVIATION: Diomedea exulans, Dio-e

CORE IDEA
WANDERING
SEARCHING FOR AN IMPOSSIBLE DESTINATION

KEY ASPECTS
CONNECTION/ISOLATION/LONELINESS/BEING SET APART
Departing is difficult. Vulnerable in contact with others.
Wanting to be seen as an individual.
Feeling of freedom even in a group.
Being alone is painful.
Being nobody in a big family. Loneliness in youth.
Homesickness.
Dream of child that does not belong to the family.

ENDLESS, TIMELESS, STILLNESS
Feeling of being endless and timeless in the water.
Transition of livelihood to stillness.

SUDDEN INTERRUPTION/INTRUSION
Sudden changes from seriousness to laughter.
Suddenly a waterspout or sailing maneuver would interrupt whatever was going on.
Intrusion by others.
Dream of bicycling accident.
Dream of entrapment.
After interruption, the group always came back to unfinished matters.
Group is threatened by intruders.
Taking one's stand; saying no to intruders.
Feeling of vulnerability in a group.
Sexual intrusion. Unicorn image.

FATHER
Death of the father.
Forgotten birthday of father.
Father as 'dykerevee' (literally 'The Reverend of the Dike'; a person of authority).

WANDERING ALBATROSS KEY FEATURES

Key Features

Unification of Opposites/Androgyny/Equality
Dream of adopting a foreign child.
A black child playing with a white child.
Unicorn as symbol of androgyny.
Dream where the roles of men and women were not strictly divided.

Thrusting Upward
Both the Statue of Liberty and the unicorn came up as prominent images. There is a certain physical similarity between the up-thrust torch of the statue and the horn of the unicorn as well as any underlying metaphorical meaning.

Death and Fire
Saw two dead animals on stroll.
Girls spitting fire.
Fire in hand of statue of Liberty.

PROMINENT RUBRICS
*Note: Rubrics marked with an * indicated suggested new rubrics.*

MIND:
    Company; aversion to, aggravates; wandering from place to place
    Confusion; loses way in well-known streets
    Delusion; body, body parts; sensation as if two sides of the body do not fit; as if there is a torsion
    Delusion; oblique lines, like a reed swaying in the wind
    *Delusion; animals, of; unicorn
    *Restlessness; eyes, ameliorated by closing
    Wander, desires to

VERTIGO:
    *Light feeling in the head; swaying sensation

THROAT:
    Lump, sensation of (water bird)

STOMACH:
> Apprehension
> *Apprehension; primal fear of life, a
> Fear felt in
> *Nausea; vomiting, sensation of, without feeling bad
> Tension; feeling of anticipation

CHEST:
> *Open, feeling of openness and burning love for life in chest

EXTREMITIES:
> Awkwardness; hands; drops things
> *Eruptions; papular; upper limbs, wrist
> Heaviness, tired limbs; lower limbs; legs
> Pain; upper limbs, wrists (ulna side)

SLEEP:
> Heavy
> Sleeplessness

SKIN:
> Eruptions; papular
> Eruptions; discharging, moist; honey, like

CHILL:
> Shaking, shivering, rigors

GENERALITIES:
> Coldness
> Coldness; fear, from
> *Shaking; fear, from; cold sensation, with

WANDERING ALBATROSS KEY FEATURES

NATURAL HISTORY

The Wandering Albatross is the largest albatross with a span of up to 12 feet long. It is nearly totally white with a few dark spots on the back and wings. The bird has webbed feet and needs a long take-off run to get airborne. They spend most of their life in flight, landing only to breed and

Key Features

feed. Distances traveled each year are hard to measure, but one banded bird was recorded traveling 6000 km in twelve days.

An albatross glides more than it flies, gaining height against the wind and gaining speed by turning around in a plunge downward to the sea where the bird catches its food by ducking its head and curved beak into the water. When the wind is strong, the wings are bent backwards in the wrist joint. While squid and fish are the preferred foods, albatrosses are often seen scavenging scraps from fishing boats. Refuse from ships and floating waste also form part of the diet. Feeding is one of the few times that birds land, and this is mostly undertaken at night.

Pairs mate for life and breed every two years. Breeding takes place on sub-Antarctic islands and commences in early November. The nest is a mound of mud and vegetation, and is placed on an exposed ridge near the sea. The single egg hatches after two months and the chick remains in the nest for approximately nine months. During the early stages of the chick's development, the parents take turns sitting on the nest while the other searches for food. Later, both adults hunt for food and visit the chick at irregular intervals.

MYTHOLOGY AND SYMBOLISM

Most enigmatic of all birds, in superstition, is the cumbersome albatross. Among sailors, this large seabird is considered a harbinger of good luck. Its captivity or murder, whether deliberate or accidental, is thought to bring misfortune and woe to the ship and its crew, and death or curse to the sailor who kills it. This superstition is best emphasized in Samuel Taylor Coleridge's poem, "The Rime of the Ancient Mariner."

Diomedes was one of the finest and bravest of Greek hero/warriors during the Trojan Wars, **whose companions were transformed into seabirds**. He was respectful to all authority figures and had little or no pride. Always wise and reasonable, he may have been the vision of the perfect nobleman. Diomedes demonstrated a great respect for government authority. He risked his own life to save the aging Greek commander Nestor and helped him escape from Hector after many other

Greeks had already fled. Diomedes did not credit himself for his accomplishments. He did not glorify his own accomplishments, but thanked the gods, and even credited previous generations for his skill and success. As well as being humble, Diomedes accepted fate and acted accordingly. Throughout "The Iliad," Diomedes is portrayed as a cool-headed individual. This trait may be best exhibited in the nighttime spying mission with Odysseus in which he completed the mission because he kept calm and did not become fueled by rage.

CONDITIONS TO CONSIDER
Repetitive Stress/Strain Injury
People who cannot settle down.
People who always feel away from home.

PROVING INFORMATION
The proving was undertaken aboard ship by a crew of Dutch homeopaths in late August, 2000, and is recounted in *Wad Stories*, Volume 1. The remedy was taken in the 200K potency.

FOR FULL PROVING INFORMATION SEE PAGE 303.

FOR CASES SEE PAGE 464.

WANDERING ALBATROSS KEY FEATURES

Provings

Homeopathy as a science stands as a bridge between the visible and the invisible; between the laws governing the matter of this world and those that rule a world we can only guess at. One doorway into this other world is the proving experience, which provides a framework through which that other world may be penetrated. In a proving, the energies of a substance can be felt and experienced directly by the participants. We offer the following provings in the hope that they will invite you into the spirits of the birds themselves.

162 B·I·R·D·S

Long understood as the primary foundation of our Materia Medica, the Proving lies at the heart of the Homeopathic system. Thus a dynamic investigation of not only the recorded symptoms arising out of provings (the totality of symptoms or remedy image) but a delving into the nature of the process itself is essential for a fully rounded understanding of this unique science.

As a discipline arising in the West, Homeopathy is (most certainly in its earlier stages) considered a science of the mind. The essential data recovered in the anamnesis upon which the prescription is based is taken in and organized by the mental functioning of the practitioner. This occurs almost always in the abstract. By this we mean that the prescriber neither participates directly in the experience of the patient nor in the vital life that has created the unique configuration of the remedy. This is not to say that no one does this but rather that it is not the norm, nor do most even experience this as a limitation.

The sense that something is missing, that life cannot be lived by the mind alone, may well be the hidden current that is surfacing in what is an increasingly widespread desire to conduct provings. It is our hypothesis that while the external reasons appear as a need for more remedies, the underlying moving force is one that arises from the feeling or the desire for the actual, visceral, concrete experience of the mystery of homeopathy. For although there are many who deny the mystery and make great efforts to explain in everyday and scientifically accepted terminology exactly what the remedies are and what they do, there are others who feel the wonder when confronted with the penetration of the everyday world by forces we cannot see or quantify or measure. Hahnemann himself strongly recommended that homeopaths conduct provings on themselves, in addition to making their own remedies, in an endeavor to meet this mystery full on.

Homeopathy is a science that stands as a bridge between the visible and the invisible, between the laws governing the matter of this world and those which rule a world we can only guess at. One doorway into the invisible world is the proving experience, a gap through which we can breach the limitations of our conventional, material world. Thus the methodology, the 'how it is done,' is critical. It is absolutely necessary to ensure that the framework of data collec-

Provings

tion is not set up to exclude, or to rule as inadmissible, the very data which carry the inner life of our science.

By way of illustration we can pose the question: at which point in time does the proving begin? Or, to regard the question from a slightly different angle, which symptoms are to be considered admissible?

It has been our repeated experience that the moment the group sits down in a quiet fashion, the feeling in the room subtly changes and begins to reflect the quality of the substance to be proven. The main threads of apparently random chatter amongst participants are seen on later review to reflect both the general and often rather specific themes of the remedy.

What is really remarkable, however, is that there exists definite evidence that the proving can begin quite some time before the official commencement. This has been observed on more than one occasion. One instance in particular stands out. In a trituration proving, one participant who spoke little English and through a set of unique circumstance was co-opted into the proving group only some 30 minutes before we began, who had absolutely no foreknowledge of homeopathy or provings, reported having had significant dreams the previous night which were inexplicable to her until the proving was underway. During the process it became clear to her that the dreams were directly related to the substance of the proving.

As an isolated incident this would have limited meaning. However, the validity of the experience has been substantiated by additional data collected by the senior author in two significant experiments designed to investigate this phenomenon.

The first was done at a five-day residential seminar in Eastern Germany in 1996. The decision to prove *Radium bromatum* was made by the senior author some 4 – 6 weeks before the seminar date. Although some of the participants may have anticipated that a proving would take place, only two German colleagues and the author knew the exact substance. At the start of the seminar it was announced that a proving experiment would be conducted and the form it would take was explained. The entire group of some 50 people was divided into three sections. The first or "sensitive" group would be those self-selected individuals who felt that they had already begun to experience proving symptoms. The second or "proving" group consisted of those who indicated that they wished to participate in the proving by actually taking the remedy. Those remaining formed the third group, which was given literature on plutonium and asked to imagine what it would be like if they had taken this substance.

The participants were specifically requested not to communicate their experience to anybody outside of their specific group. Each group then met together for one hour a day for three days. On the fourth day, a general meeting was held at which representatives from each of the groups presented a summary of their experiences. A video recording of this meeting was made. One of the reasons for the selection of *Radium bromatum* was the wealth of existing literature describing the physical symptomatology and the paucity of information regarding the emotional state. It was anticipated that if the provers accurately reproduced the known physical picture, then the image that emerged on the mental/emotional plane could likewise be trusted and indeed this proved to be the case. Especially interesting was the clear and indisputable fact that the most accurate representation of already recorded symptomatology was to be found amongst the first or "sensitive" group, those who had not even taken the remedy and yet had begun to experience symptoms before arriving at or on their way to the seminar. The video record of this was presented at the Homeopathy for the World Congress in Berlin 1997.

The second experiment was conducted in Paris in 2003. The form was of a similar but more complex construction with a little over 100 participants. *Lac equinum* was the proving substance. A standard 30C preparation was distributed to 30 people one month prior to the seminar while an additional 17 received placebo. At the beginning of the seminar, the remaining participants were divided into five groups: a self-selected "sensitive" group who had already begun to experience symptoms (some 10 people), two groups who then prepared a 3C potency by succussion from mare's milk; and another two groups who prepared a 3C potency by triturating the tail hair from a stallion. It can be seen that not only was the vital substance of "horse" being tested, we were also looking for any differences that might play out between "male" and "female" against an already proven remedy.

Provings

The groups met individually for an hour the following day and then together in a large general meeting at which a summary of the experiences of each group was presented. Although at the time of the publication of this book the final results of this experiment have not been collated, the general impression substantiates that of the earlier experiment. There was a remarkable overall correlation between the diverse groups with respect to the main themes (which correlated well with the previously published proving by Nancy Herrick), with the most precise and subtle of the symptoms arising in the "sensitive" group. It is also noteworthy that in discussion with the members of this group, after the nature of the substance was revealed, at least four members had a significant relationship with horses.

The main conclusion arising from these experiences is that the best provings are those that are constructed to include the collection of data from different proving conditions and levels of materiality. These include:

- Data gathered from journal provings, in which the symptoms have an opportunity to express themselves under the ongoing conditions of everyday life and are recorded in detail
- Data gathered from a group setting where there is direct involvement with the process of remedy preparation
- And especially data gathered from those who are so sensitive to the process as to produce symptoms even at a distance

This totality gives a more complete picture than any single method by itself.

There is one further point that involves opinion rather than fact. **It is the contention of the authors that the proving master has an obligation to bring out the central theme(s) of the proving.** While provings in which all the symptoms generated are listed without any attempt to arrive at an organizing principle are excellent sources of information for the repertory, they have much less value for practical work. The distant observer, who has not had the privilege of directly experiencing the energy of a substance, often cannot bring order to the mass of symptoms by mental analysis alone, and thus is left to the chance recognition of some peculiar symptom or other which has stuck in memory in bringing the remedy into practice.

REVIEW OF PROVING METHODOLOGIES

Throughout the history of Homeopathy, we have had a number of sources of information incorporated into our Materia Medica. Clinical cures, toxicological information and herbal lore, as well as proving data, have laid the backbone of our literature. The current explosion of provings now being carried out and those recorded in this book necessitates some explanation of the different methodologies. While it has been our experience that every type of proving is capable of producing useful, practical, and accurate data (or not!) on the physical/mental/emotional realms, not all homeopaths feel the same way. For the record, a brief description of proving methodologies now being performed is listed here.

TOXICOLOGICAL INFORMATION

While not official provings *per se*, toxicological information has always been included in our Material Medica. New chemicals and drugs are regularly producing new remedy pictures, with symptoms on the gross material plane as well as on the subtler mental/emotional one. Records of poisonings with Arsenic and Strychnine, or observations of those under the influence of alcohol and other drugs, have contributed much to the clinical picture of these remedies. **It is our supposition that each level of materiality contributes information that goes to make up the totality of the image.** The material levels are given to us; the subtler have to be discovered.

> Toxicology is included in this list for completeness' sake. The evidence borne out by modern provings, coupled with information from accidental poisonings, raises a subtle methodological question, which is: what is the role of intent? Is a proving conducted by one or more persons undertaking an experiment with intention any different from an incidental poisoning? This is an interesting question to contemplate.

HAHNEMANNIAN (CLASSICAL)

This word has become synonymous for correct, perfect, the last word in methodology. Thanks to the exhaustive research of Franz Vermeulen, we have a better insight into the early experimental origins of the Hahnemannian

Provings

materia medica. Hahnemann "proved" many of his substances on himself, his wife and perhaps one other student.

Not much weight was given to statistical verification, double or even single blind trials etc. In the search for 'scientific objectivity' currently in vogue in Homeopathy there is something that has been too lightly passed over. Hahnemann himself participated in these experiments, not simply as an outside observer, but as an active force, bringing his own vital energies into direct contact with the object of the experiment. It is quite possible that this was done, not because he didn't know any better or didn't have the resources, but rather with full intent as a preferred method with its own intelligent and sophisticated structure. Another point to be made here is Hahnemann's insistence that every symptom be included in the proving data, no matter how irrelevant or incidental it may appear.

MODERN CLASSICAL

In our time, the work of Jeremy Sherr has set a template for practical rigor in the way provings are conducted. A rough outline of this method is as follows. There is a Proving Master, Supervisors, and Participants. The proving master decides on the substance, known only to him/herself. Before the proving, the supervisors take the case of each of the participants under their management. The participants then take the actual remedy, in a range of potencies and some placebo, spread amongst the participants, until symptoms are experienced. The proving starts at the same time on the same day, as much as possible, amongst all the participants, wherever they are. The participants and supervisors record the symptoms during the specified time of the proving, noting day, time, and whether it is an old, new or cured symptom. At the close of the proving, the entire group rejoins and the symptoms are gathered into a whole, rubrics are prepared, and a picture or essence of the substance is elucidated.

MODIFIED CLASSICAL

A subset of Modern Classical provings has been used extensively by Nancy Herrick for her series of recent provings. The remedy is given in the 30C potency only with no placebo. The proving master selects the substance and keeps it a secret. Most provers are students in the Hahnemann College and thus homeopaths or budding homeopaths. They have a choice of getting a supervisor or not. Provers take three doses maximally and take no doses after a symptom is experienced. The proving starts on the same day amongst all provers. All detailed symptoms are recorded in notebooks throughout the day and night. Participants are encouraged to record only symptoms that are new or different or stronger than their usual symptoms. A group meeting is held at three weeks and each prover reports his or her experience in whatever manner they choose. The entire meeting is recorded on video and typed to add to the proving notes. The proving group (usually 2-4 students and the proving master) then assembles all the details from each prover, and meets to make an in-depth study of the proving during a 4-6 month period until they can agree on a set of themes. They then prepare rubrics from each verified symptom. Finally the natural substance itself is studied, to understand it and to delineate those areas where substance and proving themes come together.

> The one exception to this protocol was with Lotus where all potencies (not just 30C) were used. Interestingly this did not make any difference whatsoever. Some provers had big reactions to low doses and some had no reactions to high doses.

TRITURATION

A trituration proving involves the participants gathering together for one or more days to actually prepare the substance to be proven by trituration, according to protocols described in the Organon. Everyone is preferably grinding the substance in his/her own mortar. Notes are taken and experiences shared during the grinding and/or at the end of each trituration round. Videotaping can be very helpful for accurate reporting.

In addition to the three levels of trituration as prescribed in the Organon, in the last six or seven years a group of German homeopaths have taken this process a step further by adding another round of trituration. Alize Timmerman has taught extensively about the remedies made from this fourth level, referred to as C4 homeopathy. Participants in these provings find that information received from the substance during the four levels of

Provings

trituration, is very succinct, direct, and precise. It has also been the experience that provers do not "carry" the proving for so long afterward. The C4 trituration itself provides a resolution.

SEMINAR
In a seminar proving, seminar participants elect to take a remedy that has been prepared from an unknown substance. The remedy may be given out in different potencies. Seminarians report on their dreams and symptoms at various times throughout the seminar and both common and particular themes and physicals are noted.

MEDITATION
A dream or meditation proving involves taking the substance (prepared in remedy form) to be proven into one's hand or keeping it under the pillow at night, without actually "taking" it internally. Symptoms are discussed at the end of the meditation or the following day amongst group members.

PROVINGS IN THIS BOOK
The provings that follow are drawn from a number of the above methods. In general those done in California were of the trituration variety (Macaw, Owl, Pelican, Heron), using the following protocol. Hahnemann Laboratories provided a mortar and pestle, a scale, and pre-weighed quantities of sac lac. The feather was finely cut, weighed and added to a corresponding weight of sac lac and ground a few times making it unrecognizable to the participants. Some 7 – 10 provers sat around a table with each one taking turns triturating for 2 – 3 minutes, before passing the mortar to the next person. After seven minutes of grinding, the contents of the bowl were scraped for three minutes, as directed in the Organon. At the end of 30 minutes of trituration, a gram of the triturate was removed and mixed with an additional 99 grams of sac lac. This process was repeated three times for a 3C potency or four times for a 4C (Pelican).

Food was provided and the provers were free to talk, eat, move around the room or go outside. The only instruction given was to take notes of any symptoms experienced, delineated according to each trituration level. One participant was given the task of keeping time and another was responsible for entering into a computer both the thread of the general conversation and the details. The process was also videotaped.

At the conclusion of the trituration process, each prover related their experience. The triturate was sent to Hahnemann Laboratories, where it was potentized to 30C. This potency was provided to each participant who could take it or not, in as many doses as they wished depending on how they felt. The group met again some 10 – 14 days later. There was one identified supervisor who was in contact with each of the participants, to gather notes and especially to ensure that no one was without support during this time. At the second meeting each prover gave an account of their experience followed by a discussion of what the remedy might be. The journals were collected and later typed up for further review.

Provings

BROWN PELICAN *Pelecanus occidentalis*

This is a Jonathan Shore trituration/proving done in California in September of 2001. It is significant that the remedy was made up to the 4th trituration level (C4). Provers made the remedy and then took the remedy one week later in a 30C potency from either the C3 or C4 trituration.

> Everyone is aware of the terrorist attacks on New York and Washington, DC on September 11, 2001. These tragedies happened one week after we started the proving. This event had an impact on all of us and colored the proving in ways we cannot predict or separate out.

This is a portion of the verbatim conversation during the trituration process. Notice the confusion in the beginning, which is very birdlike. About 11 people participated in the proving. Only 4 knew the remedy being made.

FIRST TRITURATION
Losing my coordination already.
It's hard work.
We are supposed to scrape three minutes, right?
I thought it was two.
Just grinding…no scraping…
Should I scrape it down? (laughter).
Now we scrape the edges off for some reason unknown to me.
Now grind?
No, only scrape. Scrape the stuff off the edges.
So we've had seven minutes of grindings and three minutes of scraping?
Exactly, that's the routine. (numerology is invoked, the significance of 7 and 3 versus 6 and 10, returning to 1).

SECOND TRITURATION
Is this making people hungry?
Is someone timing this?
I'm grinding, I've been waiting long enough.
I saw a vulture at the beach the other day, feeding.
If you see that Pelican you have to duck, they'll pee on you…this is at the headlands.

They fly over the beach?
At the headlands, there's that area where the tide goes out…the birds are constantly flying over from that one rock that's solid white…and that's where they fly over my head.
I just don't believe that they fly over you and bomb you.
I don't want to worry you…but birds don't pee.
They don't have urinary tracts?
Birds just don't pee.
That's why they say thank God cows don't fly.
Except in tornadoes.
Are they supposed to break their breasts open and feed their young the blood? Is that real?
It sounds pretty self-defeating.
Sounds very Catholic.
Isn't that the Phoenix?
That's pagan. Greek Orthodox.
That's not Christian!
Jesus is turning in his grave.
I just see this purity in here.
Well that put the energy back in there. (Another little spill.)
Do pelicans dive under the water, or is it cormorants.
I don't think they go that deep.
It just seems like they'd have to go far enough down, just enough for the fish to jump in.
There's another one who's not working on my teeth (referring to the scraping sound someone is making while scraping).
I think she's working on a molar there.
That was more fun than grinding!
It hurts me! I can hear really high noises, this noise makes me kind of want to bend over.
Maybe that's the cookies.
Kind of like a cookie echo.
Or the guacamole.
That's one of nature's perfect foods.
(The scraping count is lost again, then found anew.)
We've gotten to the point where we can't count to three.
There's no more of those little hairy things in there.
We ground them down.
That's it. 3C.

BROWN PELICAN PROVING

Provings

THIRD TRITURATION
Back to 7. Third round of seven. 21.
(Two minutes or three minutes, the confusion continues
  momentarily, and is resolved.)
Who's next.
I still have a piece of the substance in there.
The first time I saw it, I thought it was a piece of my eyelash.
The funny thing is there's this confusion about how many times we've done it, and we've done it 21 times.
Everyone has a different style of grinding.
I feel like I have this past life flashback where I'm an Indian woman grinding corn or something.
Very warm in here.
Not warm, it's stuffy.
(Door opened, to general satisfaction).
My face is flushing.
Everyone is suggestible.
Isn't that the point of the group, to have everyone have the same experience?
Not necessarily?
But doesn't that magnify the experience?
Sounds like you're having fun.
I am having fun [scraping]; it's like going into the snow.
Anyone else craving chocolate?
Anyone for saké?

FOURTH TRITURATION
Now this is three, right?
Four!
No, no, four minutes.
At this level, we're getting to the soul of the remedy, getting to where the remedy actually affects the disease, into the soul of the remedy.
According to the current tradition, we're getting the keys of the kingdom of heaven.
Four is bringing things in, it's manifestation, it's the all-level. All philosophies.
Four is the last place you can be in manifestation without leaving mani-

festation. It's the closest you can be in the body to the spiritual tradition.
Fourth chakra is the heart chakra, it's the interface between heart and body.

It's the heart of the matter.

So we're like in South Africa and it's…

What….

I don't know, a long Graham Greene sentence. It's in South Africa, there's this guy who's a clerk, and then I stopped reading.

I'm feeling a lot of gratitude.

So this is the fourth, the fourth of the fourth.

I noticed at the beginning of this process it was quiet, and intense.
 And now it seems lighter.

Deeper, heavier, I feel like I'm sinking.

Should we go around and guess? Does anyone know what it is?

How can you tell the difference between what you know and what it is?

It's the same thing.

You've probably had the experience of absolute knowing, of knowing who's on the phone before you've picked it up. This is the same thing. You will know absolutely that you know.

It seems like it's going so fast.

It's faster scraping than grinding.

BROWN PELICAN PROVING

WRAP-UP CONVERSATION AFTER THE TRITURATION PROCESS

FEMALE PROVER 1:
Most of this was around my head. Even when I closed my eyes to relax them, I felt them quivering. I felt all eyes and ears. The trituration was fascinating to me; I wanted to do only it. I couldn't stop moving my feet. Needed to stretch my neck and go like this, I felt a lot of pain in the chest; I think that was around 3C, maybe around when we were talking about the pelican and the opening of the chest, it was quite an intense shooting pain. Kept going to a place in my mind where I go to Tennessee Valley, a marsh. I loved that light-hearted place.

FEMALE PROVER 2:
I have to talk now? I just want to meditate. I kept getting 'perfect' pictures, what am I supposed to do, what's the protocol, but then I let that go. By 2C, it moved out of this separate 'competition' and more about the group. I was

Provings

getting irritated with anything slightly intellectual, I didn't want to get vocal, but it was beyond my interest. Kept thinking I was going to go to sleep. Wanted to visualize the position I was in, felt very tuned in to my body, felt a tightness. Not a headache, but felt like a tube was opening in my head. Things were going in and out of focus, couldn't always see, things are in soft focus, this tube or breathing tube goes down to the place behind the heart. Kept getting pictures of dolphins and pelicans.

FEMALE PROVER 3:
Different intense feelings, maybe it's because I am in love, but it felt like a celebration. I did not want to stop. It felt like we were all drinking buddies. There was that thing that came up about the corn and the animal hunting, it was about respect. It was also interesting that people kept losing count. It was funny that one prover was sitting up on that stool going "this is heaven," and it was about the joy of singing. Felt a pressure in my head.

MALE PROVER 4:
I guess what happened to me was I immediately started itching, in my joints; I've been scratching my head all evening. I felt like I was growing hair all over. I felt like I was really getting rhythm. Started saying words that rhyme in my head, and I was hearing music, (rhyme, dime, time). Felt a lot of floating at first, less later. Very playful, making silly jokes, playing with bottle cap, then felt very nostalgic, at the end. Peace and tranquility.

FEMALE PROVER 5:
Pressure at the top of my head, while back of head was lifting up. Arms feeling light. Trituration seemed like great sport, there was a meditative state. Sensitive to smells, feeling of burnt something from the powder. Felt like someone was smoking outside. Felt hot at times. Different patterns and different rhythms during process, pictures of millstones, something very ancient.

FEMALE PROVER 6:
In the beginning I had sensations in my jaw. I kept wanting the breeze, and that stayed constant. It was also interesting to be part of a group and not have to contribute. At C2, I couldn't keep up with conversation. At C3, it seemed mundane. I went in and out, but it was OK. At C4, I kept checking in with what was really going on. I loved the purity of this remedy.

FEMALE PROVER 7:
I felt different things at different times, I felt myself observing myself. Some people said they felt high, I identified with that. I felt the energy change. I think at the beginning we were expectant of the process, but we were joking, I think I felt a greater connection with the group and the remedy. Felt hot sometimes and cold sometimes. Felt my brain, and never felt that before.

BROWN PELICAN PROVING

MALE PROVER 8:
Of the various provings I've done, I've had more experiences in this one. Everything was there right in the beginning. The sense of time was different; someone else was going to keep track of that. Serious, and quiet, but I had this great desire to laugh. And this was all within the first 5 minutes. But I think at various times all of these things came into play. At end of 1C, I felt like I was sharing some kind of secret, there was a common sort of knowledge. At 2C, there was lighter, more interaction, the intensity wasn't so strong. Then there was this feeling in my heart, and then I felt so sleepy. I had no interest in this nonsense conversation that was going on. Towards the end of 3C, there was a sense of sadness, this sense of separation between myself and the real world. At 4C, I had written here 'philosophical talk'. It came to me that this is not an intellectual talk, I felt nowhere, there wasn't a lot of mind stuff, except during 4C, there was something that was much more alert. I noticed definitely the rhythms. It was like quiet, and then there was a lot of talk. There was an easy rhythm, it was light, there was a lot of laughter.

The rhythm of the scraping brought up this story from me. My favorite story. I heard it on the radio once and did not catch the beginning. It was about a North American Indian tribe that would hunt the caribou. There was only one musician in the tribe and he was the shaman and he played a drum. They would track the caribou and when they came within distance of the herd, they would build a semi-circular enclosure with an opening on one end. In the building of it, it was absolutely essential that every move you made you had to make without a mistake. If you made a mistake you then had to immediately go to the Shaman and tell him you had made a mistake. When the circle was completed the shaman would beat the drum and the caribou would come in through the gap. If no mistakes or unconfessed mistakes had been made, the caribou would be caught. But if someone had made a mistake and not con-

Provings

fessed it, then the caribou would escape at that area. This story touches on the perfectionism and the need to do it right as well as the perfection when it is done right.

> It often happens during trituration provings that certain stories arise and are told, which upon later reflection turn out to be completely in tune with the essence of the substance.

It's head, chest, and stomach. Take more careful notes on the stomach cramps, it's very significant for this kind of remedy. It would be very interesting. Anyone else get chest pain? Labored breath, yes. Was it a group experience? It was like Thanksgiving. There's something here about getting it right. But not in the head. I felt this purity and vulnerability.

FEMALE PROVER 9:
It was incredible. I was outside, in the trees, and I felt like I just had to put my hands in water. I had everything I needed, I had grapes, I had tea. Then I came in and sat on the stool, and it was the most incredible feeling of being perfect. My nose opened up, my spine opened up. It felt like I could go outside and sit high up. I guess in a tree. (Feeling very spiritually connected with nature.) When I'm in here, I want to go outside, and be up high. Just feel a desire to move, incredible oneness with everything. The grapes were good, but they had to be sour, I just wanted to nibble. Feeling of satisfaction.

FEMALE PROVER 13:
I started out feeling very light, very joyful, felt purity. Felt great community, felt group was taking this very seriously. Noticed a lot of talking about numbers. That kept coming back to me, how many grams have you weighed out, that's never happened before. Right side of neck felt numb, forehead felt like it was starting to protrude, eyes felt like they were sinking back into my head. Kept hearing sounds. By the 3C I felt almost like I was sleeping. Then my teeth started to feel very strange, like I would not be able to use them, like they're soft. Got stomachache. By the 4C I was desperate to get outside, needed cold wet air on my face, wanted to go to the beach, wanted to go tonight. Most of all I noticed this group dynamic, like when you're a family and all connected, you don't really care if someone goes off or falls asleep.

PROVING EXIT INTERVIEW

Two weeks after the trituration the provers got together to share the experiences they had recorded in their journals. All those who triturated the remedy had experienced symptoms. Most of the triturators had taken the remedy one week after the trituration in a 30C potency. The 30C potency was also taken by four provers who were not present at the original trituration. Questions by proving master are in italics.

FEMALE PROVER 1:
Part of my body I was most conscious of was right around here [head]. Felt like a bar was going through my head, felt a needle-like pain going into my eye, some chest symptoms, almost frightening chest pain. One moment of breathlessness. There's an awesome silence and calmness that simply feels different. There's a kind of stability and calmness that I feel. My energy was really up, felt like a lot of extraneous stuff was cleared away.. The unnecessary stuff was cleared away, feeling of clarity, clear vision, freedom from worry even in these circumstances.

You were the other person who looked very different. How so?
When that happens, it's 90% accurate, the energy is just different, in that moment, there's something different. I can say my impression was, one prover looked lighter, and your face was broader, something opened up. It's nice to know there's some physical manifestation of this very subtle feeling. I still feel it, maybe it's getting used to a new fit.

Don't know if this is appropriate to comment, but I felt like I wasn't operating on an emotional level. My son lives three miles away from the World Trade Center. Normally, would have felt like I needed to get him home, but there was instead a feeling of separateness. It was OK, he was there, I was here, and it was OK.

FEMALE PROVER 2:
This remedy was real subtle, I thought there was not much going on, very little to put down, not a lot to say, felt real balanced, real solid, strong body mind and spirit, but I often feel that way, did not notice it as something I could attribute to the remedy. It felt really great. I felt sort of validated, this remedy was a validation more than anything else. I also was hungry a lot; I wanted solid foods, proteins, and sweets, a lot of yogurt, also meats, fish, chicken, eggs, protein, and craving sweets.

Provings

One interesting event, Thursday of last week, emotional outburst, emotions were very strong, could have them, see them, have them, and get an answer; they could just be what they were, have them and have them speak to you.

I was sitting paying bills and had a wave of emotions coming through me, I had an important meeting an hour later, I watched this wave roll through my body, I was getting lit up, triggered, released, whatever, it was quiet in the house, nothing was happening

Then I went to the meeting, right as I pulled up I burst into tears, and I felt my mother's pain and I witnessed it, all her pain I had been holding for her, I was crying and just having these emotions and letting them go through you, went into my meeting, very interesting, people talking about leadership, a place where I was going back to teach, we signed a contract that I would teach for 6 months; I kind of surrendered to it. Before I would have sabotaged it somehow, I would teach some and then undo it, this meeting was no big deal, I just did it, I am going to teach now, it had all been resolved, I did not walk in with my mother's pain.

I have had some headaches, in the back of head. I usually have them with the menses This time menses came 4 days later, very odd.

On the trituration evening, had the thought of balance; that this was the remedy of balance where you needed it. Kept seeing the picture of balance.

It brought me strongly into my body. It stayed with me. Instead of meditating all the time. I did meditate and then would feel my body strongly, my right eye in pain, stomach a little upset, also a hip pain right side came back a bit.

Headaches were stronger, particularly when in trance. My body spoke to me more when in trance.

Felt very balanced and grounded. Was upset over the NY stuff but not really; it felt like it was all perfect for some strange reason.

This was part of what I have been training for 20 years, just felt real in present time.

It was all just right there.

Dreams not too much; sleep deep as usual; solving people's problems in dreams like I always do.

Lot of family issues going on. They did not affect me much; I handled them.

FEMALE PROVER 3:
Overall I felt a very deep loneliness, felt like I needed to connect, but didn't know how. Ending a relationship of five years, like I want to be with people, hungry, craving chocolate, gained three pounds. Went up to Sacramento to see an aunt haven't seen in 25 years, just to connect. Worked out at gym on Friday; on Monday my left arm was frozen; could not press arms together or use left arm at all, felt like a rib was out. Came on like that. I started looking for apartments and started freaking out about the price, and I was sure I had cancer. So I'm terrified, and then I felt worse the next day. Even walking was painful, that night I woke up at 3 am and started having terrible memories of a terrible car accident I'd had. I was living on disability of $600 a month, and my rent was $600 a month. I realized it was all locked in there, so I started just trying to release this trauma. Went to the community center and started doing slow movements with the senior movement class. Got some acupuncture, had a massage, and it was about 20% better. Just releasing this struggle, like I'm not going to make it on my own, and the next day I went to my aunt, and it was 80% better. Talking about leadership, I was thinking about starting my book, did transmedium work with some healers, worked with the thousands of people who died in New York, who are in shock but haven't yet passed over. Going to get my seminars and teaching going again, and letting go of the past. Really going to be about walking my talk now. Sense of wanting to connect and not knowing what to say. Looking at an apartment and just not knowing what to say. Really want to connect, smothering my dog more than usual. Today I got the news that my ex-boyfriend is losing his job, and my shoulder started up again. Got the sense of letting go of the old, at the same time it was coming back. It wasn't until memories came up that I realized my shoulder pain in the present had to do with that accident.

MALE PROVER 4:
I guess every party needs a pooper. I had no symptoms I could attribute to the remedy. I just got a really bad cold. Really congested nasally, slight sore throat, tired most of the time. I had one or two dreams, dreamed I was on a car trip

Provings

with my mother. My best friend had cut hair pretty much off and dyed from blonde to black and we were talking to Madonna at a rest area.

But your nasal passages cleared up during the trituration? Yes.

FEMALE PROVER 5:
Worked all day in garden. Not able or willing to do 'normal' work or what is piling up on my desk. Don't know if this is because of New York or proving.

Talked with a fellow prover and that reminded me of connection problem – how interacting with people as I usually do still feels disconnected inside. I am not making my usual emotional connection even though everything on the outside looks the same, looks good. In some ways this is a relief, I am usually over-connected and I lose myself in the process. Or if the connection isn't good, I feel bad and out of sorts till it's resolved. To not care is a relief. But also a problem as I still like to feel connected! I like the emotional flow.

I feel like I live in the space between people generally, and during trituration I felt within myself, but that was OK. Part of what's going on is that Monday before the proving I was at a beach where a little girl drowned, I mention that because there was a lack of response by us on the beach, it had these overtones of a ritual play, not being real. I was still very much in that state when the planes hit the towers, which again was a very unreal event, there was incredible calmness, sadness, but it was also OK because it was supposed to happen, because it needed to happen. Giving up superficial things because they don't matter. This is the other thing… it's really hard to talk about. The words just aren't there. That's strange, but it's OK. I don't know anything, but it's OK. Running my life from my mind, having it all laid out, that doesn't even exist anymore. So the connections with people aren't what they used to be. Leadership came up, how can I best be leader during this, I've always been playing second position, but being a leader seems absolutely necessary right now.

This also brings up for me the further poignancy of the event on the beach where an 8-year-old girl was caught by a wave and pulled out to sea and drowned. What made the situation even more haunting for me was that no one seemed to be reacting to this situation. Everyone seemed calm or as if watching a movie or "it's ok", someone will do something. A complete break/disconnection from the reality of the situation. I found myself not able to act or not able to act quickly as I kept checking for external cues and they weren't there. Maybe panicking or acting hysterical would have been no better, but some action may have been helpful. I felt very cut off. Maybe that state of disbelief and shock is normal but to me it felt strange. We took deliberate action but what was needed was quick action. No one seemed to know how to work together. Solutions that may have helped came clear only later, after it was too late. That there was a slim window of opportunity and no one acted.

I had a sensation that ears had been exposed to loud noise. Not ringing per se and not stuffed up but not as acute; like as if I had been to a loud concert

FEMALE PROVER 6:
I have a strange feeling that nothing happened in this whole time, and I'm trying to bring myself into it. I had severe pain in my teeth. Woke up feeling the ribs in my back, but I also have a sort of gimpy right knee that hasn't bothered me a bit. And then this stuff in New York happened, and I felt terribly disconnected, and one prover wrote me and told me she wasn't continuing with the proving, and felt bad about that. Another prover talked with me about the weird connection with the event in New York and the proving; that both were these incredibly focused events.

The day after that I had this dream. I was in a large, dark underground cave with my son, and we had to walk through these swarms of wasps to get out. We knew we had to walk through the wasps and not show any fear. We got to the opening, where we had to climb up to get out through a dovecote that was also filled with wasps. Someone standing above the rim pours down this quantity of beer, and it wakes up the outside wasps, and then someone else started watering these wasps, and we had to depend on this person to keep watering because it caused the wasps to stop. I woke up and had no idea where I was. Then made a connection and remembered going to a balloon rally several years ago. I had a four-year-old with me who got into a wasps' nest, and I grabbed him and threw him into the crowd, and ended up with 40 wasp stings myself.

Provings

I had nausea, cold hands; my stomach has felt kind of queasy. I've done a lot more eating, pretty much all the time.

This jaw pain was very strong and it was very weird.

I had a worry that we'd done it wrong. That there was something we had done wrong in the proving that had caused something horrible to happen somewhere else.

I really wonder about this remedy – in the dream I have people I know that I take care of and there are other people who interfere (the beer thrower who woke up the outside wasps) and people who help me. I feel like I know where I'm going and what I'm doing yet these wasps are everywhere and they could turn on me any second. Very weird, **I am vulnerable but if I trust I'll know my way.**

FEMALE PROVER 7:
Dream: I dreamt that I was with my former fiancé. We were in a war zone. He was wearing a flannel shirt, his only shirt, and he wanted to have one more shirt. I tried to find one for him, but could only find a jacket. There was another dream involving my daughter. In the dream, she had broken up with a boy friend. I can only remember these snippets of dreams. Sleep was good. I didn't awaken.

I also have been feeling completely exasperated with the Republican Party in general. Because the Republicans believe in 'individualism' and 'unfettered capitalism', supposedly, they want to solve economic problems with 'star wars' technology, more oil exploration, and if all else fails, start a war. Republicans seem to feel that if my dollar goes to help you, that's bad government. The Democrats and Greens would stimulate the economy with programs that actually help people, housing programs, medical care—more of a New Deal approach. It completely frustrates me that Americans vote for Republicans. Can't they see that Republicans have nothing to offer but greed, bad planning, and programs that help only the upper echelon?

Dream: The one that I remember concerned a wonderful friend and classmate who, to our everlasting sadness, killed himself on New Year's Eve. In my dream, there were a lot of people from homeopathy class and elsewhere, and we were assembled in a home that was very dark, barely lit by candles. I was getting advice from one of my old supervisors at my job where I worked long ago, on how to avoid burnout. I kept asking my supervisor how a person can do the job in the amount of time given. Something was troubling him, and I kept asking him to talk about it, to please talk to me. I kept feeling too stupid and inadequate to be able to reach him. I'd try different approaches in my mind, and felt like I was thinking in clichés. I was quite worried about him. When I think about it now, I start to cry. I remember in my dream saying to him, 'You are the best of us.'

FEMALE PROVER 9:
Central feeling is amazingly steady, calm, I expected to be more upset after the events in New York last week, but I felt very steady. I felt like I'd been expecting things like this for quite a while, and had to be prepared, to be steadier. Good things this week for me…ran into someone, sister wanted to come to my class, amazing support when I think I'd be falling apart. Everything I was doing was coming in from some very high source and also very close to the ground. After a summer of not exercising, going to gym every day. Not wanting sugar. Cooking vegetables. But felt maybe something was going to knock this state away, maybe it's not the remedy; maybe it's the placebo. But that's how the week or ten days has been. I've been on a really good realm, where I need to be, not where I should be. Instead of going to a vigil, I went to Senior's day, where they thought we were exactly where we should be…and I skipped the vigil, took R for food, did my own prayers. Like I'd kind of assumed some leadership in a strange way.

When you say another realm what constitutes another realm?
One that's not polluted by TV and personality struggle and is by peace and direct connection. Finding myself thinking something, and then it was happening. That's when I definitely decided to go to Mexico. I decided that it was time, I was putting off magic.

FEMALE PROVER 10 (took the remedy but did not triturate)
Had a five-hour drive to Mom's 80th birthday. I picked up daughter. We had a great time driving down, really good energy. Warm connection with Mom. Everything going well till we went to dinner at a restaurant with my two brothers and other relatives. One brother and I got into a conflict over something quite trivial, and at the time I just thought I was trying to make my point

Provings

when my other brother broke in and said "stop" to us . Later I checked in with others who said it was **so unlike me to just keep going at it and not letting go.** I had had a fair amount of wine but I didn't feel that that was it. The next day I had no real recollection of exactly how it had escalated. But the night before when I asked my daughter if I had been inappropriate she said I had just kept on and on and that was something she herself hasn't really liked about me in the past – harping on things endlessly that I feel she doesn't hear or doesn't get. I felt devastated to hear this and my husband and I went back to our motel and I felt just completely disappointed in myself, very weepy and teary and upset about behaving badly when my goal had been to keep things on a high plane especially after the tragedies of recent days! My husband held and reassured me but I could hardly sleep and kept thinking I needed to move to a monastery or something to do deeper work on myself.

MALE PROVER 11 (took the remedy but did not triturate):
I was a bit more tired and less alert today. I was more thirsty than usual again today. I had a slight headache this afternoon, but it wasn't disruptive. I was more of an ache than strong and pulsing. My energy was down in general, but that may be because of accumulated activity during the workweek. I've been around people more than usual, but don't seem as chatty or verbal. I'm more aware of non-verbal communication. Despite the horrific world events, I don't feel held down by emotions. I'm very aware of co-operation and inter-connection with people. But it's not overly heavy.

I felt energetic today and fairly calm. I did not notice any unusual symptoms, although I did have a slight headache this morning. I was very active today and accomplished a lot of odds and ends. I was able to finish one project and head straight to another. I felt fairly upbeat and energized. I've been sleeping restfully since I've been on the remedy.

Again today I noticed how calm I was. I seemed to be running around less and taking things one step at a time. I was just as productive as usual, but was more in the present time. Usually I'm three steps ahead of myself in my thinking. I did not have any headaches today, but was aware of being thirsty. My sleeping and eating habits haven't changed significantly since I've been on the proving. If anything, I've been a bit more hungry. However, this might be related to increased level of physical activity over the last few days.

Aside from feeling calm and centered, I didn't notice anything specific today. I was more tired than normal and my energy level was also not as high. Despite this I still felt active and productive. I had a bit of eyestrain today, doubtless caused by not wearing glasses. My mood has been good. I've perhaps been less emotionally connected these last few days. Emotion has not been my first or second response to a situation.

BROWN PELICAN PROVING

MALE PROVER 12:
Immediately after trituration had a nosebleed. Had a lot of symptoms in nose and nasal cavities. Sensitive to smell, cannot use any of my usual products. Put on hair gel and immediately had to wash it out to take the smell away. Sensitive to smells outside, smelled really good, trees, water, or smoke, smelled really nice, wanted to get into it.

I looked really pale. I felt hot and flushed since trituration. It is the perfect temperature now, door open, air, short sleeves. Very hot at night.

In sleep, have been gripping the headboard with right hand.
Right eye very sore. Yesterday had to stop lenses, very sensitive to dust.
Strange appetites, had to remind myself I am hungry, craving salty things, fish. Loved going to the ocean and getting into the salt air.
Took the remedy on Monday, then the terrorism (September 11) happened the next day. Did not know if I could actually take it, so many different emotions and feelings, the remedy would not have any bearing on it. For two days I was glued to the TV. I think I overloaded on information. I imagined being in the planes, in the buildings, on the ground. On Thursday I finally took the remedy, felt much calmer, much more at ease, felt I could do something, about my life, about other people, I have been taking the remedy ever since, about every 2 or 3 hours, felt very calm.

Many times words failed me. What I am feeling seems to be too rich; cannot be described in words.

Kept dreaming about casinos, started out with small amounts of money, kept winning.

FEMALE PROVER 13: Started out as a very subtle remedy. I had the experience that night and then I did not feel a lot. I assumed it was not my rem-

Provings

edy, and then I realized there were a lot of things happening. I would be talking and then say, "What did I just say?", and I would struggle to try and get it back, because I thought it was important. Then I stopped; it happened too often.

Strong sense of smell. Things were too much; it was too intense for me. The fireplace would smell.

Through it all a calm sense of joy and resilience. Thinking that everything is going to be ok, that feeling, everything really felt all right with the world, deep inside, touching a place I have not ever touched before, that things were right.

Then the incident in New York. Felt a real strong observance; a need to know the information, but not a real emotional worry. Just being buoyed up, a clown you would hit and it would bounce back up, just this ability to land on my feet, I am not used to that feeling in my life, I am not really comfortable with that feeling of safety.

I watched myself create this drama where I would not feel safe. I have had a skin tag for 12 years, never thought anything about it, I woke up and was sure it was cancer, it happened on Saturday morning, I had the whole thing planned out. I also could watch myself create this whole drama and I wondered why I was doing it, and there was actually a feeling of safety there, in that process I started to realize how attached I am to situations that bring me down, or don't allow me to really be free. I started to realize that I could begin to leave people in my life, I have always had issues about being abandoned, for the very first time ever I was really able to embrace this idea that being alone is really safe. **When you follow your own personal integrity you find perfect freedom.**

Cannot really find the words. It's very new for me to even imagine a life where I am not bound to other people or the idea of being abandoned, or being alone, or being destitute. More a sense of aloneness; very powerful and wonderful to really stand alone; to have my very own power, my very own identity. I stepped down from a fundraiser that I have done for years, all of a sudden everyone wanted me to be an advocate, **they wanted me to be the leader.**

Did you have strong physical experiences from the last proving?
Not as strong, head sensations one day, but one night I couldn't stop laughing. People were asking 'what's with you.' Kept thinking of really funny things, really funny connections.

GENERAL THOUGHTS ON THE REMEDY

I thought about Pelican, I found a story about Pelicans in the paper next day.

I do not want to know what it is, I just want to soar; I think FREEDOM is the important thing, freedom from restraint. Freedom from old baggage – a new motivation to achieve, to get it done, compared to an old fear motivation. Freedom from interference as a goal. I think nature is free.

Freedom from self-consciousness, freedom from judgment.

It seems like a millennium ago since I worried about what they thought.

Permission to have your own freedom – permission to be in present time.

We are talking independence and autonomy.

There was this element of witnessing, drama of right and wrong, did not matter which team you were on.

That we are watching, but wondering why do I have to watch this?

Thoughts around birds and FREEDOM, the keyword; that all the birds have the need for freedom from something.

SUMMARY BY JUDY SCHRIEBMAN

The stories told and the subjects of conversations, in hindsight, were remarkable. One was the story about the caribou, where the ritual involved in being able to catch them meant the entire tribe had to perform a series of very specific tasks in a very specific manner. If one made a mistake, it was required that this mistake be confessed to the shaman so that there were no secrets or anything hidden. This story came in response to the intense focus and the utter inability of any of us to think coherently about numbers, timing, or any of the details of the process, even those who had done several similar provings already. How many scrapings? Whose turn was it? How many minutes before

Provings

we stopped grinding and started scraping? We'd look at each other completely blank, and try hard to figure it out, as if we were dredging up ancient knowledge from stories told to us as children. Really wanting to get it right and having absolutely no ability to even know what "right" was.

The scraping sound was irritating, like fingernails on a chalkboard, but the process was utterly engrossing. It felt like a treat to be given the bowl with the powder; finally, it's MY turn! and perfectly acceptable to pass it on at the turn's end. Complete, without any subjective chatter, other than "did we count right?" Time seemed irrelevant, neither too long nor too short. Complete, in the moment, perfectly attuned. A part of the group and yet fully oneself, which was a marvelous feeling for one who is usually overly concerned with everyone being all right and things being harmonious and what is that person thinking or what did they mean by that remark. The mind was blessedly silent and the pull to be in everybody else's business absent.

SCARLET MACAW *Ara macao*

This was a Jonathan Shore trituration/proving done in California in September 2000.

People who came to the proving wore a lot of red and blue clothing. Blue is an important color for all the birds. For this bird, we add red. Coordination and clumsiness is definitely an axis for Macaw.

The feeling during the making of this remedy was more like housewives talking - **but not about ordinary things.**
  "Speaking our individual expression is very important for the group."

CONVERSATION DURING THE MAKING OF THE REMEDY:
Feeling very disconnected, physically, a **lovely calm feeling of observing,** yet there is **a nervousness, feeling very loved and loving.**

Feel like I have had a couple of bottles of wine. Remarkable comfort being with people whom you hardly even know.

Pulsing energy feeling, out of control, a force I cannot quite explain – **a buzz – bubbles – a very calm state** – nervousness also, cannot really explain. A sensation of nervous, and not really having to do anything about it, **nervous and jittery.**

Very unfocussed feeling about the whole thing – the level of communication that we all have – talking a lot at any level and there was no judgment about what we were saying – **people were able to express themselves without feeling judged.**

Nervousness – body was nervous – accelerated feeling but this was normal. Physically separated from each other, **lightness,** not lightheaded so much, but **my bones and skeleton feeling light.**

Two themes – the journey and the searching – I can search and I can feel.

My soul is nervous, and I could feel my heart – I feel trust and love with all of the provers, dreams of family and all these are tied to her being here.

Provings

More present of myself than I usually am, a little more continuity and I knew I was here, circumstances make me feel a little self conscious. An impulse to direct things, the conversation, people were a little too quiet, but inside telling myself that I have to let them experience this.

PROVING EXIT INTERVIEW: Ten Days Later.

PROVER #1: WOMAN (*She does not speak English. An interpreter is present.*)
JS: I think we can just begin and see what comes up, so why don't you tell us what happened, even from before you took the remedy. I'm interested in what you feel are the most important things.
When I took it, I felt very tranquil for half a day. Afternoon around two or three, I had headaches. As the day progressed, I felt bothered, uncom-fortable, and on this night I couldn't sleep. I had a very uneasy sleep. The next day, I felt calm again.

JS: So on the day we made it, she felt symptoms before we made it?
No, these symptoms began when I took the remedy. When I was making the thing, I felt very strange, like I was somewhere else. The night before I came here, I dreamt of my parents, we were in a big reunion. The next day, I was in a reunion with all of you. The next day [Friday] I awoke happy, calm, I had dreamt of my parents, we were in a very clear swimming pool. In my family, these dreams mean health. When we dream of dirty water, this means illness. That was the end of the dream. Saturday, in the middle of the day, I felt that my lips had swollen. I had thick lips. As the afternoon wore on, the feeling went away. I ate normally. Also very thirsty.

JS: What did you think was happening?
Throughout?

JS: Yes, in general.
I don't know why, I feel a little strange, and I'm not sure why. Two days before our initial meeting, I dreamt of my parents. I do not know why.

JS: How does it feel to feel strange?
The night after the meeting, I could not sleep at all, and wondered why. Why did my parents appear in my dreams? Usually, when I dream of my parents, they are trying to tell me something. It's like a premonition. These dreams usu-

ally forecast an event back home in Peru. I wonder what could be happening to them in Peru.

JS: *Where do you feel this?*
In my chest, like it is being oppressed. I often dream I have lost something and do not find it again. Sometimes when I think of a friend, something happens to them, I don't understand why. I feel constriction in my chest, and something happens.

JS: *Do you have any feeling of what might happen?*
No. Just calm.

JS: *So it's changed?*
Yes, it's calm now. In the past, I felt anxious.

JS: *So this feeling has passed?*
Yes, these things I'm telling you have been with me all my life.

JS: *Was this experience different from the others?*
Yes, this time I feel calm, the other times I felt oppressed in my heart.

JS: *Usually when I prove remedies, I don't produce symptoms. But this time, I had a dream of a patient. I dreamt of a patient, we had had a disagreement over treatment. In reality, I thought we had resolved her questions, but in the dream we disagreed. Three days later, the patient called me, deciding not to continue the treatment. How many days does the dream usually precede the event?*
The next day, after the dream.

JS: *But this time nothing happened, when we made the remedy.*
Every time I dream I am driving a car, I get news that someone dies.

JS: *But this dream was about clear water?*
Yes. Every time I drive, someone I know of dies.

JS: *Aside from the swelling of the mouth, was it just the lips, or the mouth?*
Just the lips, the outer lips.

JS: *They were swollen?* (One friend saw her and noticed this. I saw her that day, they were swollen and white).

JS: *Anything else?*

SCARLET MACAW PROVING

Provings

Headaches at the end of the day.

JS: Where was the headache?
Over the front.

JS: I think that just as radios pick up radio waves, TV picks up TV waves, some people pick up people waves. So it seems that you gained benefit from the remedy?
Yes, this time I was calm, and nothing happened.

Prover #2: Woman
JS: What I'm interested in is what you felt the strongest, if anything?
The strongest theme for me started before, but it was clarified for me after the remedy; it has to do with the **individuality versus the whole group**. To expound, there had been more of a reticence to speak my truth in given situation because it wouldn't be acceptable, I noticed that in some arenas in my life, I would not. With people with whom there was a vested interest, (i.e., the husband), that I just found that I was more comfortable saying what came up in a heartfelt way. That first night, I had this dream where people were having the top layer of skin taken off, and the skin beneath was reddish. It came to me that two of the women had red on. It came to me that this might have been significant. Maybe there was a hidden meaning of being exposed.

JS: What was the feeling?
A fear. Then there was another dream, and I couldn't access the meaning or the particulars, but I saw red. This weekend we went to Minneapolis, with my family. What I got out of this was that my definition of family started to change to include friends, and that my family unit was becoming stronger because I was having heart connections outside the family. It seemed much more pronounced over the past couple of weeks.

JS: So you have found in the past, that your closer relationships have been inside a small family group?
I feel that something has shifted where **I have felt one more step closer to matching my inner prompting to my outer life without having a mask**. I feel more comfortable saying "lets talk about it." Even if it would rock the boat with the other person. I had a breakthrough about a month ago, but I did feel that there was some kind of a change, something had shifted, but I don't even know what the remedy is. It felt great though. Precognition has been part of

my makeup for a while, and I couldn't say there was any more or less. As far as a feeling level, if I can qualify it, I just felt a deeper sense of peace with myself.

I went through a cold, it left pretty quickly, If I feel overwhelmed, I allow myself to get them. This time, I said, "I'm not going to feel overwhelmed, I'm not." Then I started to feel overwhelmed, and Bam, I got the cold. But I felt fine even when I had the cold.

Prover #3: Woman
For me this has been a roller coaster ride, it's a clearing of the emotional level at whatever you're working on, and I was working it deep. And I'm not out of it yet. I did feel my head alternately would be very clear, very great, which I have always recognized as my telepathy. When I feel cleansed internally, I feel clear in the head. My sixth chakra, this part of my head was clear. When I meditated, I saw white energy just leaving. It was like clearing my son's, my husband's energy, and trying to get to mine. I felt physically exhausted; I had very active nights. Dreams were hard to grasp. I remember one dream, my best friend from college was there (I was always there for her in real life). In my dream, she hadn't come for anything. She was in color, my family was there, in black and white. There were confetti shapes all over the floor, she brought that for me and it was neat. And that was the dream.

Scarlet Macaw proving

JS: *Can you say more about that?*
She was there as a female, for me, everyone in my family was male. It was neat being matched in the dream on that feminine level. In the past ten days, there was a lot of giving up, "let it fall apart, I'm tired of it." I feel like in the past, I've given more than I've gotten. I need everyone to stand on their own feet for a while so I can get something back for myself. A lot happened, BIG things, both in the family and not. I was dealing with professionals, dealing with my son, and being clairvoyant, it is not easy to express to these people. That's what I'm dealing with right now.

JS: *This giving your heart, what does that mean?*
(Silence) It has to do with...I don't know...it has to do with giving yourself... I see the heart as giving the affinity for yourself, when others have demands on my heart space, it's a demand I can't give to myself. **I can't give to them, either, but they still demand.**

Provings

Prover #4: Man
I felt intense physical reactions. It was like a very gentle marijuana high. There was pleasure and coordination (different from a marijuana). **Felt more connection to the group.** *A persistent problem for me is tripping. I'm in my head and am not aware of the curb, etc. It was so nice to walk down the street and not have to worry about it. I felt a lot of attention in my feet. I rubbed them. Appetite was something. Normally I eat a lot of meat but I found* **I craved fruit and nuts.** *Ate an entire bag of* **sunflower seeds** *and bananas. Didn't know where the change was coming form. There is a problem because my parents are separated and there's always this rush to get up to both my parents' places. I feel like I never give my father enough attention. This time I told my father I had plans, and both parents said it was fine. Had no issue over it. Felt no issue of abandonment.*

Prover #5: Man
I did not actually take the remedy, because the symptoms began while making the remedy, and I feared for my personal safety. **It made me clumsy,** I was dropping things in the lab, in fast food restaurants, while driving. I had to drive to San Diego, and was afraid I was going to get into an accident. I bumped into my dresser, and it hasn't moved in two years. When we were making it, I spilled lactose three times, it was terrible! It was Monday, 3 to 4 days after we made the remedy, I fell down on a baggage carousel at the airport. I bumped into a door, I thought "who am I, what am I doing?"

Two really unusual dreams, I usually have very clear dreams, but one of these was brutal, very ugly. I was a witness to the rise to power of Al Capone. I was a passive, intimate witness to all of this as he murdered everyone. I wondered why doesn't someone stop him. It was about good and evil, the rise of evil when unopposed by good, about the need for balance between the two. I mean, he was a petty thug when he began, and grew through his love of cruelty to those around him. I felt like the narrator in Great Gatsby or Billy Bathgate - **able to observe, unable to change.** I remembered the discussion we had during the manufacture of the remedy, about Darth Vader.

I had a dream about bright vivid color in the tropics. I never dream about the tropics. Somewhere on the other side of the leaves, something evil is going on. Since I knew what the remedy was, I didn't know exactly what was going on over there. The stunning thing was the colors,

The clumsiness extended to drooling, I felt like I was coming apart. The exact opposite of what another prover was talking about, I had to watch every door. I had no change in diet, but even when there was no reason to be, **I was very hungry, very often.**

Prover: #6: Woman

Let me hit the physical symptoms first. The first night, **a terrible pain in the right hip** hit me. It stayed for five days. I felt it down to my right foot. My right foot felt connected to this hip. **I was starving. I could not get enough to eat**. In the beginning I was craving protein, but meat was making me feel sick. When D. introduced me to **sunflower seeds**, I felt really good.

I felt really hot, I slept with windows open, I didn't want clothes on. It was like I was coated, I wanted to shed. It would be like putting clothes on over fur. I was exhausted. I wanted to sleep a lot. I could not remember my dreams, but I know I dreamt a lot, because I woke up knowing I had dreamt.

I remember a fragment from the first night. There was a family my children knew, a peculiar family, I thought. **I was an observer, a fly on the wall**. The father would talk, and everyone would put on a show for him, pretending to listen to him. I felt very sorry for the son, who looked lost. I was anxious the first night, but the first day, this amazing calm and peace came over me. **I still felt connected to everyone**, I called them all. I saw Bonnie in the Book Depot and talked with her for 3 hours without noticing the passage of time. I realized that I had been denied a relationship with my father, because my mother wouldn't allow it. I felt fear, and went home and lay in a ball for four hours. I just let myself experience depression. About 9 o'clock that evening, I got out of bed and felt fine. I slept really well that night. The next morning it was still with me, but it wasn't something that was me. It was with me, I was partnered with it, I could be at peace with it and not run away. Peace. That's the word that keeps coming. How come before I couldn't have this peace?

Provings

Saturday morning came and it was very hectic, and that was OK. By afternoon, I was laughing, I felt stoned, and everything felt wonderful. Being touched felt very good. Life felt very 'haveable', I was finally able to have life. I felt like I was residing in life and it felt really good.

My mother was arriving in three days, my brother in two. I knew she would perpetuate more anger, and I could separate myself and it didn't affect me. It happened, but I could observe. I really loved it. **I kept calling this a love drug**. I have a disabled brother, and its always painful to see him deteriorate, but this time it was nice to see him as he was.

I decided to take a whole capful of the remedy to deal with my mother, because I felt like I would get back into that overwhelmed place where I would have to meet her needs over and over again and it would never be enough. But I said no, I'm not going to meet her needs. I let her stay in her hotel, and that's not like me. I knew it would all come together. I watched my mom and watched her do the same old stuff she always does. I wasn't going to idolize or idealize her, or pretend that what happened didn't happen. At the party, people commented about her: "strange, interesting," and I didn't argue. I agreed. I would experiment with her, using different ways to deal with her, as a lab experiment. I'd say "I don't do it that way, I'm different." I saw how it annoyed and angered her, and that used to scare me, but not this time. I actually yelled at her at one time, and she became a little girl, very reticent.

I know what the remedy is and I feel like it is from a more evolved being.

JS: Your experience affirms that the point of a life is to experience it, not to think about it. If it is possible to experience it, it can change us in a way that "working it through" could not. Confrontation is just being there. That is the evolved energy.

RING DOVE (WOODPIGEON) *Columba palumbus*

Elizabeth Schulz did this proving to C4 in Germany. The full transcript is available in ReferenceWorks. Here are some excerpts from this proving.

1. PROVER (FEMALE)
C1-Trituration
Restlessness, anger, mood swings. The **jaw muscles tense up. Cutting pain in the belly.** It feels as if the **bladder is being cut into** or as if a bladder catheter is installed. My inner voice says: "The dove belongs to *Staphysagria*." I feel **suppressed anger.** Always being a victim. Then my surroundings become a lot clearer as if my eyes could see much better. My glance becomes clear and there is a lot of love for humankind. My heart opens and tremendous softness originates from it, then changes into an incredible anger about the ugly face of the peace dove. A feeling of a lump in the throat appears. Again and again this suppression. Put finally an end to suppression! Again **piercing bladder pain. Suppression of sexuality.** The mucous membranes of mouth and pharynx become dry. Tongue burning. With a lot of effort I succeed in holding my tears back. I have such a dull feeling in my head. I am flooded with **feelings of inferiority. I am fat, stupid, and ugly.** Physically I feel great heat that alternates with feeling chilly. Pain in the cervical vertebrae. Dizziness with the feeling of flying. I see doves in a dovecote. They coo as a greeting. They are coming back to their family, back to the group, no matter what the situation looks like because their longing to be together is very big. Throat pain comes up, penetrating like angina. My trituration becomes more and more calm and balanced. The care of the brood appears. The parents take care of their babies with love and patience. **Rheumatic pain in the right shoulder.** I feel as if narcotized. Feelings of nausea and getting close to vomiting. Suppressed anger can lead to these feelings. Gas. I have strong back pain.

2. PROVER (FEMALE)
Summarized experiences: **Energy of grief.** Memories of slowly creeping processes that lead to cancer. However, people don't notice anything. They don't notice how they continue to suppress and that this is how cancer can manifest itself. She becomes very peaceful, but she senses that the appearance is

RING DOVE PROVING

Provings

deceptive. **Softness, tenderness, and gentleness are felt.** Then there is headache, stomach pressure, nausea; the headache is dull, pressing, and burning

4. Prover (male)
Summarized experience: **He loses his sense of time**. He experiences deep calmness, but also a **feeling of dizziness located in the head**. Feeling of a headache, **as if he is wearing a helmet or something is pressing from the top**. Burning pain like an arrow between the shoulder blades. He sees the image of a dove that had been penetrated by an arrow. The dove consoles the one who has to shoot the arrow. The victim consoles the aggressor. **Numbness of the hands as if they are decomposing**. He sees a stump. The hands become red and blue. War and soldiers come up. The dove goes to the soldier and puts his head against his, consoles his loneliness and helplessness. The dove makes a person able to touch aggression. A rectangular block of stone appears, something like a prison and people dressed in black. Non-violence. Those who surrender are the strong ones. This is the power the dove gives us. **The power of calmness emerges and a strong group feeling.**

He sees a lot of golden light. Within the divine there is strength. Feels unassailable and strong. **Earache**. Headache, very extreme and like dots. He wants to get out of his body through the head. **Longing for the divine light**. He feels surrounded by dust. There are mites everywhere. He is bathing himself in the dust to get rid of the mites and other vermin. Something tingles on his whole body. Doves are God's messengers. An image emerges: he sees doves as messengers in Olympia.

SUMMARY BY ELISABETH SCHULZ:
    I always have to serve.
    Strong feeling of community. Strong group feeling. Calmness within the group.
    Anger, suppression (Staphysagria).
    Great sadness.
    Softness, tenderness, gentleness.
    Grief and suppression of grief.
    Ability to console and love even the aggressor.

Headaches, nasal congestion.
Cutting pains in bladder, urethra.
Stabbing, piercing pains.

Symbol of holy spirit and divine inspiration.
Naiveté, harmlessness, innocence, humility.

Ring Dove
PROVING

Provings

RED-TAILED HAWK *Buteo jamaicensis*

Hawk is an extensively proven remedy. Jonathan Shore conducted three separate provings during seminars, one in Germany, one in Finland and one in Scotland. For the seminar provings the remedy was prepared from two different parts of the bird: one remedy was made from scrapings of the feathers and claws (T), the other was made from the blood (B). **Despite the difference in materials these two provings showed no difference at all.** Virginia Baker did a comprehensive proving in Arizona.

VIRGINIA BAKER PROVING PRELIMINARY PROVING SUMMARY
DAYS 1 THROUGH 12

MENTAL EMOTIONAL SYMPTOMS:

1) Wanting to be alone or feeling separate from the group.
KM- Dream of "feeling relieved and relaxed to be in a space where no one could interfere."
BW- "I was not wanting to be around anyone. I wanted to be in my own little state." Not wanting to deal with people.
LF - Dream- Aloof from people. I did not want to get involved. I didn't really care that much.
PB- "I felt like I did not want them to be around. I wanted to be alone and not bothered by them... I don't think I would seek people out if I had a choice."
"I had a kind of detachment and yet at the same time I seemed more sensitive. It was like I could feel the energies of people more intensely."
PV- Dream: On the other side of a glass wall there was a group of Plains Indians and I thought that is where I want to be. I could not get through that glass to the other side. Dream- Husband talking with people in a pool. She felt left out.

2) Heightened Anger/Irritability
Nine Provers felt some aspect of this. Some only slightly so that it was "a matter of speaking up more lately."
Another described it as "irritable and antisocial."

Others were more affected: "I was ready to honk my horn I was so angry. I was ready to kill her and I was definitely more aggressive than I usually am and more willing to show it, be more vocal about it."

"More aggressive and angry at the defeat of not being able to put my bird back in the cage. I was angry not at the bird but at the defeat, and not being in control of the situation."

"I was extremely irritable and angry because I felt left out."

Feeling really put out because a family member asked the person to do something for them.

"My fuse was short."

"I was irritable almost beyond my control."

3) Sadness and Depression

This varied from "nothing seems right and I can hardly get myself to do things" to a dream of one prover which produced a feeling of "sadness, futility, emptiness."

"It was that sinking feeling of depression like you are in a hole. Dismal like there is nothing to look forward to. There is no hope… a black cloud," and yet the entire thing cleared when she was out with people.

"Low again today. I just sat on the porch where the sun came in and did not move for hours, just sat there. I did not talk to anybody. I just let things pass through my mind."

Another got very upset when someone made a rude gesture in traffic and got really sad and cried.

4) Felt very strong and Powerful.

This came up in several ways. One person went climbing and said they felt "strong like an Amazon woman and could climb forever."

Another had dreams of athletic prowess, being able to do things not normally able to do.

Another prover dreamed she could "carry a giant thick plate-glass table top like it was a tray. I felt strong, purposeful, and able to do anything, totally in control, confident. It was a great feeling." A more obscure dream: Of a bull crashing through a window. "I wasn't hurt, but I could feel the force of it…a huge bull. The feeling was the power of it."

RED-TAILED HAWK PROVING

Provings

5) Feeling abandoned or neglected.
Three provers had this. One was an encounter that left the person feeling misjudged, annoyed, and feeling injured and defensive. One prover felt this very strongly and even had it in her dreams.
And if we include "wanting understanding and not getting it," six provers wanted understanding from a mate or a family member and felt they were not getting that during the proving period.
This was a gray area because some of these provers had these symptoms before and they were merely accentuated. Others actually had dreams of this. Angry with the mate. Arguing a lot.

6) One prover felt incapable of dealing with personal emotional problems.

7) Easy distractibility/More focused.
Three provers. One prover felt overwhelmed and could not get organized.

8) Mental dullness, confusion and spaciness. One prover.

9) Mistakes in writing. One prover.

10) Poor concentration. One prover.

GENERAL SYMPTOMS:

1) Low energy/High energy
All ten provers had energy drops. A few experienced energy highs before the drop.
A **nervous, undirected energy** was felt by almost every prover. Some of the descriptions were: "I think I was having extra energy but it was undirected energy... more like an anxiety or like nicotine withdrawal."
"I knew I was feeling the remedy. I felt 'revved up' with lots of nervous energy."
"Just a lot of mind activity on the surface."
"I felt more nervous this day with internal shakiness that was less noticeable than the day before."
"I continue to have that internal shakiness... "My body felt like it was vibrating internally ... I thought there was even a hum that I could hear. I felt more nervous and vulnerable like I might cry for no apparent reason... "
"I feel a general 'buzziness' or a hyper feeling like the effects of drinking too

much coffee … the energy level in my body seems to have moved up several notches to my upper chest through my head area..'"
"I felt I was having a niacin rush which is an energetic feeling like you have had a couple cups of coffee."
"Nervous like I cannot get anything done… tired and I want to sleep."

2) Periodicity
Three provers mentioned that they felt well one day and poorly the next, a "one day on, one day off" phenomenon.

3) Chilly/Hot
Two provers, one chilly and one hot.

4) Thirst increased or decreased
Five provers: Three increased and two decreased.

PHYSICAL SYMPTOMS:
Waking in the night more than usual. Four provers.
One slept better who usually wakes. Restless at night. One prover.
Headaches in the forehead and temples. Five provers.
Nasal stuffiness with runny nose or postnasal drip. Five provers.
Some became quite ill with upper respiratory infections. **Sore throats**. Five provers.
Mild all the way to quite painful. One prover had pain at night only, although this had started the day before the proving.

> The odd thing about these infections was their propensity to "just sit there" and not move up and down like a virus usually will. Two provers actually went home and slept.

Sneezing. Two provers.
Epistaxis. Two provers.
Muscle aching and pains. One prover had this quite strongly. Another only transiently. Four provers in all.
Aching in upper back, lower skull and shoulders in three provers.
One prover had disappearance of shoulder pain that had been very bothersome.
"Today I want to curl up." Two provers.
Awakened with itching. Two provers.

Provings

DREAMS:
Of ribs and needing to cut meat off bone.
Of swimming in water.
Of excelling.
Of not fitting in with the group.
Of a whirling, a movement, a busy sensation, **a zooming sensation through stars, very fast** and busy, swirling, pleasurable.
Of not being able to be with the group.
Of being in a building in a canyon on the side of a cliff.
Of feeling helpless and not being able to do anything.
Of being in a pool or ocean.
Of being dead.
Of heightened colors, small details in terms of visuals.
Of people getting divorced because the husband was abusive.
Of much mental activity like a choppy ocean in my head.
Of dog at beach.
Of bull (animals).
Of men going to attack her.
Of watching myself from above getting nothing.

SUMMARY OF DAYS 12-16

MENTAL SYMPTOMS:
Mental Dullness.
Confusion.
Spaciness.
Inability to concentrate and focus.
Easily distracted/
More focused.
Mistakes in writing, skipping words, spelling errors, writing incorrectly.
Extreme clarity of thinking.

EMOTIONAL SYMPTOMS:
Nervous undirected energy, feels like anxiety.
Initial "high nervous energy" alternating with low energy.

Anger, impatience, irritability.
Wanting to be alone. Accompanied by feeling relieved and relaxed to be where no one could interfere.
Great to be in the company of good friends vs. Depression when alone; not seeking company.
Feeling separate from the group.
Wanting understanding from the mate and not getting it.
Feeling abandoned and neglected.
Feeling incapable of dealing with emotional difficulties.
Felt strong like an Amazon woman, like I could climb forever. (Dreams and reality)
Deep truth and feeling "sure."
Just sitting on porch for hours.
Wanting to "curl up" for the day.

DREAMS:
Deep sea fishing.
Of sisters.
Of ribs and needing to cut meat off bone.
Of scolding someone for not being a good citizen.
Of old friends.
Of excelling, being capable.
Of not fitting in to the group.
Of relatives, father, sisters.
Of not being able to "get over there" with the group to which she belongs.
Of fear I was doing something I should not have been doing.
Feeling helpless, could not do anything.
Of people relating difficulty in relationships.
Of men going to attack her.

PHYSICAL SYMPTOMS:
Waking in the night more than usual.
Nervous, undirected energy. "Feels like nicotine withdrawal, a vibrating with a hum sound to it."
Eye symptoms: Heaviness; Fuzzy, dry or sticky; itchy.
Sore throat. Stuffy nose, coryza with runny nose. Sneezing. Epistaxis.
Laryngitis.

Provings

Dizzy and lightheaded.
Headache.
Numbness of the hand.
Thirst increase or decrease.
Flu-like muscle aches and pains in left chest and in hands and wrists.
General body aches.
Aching in upper back, lower skull and shoulders, Left shoulder and neck.
Awakened with itching on the left.

SEMINAR PROVING I: GERMANY, SEPTEMBER 1995

NOTE: B = Blood, T = Talons and Feather scrapings

Provers are denoted as MT = Male Talon, FT = Female Talon, MB = Male Blood, FB = Female Blood

FIRST PROVER MT:
In the first night I had five dreams and in all of them I was **naturally taking care of another person**. I was especially impressed by my thoughts about this; my thoughts of **natural loving, feeling like family**. It is natural to take care of somebody. The most marked sequence was the first dream: it was **a handicapped person** (in real life I did not know this person). In the dream I had been taking care of this person for five years and I did not want to do it any more. Nobody understood why I did not want to do it any more. But I was not upset about this, it was very natural. It was without resentment or anything, but I had done enough. The whole feeling in these dreams was natural and love.

Yesterday during the day it I went home and I was very surprised about my reaction. A cup of coffee fell down on the floor and it was natural for me to help her and take it up for her.

The other dreams I don't remember, but it was always the same feeling of natural family care. In all the dreams there was this family atmosphere. I was dreaming about friends and it was this natural feeling, feeling of everything being natural. For myself, the topic of family is a difficult thing; I have no family yet and it is a difficult situation for me. I meet my parents and brothers and sisters on a regular basis.

In the dream the person's legs were paralyzed. After five years it was enough to stop taking care of this person. It was a natural process. I did it out of affection and a feeling of being connected. Not that I was overburdened. I wanted to look after myself and see how it felt for me to live on my own. There was no resentment or anger, guilt; it was just a natural process to do my own thing. It was easy for me to do this. The people around me did not understand why I stopped this now. Everybody got used to me doing the care-taking and they could not understand why I suddenly stopped. But their attitudes did not irritate me at all. I just knew for me that I had to do it.

The feeling of deep belonging, being connected and love that was very strong. Physical pain I had since yesterday is right-sided throat pain, which I don't have normally.

Second Prover MT:
My basic feeling was relief. I had the feeling that it was not a pleasant substance, that it was an animal substance. Normally I am well connected with my dreams, but I did not have many dreams during the last two months. The dream was very clear when I woke up in the morning. I brought my little son into the kindergarten and this morning I wanted to stay there for the morning (that is real, I do that sometimes). And then I wanted to go for a walk and go there again. The person who looks after the children agreed. I was told that normally a child who's name was Lasse, disagreed, but she told me that this was a good opportunity to tell this child that it could not always go his way, that he could not have the control. And it was without resentment, the child had to accept this.

Red-tailed Hawk proving

Then an old symptom came back which was **slight pain on the hip,** on the right side. It comes every time when I have to do a step forward in my life: it is connected with subconscious fear. I have this maybe once a year. When I have to do a step forward in my life, an unconscious fear is there; before I opened my clinic, before I moved to Germany, before we got our child. I stayed with a friend this night and there a book fell from the shelf with the title, "Let Everything be Completely New." This relates very much to a Zen book I know: "Zen Spirit of the Beginner."

Normally I take my son there and go back. What is new in this dream was that I had the need to stay there. **I feel like sharing this world of the children** a

Provings

little bit more, being part of his world little bit more. The child who objected did not like the idea that there was another adult in the group. It was a good and pleasant feeling to be there, even if this child did not like it. It was clear and natural that it had to be like that. The hip pain was at the attachment of the muscle to the trochanter major.

I feel the pain a little bit, which has subsided during the day. In general there is a feeling of relief. I feel the remedy still acting and that it has something to do with me. I feel more happiness, alertness, and clarity. For the past two months, I had no dreams at all, at least I could not remember and it seems it has woken me up. Now I dream pretty much. There are phases where I feel less connected with my dreams. Usually once or twice a week I remember a dream that is meaningful to me.

THIRD PROVER FB (REMEDY UNDER PILLOW):
After two or three hours I woke up with very strong cramps in her legs, in the calf and right big toe. It was unbearable. I had to get up and it did not subside for a while. Then I had enough of the remedy and I put it away. Later I felt all my muscles, also the muscles of the inner organs. It was a wavelike movement, very slight. I had a dream; I am not sure about it. The topic was to be exploited and not be able to defend myself.

The dream was like this, I was traveling and somebody was in my house to look after it. I came home and there where several people there; I did not like this. On the table there were some things prepared, also there were some cacti and this man wanted to do something with these people, which was in connection with these plants. Then we left the house, but I did not really want to. But I went with them and there was a child who had several things in his bag, there was a camera and a magnifying glass. The child took this magnifying glass out the bag and came towards me very close; looking through this glass at me.

The feeling of being exploited came from having allowed somebody to be in the house and them taking it further than what I agreed to. The table was laid for dinner and the cacti were in various colors.

FOURTH PROVER FT (REMEDY 1ST EVENING UNDER PILLOW, 2ND PER MOUTH):
The first night with the remedy under the pillow nothing happened.

When I took the first dose of the remedy it jumped out of my mouth, so I took it again. This morning I woke up without anything having happened, but then I had the chance to sleep one more hour and after this I could remember my dreams. Normally I have difficulties to remember my dreams, I can remember only when somebody wakes me up suddenly. This morning I remembered first to be in an exotic country, southeast Asia, I left the house for jogging and saw a bird, a very exotic bird more like a chicken or pheasant or maybe like a peacock, with very bright blue feathers, my association is like a flower (Dahlia) with very narrow feathers. This part of the dream is very unusual for me; that it was like a picture in front of my eyes.

We went jogging and I had something in my pocket that was disturbing. I took it out and it was a film and I left it in the hotel. There was somebody from this group and (she or this women) asked if I was dressed appropriately. I need a long T-shirt and this woman said, "Yes, it is important because otherwise it can hurt a lot." I don't know what it was but there was a feeling of danger.

I remember two other pictures, one is from my family, and my mother or sister or myself was thinking about whether I have enough bed sheets or if we have to borrow some. Poor Henrietta has to change the bed sheets every night because the son was wetting the bed or something like this.

The third picture took place in a large room at our neighbors', there where several people, they have two children (girls) but here appeared two boys. The younger child came to me walking on the knees. There was a group communication.

FIFTH PROVER FB:
Felt like flying, very high in the air as having taken drugs (I have never taken drugs). It was like floating in the air, I did not move my wings and I saw birds' heads, birds of prey, and there was an **incredible yearning for freedom**. I had the feeling that we were hawks. There was a leash and a leather glove and I had to go back to this hand to which I was connected with a leash. The yearning for freedom was very strong.

After these pictures were over, I had a feeling that this remedy released one aspect of my personality, the feeling of a deep cure. The feeling of deep con-

Provings

nectedness and oneness. A very strong pain in the left breast, dull and boring. Itching skin on the toes, and the feeling of difficult breathing. Then I fell asleep and woke up several times. I had very acute hearing. I woke up at a quarter past midnight and had the image of somebody shooting lots of knives into my body. Visions of birds, ducks and owls and then a story appeared, the name of the film is **'The Call of the Falcon.'** The topic is of a curse and a love story. A jealous man changes the woman into a falcon and the man into a wolf. And the falcon lives during the day and the wolf lives in the night. And they can see each other when the first sunrays are there and then a change is there again.

At four o'clock I had to urinate again (I had to urinate frequently during this time) and I saw an eagle. It seemed to be connected with a leash again and tried to free himself. I turned the light on because I was very afraid. This eagle reminded me of Prometheus, where the eagle keeps coming to take out a part of his liver.

I had a discolored yellow stool. The mucous membranes were dry. Yesterday I had to leave the seminar because of my family, there was a feast. I was not able to communicate with the adults there. I played with the children there **and I got a lot of love from these children**. I wanted to stay there with the adults but I could not bear the restlessness there.

Then I went home, last night I did not dream at all. Normally I dream a lot. I grew up ... I use wrong words ... and feel torn between my feelings and the needs of other people. I am afraid in crowds and feel better in a distance where I can observe. A great fear of burdening other people. Where is my place in this world? I cried a lot this morning.

A dull and boring pain in the right hip (I don't know this pain at all.). The menses came early. **A strong menstrual pain**, which I never have. As if sticks are pushed into the pelvis like magicians cutting women into pieces. **A nervous restlessness**, I was at a great hurry. The reaction is slowed down. I drove through 5 red lights which I never did before. I took the wrong way several times. Delusion of greatness. I spent a lot of money. I had to buy things all the time. Luxury articles, food, glasses, desire for cereals. I spent 500 German Marks for books. I feel embarrassed but I could not help it.

This morning, after I cried so much and felt so nervous, I thought the only thing which could help me would be to look again at the inner pictures. I sat down and saw many wild geese and I became a stuffed goose (I had the association of a goose for goose liver pate). Then I landed on the water and put my head into the water and was quiet there.

Flying was a feeling of being completely disconnected from the earth, a feeling of unlimited freedom, a feeling of having this overview and of being completely alone. The first image was this incredible freedom and then it changed. Then this feeling of being connected with this human hand and fighting for food. Feeling of being everything, like being the air and being in contact with the earth at the same time. I never had this feeling before, I can't describe it differently. I felt it released something in me, like something that had been closed up inside me for a long time. The wind runs around my ears and I have been in contact with the element air.

SIXTH PROVER FB:
Before I took the remedy I held the remedy in my left hand while driving and had the feeling that my upper jaw was affected. In the left arm I had the perception of it being pulled out or cut off. I felt the tendons of the right thigh, as if somebody was pulling there. I had a feeling of non-substance. I tried to describe it, but I can't. Not like a vacuum, but just not substance. A lot of physical things, saliva suddenly, my menses started 4 days early (which is regular normally). I had a totally different type of pain, which started in the afternoon in the stomach area something like claws drawing something apart there.

After I took the remedy in the evening I went to bed. The bed cover was floating down on me, like goose feathers. I had an intense awareness in the third eye, as if a nail was driven into it. My perception was that the right side of my face was radiating in a bright light. The left side was dark. The association was with Jesus Christ and the Third Eye.

I woke up at 7:30am and **was very sensitive to noise**. I remembered my dream very exactly. I listened to an interview of my father with a patient. He had cancer in the rectum and he was treating him homeopathically. The patient was not content with the treatment. The cancer was growing more and more. I spoke with my father and said: "What did you look up in the repertory." He

Provings

said he has no repertory and I was shocked. There was a conversation about this issue. He should instruct me how he found the remedy. And he said the tumor had shrunk and not grown.

The next dream was about a gay man and I fell in love with him or found him very attractive. He said to me that I have an extraordinary beauty and that I have **blue wings**. He spoke about colors and shapes. That was exciting.

Another scene with a dentist who was very cruel to me, he gave me at least 10 injections. I had to run away. I got out of it; I knew that it could be very bad for me.

Symbols of butterflies and dragonflies. I noticed that a butterfly tried to get in here and today he got inside and sits up there. Another feeling was of inner release. Not so sad and serious. There was some lightness in the sense of light without weight, an inner happiness, like an inner dancing.

PERSON WHO DID NOT TAKE THE REMEDY:
Had the feeling of an increased inner alertness and I was afraid when it was getting dark. I felt I have to go back to my nest. When I was driving back to the place where I live, I lost my sense of direction. I did not find my way several times, which is not usual for me. There was an inner panic and the sense of vision was acute, especially the sense of movement. Inner alertness, being on guard all the time. When a bicycle passed, I turned around immediately to look what was going on.

ELIZABETH SCHULZ REPORTS HER OWN EXPERIENCES:

I took the remedy in the evening before sleep. I had the feeling that I was flying, very high up in the air. I didn't move my wings. I had the feeling of seeing birds' heads. There was an incredible yearning for freedom. There was a hand wearing a leather glove and I had to come back to this glove, to this hand. And then this yearning for freedom was very strong. After these images had passed, there was a very deep feeling. The remedy released one aspect of my personality. The feeling of a deep cure. The feeling of absolute connectedness into oneness.

I stood in a group of women and we stretched to warm up for the coming exercises. However, **my right shoulder joint painfully refused to do what I want-**

ed. In spite of the pain and tormenting symptoms this was my most beautiful remedy proving. The pain in the shoulder joint was **piercing and gnawing**. I had an unbelievable longing for freedom and a **deep need to follow my own instincts and intuitive impulses**. I had a desire to move myself quickly through fresh air. **Bicycling** became an addiction, the faster the more beautiful. I felt my body more intensely and my eyesight became sharper. It was almost as if I would absorb the stimulation and impressions of the outside world with my whole body.

Sleep becomes restless. Often, I wake up at night with the feeling of suffocation. I am struggling for air and in spite of deep breathing my body does not seem to be able to absorb enough oxygen. After this I fall asleep again. The attacks that wake me up only last a short while.

Then I experience one of the most beautiful and clearest dreams of my life: I am aware of myself and suddenly become blind. Invisible powers push me back and forth. I can no longer walk or stand. I stumble and everything is lost in the darkness. I am afraid. Suddenly, I can see through the darkness, sharper, more colorful, clearer than ever. There is a Buddha sitting not far away from me. He is alive and completely dressed in gold and silk. I am standing behind a little wall and look at him. "Sleep with me," I say to him. He answers: "You may enter the shrine." I walk towards him and we kiss each other. We kiss and I awake bathed in an intensive feeling of happiness.

My aversion against driving has completely disappeared and I enjoy guiding the car quickly, nimbly, safely and skillfully through traffic. My sense of orientation becomes bad and I do not recognize usually well-known streets. My colleagues experience the same and during those five days several wanderings occurred. As soon as I took the pellets into my hands, my knees started trembling. I became very excited and nervous and my body wanted to fly down the staircase in a dive. I grabbed quickly the banisters to avoid falling down the steps. Another activity was getting food. More or less **I was constantly busy with eating and searching for food during the breaks**. Delusions of grandeur took place. I spent a lot of money on books, but felt ashamed about it.

I give this remedy time and space and ask it to show me something about its essence. In the evening I enter a quiet room, lay down on my back and let the

RED-TAILED
HAWK
PROVING

Provings

pellets dissolve slowly in my mouth. I want to get into contact. After a short while I had the feeling of being a bird flying over the land. I saw the head of a bird of prey. There is a ribbon and a little bell and I fly back to a human hand that wears a thick leather glove. The ribbon is like a connection to human beings. **I am in conflict between my own need for freedom and the restriction of my freedom through the attachment to humans**. Then, I feel that the remedy releases something deeply within me. This something has no name yet, but it leaves a wonderful feeling of happiness within me. I have a strong longing for this aspect of my personality and a deep healing takes place.

Dull and pounding headache, **strong throat ache around the tonsils,** first the left one then on the right side.

The mucous membranes are very dry. Then I see a huge bird. The bird seems to be tied down and fights to free itself. The images change and a big eagle appears.

I have **pain in my left eye as if a needle was pricked into it**. Eye burning. Constantly the feeling to be a burden for other people. I don't want to impose myself.

The colleagues are trying to convince me to stay. **Again, I experience an awful conflict between accommodating my need for free decision-making and other people's needs.** There were the children. They lured me into the dusk. I got along well with them. We played ball, laughed and went wild in the grass. Among the children in fresh air and surrounded by trees, I felt good. Here I felt free.

Physical symptoms: urine is yellow like lemons; frequent urination. **Menstruation** is three days early and **very painful** in the lower back area. An image that comes up: as if someone puts sticks into my back, like a magician who penetrates and divides a woman in a box with swords. **Pain in my right hip joint**, dull and gnawing. Rheumatic muscle pain. **My skin turns yellow.**

Clumsiness and difficulties with coordination. Lack of orientation, worse in the dark. That morning I think a lot about my fears to impose myself on others. A feeling to never do it right for others. At the seminar I noticed that my cervical vertebrae have become very flexible.

SEMINAR PROVING II: FINLAND

FEMALE B:
Heavy headache on right side. Woke 6 am. **Right eye like digging the eyeball out**. All day feeling in this eye. Swollen feeling as if closed. Headache behind right eye. Information in her work cannot reach her, **as if drugged**. Didn't like the feeling because got evaluated and criticized at work. Annoyance that couldn't do the work the way she wanted. Absent minded. Small mistakes. Couldn't do a practical job as she should. Got confused about the vagina and rectum in nursing.

FEMALE B:
Took a 2nd dose because nothing happened. Odd pain in hypogastrium low down extending upwards. Desire to urinate but unable to find the right position. Went away in one hour. In bed in the evening waking dream. Big space like a sports field. Everybody knew there was a center in that field. Some people faced the center, others stood with their backs to the center. Two groups moved together and fell down, like round people without the weight, light and very round figures. Human head but not the body like foam body. Repeated exactly same experience 4 or 5 times. Thought it was very funny because they were so light and fell down. They all had fun, like a game they were playing. Then had a dream about my 18 yr. old daughter who has just broken up with boyfriend and new ones are coming. This is reality. In the dream there were three boys one of whom she knows. Boys live together in an old **blue** house. Didn't know where daughter was and went with husband to look for daughter, who was not in the house. The third boy began to cry whenever she looked at him. He wanted to leave his home and move in together with the other boys. He wept a lot, she woke up. Anxious because couldn't do anything for the boy. Same situation in her work where she would like to help but cannot; sometimes you are stuck. He was crying so much that she could not communicate with him. Helpless and anxious.

FEMALE B:
Shortness of breath 5 minutes later. Sneezing. Small occipital headache. Short duration.

RED-TAILED HAWK PROVING

Provings

Dream. **Taking child to caretaker and forgot the child there for many days and then suddenly remembered and was terrified when she remembered that the child had been there for many days**. The place where she took the child was a strange place, as if she had taken it to some unknown person who had just offered to do the caretaking. Another dream. Chaotic situation in the world, natural phenomenon. **Very big waves** and the ground moving like earthquake. As if aliens came from space and came to conquer the world. Felt like a child and wanted to hide, then woke up.

Pain in neck now. Feels OK but her children have been irritated and she has been irritated. Usual situation.

FEMALE B:
Headache on the right side on waking in morning. Pulsating pain. Lasted 15 minutes. Better on moving around. Slight vertigo. Stuffy feeling. Woke in middle of night and saw vision of one of the video cases of *Platinum* in front of her face. Had *Graphites* in her mind. Another short dream. Saw a cow and told the boyfriend to write down the cow and the milk. He said you are the cow. 3rd dream. Situation with war veterans. Yesterday felt **as if someone put a stick in the right eyeball**. Lasted a few minutes. Had iritis on left one week ago. Last night dreamed about well-dressed friends in a hotel. Girlfriend had short hair and brown fur coat.

FEMALE B:
Short dream. Colleague from work place who in real life has just taken a job as accounting manager. Middle-aged little obese female. In dream she had a mini size fur down to upper knees. Fur was too big and didn't fit her. Looked very fat in this fur. Brown maybe like mink. Astonished because the boss was dressed like this. Next morning very tired and eyes dry especially the right. Now feels OK. Better than before took remedy. Difficult to understand yesterday. Stuffy feeling as if hadn't slept at all.

FEMALE T:
Usually so stressed. Felt so good after the remedy. So wonderful to have no stress.

FEMALE T:
Usually **hard to focus before putting on her glasses, but this time saw the needles of a pine tree 100 meters away** without glasses.

FEMALE T:
In the night it felt **as if a spear through the body** from chest to back.

FEMALE T:
Flu, vertigo, confused dream. Two messages from the dream; loneliness and to be ahead of her time. **Woke up and said to her husband "I have lived 45 years and will not be ordered around any more." She has never spoken to her husband like this before**.

FEMALE T:
Dream. High up looking down at beautiful island called Bolivia. Looking down from high up.

FINLAND WRITTEN RECORDS
(Notes kept in English by Finnish recorder)
Scale visual analog 0 to 10: The remedy affected me in general: 0= not all; 10=very much.

FT scale 1. Occipital headache in the morning lasting a few minutes. Dry mouth in am.

MB scale 0-2. Woke 5am - 5.30am on 2 nights

FT scale 3. Headache in morning, forehead lasting 15 minutes. Dream: high building. Walked up the steps and saw this great view. Both headache and dream are usual to her.

FT scale 1. Occipital headache in the morning lasting a few minutes. Dreams: many. Can't remember. **Water, sky, space, feeling very free**. On the third day still dreaming high up between water and sky.

(Unknown prover) scale 3. **Marked numbness left leg at night**. Next night much lighter to breathe after waking. **Changed eyeglasses** because they did not feel right.

MB scale 2. Put remedy in pocket. While walking home from seminar **suddenly had the feeling that walking is like flying**. It was so easy to walk, as if the feet were not completely on the ground. I was late and had to run and there was almost no difference in my experience between walking and running. I covered the distance in what seemed a very short time. Inside my head

Provings

there was a fresh sensation, as if it was full of air. I have been rather nervous during the whole seminar.

FB scale 2. Immediately on taking the remedy, while lying in bed, I felt a light sensation as if I could fly. Many dreams but hard to remember. Disappointed because couldn't remember dreams. **Grayish blue** with two white figures, one like the tail end of a horse running away from me; the other figure was something which was following the horse high up in the air. Disappointed. Dreams had passed away and the horse was also going. On the 2nd day bright red almost orange menstrual flow lasting from 1 pm to evening. Menses was 12 days ago and I have never had this before in my life. The color was unusual as well.

FB scale 1. Cannot remember dreams. Slept so soundly. Disappointed. Took another dose. Woke early. Asleep again and 2 dreams. Dream. Tried to contact different people Had to do with communication and an unknown man Going from one place to another and in each place was a telephone as a central element. I did not talk with anybody on the phone and the presence of the phone was disturbing. The phones were of different models, colors, and sizes. With the last normal-sized and -looking phone I tried to dial the number of some person but I failed as wrong numbers could be seen in the selection table. Next dream. **I had planted some plants in the countryside. Many days later I remembered and was shocked as I had forgotten to pay attention to them and so they had not gotten any water, etc.** I rushed immediately to the plants and noted to my surprise and relief that they were alive but huge buttercups were overwhelming the area. I started to pull up the buttercups. It took great effort with both hands and the energy of my whole body. In some small areas it was difficult to separate the buttercups from the other plants.

MB scale 7.5. The next morning I felt very sharp. My energy on waking was very high. In the afternoon and evening I felt great tiredness and went to bed early. **A funny feeling in my left eye, a sort of pressing. Vision was diminished.** While lying in bed at night **very restless and pressing feeling** in my legs. 2nd night a heavy feeling. Saliva thicker than normal after 2 days. Dreams: 2 very confusing dreams. People were chasing me. Then I was caught and somebody punched an injection needle into my side. The place where the needle entered the skin began to break as if the skin was made of paper.

The wounded area with red flesh under the skin started to appear. My feeling was to get the needle away from the people so they could not make more holes in my body. I got the needle away and began to punch it into the people around me and was thus able to run away. In the same dream there were **knives** flashing. A woman took a knife and tried to cut/slice me with it. I also had a knife with which I defended myself. I cannot remember the 2nd dream.

FB scale 9. All the night I was in the country where I was born and lived the first 18 years. It was a beautiful light summer night. I was in the garden looking into the house through the window. I saw some woman moving inside. I remember the motion as if I were in a swing. I saw a view from very high in the air, a field near my home was full of runways like an airport but there were no airplanes. I was very high up. Next I awakened at 7:26 a.m. with a good feeling. Not tired, very energetic as if it were sports racing. I took care of two beautiful Chinese children about 7 years old. I covered them with my son's **blue** blanket, as if a bird with her wings. I saw, too, my old neighbors who died 10 years ago. They were repainting their house. Inside the house was full of wooden toys **red**, white and **blue**, some of them quite large from wall to wall. It was the first time I saw my dead neighbors in a dream. They were very close to me. It was an exceptional night. I awoke at 8.30

SEMINAR PROVING III: SCOTLAND, SEPTEMBER 1995

MT: I heard a voice. My father always told me to do it like this. Then **an image: Black glove**. Hairy arm. Then woke up.

MB: Slight headache right eye. Frequent waking. Dream rugby scrum. Front row. Locked horns. Pushed the scrum to the other end of the field and scored a goal. Sentimentality. Beach Boys on radio. Woman's name. He missed her. Sentimental about the oneness of the universe. How it all fit together. Jigsaw puzzle all fit into place. Reason for things.

MB: Disturbing dream. Horse face in front of his nose. Cats across path in front of him. Then disturbing dream. Know they're all rules but no one told you. Knitted purse like chain mail. Put money in this pouch. I have put too much in. Pouch designed not to release money. Cut a hole in pouch. Hope no one sees him. Store detectives, "Come with us." Shoplifting. "We have you on camera." Unfairly treated. Wanted to be let go but they wouldn't. Then

Provings

lying on floor. Guard said "We have got you now. You used this card. It is against the rules." Feeling that he was in everybody's way. Female vomited next to his belongings. Bothered no one. Policeman slouching at the desk. Bloodshot eyes. Sneering. Got you now.

GREAT HORNED OWL *Bubo virginianus*

Jonathan Shore proving, 8 provers present. Trituration/proving up to C3 done in California in 2000.

Bursitis during night of proving. Couple of hours here were worst. Cancelled golf the next day. 3 days bad, then totally gone. In the couple of hours during the proving, it went from a twinge to really bad. **Pain in the joint (indicates right shoulder.)** I couldn't take my clothes off over my head.

The other thing I noticed was, I've had migraines for a long time. They were just recently diagnosed as migraines. I was away and ran out of my prescription. The night I was here, I didn't have a headache. On Tuesday after I left here, I got a headache again, another one of those that will last forever, but it went away.

Had earache. Bad, remembered hot oil mom dropped in ear. Had to fly to San Diego on Wednesday, very afraid of ear problems on the plane.

Dreamed a wagon was going around like the old west, everyone else was walking. Received a gift of a corset woven out of leather straps, like Madonna. Surprised that it fit perfectly, refused to buckle the belt buckle at the crotch. Given boots by a Japanese man. Boots had silver stars on the toes. Sepia toned, dark like in museum. **Huge dog, jumping over me**. I have a fear of dogs, but in the dream there was no fear. FELT LIKE I WAS OBSERVING. The leather corset is something that holds you in, but it didn't feel too tight. Felt sexy, I don't usually wear sexy things. In the dream I felt quite sexy, because it was a gift. I felt very beautiful and gifted. Very old west.

Dreams of water, drowning.

Feeling of calmness stayed with me, felt very good. It's still with me. Wonderful to be so present, so watchful, it's nice to be here just taking it in.

Had issues with knowledge and wisdom, and also fairness. I actually caused a seating arrangement at a seminar to be rearranged to allow people in the back to sit in the front. Not a big confrontation, but I would not let it go and it worked. At another time, a person in a clinic didn't get a turn to speak and I called this to the attention of the teacher.

GREAT HORNED OWL PROVING

Provings

Also talked about associations with owl. **Visual strangeness** continued. I couldn't see letters during trituration; I kept wanting to put my glasses here (indicates forehead.) Made lots of **spelling errors**.

Issue of safety, think I felt that connectedness with the substance, it relates to this thing in Holland where we had this owl on TV who told the little children stories at seven o'clock every evening. These stories had a moral.

Maybe more of a **teaching element** in my work, **I see myself as more of a teacher**, more of a solid guide rather than a California loose and flaky one. I have a feeling about teaching, settled more in a part of myself that's already there.

At night, I usually listen to tapes in the car, but on the night of the trituration I just drove in silence and enjoyed the view, the moon, the Bay. My perception of the night was very clear and different.

It made me feel **very calm and wise**, but very **detached** at the same time. The first few days **I was observing my own life rather than living it, watching the world go by.**

I felt very unruffled. Work was hectic, but I was not affected by it. I was the calm spot in the center of the hurricane.

It affected my body clock. I could not eat for days after the remedies, but **at sunset I would get ravenous, especially for meat, chicken.**

VISION: Blurry. When driving, losing three-dimensional orientation. Had to be careful when changing lanes on freeway. It was a depth perception issue.

DREAMS: **jumping dog,** in a house upstairs and chaos was breaking out. Everyone was talking at the same time. The dog was barking, someone was pounding at the door then the dog flew up the stairs **over my head** and landed and that was the end of the dream.

DREAM: back in an old house, sitting in old fashioned porch swing under a redwood tree that grows in the back yard. The swing was not attached to anything, I was swinging in mid- air. I first worried, then was swinging higher and higher. Eventually I let go of the swing and flew around everything. I really enjoyed that dream.

EARS kept getting plugged up and unplugged. I could feel something rattling around in my ear, went under water and goo came out of my left ear, gummy like rubber cement, something new, it was the color and consistency of rubber cement. I thought I got glue in my ear.

I felt, especially at work, like being **guided by an inner wisdom**, giving me all the answers I needed, giving me all the knowledge and answers I needed, did not at all feel afraid.

Tingling and circulation stuff in arms, tremendous amount of neck pain, still have it. It got very bad. I felt **like I was losing my neck, like it was fusing onto my head.** I was ok with all of that.

I had a hard time with talking, all the talking in my life. There was no place I could go to be quiet. All I wanted to do was to go in the wilderness, camping, far away.

I have gotten more personal power and strength than I can remember, a real self-awareness and a real **wisdom**.

I have issues with vision and I totally gave that up. I completely surrendered to having no sight.

HEARING would come and go. I was hearing things on a completely different level than I had before.

I would hear a voice calling my name, hear a sound that made no logical sense, a vague kind of thing, very much in tune with different sounds. Like a clock ticking, the hum of my computer was unacceptable, it was so loud, I could not deal with it. That lasted the whole two weeks. My ears would get plugged up at various times, it came and went, it happened a few times.

I almost could not read. The words would get blurry, or I could not focus. I would get a headache. In general I could not focus on specific things. It came and went, but since taking the remedy, I notice it very soon after I take it. It is very intense. I had to be careful driving; it limits my sight.

GREAT HORNED OWL PROVING

Provings

Needing to know the truth and needing to know what was going on. I had a lot of insight coming to me in conversations and in books, **meaningful insight**, thoughts would just come to me.

I didn't want to have conversation, and **I really didn't want to have MEANINGLESS conversation**. I was very restless with having interaction with people that was meaningless, or babble.

I wanted to eat more, and wanted to think more about food than before. Eating food became more of a sensual experience.

I've had a lot of sleep problems, and these problems went away on the remedy. Have had a few nights of 9+ hours of sleep, but not feeling groggy or drugged. Woke up refreshed and ready to start the day.

Thought I was getting a cold or an ear infection: **sore throat, earache**.

I noticed I was waking up early, bright and shiny, felt like I got a good sleep, like I got complete rest during the night. Completed tasks during the night.

That day, and every day after, I felt tightness in the jaw and my ears hurt. More on the left. My teeth really bothered me, like they were too big for my face. Thought I had gum disease. It was funny; it was all teeth and ears.

Tremendous pain in the back OF MY NECK around the time of my menstrual cycle. My eyes were also focusing weirdly. **I was aware of eyes functioning separately;** am I seeing with my right eye or my left eye? Every room in my house seemed too dark. I also noticed depth perception was off.

One more thing, when we started the word I used was clarity, the past couple of weeks have been so hectic, but so clear.

Thirst was just awful; lips are completely chapped, peeing all the time. Thirst for water. I went through two gallons of spring water in about 2 days. **I did not want to be IN water, and that's really unusual. I perspired a lot on my hands AND ARMS particularly.**

GREAT BLUE HERON *Ardea herodias*

GREAT BLUE HERON PROVING

PROVING METHODOLOGY: This was a Jonathan Shore trituration/proving done in California in 2002. Seven people participated in the trituration of the remedy, 5 women and 2 men, ranging from ages of 20 - 55 years old. The feather came from a Blue Heron rookery in the San Juan Islands of Washington state.

PROVER #1, WOMAN
PROVER #2, WOMAN
PROVER #3, WOMAN
PROVER #4, MAN
PROVER #5, WOMAN
PROVER #6, MAN
PROVER #7, WOMAN

GENERAL CONVERSATION DURING TRITURATION

FIRST ROUND OF TRITURATION
Seven people grind for one minute, then 10 people scrape for one minute.
Timing of everything is becoming a minor issue already.
B. asked a question if it would make more sense to have one person grind the matrix. Four people in and we've lost track of time. Is it all mutual suggestion?
The movement of energy from one person to another suggests it.
After this first round, go three minutes, instead of one. Too short to develop some sort of rhythm.
Something funny about all of the timing.
Everybody's pretty quiet this time.
A little discussion on the process, what's to come when were done with the base substance?
I think this is about fear.
What does the French phrase *laissez faire* mean? Let it be?

SECOND ROUND OF TRITURATION
Has anyone ever done a human remedy?
Yes, breast milk. There are also pituitary remedies, from bovine glands, but breast milk is done from humans.
Only one spider cares for its young; it's used for unrequited love (*Tarentula-cub*).

Provings

What about dolphins, whales?
Yes, dolphin milk, ambergris are used.
A little girl had always been fascinated with sharks, she had nightmares, and was given dolphin. She was outgoing, athletic, gymnastics, but was afraid of being rejected at school. She wanted to be a marine biologist since age of four. She'd rather be a dolphin than a shark.
Also used on a guy in his 50's with nasal polyps, also a surfer.

Third Round of Trituration
Everyone is having issues with vision.
Constriction in throat. It's almost like a vibration.
Numbness.
For less than a minute it was tight.
I feel like I'm missing something, as if maybe there's something going on under the surface, and I'm not in a place where I can contact it. This is an energy I call hiding. It's like a family dinner, there are things going on under the room, but no one is talking to it, only over it.
I don't feel the rest of my body, just the head.
He looks tired; we are going to see him on the floor any minute now.
Do you feel the information not just of the animal in general, but also of the specific individual?
I feel like this animal may have been separated from its flock or group.
The wonderful thing about remedies is that every substance has feelings: rocks, trees, bugs.
So it does have to correspond. That's what's interesting, trying to enter that substance. I'm reminded of one of my favorite stories about **purgatory.** My friend was Catholic. He lost his faith because he had no idea of how long his time in **purgatory** would be when compared to the whole. If it's 100 years out of 10 million? That started a whole logical analysis and he lost his faith.

WRAP-UP CONVERSATION AFTER TRITURATIONS
Prover #1
Trituration 1:
Eyes were itching for 2 days before the proving. Got worse, dry and hot tonight. **My teeth hurt,** since a couple of days. The trunk of my body feels heavy, thick.

Calm, detachment to interaction, felt separate from the group in a good way I liked listening to the stories Jonathan told, it was mesmerizing My mouth and lips tightened and getting small. I could not control anything, everything started to move separately. My reaction to it. **Everything was moving at its own pace and time.** Heat was distinctive, started in the legs, kidneys, **the heat kept rising.**

GREAT BLUE HERON PROVING

Trituration 2:
Heat went up in the face and neck Detachment and calm. Surrender to make anything work in a particular way, congested. All was separate, even the food. **Separated from the group.** Itching eyes, and the closer the mortar the hotter I felt. It got very clear, not on a mundane level, at a level I do not get to very often, and I liked it.

Trituration 3:
I was just staring, not connected, enjoyment, no fear, detachment. **Lips and eyes itching.** While **grinding, pain in the liver**, suffocating. **Tight jaws**, not comfortable Felt I wanted to fly away, and I was ready to leave the group. **Neck pain**, left.

PROVER #2
Trituration 1:
Dizzy, lightheaded, spacey, focused on details. **Stiff neck.**

Trituration 2:
Isolating event, not uncomfortable to be quiet with each other, but weird.

Trituration 3:
Spacey, dull. **Throat constriction**, pain in or around the heart, easy to get loss in the task with no care what is going on, but aware of the silence and every sound around. Headache on the right, light.

PROVER #3
Yesterday I was with my family; they were playing golf, I don't play. But I played. My eyes focused in a strange way on the orange ball. I was aware that the focus went in and out of this ball. I was so calm and so relaxed. **I sent the ball to the green every time**. I was playing with two men that are wonderful golfers and their play fell apart watching me. I didn't care, I never got frustrated, never got upset, watched them fall apart, I kept focusing on the ball.

Provings

I woke up last night around 5 o'clock, **my eyes were burning so badly** I thought I must be sick; it hurt so much I could hardly go back to sleep. When I got here tonight I was aware that my perspective on things was moving way out, back and above and I was **becoming some kind of an observer**. I too experienced falling into details, music, shine of an apple, all these facets. I was aware of all of them individually without blending in together. **I had heat in my body**. I had a sense of my emotional body vibrating in some kind of expectation, especially while pressing the powder.

Trituration 1:
I had a real sense of this vibration I was into experiencing. It had not been able to fully express itself in this dimension. There was **this quality it had, this vibration to all of us that was not able to be expressed**, to be accepted. I had a sensation of tearing (eyes), yawning, wetness, something happening to my thymus, thyroid gland. My breathing deepened, I was not pressing to breathe deeply, but I was **breathing more and more deeply, taking longer and longer breaths**. I really experienced my breath. I had a tightness in my solar plexus at the beginning that cleared. I had this **stiffening at the back of my neck** to my scapulae. It felt like an **all over allergic reaction** to something. I was continuing to yawn.

Trituration 2:
I had a sensation of being watched, even hunted; I wanted to get away, to leave. I wasn't feeling frightened, I just didn't want to be here anymore. I wanted to leave. I was kind of aware of some kind of energy to do with rules, expectations, even perfection; it wasn't moving. There was a 'something' that was beautiful, but the energy itself was not moving. I felt suffocated in my body, I wanted to get away and I **felt unable to express myself**. Again sounds.

Totally in my head. My **eyes are burning, vision spread out**. Static feeling, temporal pressure, shoulders, a lot of burning, tensions into the kidneys. Yawning, start to release. **Deep breathing, feeling of pulling air into the body** to keep myself here. A lot of **burning in the eyes**, a **lot of heat** there.

Trituration 3:
I was totally aware that my eyes were still not focusing. I had that **panoramic vision**, an awareness about that. Dullness in my head, experiencing that

I was unable to take any thought; that dullness which is like a curtain had fallen, I was just watching everything at that table, and it was very funny for me. I had more tingling in my fingers, and a sense of just wanting to get out and away. There was a heaviness present in my body that I was aware of. I mentioned the hiding, that strong sense of this not being expressed, this vibration. I again had this strong sense of expectations, judgment about not being able to speak, express this vibration out. Almost a fear of judgment, almost like: you can look and see all the details, but don't look, just dream back, don't see. Kind of dreamy state. I wouldn't call it Detachment, but **floating, just floating out of it**. I did not really have a strong sense of my body, of isolation. I couldn't feel the judgments, I wasn't in the pain, I floated out of it. I did not really have a strong sense of isolation in my body. I could *see* the isolation, I could just see it; my body was kind of numb. I was aware of the isolation, vibration, but my body was numb to it, floating. It almost felt like I was on drugs.

*Jonathan: The issue of **absinthe** was raised. This was no accident; I felt it very much.*

Prover #4
Felt hot in the last couple of days.

Trituration 1:
Eyes watering, post nasal drip, in the throat now. **Felt teeth folding** in, sensation of elongation except my fingers felt thick. **Tingling in fingers and feet. Vision double**, could not focus on computer. Focus came back, but double. Sensitive to smell and hearing, vision was going, changing, eyes were moving somewhere out, sensitive to odors and sounds. **Detached** about the whole thing, I did not care about people talking. Feel swollen, flurry in stomach. **Waiting for something, detachment comes from this waiting.**

I felt waiting for something, I felt detached, I don't know what I'm waiting for, but I know it is coming and that everything will be fine and everything outside of that is not important.

Prover #5
Trituration 1:
Felt drowsy, moderate energy, comfortable silence, no need to speak.

Provings

Spacey feeling, at every step, HA shifting to vertex then dissipated. Grinding seemed to go slow.

Increased sensation about color, light got brighter. I was aware of the outside noises like wind in the trees which is unusual for me. The grinding was too slow, surge of mirth, sounds were coming through. **Nose drainage internally**, eyes not focusing. **Discharge in nose. Choking sensation that kept building**; that made me nervous. Everything was distracting me, even a fly that flew by. **Face flushing**. Sense of hilarity and **time passing slowly**.

Trituration 2:
Fun to nibble on the snacks. **Trouble spelling**. Nervous energy shifted and I felt dreamy.

Itching in the shoulder, and nose, center of vision focus got blurry. Sensation of **headache on the vertex** came back. Concentration bad. Sensation in eyes. Hands got warmer, more relaxed, felt like sliding down in a chair, **dolphins, sharks**, felt in the water with the sharks. Calm.

Trituration 3:
Strong dreamy feeling. Awareness centered around my head; usually aware of my whole body. Focus up in the head.

Feeling **I did not care about anything**, what was a relief, not cold. Noises outside are prominent; the grinding in the bowl. Physical shock about **separation from the flock**. Pain in the chest with pressure, anxiety underlies everything. **Sore throat**. Colors and jewels that glitter captured my attention. After the shock, came sadness. **Heavy anxiety in my chest again**. Did not want to hear about the **purgatory** when the discussion came up.

Prover #7
Trituration 1: Felt excited, joyful, mood uplifted, more energy, more awake. **Body temperature rose**, awareness of heart, lungs, throat; euphoric sensation, energy coming up the legs. **Lost focus** easily, scattered, became dreamy, pressure on eyes. Wanted to start **flying**.

Trituration 2:
More dreamy. Vision of ocean and nature, euphoric, spacey and quiet.

Trituration 3:
Tired, memory got short, **vision wider**, pressure on skull, pain in the eardrum, awareness was above me, withdrawn, sensation of being alone, heart beat faster, sadness, **separation from the group**, **burning eyes**, calm.

Prover #8
Trituration 1:
I will try to make a coherent synthesis of my experience. I will read what I wrote down, which isn't much. I wrote down: Philosophy, laughter, gentle. I definitely had the feeling this is a gentle remedy. The last proving, when we did the proving, the scraping was loud and strong. Here it was **gentle**. I noticed I was **sighing** a lot, and I definitely saw that others had this too. And **yawning** too. My **eyes were tired and burning**.

Trituration 2:
There was this desire to explain. I was sort of bored at times, nothing was happening. At the same time I had this sense I was missing something, and that what I was missing had to do with some other level of **vibration**, which despite the fact that I was quite quiet, I wasn't quiet enough to contact. I was still too distracted by my experiences in my body, the feeling of this, to really touch this other energy. I noticed I was **burping a lot**; I also notice other people were doing that; there was definitely some digestive element (not uncomfortable).

I forgot the camera; I went back into the house 3 times before I managed to leave (but still forgot the camera). At the same time, my feeling was that this is a serious remedy, but not serious-heavy.

It was very quiet, **an extra-ordinary quiet**, in terms of proving sets we have done. Yet when people talked, there was nothing particularly frivolous, it was not a sort of chatter, it was to the point, **transmission of information**. In that sense, it seemed that the mind worked quite well. It wasn't that you could not gather your thoughts, if you wanted to say something it was possible to say it, very clearly and directly and in that sense, there wasn't that spaciness. I felt this laughter in the beginning, which came up quite strongly. And very quiet, not quite detached, but this mostly in myself. The noises were not really distracting, they were there but they did not penetrate very far, so it was mostly a **very contemplative experience**. Just really quiet, contemplating; **not a lot of activity in the head** and there was some tension around that, like being

Provings

bored, because my mind is used to more stuff going on, to more action. At the same time it was just not much going on, not necessary.

SUMMARY REMARKS
PROVER #8
I have the feeling I am missing something, like **something going on, sort of under the surface** and I am not in that place to contact it, exactly. Either it is this sort of no experience, or my perception is not active enough to see what is underneath the no experience; I know there is always something going on.

PROVER #7
I have the feeling that I am way up here (shows up), and a part of me is feeling what is here. Something up in the sky. I look around up there, vision of the sky, vision of the ocean.

PROVER #3
Hiding, this is an energy that I call hiding. It is oppressive. Everyone is just sitting, looking around, quietly engaging, eating, like a family dinner, a gathering, a group of people not having seen each other or have seen each other. There are a **lot of things going on in the room. People talk about or below it, but no one is talking to it. What is going on**, what is happening in your body, what is your body feeling? It is uncomfortable.

PROVER #5
I have more the feeling that all is here, not that I am nervous about the situation. I check where is the rest of my body.

PROVER #7
Sensation that this creature got separated from his group.

FOLLOW-UP SESSIONS 2 WEEKS LATER
PROVER #5
I had to juggle things; this week I kept dropping the balls. It is unlike what I do. I appreciate the difference. My **spelling was bizarre, lot of problems spelling**. I couldn't get the spelling of words, it is unusual for me; I am not the best speller in the world, but this was extreme.

I like singing and driving in the car at about 50 miles an hour. I was listening to a certain kind of music and singing, which was really fun; I want to get it out of my system before I go away on the weekend with my husband.

That was weird; I don't usually do that.

When I left last week, the next day I had this incredible craving for **cold apples and grapes.** I usually like bananas. That stayed with me for the week. I was much less sensitive to people, and I liked it (just "give me the facts, ma'am, ... ok we are done now" kind of thing). They come late or they come early, and usually I get a little anxious about it. **And I just did not care.**

Jonathan: When you say sensitive to people, what do you mean?
I really **pick up people's energy**, and even though I try to be myself and don't try to pick up people's energy, I'm very sensitive to it. So it works in my practice. And when the remedy leveled off yesterday, I ran out and did some errands. I interacted with a couple of people and I was like.... wow! I was just right back to where I was and I was "I don't like this", I liked the other way. I'm definitely going to take the 30C. So up to then, that was the effect of what we had made, the 3 triturations and this was pretty good, but then it just went boom (she motions down).

Jonathan: Explain to me more.
I went to do errands, and I lined up four errands precisely, instead of my usual thing. The first errand I did I bought bottles for my business and the guy was uptight and I felt so uptight interacting with him. And then I went to buy gas and I went in the wrong direction and this guy was standing there yelling at me "next time don't come back in this direction" and all this stuff. I was oh my god, what have I gotten into, and then I just went some place else and I was still **just very sensitive to people around me**. An exaggeration of my usual state. So I was very happy to feel that again. And today I'm doing this major writing project and I **just disconnected the phone** and did it Because otherwise I just answer the phone and I do this and I do that. So it felt to me that the remedy is still working; I can't just juggle things like I usually do, which again is still a relief. I had two dreams: the first one I had a couple of nights after I took the remedy and it was really bizarre. In this dream, there was a herd of goats and somebody said, "Here is a club and we going to club this herd of goats to death." It was like this is what we are going to do, so it wasn't like we did it,

Provings

but I could preconceive of it and I thought, "This is archaic. I'm not doing this," and then I woke up. I never dream about goats. Sometimes I have violent dreams, but that was just so first-hand; we are going to club this goat to death. So I wrote it down because it was pretty strange. And then the second night, I had this intense grief dream about my dad and it stayed with me and it is still kind of strong. I felt like this thing **lifted off my heart** afterwards. The rest of the days I did not dream enough to remember. A couple of people thought I seemed more centered. And then I was just super, super industrious, and I am always industrious, but this was just like **very industrious** and I thought maybe it is a bird, one of those that is always busy. I just got everything done. Maybe it was more organized, so I had high energy during the proving.

On the issue of loneliness:
I **felt myself alone** a fair amount and I'm very **attached** to my husband. I was very affectionate with him, and we made much more improved negotiations. I expected a lot of social activities, when usually, because of my sensitivity, I burn out, and I usually like solitude. I had a lot of **social activities**.

PROVER #7
I had a very different experience from that. I was actually pretty opposite. I was very sensitive through all of it. I was not insensitive to other people, but I actually **became more detached from other people than I usually am. Especially from people that I actually have very strong attachments to**, I became detached in a very nice way. **I just became more sensitive to myself and my own emotions.** I have a lot of releases in my body and on a spiritual level. I was very emotional the whole time; it was very consistent. I did not have a lot of energy and my body was tired. With the changes that were happening in my body, I was tired the whole time. I had a lot of body pain, but I was very emotional and that was great, that was really interesting. A lot of my dreams were emotional; a couple of dreams I was angry and yelled at people I had wanted to yell at, which was great. My **eyes have been sensitive** the whole time. My **appetite has been very awkward, I can't handle a lot of food; I had to have small amounts of food. I didn't want to eat fruit**, and usually I eat a lot of fruit. I mostly eat fruit and vegetables. I wanted grains and stuff like that. And meat I did not really want to have it. My sleep is different. One great thing that was the effect of this proving is that **I am a smoker and I didn't want to smoke** or

only in very small amounts. It totally changed for me which is the greatest part of that. For a long time I really wanted to quit and for whatever reason it pushed that for me, which was really great.

Jonathan: When you say emotional, what does that mean?
My emotions are stronger or maybe I was more in them than I usually am. I was more aware of them, no I wasn't more aware of them, but they were stronger.

Jonathan: Emotions like?
Call it anger, not that I was sad; emotions I can't describe, probably **emotions in my body that I don't have a name for, not in my mind.**

Jonathan: You actually got sick?
Yes. I got very sick with a temperature.

Jonathan: It started right that night?
No, actually this started for the past two weeks; it has been like this. It started on the Saturday before this proving. Then I would feel better, then I wouldn't feel good again. I would feel a little better, and Thursday a little better and a little better on Friday and then awful again, very tired on the week-end and Monday it hit. I felt awful, I had a high temperature and could barely move.

Jonathan: This actually began before we met?
Yes, but I think it had to do with what we are doing here; I just started it before I came.

Jonathan: What makes you think it has to do with what we are doing?
Because I look at it and that's what I see. I know what is going on with me and I know why.

Jonathan: You feel that there is some benefit from this process?
Yes. Absolutely. I'm not sure that everyone would see that. I appreciate all that stuff coming out of me. I live for that. For me it was great. Sometimes when I thought it was horrible, I wanted to shoot this bird or whatever. When I look at it, I feel different. I feel I have a stronger sense of myself. I feel that a **lot of things are unimportant to me.**

Jonathan: Do you generally get angry?
Yes.

Provings

Jonathan: So that is generally not an unknown?
No, but it was a really great angry state and I was in a dream and **I did not care how senseless it was**. It was me. I was in the dream space; **I got to do wild things that would maybe not be ok in my dreams**. Usually everything is ok in your dreams, but I got to try some raucous things that I wouldn't say on the tape. The anger part was good.

Jonathan: The wild stuff had to do criminal activities, sexual activities, torturing?
(Laughs....) I do have to say it was **exploring emotions inside of me that were taboo**. I do not have anything else to say because I got real sick.

Jonathan: Worst symptoms?
I could not do anything, I could not get up and get myself food or things, and it was very painful physically.

Jonathan: Emotionally, physically?
Temperature was very high, my ears, I went deaf when I was a child and my ears hurt so bad.

Jonathan: Is your hearing ok now?
I haven't noticed anything. I can hear myself.

Jonathan: On issue of loneliness?
I just said it felt good. I was detached.

PROVER #6
It has been mild compared to Prover 5. I found myself **quite driven, work-wise**; I put in **an inordinate amount of effort working with the people beside me**. The weekend I had scheduled camping with friends at Big Sur, I was kind of lukewarm about that. I brought my tent to a friends house, it was good to see him, I saw him the week-end before, but in a way **I felt a bit lonely, I was surrounded with people I was friendly with, but I felt withdrawn**. I would engage, be social, but I expected to be more. They would talk about their experience in college, pranks; I had heard it before. I said ok, let's talk on a different level. I was beyond the drug pranks. I was not clued in and found my mind wandering. That night I forgot my sleeping pad, I wanted to bunk in with people that had one but I couldn't do that so I ended up taking the seat out of the back of my car and sleeping in my tent. It was difficult to sleep. The

wind was blowing quite a bit. I found my appetite quite normal. At the end **I was not connected to anybody like I wanted to be; I felt lonely**.

On Sunday, people were going for a hike, I bowed out of that and left mid-day. **I did not feel like I wanted to be part of that group** at that time. So I left. The rest of the week work-wise was sub-par level and today I found myself with a slight eye-infection on my eyelid (points to his right eye). I felt myself concerned with my appearance a fair bit, looking at myself in the mirror for instance, but that is about it.

Jonathan: I think loneliness is an issue which came out in others.

I found myself not working, I rented videos. Just a general level of not being concerned with what I would normally be concerned with.

Jonathan: Just now, why would you say you put so much effort in what you are concerned with?

I found myself less enthused with things, just more slowed down and relaxed. With slowing down I noticed, 'my god there are people around me that come around.'

Prover #1
Right after the proving, I got a **tremendous energy, very industrious**, it was unusual for me to have that much energy, and then **I found myself unusually tired**. Low energy. But part of that is that I tend to have high energy anyway. I could feel this real shift in me about **detachment, detachment not just from people but also from my life**. And what I started to see during the proving and later, was this construct in my life. Like I built this framework I was supposed to live in and I was able to step out of that and I realized it wasn't anymore real than anything else that I could create or identify with. It was incredibly liberating for me, it was the most liberating experience for me mentally to let go of roles and ways of thinking. And I'm also **very sensitive to people**, so I have to be careful to who I let in. This remedy really helped me to do that. I was able to put up better boundaries or people weren't attracted to that energy. I didn't feel invaded. I felt like I was given a lot of space to do what I needed to do.

Great Blue Heron
proving

Provings

I've slept better in the last week than I've ever slept. I tend to wake up a lot at night and I start thinking, I can be awake for an hour off and on, and I slept really well. **I was very hungry; I really craved proteins and fish a lot.** I would even go hiking and cut my hike short because I was so hungry I was convinced I could not continue the 30 more minutes to get home to get something to eat. I craved fruit; **I ate a lot of fruit**, more than usual.

The other thing I noticed was my senses; while hiking, I could hear the grasses blowing, it has always been there but I never noticed it. I could separate sounds out, I have a hearing problem, so sometimes all the sounds blend in. If I listened to an orchestra, I can't always separate strings from percussion, with almost everything I could clearly delineate what sounds were coming from where.

The other thing **was touch, and incredibly sensual**. Wonderful, and **a lot of body connection**, it was really pleasant. And then I had this dream, and this dream stayed with me for a couple of days and it really had a big impact on me. I taught that day and V. and I had spoken and I checked with everyone in the proving and we were talking about our old neighborhood. I moved away about 5 years ago, and I had this dream: I went back to my old house. I did not call anybody to tell them I was coming to go into that house without anybody home. So I came down the driveway and for some reason, I parked right in the middle of the driveway, and still felt stealth, and felt I would not be seen. Even though there were cars there, I was convinced no one was home. And I went into the house and not a lot had changed, but **I knew of secret places** that the current owners would not know about, in fact they never really existed when I was there. Cabinets behind tables, and **I went to these secret places** and there were these really beautiful clothes, **really colorful, floral clothes**. Clothes I would normally buy, but hide in a drawer and say "oh, I should wear them one day." I was so pleased I found them and took them, there were some left there in the drawer but I took some with me. And people came, I could hear them; I've got to be going, **I could sneak** out and sure enough, they were right there, but I got out without them seeing me. I just walked out and got in my car and drove away. As I was driving away, she said "oh someone has been in our house; who could it be?" She tried to follow me in the car, and I have a big car, and **she could not see me but I could see her**. I was really fascinated by that, and I woke up and I couldn't stop thinking about that. It was like reclaiming something that was mine; it was really beautiful, like a treasure in a secret place. It stayed with me all week; that dream.

I'm going to continue taking the 30C, I really like this remedy, it has really slowed me down, it has given me a perspective. I have become a nicer mom, I do not yell as much, I've let a lot go, it has been good for me. And I've not gotten eye problems, I look at my eyes and noticed they were a little red, but I'm not having the pain.

GREAT BLUE
HERON
PROVING

PROVER #2
Adventures of the week: You know for me it turned out to be a very casual remedy. I didn't notice a whole lot of change emotionally, or I didn't notice much that I have to say. Whether I was **less detached**, it seemed pretty much normal to me. I was pretty steady energy the whole time, that didn't seem to make a change either. So I kind of felt like I didn't change that much for about the first 3-4 days. Except for my appetite, little body pains, little physical things. **A lot of digestion rumbling**. Just rumbling in my digestion. Also pains in my ovaries and in the whole lower abdomen. I could feel a shooting thing like that. My digestion just wasn't friendly. **I was craving fish. I ate fish for breakfast, lunch and for dinner. I ate an entire salmon in one sitting,** maybe two sittings. I couldn't find anything else to eat. I would open the fridge. I would try vegetables, they would nearly make me throw up, when I ate asparagus one time. The only other things I could find to eat was nut butters. I went through 4 jars of **almond butter**. What a combination! I think it was the oil, isn't that funny. Almond butter and fish that's what I've lived off of the last week. I munched on nuts in the car, almonds and walnuts, though the walnuts kind of made me sick. I could eat salad. Salad, that was about it. I think it was the oil I seemed to be **craving oils**. I'm not sure about that but it seemed like it. It wasn't specific. It didn't have to be almonds; I went through a jar of cashew butter. **Any nut butter and almond butter**, and I didn't eat anything else. I wanted you to know (laughs).

My body temperature fluctuated a lot during the week; I'd get like my whole body flush. Usually in the afternoon I'm hot, but not real hot, just mild.

Provings

It would last maybe 1/2 an hour to 45 min, and then it would taper off. It wouldn't go to cold; it would just go back to normal. Felt like this big flushing was happening. I would feel kind of light headed or dizzy when that was happening.

I had a **sore throat** the entire week and I still have it slightly. Every morning when I wake up I would have a sore throat. It's the kind of feeling like just before you get a cold. You wake up in the morning and like an hour later after you eat or drink something it's gone, except it's not. It's that little itch in the throat, or like for me when I eat sugar before I go to bed sometimes I wake up with a little sore throat. But I haven't had sugar for months and I didn't have any this week either. It was that same feeling every single morning, and I had it all the way through. It never turned into a cold, never got a sore throat, it's just constantly right here (taps the neck). I felt this **lump in my throat** the whole time. It felt like my thyroid was off. Sometimes it was **hard to swallow, that feeling of, you know, like something is there**.

My eyes were burning through most of it, till about maybe two days ago. Especially my **right eye, it was stinging. It would tear**. In fact it **teared so much, the first 3 days, it was raw underneath. I had to put oils on**. It hurt.

Jonathan: So the tears were actually acrid? It irritated?
Yeah, they felt kind of salty, cause they kept coming. I had to go like this (rubs eye) to get it away. Then it would taper off. It was like a slight stinging that would come and go. Sometimes I would wake up in the morning and it would go.

I didn't feel a whole lot emotionally, until all of a sudden, three days ago (and I thought this is weird) **all of a sudden I just burst into tears. It was like one of those really deep under current things that's happening. You have no way, you didn't see it coming but when it came you say, "oh, I've been working on that for a week."** It was one of those, and it was all very clear when exploding, but it was like I had no warning. It didn't relate to my life, or what was going on in my life. It was just something coming up and out and that fascinated me cause I wasn't looking for that. That just came and then I was kind of teary throughout the day. It would just come in waves, just coming through. That was a couple of days ago, and then I felt like the remedy started to taper off on Wednesday, and I started to get part of my appetite back. I was thinking how this is starting to taper off and that night I had another emotional explosion. It was not really on explosion, it was quiet. I'd gone to a seminar and come back and got in the car. I had nothing to do with the seminar. It wasn't anything we had talked about. Again the thought came up and I burst into tears driving home, crying; thinking this is weird. The pictures came and they were very similar to the first pictures. It was another layer of it. There was a connection. **Things I'd never seen before on a really deep, deep level. I mean it was so sudden, but deep, the things I would see would be so true for me. Some of it was sexual in nature, but not just sexual nature**. It was my relationship to that. On how I related to people or what I allowed to happen to my body. That was on an abusive level. Obviously I've never had any rape, you know, I've never had any kind of incest. I have not had that in my life so it wouldn't be a place I looked at. It sort of surprised me that a whole new definition of that came out. That in fact I had been victim to, not actually victim to (I didn't see it that way), but a party to. So I could sort of own that in a different way and change that relationship and choice within me, and with my body. So it was a very deep body level. A body response that I couldn't have come up with threw my mind. That, I couldn't see at all. So that was probably the most interesting thing; that just happened yesterday. That was pretty good. I felt like that was pretty resolved. You know it was like "wow, that was interesting."

Jonathan: That is interesting, because it was definitely my experience making the remedy. That something was taking place just below the ability to penetrate to that place. It was **very subtle** I found, having done the other birds, this was so interesting to me because this was so subtle, but **really deep** and so nurturing in a way. Self-nurturing. I felt it went right in and cuddled you inside and brought it out. It didn't do it with any force; there was no aggression. There was no force that was needed, no conversation that was needed. It was all right there; it just was a cuddle that came out (arms in front of chest then expand).

Jonathan: You said that the first night when you left, you said you felt cuddly…
Yeah! Did I say that? It's like this nurturing thing, yeah, I thought it just wasn't a forceful kind of thing. It wasn't a thing I had to force or deal with. It just was there and yeah I didn't feel particularly fragile, allowing that to release. You know when I went to a deep place. When I was crying I felt a lit-

Provings

tle loss, but not for long. The picture was right there, the answer was right there along with it. I could see it, accept it, the way it should be and use it. It was neat (giggle) and I'm still **wanting fish** (laugh). All kinds of fish. Oh, one last thing I noticed was that I didn't drink that much. With some of the other birds I was so thirsty constantly. I didn't drink very much at all and I didn't have that usual peeing constantly like other birds. In fact I was more constipated then anything with this one. So just because I had that reference I was kind of looking for that. I was barely drinking on this one. **My eyes teared**. I had to force myself to drink. Say, oh I'm thirsty maybe that's why my thought is like this. Drink something; I had to tell myself to drink. That was fascinating. That's it.

Prover #3
Well, I'm trying to put together the week, some interesting things. I lost my purse the day before the proving and it had both of my watches in it. I went to buy another watch and just couldn't buy it. Which has made me late or early for a lot of things. I actually experienced a lot of emotions. A spaciness; **detached** to schedule is what I would call it. I did go through a period of hopelessness on the Friday after being here. If you would have asked me I wouldn't have been able to find any reason to stay in this hideous world. That's just the way I saw it. **There was nothing worth sticking around for. I was left alone**. Everyone was gone from the house for a few days, except for my cat. She bugged me to no end. Screaming at me, waking me up at 5:00 AM. In my face. So I threw her out. I had some **violent bursts of anger**. I told M. (fellow prover), I was struggling with my toothpaste. It just wouldn't come out. I just screamed and threw it into the garbage, cursed it. That kind of thing. Where did that come from? So I've had some of those, and I've had a general sense of overwhelm. **I've preferred to be alone**. I haven't really solicited any kind of contact in my life. I've just been very happy doing the kind of things that I do. It became very important for to simplify my life. I just didn't want a lot of business. At one point I decided to move from where I was living. I just did not want to be there anymore. So I threw out a lot of things. I don't have many things, and I packed them into boxes, so I could quickly do anything I wanted.

GREAT BLUE HERON PROVING

Jonathan: Is this characteristic?
I'm pretty free flowing and spontaneous, so it's not totally uncharacteristic, but I don't generally do this. I had experienced not really a dream but a connection to my life and my dreams while I was walking around. I'd be aware of myself in other places. I had a strong sense of wanting to gather myself up, from wherever. It was a very strong sense of that. I had a really unusual experience where I went to my first ever, and maybe my last, IRS audit. I was being audited in a home office, and I had a perfectly wonderful reason for having a home office. There was nothing, I just went. Before I went, I contacted some CPAs. I went to just get adjusted, and see if everything was in order. They really didn't help me. I contacted the IRS, and got this gentleman who said, "Don't be ridiculous, just come on in, don't be afraid of what I do." I said I really wasn't worried about that, I'm not afraid of the interview. **I just wanted to come in organized**. So I came in and this man was sitting across from me. He reminded me of myself being in the school system for years, and trying to take this archaic system that doesn't work and try to make it better. I watched this man for an hour flutter over my things, trying to make everything come out, which wasn't really a big deal to make it come out. I watched him do this, and then at the end of this, he said, "Oh, we have it now." I thought okay and then he looked across at me and leaned across and said, "Do you think I'm weird? What is your take on me?" I told him exactly what my take on him was, that I had been sitting there observing and what I'd been observing. Then he started to cry.

I was talking to some people today about what I was observing. **My observation today made at least 4 or 5 people burst into tears**. The thing that I'm most aware of **is this coming together of where I dream and where I go into my imagination and would just call it an energy there that has been controlling me**. Out of my body and the energy has been coming into my body and exhausting my body. **I haven't been able to make a separation between — I haven't been able to protect or detach my body from what's happening in my dreams**. Now I know why I'd been **feeling exhausted**. I've been feeling exhausted! I've been experiencing some nausea but mostly what I've had is intense tiredness, and so I've been in my **detachment** of people. Which is not totally about them. I care. I'm just not getting drawn in. It's like **I'm a witness** and I just tell them what's happening and then I have this response, and in a

Provings

way I'm doing that for myself, so I'm able to create it out here and it's profound. So whatever it is that is controlling me, it is very old and deep, and it's not from this life at all, and it's on the planet. It's very here! For me it has an almost Tibetan, Buddhist, ethnic quality to it and that information has been more important than mine.

So making this separation somehow, and my body is so happy. It's so, "Yes! Now we can do what we've actually come to do today." Today I was walking by a market and there was something that said, just walk over there. So I walked over and there was this little thing that said something about a woman and an **autistic child**. I've always been interested in autism. I don't actually see it like other people do. I see it something like Alzheimer's, as something some beings do when they don't want to participate. **They actually detach.** I ripped off this information, and went home and called the woman and talked with her for a while. She said, my daughter is coming along, but there are students and kids out there that aren't making it. I thought oh, I can easily communicate with these kids. I just heard myself say this and said," Give me the worst ones you have." Gave them my number and hung up, and thought, where did that come from? That's it for examples of what's happened. I seem to have found this place within myself that is calm and isn't concerned with what people think, and feel very much; like it wants to express itself, but it's not pushy. I'm not on a cause to save the world at all.

Jonathan: This is connected with the experience of the loneliness?
Well I don't know that I experienced loneliness so much as hopelessness. The hopelessness was what was really strong for me. So now I'm not in the hopelessness at all, but I really went into it.

Jonathan: So, I'm just curious, how did you experience relationships with your state and your experience of hopelessness?

Well, the relationship would be that I was swinging at one end and came to the other end of it, where I'm seeing the world half-full instead of half-empty. I just slid into that.

Jonathan: Do you live in a group?
I actually have a partner, and we have houseguests living with us upstairs.

Prover #4

Overall from the notes I've taken, I noticed that this remedy made me feel like an **adolescent** again. My particular adolescence being re-lived again. I felt so **clumsy** and so stupid for about a week now, I mean I couldn't finish sentences. **I cut myself 3 times over the last 3 days**. Once really deeply on my fingertip and I am usually very careful when handling knives, needles and cutting tools. This time all of that went right out the window. I **sliced my hands to ribbons and banged my head on a nail in the attic**. I've still got a sore on it. I almost went through the floorboards in the attic, the day that you instructed us specifically to be careful. I lost my balance and almost went right through the whole thing. It's fine though (group laughs). What else...? A lot of stuff happened around **my eyes**, a lot. I was having **vision problems** the night we were preparing the remedy. I couldn't wear my contact lenses for 2 days after that. Painful to put them in, literally. This is after I used the mildest disinfectant I own. So when I'd use it, my eyes would get very red. Yesterday I could only wear them for half a day. Today is the first day I was able to wear them all day long. I felt my **eyes were both dry and teary at the same time**. I could also feel a lot of **heat around my neck**, like breaking into a rash or something.

I have had really odd food cravings, for **very spicy food**. I finally got a burrito at the burrito place the other night, and got the extra hot salsa and brought some more different extra hot salsa home, which was a bad idea. Apparently it's toxic if you don't have anything with it. It felt like something I should be putting in my body at that particular time, and I can't explain the impulse, because it is completely gone now. Three days ago, in the middle of last week, I would actually like to hurt myself with my food. Something that would actually make it taste like poison would be great. Yeah! I love that food that actually makes me cry. Some kind of tapeworm or something. Ya! (Laughter) Ya! I also felt like I had **urinary problems too. I couldn't urinate.**

I was drinking and I **urinated, but I didn't feel like I could get rid of all of it** and I would have to pee again. Then I got up to use the bathroom and have to pee some more. Finally, in the end I did feel if it went on much longer, I would

Provings

have had to go and see someone about that. That was really strange. Again it felt like a **kidney infection I had when I was about 13 or 14 years**, I think, cause I was in 8th grade. I just now realize this cause that is exactly what happened to me. Anyway what else? Dreams: **that waiting thing kept coming up**. I had a dream where I went to the symphony late opening night, and went to a great deal of trouble to the orchestra seats. It ended up being a stadium theater and we were in the way back of the orchestra and it had an obstructed view, like this (holds up his notebook, in his face). So you couldn't actually see anything. So I said, just sit and wait and I'm sure it will be fine. So we sat down before it started and our section, (just us), picked up and went underneath everyone else and ended up in a special area close to the front where you had special dancers and Bob Dylan performing.

Jonathan: This was a dream right?
Yes. This was a dream. No, Bob Dylan didn't play with the symphony, but they were doing folk songs, they had Drawershot and Dylan, and we had Dylan performing for us, performing his music and that was kind of fun.

Also in waiting I got a **job offering at a national bird observatory**, ironically enough, which I was waiting for. It is a process I started almost a month ago, when I first sent the resume and I went for an interview, and they wanted this and that and finally I talked to them. Got any jobs here? So that was exciting.

Jonathan: And the job is doing what?
A couple of things; upgrading web sites for their web page and taking data from their field work, and making sure that it is accessible to people in the organization. Basically publishing research data on the web. Basically the kind of job I've been looking for, forever since the Internet went booming. I've been looking for something using technology and it's thrilling.

The eye thing. Then I got **a pimple on my eye**. The eyes have been insane. My eyes have been bothering me so much and this never happens. My contact lenses have never given me trouble. I can forget them. I'm supposed to take them out daily I can forget that I have them in for 2-3 days. These, I couldn't wear them, which again is a problem I had when I was younger. I got these terrible contact lenses and I couldn't wear them. I tried to wear these lenses in the middle school, but they were too painful, so I went back to my glasses.

Jonathan: You would injure yourself when you were younger? Bump into things?
Oh, always, **really clumsy**. Always tripping, tripping in class literally over nothing. There was the carpet. Kids grow really awkwardly; sometimes their feet grow before everything else and trip over their feet. Things like that happened to me. Plus I got tall really quickly, so I don't think I was quite used to my body size at that age.

Jonathan: So from what age to what age are you talking about?
I think really 5th or 7th grade, an awkward time.

Jonathan: And what age was that?
10 to 13 and a half.

Jonathan: Sort of curious why it would pick that time, some sort of remedy for adolescence.
I just put it together, as I was sitting here that this is all stuff that happened to me from that time in my life.

Jonathan: There was something that sort of characterized that time in your life. I mean it was a separate time? Separate then from what went before or what went after?
Right.

Jonathan: And so what was the guide or spirit of that time would you say?
Actually, it was not a happy time. Really, and I haven't felt any of the emotional flashbacks from that, but I was pretty miserable as a middle schooler. I had some friends who beat me up. Socially I was happier when I was younger and I was a lot happier in high school.

Jonathan: So maybe it was that feeling of separation that pours down on you, that it has picked that time?
Yeah, because I missed what other people were talking about, but I didn't focus physically on what was happening at the time, when I was most **isolated**. Even 8th grade was better, but 7th grade just sucked.

Jonathan: They separated him from the group for being so smart, and they really looked down on him…
In middle school there were three teachers who taught in a pool (6th, 7th, 8th grade); and then I was supposed to stay with them through 6th, 7th, and 8th grade but they changed the program. So in 7th grade I went back with the old

GREAT BLUE HERON PROVING

Provings

7th graders and I sort of thought certainly that I would be with the same group of students. Instead of having two teachers for all my classes, I had 6 different teachers for all my classes. So I had a disadvantage because I didn't have the preparation that students had that went from regular 6th grade to regular 7th grade. I got thrust into huge classes with different kids all the time. I hated it.

BALD EAGLE *Haliaeetus leucocephalus*

Complete proving information for **Haliaeetus leucocephalus** may be found in *Dynamic Provings, Volume 1,* by Jeremy Sherr.

EAGLE'S BLOOD PROVING by Divya Chabra
Dreams of animals free, not caged. People naked and bathing.

PROVER 1:
World full of fights, quarrels, selfish. People kill others. Riots. See a man who says hide or I will be killed too. Man dies of cerebral hemorrhage.

PROVER 2:
Selfish society. Only concern with selfish. Poke nose into the middle.

PROVER 3:
In cage father has clapper, long, and he is hitting me. Mom said why? I come out and said I didn't do it. Go into cage. People blame you for what you have not done. Kill me, go ahead. Corrupt people who cheat you.

Fear of hurting another if I express anger. Sister makes noise. I am sensitive but can't tell her. **Won't hurt them**. World of fights, cheat, corrupt, selfish but don't speak to avoid hurting. So rise above. To fly away. To rise high above your fears. Be free of obligations in the world. To rise above negative feelings within you.

I am dominated by the world, better when I am high above and not being pushed. People put me down. I rise above negative feelings inside. I am superior. Something above the normal person. Walk boldly like a male. Walk like a hero. **Puffed up feeling**. All others low down. I am a tall person. Eagle? If people see me they look up. Strength to fight which they don't. **No one dare touch me**. I am superior. Refined. **Above them**. They can't put me down. Not physical but through intelligence. Get above negative qualities inside of me. But use it in a constructive way. Will be better. Ask them to absolve you. Free guilt from sins.

Provings

Dreamless. Dirty. I must get above this feeling. Should go alone for a walk. Decreasing attachments. Desire for freedom since the proving of eagle.

Responsibility/commitment. Rise above fears. Get above. Be bold so no one touches me.

> Comment: The harshness and cruelty of the everyday world and the need to escape to a better place is clearly brought out. This escape takes the form of rising up; to be higher; to be above. The world of dreams is not identified here. It appears as if this rising up above it may be an earlier stage of entry into a different world.

RAVEN *Corvus corax principalis*

Greg Bedayn organized and directed the proving on Raven's blood (*Corvus corax principalis sanguis*) during Lou Kline's Master Clinician course in Berkeley in 1996. Kim Baker assisted in the proving and Jessica Jackson extracted the rubrics.

Corvus corax principalis (sanguis)
A new proving of the blood of a North American Raven

Greg Bedayn, RSHom (NA) Director
Kim Baker, Co-Director
Jessica Jackson, LAc, extraction of themes, and rubric selection

> *This proving is dedicated to the loving memory of my mother, the late Barbara Bedayn, international ornithologist "par excellence."*
> *Greg Bedayn, Editor*

GREG BEDAYN WRITES:
I have had a life-long fascination with Raven, and once, having taken months to nurse a young road-accident victim, "Juaquin," back to airborne-health in the 1980's, when I lived on Puget Sound's Salmon Beach, I developed a first-hand knowledge and appreciation of this creature of global fascination and lore. It was during Lou Klein's Master Clinician course in Berkeley in 1996, that I first decided to organize, then direct, a proving on Raven's blood (*Corvus corax principalis sanguis*). On March 17, 1996 I asked my friend and colleague, Kim Baker, to assist me in the proving.

The proving went well and the final provers' meeting, weeks later, in my office at The Center for International Medicine, became more and more fascinating. As the evening wore on, mischievous Raven finally revealed itself in its medicinal form.

I remember how the eight provers, one-by-one, got into the "hot seat" and reported their individual experiences to the assembled throng, and how most

Provings

reported what became a similarly hilarious experience for all. Each prover basically told his/her story of how their appetites had GREATLY increased during the proving - one prover had even developed the habit of standing in front of his open refrigerator, methodically eating his way through its contents, unable to stop until the last kernel of leftover rice casserole (etc.) was gone. It wasn't actually funny until about the second or third prover confirmed that same symptom and the provers group howled with laughter over the peculiar similarity and then the next prover confirmed it again, and so on.

The next day I was driving into Berkeley, deep in thought over what the similarity of increased appetites could mean, when I suddenly realized the rubric was ravenous appetite and I nearly drove off the road when I just as suddenly realized the source of the word: ravenous! I later decided I was too close to the remedy-source to be fully objective during the extraction process so I asked my colleague and fellow graduate from the Hahnemann College of Homeopathy, Jessica Jackson, to develop the theme and rubric-extraction sections. An objective extraction is a difficult thing to be performed by any account. I feel the high quality of Jessica's work speaks for itself.

JESSICA JACKSON WRITES:
While doing the extraction on Raven's blood, I realized this was not a simple remedy. There's a complexity and intensity to it that I am in awe of. Spending time at the Grand Canyon over the holidays with my boyfriend, we saw many, many ravens there. Now their countenance and manners are indelible with me.

These quotes were my guiding lights during the Raven proving:
"Each individual symptom must be considered. Every symptom must be examined to see what relation it pertains to and what position it fills in the totality in order that we may know its value, whether it is a common symptom, a particular symptom, or whether peculiarly a characteristic symptom." J. T. Kent

"When a person presents a peculiar symptom, a dream, a modality, or an experience, clearly, intensely and spontaneously: find it directly in the materia medica or repertory; see the feeling it creates and connect it with the overall case; it is directly connected to the source of the remedy. Any marked thing can be understood in this way." Dr. Rajan Sankaran

White Raven

This special albino Raven was hatched in the spring of 1996 at Port Clements in western Canada's Queen Charlotte Islands, to black raven parents. It was the only baby in the nest. Human companionship and feeding seemed important to "Lucy" and her survival.

Lucy's habit of frequent highway walking caused "White Raven Crossing" signs to be erected on both sides of the town. It seems that crows used him as a meal ticket and were with him when he flew into a transformer on November 30, 1997. He died instantly.

The Haida peoples tell us that in the beginning all ravens were white. Lucy was very tame and gave islanders and visitors much pleasure!

EXTRACTION BY JESSICA JACKSON, LAc
Separate Realities; Not of this World; Not Belonging to Earth or Body

She felt she was not really belonging to her body.
I feel a little separated from myself as if there's a gap between my thoughts and my body.
General feeling is dull, not really here, spaced out.
Felt like I was not reacting fast enough or like I was missing depth perception.
I am unaware.
Reality seems to come and go and conversation seems almost surreal. Someone spoke and the words were right there in my face but almost delayed... Something becomes a distant memory really quickly, like I smoked some pot. A friend commented that I was "out there."
Very short snippets of distortion, like sounds are amplified. I smelled cocoa when there isn't any around.
Unseated. In and out of other spaces.
Her husband said to her, "You are like in a shell, in your own closed world, you don't seem to feel good."
It's like an LSD or mushroom trip. You sink into the hallucinatory phase and you think that that's the way things have always been and will always be. It's "reality" and then something clicks and you're back to real reality so in a way it's as if I'm floating between two dimensions...

RAVEN PROVING

Provings

Looking in a water jug I thought it would be great to be in there swimming around. Part of the appeal was how simple it looked in there. The other was just thinking how neat it would be to be really small like that. And knowing I would never be able to do it. [Supervisor] told me there was a comet hanging out near earth right now. I finally found the comet in the sky and am transfixed by it. I find such "otherworldly" things so moving. They remind me of the beauty and power of creation which can, I hope, transcend the destruction humans have wrought.

Flashbacks into the past: all of a sudden I was back in a farmhouse, remembering smells.

"Hooks are what keep us going in society. Otherwise it's free falling out of a plane without a parachute. If you take that away then you realize you're not like you thought or who you thought you were."

My sense of time is slightly confused in that I can't quite tell whether it's morning or evening.

My husband keeps wanting to talk to me but he can't really reach me.
He says, "You're so far away, as if not here." For me it's normal, only when he says something I feel how far away I am, how spaced out.
Sitting at a table staring but not seeing anything.
In and out of body. Contractive physical feeling.
Empty space around me. As if in space. Spaced out. Not reacting properly, not fast and not aware.

This proving has given me clairvoyance, feeling others pain, not as in this world as I used to be. I'm on the divide between two worlds with decreased attachment to the physical world. I can sense what's going on with other people. The feeling is hard to put into words but it is something like being not "in" this world as I used to be. It's a kind of clarity about other people's feelings.

Thirst has decreased which I related to this detachment from the physical world.

Delirium as if floating in a velvety, black, brown space. Felt warm. Not being really conscious, not being really here. Like a higher dimension. Kind of lost, like free floating and not belonging anywhere on earth.

Hearing things like someone knocking at the door, someone calling my name, the phone ringing but nobody knocked, no one called.

Surviving Theft, Deception, Trespassing and Invasion
A gang took my Harley Davidson away. They were threatening. I was in a room lying on the bed, knowing they will come in to rape me because I was not impressed or afraid by their threats. I knew where and how to escape.
Dreamt I was shopping, making deals and stealing. The feeling of underhandedness, getting ready for something, anxious and nervous.

Dream of being in a house with my friend, sleeping in the basement. I went to lock the patio doors when a stranger, all covered with a large coat, with a hood over the head and face, came barging in and kept barging around. I edged towards the basement door and called for my friend. Then I woke up.

The prover has become a conservator for one of her elderly female clients who is losing her faculties. Someone recently "cleaned her out" by making her sign over her money. The client had no idea what she was signing. The prover was outraged. Recently, they located some untouched money and will use it to put the woman in a nursing home.

RAVEN PROVING

In a dream, a woman had taken a section from my own personal journal and read it. How she got it I don't know and she would not tell me. I asked her where she found my journal. She would not tell. I became very angry and threatening toward her. She was quite indifferent to my feelings. The angrier I became the more she ignored me. The next scene was a crowd of people. She was there. I went and confronted her. She tried to ignore me. I pushed her, yelling, threatening. A woman came to me and said something mean. I pushed her away. The woman who took my journal said she didn't know where the journal was because she had given it to other people to read. I began to scream at her that I was going to kill myself and she'll be sorry. She'll see, I'll show her. I felt humiliated, trespassed upon, ignored, disregarded, my privacy totally invaded which created anger and violence in me.

Dream of testing a friend and finding he had Lyme disease. I didn't tell him. A client had lied to me. I was misled.
I told a small lie at work and it's really bugging me. Usually it's fairly easy for me to lie.

Provings

The dream made me feel dishonest and disgusted with myself. I was not honest with myself or with my friend.

Dreamed she was a member of the FBI and is way, way, way under cover, investigating a man with a strange Batman like house, all white with moving walls operated by buttons. Rowing up and down canals, trying to find these people involved in smuggling.

Dream of a garlic festival and the man in charge decided all the vendors should close at noon to give them a break so they would be refreshed in the afternoon. People were furious. People formed huge mobs and started looting all the vendors' booths.

A designer took my designs, $10,000 worth. This project represented survival. It was a major deal. I must prevent this from happening in the future. I must protect myself.
Tired of fighting, cajoling. Desolate to live this way, constantly trying to protect myself. Survival issues.

Dream I was the sister or wife of one of the Romanovs. We lived in this huge palace and there was a revolution. At first the commoners only took over the ground floor of the palace and left us alone but then there was a crash at the door and in they came. When they addressed my husband I would correct them if they didn't call him emperor. The emperor and his brother were tied in chairs and their hair was cut off. Then the revolutionaries went through all our stuff. They admired the golden spoons and let us have a cup of tea on the condition that we return the valuable cups and spoons when we finished.

Got ripped off by another designer. Needed to borrow rent money.

Dream of a little boy who is sick and his parents asked her to look at him. She agreed. The boy was climbing on these crates and when she wasn't watching carefully he fell on his head and neck. A breath noise came out of him and she feared he had broken his neck. He said he was okay and was playing. His mother came out and she told her what had happened but minimized it for fear the mother would be angry. She told her the boy fell from the second crate to the first when it was actually the third to the second. Again, she was lying, minimizing. She felt trapped lying. The woman gave her a look like she knew she was lying but since her child was okay she wasn't going to say anymore.

In the end of a dream she is walking with a man and tells him she took a pinch of some seed. She realizes she thought it might be stealing. She apologized for not asking first. It was hard for her to say that. She thought they were going to go off and have time together but instead he got real mad and cast her away from him. She followed him but tripped and fell. No one would stand up for her. Then she was on this lawn on the edge of a farm, flowers from a bouquet on the grass, sobbing, wondering why no one will forgive her.

A Rush of Emotions: Anxiety, Fear, Panic, Pain and Sadness
Short tempered, anxious, speedy, like I want to jump out of my skin!
Felt wired and depressed at the same time.
Feeling a little scared, close to tears; have to hold myself back from emotional breakout.
She described herself as scared, anxious feeling. Close to tears. If an aggravating factor such as an accident in front of her or if she needed to defend herself or if there was emotional or physical exhaustion, she wouldn't be able to breath.

RAVEN PROVING

It is very scary when my lungs are not working fully, panic, anxiety. I need to force myself not to flip out. Very teary, oversensitive, slightest event causes rush of emotions. I am consciously calming myself. Any slight event, somebody walking by, a car driving too fast, causes a rush of anxiety.
An ambulance racing down the street causes a rush of emotion, makes me want to cry with pity.
She felt agitation and a rush of feelings, the hectic feelings of an emergency.

I feel as if I am on speed. My mind is racing and I can't keep up.

Anxiety dreams of being in a hotel room, trying to pack to go home with lots of people in the room. We were going to miss the plane. Finally on the plane, there were problems with the seats.
Financial and business world fell apart. Waiting, waiting, waiting, this is when the waiting began. Fretful, anxious.

Provings

I feel like I'm spinning out of control. It's a bit scary. In the shower I couldn't get the water out of my ear. I felt deaf and therefore defenseless. I need to be able to hear what's going on around me but this was on the verge of panic.
My thoughts, rather my feelings, are all over the place but definitely on the fear/paranoid end of the spectrum.
Talking with my supervisor really brought the emotional reaction which started with a dream. I was trembling and on the verge of tears several times. I'm a little afraid of going to bed. All this emotional energy has to go somewhere. I wouldn't be surprised if I had another nightmare.
Feeling jittery, nervous and trembling.

Feel less frantic this afternoon but I have the sense that it could easily boil up again. Feel sad, wanting to cry. Weeping. It took some time to cry, though it would help me out of this sadness.
I feel sad, on the verge of tears again.
Weeping in the car driving home. There is so much PAIN in this proving - emotional pain!
She talks about so much emotional pain, like she wants to cry. A really short fuse. She feels like she's lost her balance emotionally. Feeling sad and crying with the emotional pain of wanting to be free and not being free. Nothing gives her comfort. She felt like crying, on edge. Shaking "like an idiot" again in her legs, chest, and belly, in waves of quick succession much worse from emotions.
I feel like crying or exploding. I need to release this somehow.
Extreme feelings about a concert she went to. She was really upset and went to the artistic director about it.
Hard not to cry, every fiber of my being wants to cry. It definitely helps talking to people.
Trembling with emotions. If I can't handle the thoughts they spiral down into the physical. Once in the physical it's really hard to get out of. Better from distractions, from talking to people.

Bad day today. My husband has returned with another woman and it's thrown me off-balance. A lot of the pain, anxiety, thoughts of revenge, anger and sadness as well as the trembling are back.
Confusion. Parade of experiences. Sad, sad, sad. Worried, worried, worried. Preoccupied, obsessed, sad - usually I move on.

I feel uptight and emotional. My neighbor snapped at me about the noise of our slamming gate. I feel hurt and pissed off. This isn't unusual for me. Hanging on to these feelings of anxiousness is.

Woke up this morning and felt anxious and uptight. Went through everything that is not right in my life. Everything I have done wrong.

At a funeral I cried so hard and yet not enough. I would have liked to have wailed.

Retrospective of the entire proving: it was a period of feeling very down and sad. Almost like a depression with low energy and crying, not knowing why. Falling apart emotionally, thought I can't name any specific reason. I didn't want to write or talk, just go closed, into myself, to suffer on my own and not come out again.

Screaming, Yelling, Outrage, Telling the truth
Yelling a lot, short fuse.

I thought of the resistance I had last night to writing in this journal. I was so angry I started yelling and screaming, "I don't want to write, I don't want to write." Repeatedly screaming these words out loud and very hysterical, body shaking and trembling.

Dream of an explosion…to my utmost horror I began to see it mushroom out. I started screaming…

She feels like screaming and she feels impotent. There's nothing she feels she can do about these idiots doing things to our planet. A rage feeling, not as in anger, but she would like to rage. It's so global, so big, injustices, ugliness and death.

Leaving the store tonight, while getting into the car, I let out a happy yell. I don't know why, but it felt good.

She said that, "something is free." She was screaming with joy in her car.

Dreamt my mom had absolutely no sympathy for me. One of us was yelling, I can't remember who now.

In a dream, I confronted [the woman who had taken my journal]. She tried to ignore me. I pushed her, yelling and threatening…When the woman said she didn't know where the journal was because she had given it to other people to read I began to scream at her that I was going to kill myself and she'd be sorry…[discovering someone else reading my journal] I began screaming at her, "Why are you doing this, I'm going to kill myself!" In the next part of the

RAVEN PROVING

Provings

dream my father...got up saying, "We'll publish her story. We will publish the truth." As I heard this I began to feel better...In the dream my father supported me. He would write the truth and get all of this mess cleared up. He would write the truth about me. In real life my father always supported me.

When I try to breath normally or try to move it hurts so much I have to scream.
I was screaming at him in my mind, accusations, look what you've done!
Still getting spasms of anger at my husband where I just want to shout insults at him, slap him really hard or push him.
A dream that reminded me of "The Exorcist." It was a very loud dream, shouting, slamming, special effects type of noises.
I saw my husband from a distance, still screaming at him in my head. ANGRY. It still feels raw.
Dream with the theme of outrage: everything is pristine and pure. Then I noticed dirt and evil, the intransigence of people who have the power. I'm screaming, "Can't you see it?!"
I had to go to Switzerland, an emergency. I had to go there to speak up for my feelings, for what I know is right. Normally, I would not say anything, thinking "they know better." I speak up for what I now know is true for me even when I can't fully explain it or prove it. I scream at authority. I have never before even said anything against his standpoints. Speaking up. Of course, this is the result of many years of work on myself but the proving might have given me the courage.

Prison, Torture, Protection and Escape
Dream of my husband or brother, sister and I are in prison. I can't remember why but we are being beaten and tortured. It is a prison infamous for this. We keep trying to escape but our attempts are foiled over and over again. There's a dark staircase that we use in several of these attempts, running up and down stairs or down and down. We are the only prisoners and there is one warden, the "baddie" who keeps catching us. We finally make it to freedom and immediately go to the prison authority to complain but my brother has been talked into denying that there was any torture by the warden so it makes my sister's and my claims look like lies. It's the usual bureaucratic bullshit, forms to fill out, skeptical paper-pushers. A nightmare until both of us are even doubting that the torture happened. Then I find big bumps and bruises on my left arm and

elbow and both of us know that there's only one way I could have received those...There was a feeling of being constantly chased in the dream and a desperation to escape the prison, the poor conditions, the lack of light, the warden. It wasn't a terrifying dream, just painful, immense frustration and always this being chased up and down many flights of stairs.

In a dream of a huge, fenced in part of the Wilderness, I try to get animals to go into a fenced area, otherwise they are in danger...The animals are afraid of people and run away when humans approach them. Except one big sheep. I have to grab the sheep on its thick wool, lift it up and turn it in the direction of the fence gate. The sheep will walk into the gate and all the animals will follow. The feeling of being stressed, the danger to lose the animals, and being super cautious not to scare the animals away with a wrong movement...In all these [proving] dreams I am in the leader position. Protection is a theme going through, to animals, to kids, to me, to my feet. All is happening outside in huge, huge wilderness fields. Stressed in these dreams. I was the only one to really do the tasks. Others that were present didn't care. I was the only one doing the safeguarding. [A dream of] my father [who] is sitting in the entryway of this building with his back to the door, not letting anyone in, protecting me from the public.

RAVEN
PROVING

Feeling powerless and confused. I must prevent this from happening in the future. I must protect myself.

Dreamed of torture victims. I just remember a snippet of seeing a male torso with a huge cut in his right groin and his penis cut off. He was dead.

Dream of entering a triage area...I made a quick assessment of all the patients. There wasn't a lot of blood and guts, but one patient really worried me. She was a woman with a huge hematoma on her left thigh and groin area. It was deep red...the nurse in charge was also assessing this woman. I thought she might have an intra-peritoneal bleed so I asked her if she had any abdominal pain. She said yes, whereupon this nurse began palpating her abdomen really hard, dragging her fists in, even her elbows. The woman was in agony.

Dreamed I am locked into a room, way up in a high skyscraper. I am a prisoner of an approximately 45-year-old man in a suit, with dark hair. It is a high stress situation for me. Panic. I know something terrible will happen. They

Provings

don't kill me because they need me for???? I have information. I know people. I know if I try to escape they shoot me immediately. I manage to escape anyway, climbing super cautious over a highly sensitive security system. Running through many hallways, down an elevator, on the street. I see two people I know. They would get into danger if I stayed in their house. So I run out again. A woman hands me fast and secretly a key which is a skeleton key. I have to go back so they don't discover that I escaped, that would be fatal for many other people. In horror I realize I don't remember what floor I was on. I ask three men on the street. They are so slow! I'm back on the street and go up with the elevator, run through a hallway and realize I better escape completely otherwise I will never get out of there alive. Suddenly I am in [my native country], jumping into a tram, realizing in terror that this is the tram that goes to my parents' house. Me being there would bring them in danger, because "they" would come after me and of course check my parents' house. My husband drives by. I stop him and jump into the car and drive up the street to my parents' house. It's too dangerous. My sister, my husband and I feel we have to get out of the car and run away and hide. A woman walks up to us. "Passport control," she says. We know immediately she is one of "them." The feeling is I am in danger.

Resistance, Frustration, Stuck
My supervisor called and I gave symptoms. I don't like giving symptoms. I feel like I'm whining about myself. It feels forced.
The structure of the proving was really bothering her. She was feeling really resistant. I don't want to write. I want to cry. I have resistance and anger about having to write in this journal: RESISTANCE + ANGER = FEAR.
I don't like doing this. Not at all eager to talk about the days' events.
Restless, frustrated kind of energy, not really content.
Couldn't accomplish anything today. Everything went wrong. I kept being unsuccessful at accomplishing things and feeling frustrated.
I should do so much but I don't want to. Feeling sad and wanting to cry. Hard to do stuff, running around. Frustrated because of sadness and agitation. Frustrated, wanting to feel better and get more stuff done.
I feel really frustrated and angry this afternoon. I am so frustrated that everything I am trying to do takes so much effort. Usually with my frustration I don't feel angry like this.

Completely sluggish, useless day. I have been unable to focus or get anything done. I am stuck. I am getting upset with myself that nothing is getting done. A horrible day. Frustrated with myself. Everything is so extreme, unable to move, stuck.
Didn't want to do anything anymore.
No inspiration to paint.
Did not want to draw.

In a dream she felt like she had totally blown it. No way out. Stuck in that state.

Antagonism with Family, at Home, with Damage, Destruction and Injury
A dream I was in conflict with my parents. This is a usual thing for me to dream about but [what is unusual] is I wasn't upset as I usually am. My brother was throwing glasses down at the floor because he was so upset. I was concerned that he was doing it but also aware that it was totally necessary for him. In the dream I decided to run away from home.

Dream of someone playing the part of me. She was a young Caucasian woman (I am an African American). She, who was I, discovered her mother going through all her journals. She asked her mother why she was doing this. I began screaming at her, why are you doing this; I'm going to kill myself.

My father and I are looking at our house...Something was getting damaged on the roof...I see that the roof is partially gone...In the next scene my father and I are driving a carriage...over a bridge to cross a wide river. All of a sudden a piece of the bridge is missing...We look at the damaged part. We can't understand why a piece is missing. At home my mother explains that she tied Mozart down on this part of the bridge and blasted him and that part of the bridge with dynamite. She says cruelly, laughing, "Now he's rotting down there," meaning on the bottom of the river.

Dreams of work; feeling aggressive and spoiling for a fight. Feeling angry especially towards those close to me.

Dream of two brothers, one "good" and one "bad"; it was a battle over right and wrong. They had these intense fights, eyes flashing, telekinetically smashing each other against the wall. One brother, the "bad" one was twisted with hate.

RAVEN
PROVING

Provings

I dreamed of four young boys, African-American, and four or five adults, all connected somehow, related. They were all the family each other had. Something happened, someone died or was injured.

I dreamed I was angry with my sister-in-law. I wouldn't talk about it and my family kept badgering me to tell them what I was angry about...

Trickery
The Deal Dream: Everybody is sitting in a row. A woman on my right side, a man on my left. We are discussing business, it feels like a complot [conspiracy]. All of a sudden the man on my left flips in one hop in front of the woman on my right. He has a yellowish mouth. He tells her he gave all his money to her, both are laughing, tricky, mischievous laughter.

I dreamed I was in a huge building, dark interior...A small group of people walked in looking somber, almost zombie like. I noticed an African-American woman looking straight ahead, somber face. She stared, no expression on her face. They all began to sing. She was leading the song. Her voice was beautiful, her expression completely changed. There was a pleasant smile on her face and her voice was beautiful. I began to notice her voice was so soothing to me, but I began to feel the song taking over my mind and body. I put my hands to my face, my ears, trying to drown out the music, even though it was beautiful. I felt it taking over my whole person. I fell on the floor moving my body back and forth. A man friend tried to console me but to no avail. The music and singing was trying to control me. The next scene was in the same building. A dark, frail, sickly man came in the building. I realized he had these people under his spell and was trying to get me and my friends. He had helpers. It seemed he spoke with his eyes. His helpers were trying to connect me. They gave us toasted bread with a yellow spread for us to eat, then we would be under his spell. I saw my friends eat and it immediately happened. I said, "No, I will not do this." I was adamant that I would not eat the bread. The man who was standing next to me did a magic trick on me and before I knew it I had eaten the bread and I was under his spell.

Injuries, Explosions, and a War Zone
I hit myself with the door of the kitchen cabinet, which I opened. My lip and front tooth on the right side are hurting so much that I have to jump around the kitchen. I'm getting tears in my eyes.

Dreamed of looking for the comet. On the horizon I saw something, it looked like an explosion, white spray, etc. I looked to my left and saw another explosion. This one had a dark cloud and it grew and grew, black, huge, it grew vertically into the atmosphere and to my utmost horror I began to see it mushroom out...People looked up to see the deadly shape of a huge nuclear blast. Then the sound and the heat of the blast hit us. Everyone had already run into the sanctuary of a church. I was the last, transfixed in horror by what I saw. The blast was beyond anything I'd ever experienced and as I dived through the door, the flesh of my legs, the last part of me exposed to the bomb, was seared off my bones. A real nightmare. On waking I felt a sense of impotent anger and despair about the savagery and utter stupidity of humans, and a fear for the life of the planet. A kind of hopelessness I sometimes feel in my waking life. How can we do these things when there is so much life and beauty which gets destroyed.

In a dream I hurt my right ankle, where I'd had a bad sprain in November. I thought this was significant during the dream and I would be better balanced because of this.

Raven Proving

Dream of being with a friend who was my brother or my husband. We went back to his place in an old apartment building. We had to be careful because he was on the edge, literally one house away from Sarajevo. There was a line that delineated the war and peace zones and he was extremely close to the war zone. We sat on his verandah and looked for the comet and saw comet-like flying things, flying in all directions. It looked a little like fireworks. We were afraid these bits from space could actually hit us sitting there and we hunched low although continued to watch.

In a dream (a doll came alive). She had some type of head injury; a lump on her forehead and no one knew where she was from.
Old broken arm is aching again. Dream of a family who had to separate because someone died or was injured.
Dreamed of a boy climbing on crates. He fell on his head and neck. She feared he had broken his neck..

In a dream I saw a plane crashing into a little shopping area. It looked like a sci-fi type of flying thing, like flying doors. I thought I should go over to the

Provings

crash to help out since I'm a nurse. [When we found it] I was told I was desperately needed. Just before entering the triage area I remember steeling myself for what I was about to see and do...

Death, Dying, Suicide, and Killing
My daughter is depressed today. She talks about killing herself. It gets to me.

She dreamed of her sister, who has a lot of trouble in life at this time. She dreamed that her sister was leaving and she had a black parrot, which she killed. She asked [the prover] to cover up this fact that she had killed it, as if it didn't matter.

A dream all about my friend who died. He was my closest friend. We were together. Walking...talking, being very close, a very intense feeling of warmth and deep friendship between us...the feeling of crying a lot since he died. The most striking thing was realizing in the dream that this was a dream and to enjoy him while he's here, glad to be with him at least then...Sad, tired and unbalanced upon waking after this dream. Miserable memories of how sick he was; how at the end he couldn't talk. He wanted to die, creating symptoms to die. Grieving over his mother's death, he couldn't get over it. He lost his will to live.

In the dream I began to scream at her that I was going to kill myself and she'll be sorry...I felt using the threat of killing myself would get a response from her, or at least make her feel bad for her action
Had a long discussion with her supervisor about three people she knew who had committed suicide in the town where she moved from.
The heart pain scared me a lot. I thought I was dying.
Thoughts of death, looking at the Moon and Venus, feeling tired, so welcome it seemed, benign. Usually thoughts about death are darker and wrought with fear. Suicidal feelings during the day. It seemed like a way out of the proving.
In the dream I thought I had somehow given up myself, and given someone or something power to control me. In allowing that to happen I had no life, nothing. I die, my spirit dies a slow agonizing death.

Dream of being in medieval times. I am lying under a coach wheel made out of wood that was getting burnt. Only a half of the wheel is left, the black, burnt piece above me. I am lying on my back. Fire around me. People running, screaming, disaster, hectic, panic, war. I am wearing a long light brown-red, now dirty, dress. I am half dead probably because I can see part of my surroundings but I don't feel any pain even so I am probably deadly wounded. No anxiety, just calm witnessing goings on around me.

Dream of a woman sinking into quicksand mud. Two tigers are there. I feel so bad I could not save her. Touched some deep feeling of responsibility. I could do nothing but watch her sink and die slowly. It was horrible. My husband said, "You didn't kill her." Really feeling sad.

I dreamed I was with a friend and we were talking to my friend who died. He was joking around with us and we were laughing away. He was talking to us in "rap" about dying. He changed it around in this song saying, "What if you woke up one day and you were the only person alive, would living be so great?" We were shaking our heads in amazement at him and his funny ways...

Got a lot of bad news last night. One thing was that her cousin, about her age, had died.

The symptoms of this proving went to the life center: heart and breathing. The feeling of what it would be like if I were dying.

Pity, Sympathy, and Sensitive to the Pain of Others
An ambulance racing down the street, causes rush of emotions, makes me want to cry with pity. Feeling "glad it's not me" or "poor guy."
I was having lunch with a friend and she was telling me her marriage was probably ending. Even before this I got an emotional hit of her pain but when she told me I felt like I was experiencing her pain myself, physically and emotionally.
A skunk walked by my window three times. It gave off its scent. I had pity for this poor creature, going through the world, being smelly and everyone reacting to him negatively. Wouldn't want to trade places with him.
This proving has given me clairvoyance, feeling others pain. I can feel her pain physically. It's kind of a clarity about other peoples feelings.

Provings

At the end of a long disturbing dream, a man slapped my youngest brother, really hard, for something he hadn't done and it gave me so much pain to realize my brother was being treated this way.

A dream of a woman working in the clinic who is crying while she works. (The man who should be helping) doesn't help her. She is tired out, 2 kids and works 2 jobs. The dreamer felt very sorry for her, wanted to help her.

A dream of studying in front of a monastery with my study group. It starts to rain very hard. All the material needs to be carried inside. One woman gets immediately deadly sick because she got wet in the rain. I feel enormous pity with that woman.

Lonely, Abandoned, Needing Company
I can't wait to call my supervisor. Just 10 more minutes. I need contact. If I can force myself to do something I'm fine but it's hard to collect myself and concentrate. I really don't want to be alone right now. I'm calling many friends to talk to but no one's home.

I feel needy and called [the master prover] for no other reason than to chat. I'm looking forward to my talk with my supervisor tonight. I feel I need to talk about this stuff, especially my dreams. I feel sad in a needy sense. I want someone to comfort me and take care of me.

This morning I was listening to a Bach CD and realized that it was partly to do with my craving for company and comfort. My brother sings on the CD and it was soothing to hear his voice.

Feeling uncomfortable about a client I was waiting for. I felt I was being abandoned. I definitely desire comfort and sympathy from others. Usually I'm kind of prickly about my privacy and solitude. It's interesting I have no qualms asking for it. Usually I wouldn't ask out of pride, fear of rejection, etc. Not now!

She wants to interact with people and have them take care of her.
I feel so alone. I need company. Got a buzz when people started calling.
I was abandoned by people throughout the proving. It almost killed me. Loneliness is a major theme.
Feeling unsupported. It didn't occur to me to call anyone.

Waves of Symptoms and of Water
Both hemispheres are contracting severely.
Three waves of contracting in about five minutes.
Another wave of lung symptoms.
Numbness and headache waves still there.
Next wave of lung symptoms...
Dreamed there were tidal waves. At one point one of the waves came over me. I held onto something as it washed over me. I would stand there and I knew the wave would go away soon. Each wave that came, came bigger than the last.
At one point in the dream I was lying face down on the beach, which was wet and packed down. Suddenly a wave came washing up and under me as the tide came in.

In a dream everyone was naked and the tide came in. It's hard to describe but with every wave coming onto the shore the water level rose all around us. Walls of water towered over us and subsided. There was the loud sound of moving water. Then a really strong wind picked up and started blowing sheets of water off these walls of water and we ran inside.

A dream with a strong verbal message, "This proving is about being upside down in a waterfall."

Another dream about huge waves. M. and I were standing up against a sandy cliff wall and the waves would come up and over at us at regular intervals. I concentrated on holding my breath through them and not taking in a breath.

Frightening Dreams without Fear
Dream of tidal waves. I was trying to get up high enough to get away from them. It was on a mountainside. I was not frightened in the dream. I just worked at getting away from the water...
Dream of being in a car with a friend who was driving to get his driver's license. As we drove we came up to a big cliff/hillside. He tried to turn the car quickly but he was too late. He looked at me apologetically as we headed straight down. I wasn't scared as he somehow maneuvered the car.
Dreamed we were on the island I spent summers on as a kid. We were in a field and some people had guns. They shot at something and there was some under-

RAVEN PROVING

Provings

standing that it wouldn't hurt anyone. I took my daughter and her friend into a building and tried to hide them under a bunk bed. I was not frightened.
I had a dream of a dog trying to bite me. I was holding its mouth shut. Its mouth was like a beak. I've been having frightening dreams with no fear.
Dream of myself and someone else walking up a flight of stairs. One way looked broken down so I went a different way. The stairs began to crumble. I changed directions and went another way. The stairs broke that way too. Two of us were left hanging quite a ways up, trying to figure out where to go next. I had no fear. I just hung there with total ease.

Black and White, Light and Dark, Clean and Dirty
She was napping and woke and told me she was just having a delusion of grandeur: The pope was coming to visit. She had to get ready and clean up for him.
Dreamed of visiting a former boyfriend...his house is still an incredible mess. The mess bothered me a lot...I desired to walk because the house was dark and messy.
Dizzy when looking down on the floor...Consciousness gets black for a moment.
In the dream there was one big old lumpy bed with stained covers and one lumpy couch where the children were sleeping. Between the wall and the couch there was debris. It looked as if it had been there for weeks. I remarked that I had forgotten to clean. My friends were really shocked. I decided to move the couch away from the wall. There to my amazement was a tiny little animal, which resembled a lion feeding on the garbage. Something about the little lion disgusted me. He was sort of glowing from slime. I said I'd better check the children; they may have black bugs on them. Sure enough, they did.
I signed up to clean my teeth. I haven't done that for three years. Now this urge, it has to be right away. I also bought dental floss and floss every single evening, which I haven't done for many months.
I dreamed there were people who wanted me to join their church, which was out of town, but I would commute when they had services. I would pack a bag of clothing that was simple, neat and clean. In a house watching a lady change a lampshade: the old one was dusty and dirty. When the new lampshade was put on everything was light and bright and there was a dark gray dirty rock

floor. There was a pile of dirt with a dirty diaper on it. "What should I do with this pile of dirt?" The woman said to spread it out. I did not feel right doing that. But I did it and felt as dark and dirty as the floor. I was in a room with a broom. There was a lady sitting in a chair across the room. She looked like she didn't care, "just spread it out." Everything was light on the top and dark on the bottom.

Dreamed I was vacuuming and the vacuum wasn't sucking up anymore. I opened it to find that the hose was crammed full of stuff. I tried pulling stuff out to clean it.

I want to stop thinking. Things look physically dark, as if there is less light in the world.

I have a feeling of clarity and lightness.

Ravenous Hunger and Eating
I started to eat. Pickles, Cherry Garcia ice cream, crackers, croissants. Grazing in the fridge. Constant eating. Enjoyable. It was about taste, biting, smelling. Very sensual and sensory. It wasn't about lack. It was about fun. This lasted several days. Eating was the most important thing.

She's eating a lot although she doesn't have an appetite. She's disgusted with how much she's eating, losing control of what she eats.

I've been eating well.

Another day of eating.

The last few days I was INCREDIBLY hungry. Grazing through the refrigerator, looking for anything edible. I am hungry all the time. I have to cook immediately, big meals, good meals, and I enjoy it tremendously. I prepare a lot. I eat everything, even the crumbs. I eat more frequently. I get a little worried if I see that my husband seems to have a bigger portion on his plate. Normally I finish all my duties then I allow myself to eat. Now I let everything wait and enjoy eating a lot. It seems very important all of a sudden.

Dreamed of a fish in a little bowl. The fish kept getting bigger and bigger and eating everything that was there. She was wondering how it got so big, it was filling the whole bowl. It was all mouth, a huge mouth. She had another dream of a giant fish in the ocean, eating everything. It was eating everything in its path.

RAVEN
PROVING

Provings

Teaching and Socializing
Many, many different dreams all about family members or friends. Everyone knew each other. Lots of people, being busy, with talking, discussions, money, working...the feeling in the dream was very social, busy, entertained.

Dreamt I was in a teaching mode, sharing information.

Kids dream: I had to teach/watch lots of kids, twelve children between the ages of three and six. They ran away to go play in a huge field. With a lot of effort, I find them and convince them all to come back in the house, my parents' house. Finally they all sit in a row so I can continue to teach them. I have to go to the phone. They all run away again, not mean, but because they want to play. I find them on a huge field across the street. There was a feeling of being stressed, of danger that the kids would get hurt or lost.

Dream of a long pilgrimage parade with a number of people, teaching, watching, kids, rocks, hills. I organized a celebration. I'm told I won't be needed ... relieved. Steep hills. Looking onto an Indian village, a woman grinding corn. She looked up at me and it was a wonderful feeling.
Dream of being in a huge old house working with children...
Dream of having a therapy session with kids. I'm in the role of therapist/counselor/teacher

Major changes in my life now with connections to the proving: I'm heading for working with children as an educator, with parents, in counseling therapy, workshops and groups. Working with kids on communication skills and to resolve conflicts.

Lots of people in my dreams: Light, outside, in nature, like in a big field. People scattered around the field. Adults; not kids. Feeling of huge, immense field. If I think about it I was small but I didn't feel small in the dream. There was some kind of social purpose for being there. A group feeling but people weren't talking with each other.

Dream of being with her husband in Brooklyn...On the corner she sees Michael Jackson, his sister and some other black star. Kids are playing in the street, ignoring him. Kind of like it is his home neighborhood...

Powerful, Proud, Queen-like and Beautiful
My chest in the breast area feels enlarged tremendously, like the ribs are bowing out... Feeling very good, clean, strong, proud, 'unwoundable,' like "shoulders back, chest out." Generally feeling really good energy, feeling strong, proud, queen-like. Firmer, straighter, walking, talking. Feeling free and powerful.
I dreamed I had a beautiful house and I was showing it to some people. It was actually like a dollhouse, with the front cut out, so you could see the inside. It was lush and rich with lots of rooms, lovely old carpets. That's what's inside me.
I make beauty.
I am a little tougher. I was too friendly, much too pleasing [before the proving]. Now I feel just "Be me." Not having to smile all the time, coming from my higher self, [not] from "the pleaser" role.
I feel like I never look beautiful.
Dream...everything is pristine and pure. Then I noticed dirt and evil, the intransigence of people who have the power..."How can you destroy this beauty?" Feeling powerless.
In a dream she dresses up...putting on a beautiful blouse like the one her sister brought her from Paris. She's waiting, dressed up, holding a bouquet of flowers...

The remedy has shown me I have the power to fight for myself. I am now working from within not without.

Pestilence and Poison
I'm slightly paranoid about the foods I'm ingesting. The irradiated milk? The meat? Is it all healthy?
Very congested nose all of a sudden...burning, watery eyes. I keep thinking they had an accident in a factory with poison gas, but my husband next to me has no such symptoms.
I dreamed of a scorpion in my hand. My hands were protected somehow. I was following some instructions that told me to cut part of the limbs off the scorpion. I did this and then shook the remaining part of each limb, on either side of the body. The poison of the insect then spilled out on to the bed. During it all I was reading or receiving instructions or lessons about the poison of the scorpion.

Provings

She was real sick last night. She thinks it was something she ate (food poisoning).

Dream of staying in the mountains with my family. It was beautiful until we noticed the oil refinery down the slope belching out huge clouds of a poisonous yellow smoke...

In another dream there was a beautiful, verdant lush field and there were holes all over it. Small mines where people were digging for gold. Again there was a theme of pristine nature ruined by man. It makes me feel humanity is pestilential.

Old Boyfriends
Former boyfriend dream: I go visit him to try to resolve old issues. His house is still an incredible mess, which bothered me a lot. He is still overconfident, the general attitude of "I didn't do anything wrong." ...I desired to walk so we could perhaps talk about old issues, and because the house was dark and messy. I wanted to go to an open plaza...he wanted to go uptown. His face said, "Oh you again, always do what you want to do." This dream was somehow about protecting myself.
Dream of an old lover.
Doing the "poor me" with my ex-boyfriend again.
I dreamed of one of my high school boyfriends. He was interested in dating me but I was not. I was using all kinds of tactics to avoid him. He was in trouble because he was late for class. It was raining. He didn't have an umbrella. He was crying. I made the decision to help him so he would not get wet going to class.

PEREGRINE FALCON *Falco peregrinus*

The proving was conducted under the direction of Misha Norland by the School of Homeopathy in 1997 in England. Published in the 1999 edition of *The Homoeopath*. The full proving can be found at the School of Homeopathy's website: www.homeopathyschool.com.

INTRODUCTION

The proving of *Falco* would not have taken place had it not been for a patient. Her story is told in the introduction and case example to the AIDS proving (found on the website of the School of Homeopathy: www.homeopathyschool.com). What follows here is a continuation of that story. During this period she felt increasingly claustrophobic: trapped in the office, while others were being funded by her efforts to set up and experience homoeopathic health projects. During this time her father also reappeared. Menaced by fear, wanting to escape, yet bound by obligation, she consulted me once again.

Receiving her case I could find nothing new, yet found an intensification of her state, which a previously prescribed AIDS 200C had not alleviated. Therefore I set to ruminating: what is there in nature, which mirrors her state? I could only think of a human situation, for there is nothing in the world that I know of which could behave in a manner such as her parents had, other than humans!

I set to thinking about a situation, which is even more extreme than that of the chained dog (*Lac caninum* had been a remedy which had helped in the past), more frightening and alienating than an AIDS situation. And I came up with the trained Peregrine Falcon. I remembered her love of running and climbing the rugged rock face (ledges on sheer rock-faces are used by Peregrines as nesting sites). But most of all I brought before my mind's eye the picture of the training of the falcon, involving starvation, being tied by the ankles and kept prisoner in a dark place. I thought of the perverted bond of persecutor and victim - the 'no escape' situation of the bird until, once trained, it is allowed its flight, yet returns when summoned by conditioned reflex to sound of whistle and sight of lure.

Provings

Mentioning my ruminations to her led to the interesting revelation that she knew a vet who ministered to an aviary of hunting birds! Thus a wing feather clip and blood spot were procured, sent to The Helios Homoeopathic Pharmacy to be run up to the 30th centesimal potency. The pharmacist who did this provided us with a report of her experiences - the first proving, while the patient subsequently benefited from the dose: she lost her fear, her sense of disempowerment, quit her stifling job and is currently living in her beloved Scotland where she can roam free, making her peregrinations.

The proving was conducted with students at the School in 1997 using a unit dose of the 30th centesimal potency and following the protocol given on this web-site. We recorded our experiences some minutes after beginning the proving. During the course of the School weekend (Friday through to Sunday) we took stock of thoughts, dreams, sensations, feelings and outer world happenings, using transcripts of tape recordings to insure accuracy. Supervisors and daily proving diaries filled in from month to month.

As usual, some members of the class did not take the dose, yet of these, two were affected. **The psychic field effect of group proving is such thatit is not possible for susceptible persons to absent themselves.** Recording spanned a period of three months.

During this proving I wrote the following poem as witness to my involvement in the spirit of Falcon.

FALCON AND FALCONER

By lakeside, amidst violets white and blue,
amongst boulders sculpted into forms of sleepers
in love's embrace, hunted we two,
knowing that our past held a hidden clue
yet to bear fruit or be harvested by autumn reapers.
As seed is cast into fertile earth by careless breezes
or by sowers' hands, so shall our compound of love
raise flowers, lake, boulder, swan and dove
and make a nature which embraces what pleases,
for as seeds root below they blossom above.

*We sanctify the soil and soul which dwells within
by our actions. So let us take care
to be full of heart and not to act upon whim,
or profanely speak when we intend to hymn,
or set a poisoned trap or baited snare.
We may be tormented by our hunger, by sin
Which burns, desire which turns in falcon's gyre
upon up-draft above the raging fire
which we have lit. Our terror is that conflagration
consume the world and become our funeral pyre!
Then falcon would have no returning
unless transformed to phoenix it aspire out of ashes
its nest to make! We must take heed of motives
if we are not to cinder in the burning
when flashing storms crash upon the lake.*

PHARMACEUTICAL PREPARATION

The substance of the remedy was taken from Nesbit, a captive bred Peregrine Tercel who was about 2 years old and had been trained in the traditional way.

Nesbit had been acquired when very young and had been brought up in his owner's home. Even for a Peregrine he is a bird of considerable character and charm.

A small piece of feather and a sample of blood were taken from Nesbit by his regular vet. The blood and feather were triturated in lactose as specified in the footnotes to paragraph 270 of the Organon up to 3c and then succussed up to 30c.

FALCON PROVING

PROVERS
Nine persons took a single dose of 30c potency.

MAJOR THEMES:
- Spirals, Waves, and Colors
- Carefree
- Careless

Provings

- Freedom and Speed
- Floating and Flying
- Empathy with People
- Confidence
- Anger
- Unfeeling
- Controlled by an Alien
- Guilt

SAKER FALCON *Falco cherug*

The Saker Falcon was proved by Elizabeth Schulz in Germany. It was a trituration/proving to C4 using a feather. We extracted the following pertinent parts from the entire proving, which can be found in ReferenceWorks.

Elizabeth Schulz:
I decided to take *Falco cherug* as a proving remedy for a weeklong seminar on biodynamic homeopathy. The theme 'search for acceptance' is important for people in healing and helping professions. We could also say it is 'about the addiction to being needed.' I wanted to grasp this part of the theme. Within a week the falcon led us into painful depths. We triturated from the 2C to the 4C potency.

Since the processing leads us into deep regressions we came in direct contact with the child's wounded soul. The first and most common theme was the **loss of the parents.** In many ways we could recognize this theme through the biodynamic processes and could allow ourselves to feel the repressed feelings of **abandonment, grief, and anger.** Most of the provers experienced **shame** about the neediness of their soul:
"I lost my parents and stood alone on a meadow. The child cried a lot until after a long time the parents showed up and hugged their child."
"My parents never had time for me. I always had to go places by myself. Even for my first day of school and the party afterwards I was alone."
"My mother left me." (In actual life she died).
"My mother had no time for me. I was a baby, and I always had to be alone."
"My father lied to me, and he left the family." (The prover was four years old when her parents separated).
The next important part of the theme was **sexual abuse**. Five participants (male and female) remembered sexual violations in their most intense forms. One female participant said in deep regression:
"My dad is crazy but despite everything that he does to me, I want him to become healthy because I love him."
This sentence shows a main theme: **the pain of experiencing the loss of love is much worse than the pain caused by sexual abuse**.

FALCON PROVING

Provings

PHYSICAL SYMPTOMS
Neck pain, pulling, piercing, sensations of cold and stiffness.
Back: strong tension between the shoulder blades with pulling pain.
Rheumatic pain in larger and smaller joints.
Visual defects.
Varicose vein complaints.
Flatulence.
Complaints during menstruation, menstruation **too early and too painful.**

A DREAM:
I am looking down on the ocean, light blue clear water. Suddenly the waves become very high so that people are tumbling. I am afraid and observe everything from the outside and above. Then I am in the water myself. I take a child that is in danger to calmer waters and protect him. It was as if I had spread my protecting wings so that the waves couldn't harm the child.

This dream touched me very deeply. At that time I didn't know that **Horus, the Egyptian falcon god, protects children.**

PROVER 1 (FEMALE)
1C Trituration
Strong allergic nose itching. Wanting to be the fastest. I think about giving up my freedom, giving up freedom in exchange for admiration, acceptance, and love. Throat pain, piercing pain in the left tonsil. Uncomfortable feelings in the genital area like piercing, itching, burning. Difficulty breathing. Pain in the right shoulder. Rheumatic muscle pain in the right upper arm. An incredible longing for the knowledge behind things. Cramps in the right hand. Sensations of paralysis in hands and arms. Clumsiness. Great hunger. Itching skin.
The wish to observe: I could sit here forever and watch trees and bushes.
Pain in the varicose veins.
Piercing pain in the costal arch. Piercing pain in the wrist. Scalp itching as if many ants are crawling on it. The eyes are itching, swelling, and closing. Eyesight worsens.
Tight jaw and neck muscles.

2C Trituration
Thoughts about money and perfection.

3C Trituration
Mild nose bleeding.

PROVER 2 (FEMALE)
1C Trituration
The skin's surface is itching. Bad eyesight. Headaches starting in the neck region. I am just a witness, and this doesn't concern me. Feelings of infinite freedom. Varicose veins are aching, stagnation in my left leg.

2C Trituration
Wanting to be faultless. Stretching one's neck to be equal with the others

3C Trituration
Tension in the neck, in the nape of the neck, in the shoulders. Sighing, sadness. Having no family, no support, no work. A handicapped child. Despair, no prospects for the future.

4C Trituration
I am easily bothered by small things. Yellow light and a lot of sun energy come up.

The triturations led us again and again into deep processes. After a long walk through the beautiful landscape we returned tired. Of course, we saw birds of prey everywhere and it was as if they accompanied us.

FALCON PROVING

Provings

TURKEY VULTURE *Cathartes aura*

A proving of Turkey Vulture (*Cathartes aura*) performed in Phoenix, Arizona in the fall of 1999 under the direction of Todd Rowe, consisted of 18 subjects who began taking *Cathartes* 30C on September 1, 1999. There were 3 male, 16 female and one dream prover. The participants' ages ranged from 21 to 65 years old. Eight proving supervisors monitored the participants closely for the month following taking the remedy and the proving supervisors reported directly to the proving coordinator. One of the subjects took the remedy again at 200C potency six months after the original proving. All participants gave informed consent to participate in this study. This was a partial proving. Each prover was instructed to take a single daily dosage for a maximum of three days but to stop after any symptoms became apparent. Participants recorded their symptoms in journals over the space of the next month. The specimen was obtained from a fresh automobile road-kill in Northern Arizona. A turkey vulture primary tail feather was triturated to C3 and then hand succussed to a 30C potency. The remedy is now available from the Hahnemann pharmacy and others.

The proving was a double blind test: neither the provers nor the supervisors knew what the remedy was until after the proving. At the end of the month, provers participated in a videotaped exit meeting and the participants' written journals were reviewed separately. Any participants who had residual symptoms or improvement following the one-month interval were followed subsequently until the symptoms resolved.

The entire proving is available in ReferenceWorks.

WHEN VULTURES DREAM

The hovering dives
Of the birds
Haunt them at nights
When the sky is dark
And carcasses and bones
Are like stones
Sitting still but,
Hard to be broken.
The leaves ooze
Singing and clapping
Their hands
By the wind blowing
And the trees whispering,
So, gentle sleep
Creeps into their minds
And,
Awful snores
Fill the
Mountain heights
And the craggy forts.
Sleep,
Ravenous birds,
The night is yours
And,
Snore ......
And,
Dream .....
And,
Bald heads
Dream!!!!!

           Segun Ige '96

TURKEY
VULTURE
PROVING

Provings

SOME PROVING EXCERPTS:

P‍ROVER #1
Dreams:
>Condemned buildings.
>Conflict.
>Kidnapped children.
>Attic of an old house once lived in.
>Criminal activity.
>Threats from gangs.
>Squirrels and lemurs.
>A dog jumping.
>Secretly foraging for food.
>Spacious mansion.
>Secrets.
>Family and friends.

OK to break rules; rules can be broken.

P‍ROVER #2
Dreams:
Disgusting, disturbing dream that lingered for several days; anger and disgust; two friends she knew were boyfriend and girlfriend; on her birthday, he violated her and forced her to perform sexual acts in front of two or three other people; she came to my house very upset but went back to him the next day. I went there to protect her and other men started doing sexual acts to provoke me.
>Got a computer virus that would not let me exit while it destroyed all my memory.
>Test driving cars without any intention to buy one.
>In high school doing dangerous and exciting things; sexual dreams.

P‍ROVER #3
Dreams:
>Unable to get somewhere or something.
>Black and yellow striped snake (which she saw in her garden the next day).

Cleaning out and going through papers.
Traveling.
Getting rid of stuff from husband who died 13 years ago.
Industrious.

Prover #4
Dreams:
> In fire got eyes and hands burnt; skin tried to grow over these empty holes in hands and eyes.
> Grass full of snakes.
> House rafters.
> Stealing.
> Large house.

Felt crowded being in city. Irritated by people and traffic.
Let go of a relationship that was dragging.

Prover #5
Dreams:
> Big dogs like coyotes.
> Sailing with inexperience people and ran into gale force winds.
> Rooms of office furniture.
> Cliffs, rocks and ocean.
> Bony structure like human spine.

Theme of death and sudden death.

Prover #6
Dreams:
> Bugs or ants on bottom of feet; infected blood on my face; hospital.

Prover #7
Dreams:
> Wedding near ocean with unique furniture.
> Evacuation.
> Children.
> Skyscrapers.
> Prisoner where I learn you have to be humble to leave.
> Frustration and alienation.
> Reaching dead ends.
> Encountering dangers which I barely escape from.
> Being a spy and tour guide.
> Secrets.
> Sick child.

Turkey Vulture proving

Provings

Dreams complex, hard to capture in writing; feeling of receiving messages that couldn't be grasped; like being viewed through a veil. Missions uncompleted yet did not know what they were.
Treated as if I were invisible; how I felt as a child around my parents.

PROVER #8
Dreams:
>Sexual dreams.
>Sneaking.
>Ocean.

PROVER #9
Dreams:
>Four identical children.
>Red rocks with green veins.
>Two groups of women in swimming pool; girl in green and white.
>Dog with hurt leg.
>Friendly snakes and leopard.

PROVER #10
Dreams:
>On island.
>Alligators and scorpions.

PROVER #11
Dreams:
>Many friends, people in yellow robes.
>Phoenix rising from ashes.
>Transportation and a journey.
>Children in basement with paper floor and no fear of falling through.
>Two men romancing me but left when saw each other (competition).

PROVER #12
Dreams:
>Aliens, who were friendly.
>Man pursuing her.

>Babysitting for $100/day.
>People with diseased arms with skin red and raw.
Felt totally unsupported in the world; abandoned by my mother; no family.

PROVER #13
Dreams:
>Lack of support from husband.
>Traveling in huge camper with dog.

PROVER #14
Dreams:
>Frustration.

PROVER #15
Dreams:
>Having affair with attractive brunette who lives on the beach & has a protective dog.
>Dreams full of color and sound.
>Flying in a jet.
>Mountain lion.
>Horseback riding.

PROVER #16
Dreams:
>Large business place with different rooms.
>Spying and picking up secrets.
>Communication room.
>Transparent blue stone floating in space.
>Floating in water.
>Wooden house with wooden floors.
>Feeling like the ceiling or floor dropped.
>Man sick because not open to lifestyle changes.
>White structure that looks dead, which I criticize but it turns into a beautiful face; on a ship.
>Leader kills someone.

TURKEY VULTURE PROVING

Provings

PROVER #17
Dreams:
    Motorcycle stuck in sand.
    Gophers.

PROVER #18
Dreams:
    Giving an address.
    Bit by a rattlesnake on finger; in hospital.

PROVER #19
Dreams:
    Taking care of children.
    Gold balloons.
    Island retreat center for working out family issues.
    Working through old issues.
    Transformation and releasing old stuff.
    Sexual and romantic dreams.

PROVER #7 (repeated 200C)
Dreams:
    Room guarded by vicious dog.
    On taxi ride with lascivious stranger.
    Don't know where to go.
    Eating in a group.
    Arrogant, negative person; jumping from a balcony.
    Security guards checking badges.
    People playing in tub of chicken shit.
    Car with dead battery.

ANDEAN CONDOR *Vultur gryphus*

This is a proving extract from a proving conducted by Elisabeth Schulz in Germany. The full proving is available on ReferenceWorks.

ULI RIMMLER:
The trituration of a condor feather was my first experience of making a homeopathic remedy. Before, I didn't know much about this ingenious procedure originated by Hahnemann. With a mortar and pestle a substance is ground and then later triturated into higher and higher dilutions. I was very curious about this experience.

We were unaware that the day Elisabeth and I chose for the trituration a total lunar eclipse would occur. This is an event that occurs only every few years. C.G. Jung called the phenomenon of things that are actually totally unrelated but seem to be connected on an inner level synchronicity. These are coincidences that drop into our laps so that we are spontaneously inclined to want to see an inner meaning. That is why it made sense to us that this very impressionable lunar eclipse and the homeopathic remedy *Vultur gryphus* were connected.

While we were triturating the remedy, the moonlight was shining directly through the window into the room. During the trituration we could see the entire eclipse: the moon's disappearance, total darkness and then its slow growth toward a full bright disk. Throughout all this, the atmosphere was as if we had emerged into a magical space. With the steady turning of the pestle in the mortar it seemed to me as if I were in a different historical time performing a ritual.

ELISABETH SCHULZ:
I was surrounded by darkness. I had fallen far and all of a sudden there was fire. My body was burning; everything was burning. And then the miracle happened: transformed as *Phoenix* I rose from the ashes. I flew freely. I looked back, sad because I had lost everything I loved and that belonged to me. From way up high I looked down on the old, dead, and burned. My old life was lying broken under me.

Provings

As *Phoenix* I sat high above and looked, calm and surprised, at the new.
(Inner images after taking *Vultur gryphus* 30C)

1C Trituration:
(7:30 P.M. September 16, 1997)
Shoulder pain on my right side, piercing.
Hot flashes.
Inner restlessness and then sadness because I think of the two airplanes that have just collided. Children lost their parents, women lost their husbands, many people died.
A feeling as if there are parasites on my skin, a subtle stinging sensation.

2C Trituration:
(8:30 P.M. September 9, 1997)
Skin is sensitive.
Right upper arm is itching.
Narrowness creates fear.
Stinging pain in my right ovary.

September 17, 1997
Headache.
Sinuses on my left side are swollen.
Desire to clean up.
A lot of power!

September 18, 1997
Dream:
I bought a Porsche. The top is open, and it is a bit too small for me. I race through the streets, pass men driving and drive over 60 miles per hour. What if the police catch me! I feel faster than lightning. The men admire me for my speed.

Back pain, on the right side of the thoracic vertebrae, 'pulling' muscle pain.
Feeling as if no one wants to have anything to do with me.

3C Trituration:
(6:55 P.M. September 26, 1997)

Chopin's funeral march.
Headache and pain in the skull.
No one wants me; am I that ugly?

4C Trituration:
Tired, yawning, quiet, silence.
Losing the light. Light is hope.

September 27, 1997
After the 3C and 4C Triturations
Dream:

The old key.
I see a bunch of old keys hanging on my mailbox. I don't know to whom it belongs. I ask a woman. She is making a lot of noise with her car. A child comes running down the staircase. The horses are bolting. Beautiful horses are running. I have to save the child. The woman is screaming.

ELISABETH SCHULZ:
I ask myself: Is it of use to pass on unproven bird remedies? Is the reader bored by the symptoms of the trituration? Is it actually possible to see a picture? Doesn't the condor resemble the eagle too much? So many questions. However, perhaps the condor will one day help even one person to bear, understand, and transform his suffering so that he can experience the miracle of transformation, healing, and death just like *Phoenix*. Then this work has meaning.

PROVING REPORT
ULI RIMMLER:
The experience of the condor trituration was incredibly strong and moving. During those four hours (each potency is triturated for an hour) I had a real flood of inner images, mental associations coupled with sometimes intense physical sensations. At the end of all four triturations I mostly felt better, and the unpleasant sensations totally dissolved except itching on the head and body. Interestingly, while I was typing my notes my body was itching strongly so I made many errors and became upset about the distraction.

Provings

Notes of my inner experiences, images and feelings during the trituration:

1C Trituration:
First feeling: **sadness, sad heart, sharp heart pain**. Pulling sensation in right groin. Genital area is cold. Scraping out the womb after an abortion.

2C Trituration:
Toothache in the upper left area. A gynecologist's blood-smeared white coat after an abortion surgery. Itching. Scratching is funny, we laugh. Pulling pain in the right testicle. I become fidgety and impatient. Effort, genital area hurts. Image: scraping dried blood and meat off a butcher's metal tub. Lower back pain.

3C Trituration:
Scratching the head, itching of the face.

4C Trituration:
Testicles are hurting. Thoughts about being humiliated and humility. Pride goes before the fall. Totally chewed up finger nails that are already bleeding. Nausea (bad taste in the mouth). Other children that tease children. Grief about death and the fact that things are simply gone. Search for consolation. Head itches.

It is obvious that during the trituration some themes came up repeatedly for me:

- Themes of morbidity, destruction, and death
- Themes of nourishment and food (fear of not getting enough)
- Sexual theme
- Religious themes
- Violence, addiction, and despair
- Grief and hope

EXPERIENCES WITH THE HOMEOPATHIC REMEDY VULTUR GRYPHUS:

ANDEAN CONDOR PROVING

Before the condor-trituration I dreamt several times about the dead and the living.

One dream: I was walking through the streets and saw dead and living people. I was surprised and amazed that the dead ones looked like the living ones. They looked so normal and mundane, and yet I knew they were dead. To find out who was dead and who alive I asked some "Are you dead?" They replied: "What? You can see me although I am dead?" The dead people were sad and hopeless because they were no longer seen by the living and could no longer communicate with the living. The dead people walked through the streets like lost souls.

Another dream: Elisabeth had a camera that can take pictures of the dead and the living people. I took pictures with that camera and a normal one, so that I could compare pictures of the same situation afterwards.

These dreams can be interpreted from several perspectives. Obviously, they are about the relationship of two worlds: the world of the dead and the living.

Dream fragment: Then I went down, deeper and deeper and I fell and fell. I fell with an incredible speed. The speed was so fast I couldn't perceive anything about my surroundings. I relaxed and trusted the free fall. There was no ground under me. I fell and fell and had let go completely. Eternally falling, continuing to fall and simultaneously being taken care of. It was like the center of the cyclone. On the outside the surroundings through which I fell with an incredible speed, and myself in the still center.

What is left is a message for me: I can let go and trust. I am totally protected when I let myself go completely.

Provings

HUMBOLDT PENGUIN *Spheniscus humboldti*

The complete proving of Humboldt Penguin took place in Munich, Germany in 2002. The complete write-up is not yet available. Following are notes by Jonathan Shore taken during the trituration proving in Munich, Germany in the year 2002:

C1
Detailed, exact instructions 3x 6x 6 minutes, on and on (Does this have to do with Germany, with the C4 idea or what?) Irritation.
Happy, funny.
Everybody will not get a turn.
Take what comes.
(People are whispering to each other, giggling. They talk to the people next to them. **Little groups like cliques.** Laughter gets louder, sounds of suppressed laughter)
Feeling of **social restraint**
Stiff neck.
Talk about rules. About doing it right.
Not much feeling, then inner silence and in the silence is a sadness. Then a flash of frustration at people; **anger at people with no reason.**
This will take forever. It is only 6:20; I thought it was at least 8 pm or later.
(Someone directs the proceedings. More discussion about methodology. People are singing and humming).

C2
Very fast trituration, intense rapid activity. Like a train going chuff chuff.
Alternating energy and fatigue .
Need to find energy. Look for ways to do this. Go to toilet, eat, go outside, do tai chi.
I have to draw on my resources, to find my resources.
If I hear that sound again [scraping] I will go nuts.
My head is tired not my body. It takes all my attention to stay in my body and out of my head. If I can stay with the sensation of my body I do not feel tired.

EXPERIENCES OF OTHER PROVERS:
In general there was a lot of heavy and intense negativity.

Respect and deception stabbed in the heart.
Do it right.
Clean and dirty.
Mistrust of others. **Paranoid mistrust**. Threatening spirit in the group, which prevents us coming together.
Yearning to be together.
No contact at all with anyone.
No group. Everyone just does their own thing. I do my thing, they do theirs
Let it be. Ok how others see me.
Tension between head and feeling.
Alternating interest and boring.
Social rules.
I am what I am and others are what they are.
Feel distant from the whole thing. That's why it doesn't matter.
Coldness of extremities. Coldness in general. Coldness with perspiration. Coldness in hands, in feet, in head, in nose.
Trembling extremities.
Desire to take a deep breath.
Pain in the big toe.
Heaviness in extremities. Heaviness in chest.

The whole thing was a heavy and unpleasant experience. It was as if the effect of the seminar had been antidoted and we all came down into the heavy realm of everyday ego emotions.

HUMBOLDT PENGUIN PROVING

Provings

WHOOPER SWAN *Cygnus cygnus*

Cygn-cy is a proving by Jeremy and Camilla Sherr, published in *Dynamis Provings Volume II*. An article about two *Cygn-cy* cases was first published in *The Homeopath*, October 2002, No. 87. Here are excerpts from this article, pertaining to the proving, reprinted with kind permission from Nick Hewes, Editor of *The Homeopath*.

Camilla Sherr:
In the summer of 2001, Jeremy and I were on vacation in the Finnish archipelago. Jeremy had been experiencing some nasty neck and should pains for two months and our visit to the summer cottage seemed to offer him the chance for some needed rest. Coming out of the sauna one day, rubbing and twisting his stiff and aching neck, Jeremey searched his mind for the remedy that would ease his pain. At that moment, the most beautiful swan floated by, head poised elegantly on a long, thin neck. We both took this as a sign that the Whooper Swan, *Cygnus cygnus*, was to be our next Dynamis proving.

Cygnus causes profound feelings of sorrow, relating especially to the death of a loved one:

> "Overwhelmed with massive sadness… It's mine; it's about me as a mother…with our second daughter, it was a normal delivery, but she was born prematurely, and rushed into intensive care, where she died. I NEVER EVER HELD HER. There is something inside me still crying out for that experience…crying and crying all the time."
>
> "Definite sad feeling, as if someone had died, someone close."
>
> "Felt grief for mother who died three years before, deeper than before."

Grief in *Cygnus* is indeed the central component of the remedy. Related to the theme of sorrow is the sense of a deep connection to the past. We see this very clearly in the comment from a case, "The grief is there all the time. It's like it all happened five minutes ago. I can't escape it."

Many provers dwelled in a similar way on incidents which happened long ago, sometimes as if the intervening years didn't happen.

"Thoughts on my birth and the hesitation I had about being born."

"Memories of water breaking with first daughter."

"Feel as if today some bit of me from way back is coming out. I was going back to being very young, maybe four or five years old."

"I had feelings related to the past, like I am fifteen years younger. Time was rewound fifteen years back."

"The unraveling process has taken me back to the beginning."

There is a strong emphasis on the history of abuse in the case and we find similar imagery in the proving:

Dream: A baby had three abortions because he had been raped.

Dream: "We were staying with our grandfather. I spied on him sexually abusing a young boy. I could see that he thought the boy was enjoying it and I could see that the boy was terrified."

"It feels as if people torture me before putting in the knife."

The proving is full of water imagery:

"Really enjoying water. I'm in my element."

"Strong desire to go swimming."

"The sound of water was beautiful."

"My head is full of watery metaphors: I'm drowning in work. Without that we're sunk."

"Feel as if I'm swimming in a different stream beside the main stream and it cannot merge with the other."

There are many throat symptoms in the proving:

Sensation of lump or small constriction in throat.

Heavy pressure high up in my throat.

"My throat feels tight; suffocation."

Tense feeling at top of throat.

Some provers experienced more general sensations of narrowing in the chest and throat area:

"The feeling of being stuck in something, can't get out of it. Maybe it's important to stick to my empty feelings. I'm going through a hole."

"My lungs are empty, an empty feeling in my chest."

Provings

CAMILLA SHERR COMMENTS:
These sensations again suggest a constriction in the throat or chest area, and this of course reminds us of the shape of the swan, with its long, thin neck tapering up from a large and powerful body: a perfect natural symbol of the constrictive nature of silent, unexpressed grief. In this context, one can see that the Doctrine of Signatures can sometimes serve as a useful adjunct to the pure information enunciated by a proving.

MUTE SWAN *Cygnus olor*

This was an Elisabeth Schulz proving done in Germany.

Below are some pertinent points extracted from the complete proving which is available in ReferenceWorks.

One participant who was brutally abused by her husband and now lives alone said with deep longing in her voice: "I want to meet my soul mate and to be with him the way I am and to be loved like that." The search for the soul mate was only one part of the theme.

The other was the sexual relationship. The refusal or rejection of sexuality by the male life partner or spouse was also present. Rough sexual treatment by men, sexual abuse of children, and child pornography were themes difficult to confront during this trituration.

A female participant's dream:
> My ex-boyfriend is visiting. We talk about our past. I know why he came. He wants sex, but I don't want it. I know his sex. It has nothing to do with love. In bed he is clumsy, egotistical and only after his own pleasure. I need more feeling to be aroused. Not only my own feelings: I also want to feel that my partner participates wholeheartedly. This man cannot respond to me emotionally, sexually, or intellectually.

One participant saw herself lying on a horse carriage, and she lost her child. It died during birth.

Another female participant was the newborn, and her mother lost her life during the delivery.

PARTICIPANT'S DREAM THEMES:
- Animals
- Being able to see and breathe under water
- Being betrayed for money
- Being robbed of something
- Broken glass
- Burglars

SWAN PROVING

Provings

Burns
Clairvoyant dreams
Color white
Death and dying
Death while traveling
Deceased people
Diving
Dogs
Erotic dreams
Fear of crowds
Flying
Funerals
Great efforts
Impotence
Money
Snow
Territorial fights
Traveling
Water

In our opinion grief and loss show up as significant themes in this proving and thus should be added to this list.

Physical symptoms

Complaints about the sinuses, excretion of bloody mucus.
Dry mucous membranes.
Eczema, itching, red and scaling.
Flatulence.
Frequent urinating.
Neck tension.
Pain in left shoulder joint.
Pressure on the bladder.
Rheumatic pain in all muscles.

WANDERING ALBATROSS *Diomedea exulans*

A proving was done by a group of Dutch homeopaths as reported in *Wad Stories: Homeopathic Lectures From a Sailing Trip on the Wad in the Netherlands*.

NOTE: There is a song by Rod Stewart, called *Sailing*, which expresses the feeling of this bird beautifully. "We are sailing stormy waters, to be near you, to be free."

THEMES OF THE REMEDY
Freedom
> Vision of the Statue of Liberty. Some provers had a flying sensation.
> Feeling of freedom even in a group.

Connection and Isolation
> One prover had no contact with the feeling of other people.
> On the other side departing is difficult (in a prover's dream and in reality).
> Vision of masks. The owl as symbol of intimacy.
> Feeling of vulnerability in the contact with others.
> Wanting to be seen as an individual.

Loneliness
> Being alone is painful (in a prover's dream).
> On the other hand many provers had a feeling of being more easily themselves in this group than in other comparable circumstances. Feeling of being unnoticed in the group, of not being an individual, a nobody in a big family.
> Loneliness in youth. Homesickness.
> Endless, timeless, stillness.
> Feeling of being endless and timeless in the water.
> Visions of sunset in India, the transition of liveliness to stillness.
> The polarity is setting boundaries. And the entrapment in a very small boxlike house in a dream of a prover is the opposite of endlessness.

WANDERING ALBATROSS PROVING

Provings

Peace
Sensation of peace. Sensation of serenity. Sensation of a fan-shaped restful energy.

Sudden interruption.

Sudden changes of atmosphere were noted, for example from seriousness to laughter. Suddenly a sail maneuver, a water spout, or another incident would interrupt the ongoing.

Dream of a bicycling accident. Suddenly there is intrusion by others (see seduction and intrusion). Sudden change at sunset.

But all the changes were with flexibility and care. The group always came back to unfinished matters.

Ascension
Shortly after the remedy was distributed, during a short meditation a waterspout interrupted the serene atmosphere. Fan-shaped sensation. A sensation of heavy lightness. The Statue of Liberty was seen as image. The whole atmosphere was light and elevated as if we were all functioning on a higher level.

Crooked
Sensation as if two sides of the body do not fit, as if there is a torsion.

Seeing oblique lines, like reed swaying in the wind.

The waterspout rising to the sky. Association with a double helix.

Group and boundaries
The group is threatened by intruders. Taking one's stand is a theme. Saying no to intruders. Intrusion by phallus. Feeling of vulnerability in the group.

Feeling of vulnerability and loneliness on deck. Dream of stopping the killing of an Arabian woman (with a knife).

Lost children
A book about a black boy who wants to go to the Eskimos. There is a dream about a child that does not belong to the family. A book about adopting a Nepalese daughter. A black child playing with a white child (Sabian Symbol card).

Father
The father theme was stirred up in different provers: death of the father, father as 'dyke reverend' (someone who oversees the land surrounded by dykes), the forgotten birthday of a father.

Androgyny
>Unicorn as symbol of androgyny. The roles of men and women were not strictly divided.

Laughter and quacking
>Many bursts of laughter; fits of giggles; animated and loud conversation; we made as much noise as the quacking seagulls.

Seduction and intrusion
>Four girls on the quarterdeck were seducing. A man on the boat alongside was claiming a kiss for a mussel. Overriding boundaries was a common theme.
>
>The unicorn as a symbol of the phallus is part of this.

Death and fire
>Seeing two dead animals on a stroll (a dead seagull and a dead cat). Girls spitting fire. The fire in the hand of the Statueof Liberty.

The one-liner summing up the sensation of *Diomedea* could be:
I am a poor lonesome cowboy and a long, long way from home.

PHYSICALS

MIND:
>Confusion, loses his way in well known streets
>Dreamy, not focused, distracted, confused, misty in the head
>Restlessness, ameliorated by closing the eyes
>Unreal sensation

VERTIGO:
>Light feeling in the head, swaying sensation

HEAD:
>Glowing sensation, forehead, left
>Heavy sensation, forehead, right
>Heaviness of head
>Pain above the eyes
>Pain deep behind the eyes
>Pain occiput
>Pain, forehead

WANDERING ALBATROSS PROVING

Provings

Pain, occiput, extending to vertex
Pressing pain inward, occiput
Stitching pain, forehead, right

FACE:
Cold wind sensation
Pain, mastoid
Twitching left cheek

THROAT:
Lump in throat

STOMACH:
Eructations
Fear in stomach/abdomen, a primal fear of life
Feeling of anticipation
Nausea
Sensation of vomiting without feeling bad
Tension in stomach

RECTUM:
Constipation
Diarrhea at 6 o'clock
Flatus

CHEST:
Feeling of openness and burning love for life in the chest
Oppression in the chest
Pressing sensation, sternum

EXTREMITIES:
Circumscribed spot pain in right upper leg
Heavy sensation in leg, right more than left
Pain in wrist, ulnar side, left more than right
Perspiration fingertips
Right hand colder than left
Tendency to drop things
Tingling in legs

    Warm feeling in legs
    Wounded left heel

SKIN:

    Papular eruption on wrist, hand, and back of feet with honeylike discharge

SLEEP:

    Sighing
    Sleeping as a block
    Sleeplessness
    Yawning

GENERALITIES:

    Cold sensation
    Shaking from fear
    Shivering from coldness

WANDERING ALBATROSS PROVING

308   B•I•R•D•S

Cases

Although provings are the basic building blocks of our remedies, it is in the cured cases that the final form, molded by the forces of life and experience, is given. It is somewhat analogous to the difference between looking at pictures in an anatomy book and doing surgery on a live subject. This is especially true in the early stages of experience with a remedy where the central feature, the "image of the essence," is barely perceptible to our vision. Thus cases such as these are a most welcome addition to our growing ability to discern what will truly separate one remedy from the next.

Cases

BROWN PELICAN *Pelecanus occidentalis*

CASE 1:

The following case presented in the psychotherapy/homeopathy practice of Anneke Hogeland about one week after the proving was concluded.

A 46-year old woman comes for hypnosis to help deal with side effects of chemotherapy and to prepare for mastectomy and further breast cancer treatment. She mentions that she has taken some *Arnica* and 'detox combos' as well as some *Cadmium sulphuricum*.

She relates her story as follows: her mother was a French socialite who married a US army officer near the end of WWII in Paris. She followed him to the center of the California agricultural community after the war and had her first child, the patient, soon after arriving here. The father had 2 children from a previous marriage. There were 2 other children in the second marriage. The father was a tough disciplinarian and the mother was completely lost and estranged and became highly irrational and violent, especially towards her first-born daughter. The daughter often endured physical beatings and the only way to get the beatings to stop was for her to verbally state "I wish I were dead" and say it with conviction. She had her head stuffed into the toilet on numerous occasions until she would repeat that phrase.

The client left home early and married a man who is not present for her in any significant way. They have a daughter and divorced when the child is 6. The child spends 3 days with mom and 4 with dad and a stepmother.

The woman relates feeling all alone in the world. She states, "There is no connection" and feeling very small. She talks about her Aikido training and not being treated well by the leader of the Dojo. Again and again she talks about feeling as if she does not have connections or any knowledge about how to be in the world.

> COMMENT: *In explaining the possibilities of homeopathy and cautioning her regarding taking combination remedies and just any kind of remedy, I related some of the story of the Pelican proving to her and she spontaneously asked if she could take this remedy. I consented and gave her one dose of Pelican C30/4.*

4 MONTH FOLLOW UP:
Since she took the remedy this woman has made many changes in her life. She relates taking charge of the relationship with her daughter and acting much more like a caring, responsible parent. She has left her Dojo and is experimenting with different teachers. She has also left her church where she felt judged and criticized and has connected with another spiritual community where she feels she belongs. She has started taking care of her house. She has recovered quite well from the surgery and subsequent chemotherapy treatment. She is figuring out how to restructure her nursing job to suit her temperament better. She is also reconnecting with the mother and beginning to have some conversations with her.

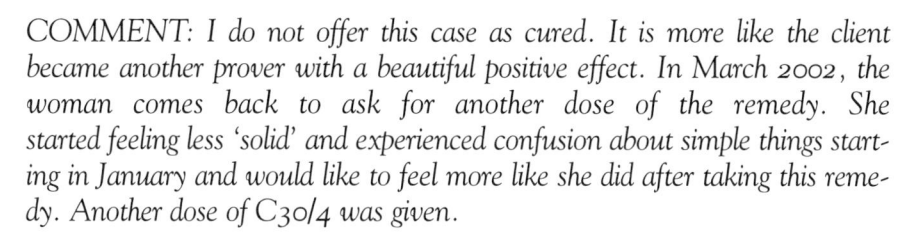

> COMMENT: I do not offer this case as cured. It is more like the client became another prover with a beautiful positive effect. In March 2002, the woman comes back to ask for another dose of the remedy. She started feeling less 'solid' and experienced confusion about simple things starting in January and would like to feel more like she did after taking this remedy. Another dose of C30/4 was given.

CASE 2:

Case taken by Jonathan Shore.

Woman, 40ish, brunette hair in upswept feathery cut, furrowed brow and pinched between eyebrows, Latina good looks. Does neck rotation while JS reads over chart. Eyes bright and large. The case is transcribed from edited videotape.

Chief complaint: Headaches

Why don't you go ahead . . .
44 year old female that been relatively good health. I jog from the git go. I'm always running around, except past 4-5 years. About 3 weeks ago, started getting this headache. Two days later ended up in emergency room. They gave me a couple shots of Demerol but after getting out of drug haze, pain was still at 2-3. It never went away. Had blood work, MRI, CT scan, seen an ENT, my regular internist, a neurologist who admitted me to hospital. Thought I had optic neuritis. Best guess of optic neuritis with atypical headache. Never had headache before. Have high tolerance for pain; have had endometriosis for 17

Cases

years. Told that was my downfall because I can take pain to "5" without taking anything. They said usually headaches don't last 2 weeks. I'm not a headachy person. This isn't normal for me.

I retired from Air Force reserves after 23 years. Don't think I've quite come to grips with that. It hit me harder than I anticipated even though I was ready to retire. I work in a hospital; the head of biomed. My staff maintains medical equipment. I run three hospitals. I like what I do. 80% of my job is public relations. I like to go-go-go. I've gone too much the last 18 months and feel I haven't been good to my body and soul and it's not been good for me. Been a rough 18 mos. I was put on active duty. We had joint commission and accreditation and every time I turned around, there was another regulatory agency coming in. With medical equipment, it's a big thing. I had my job threatened; that I had better do well during joint commission. I'm in a very male dominated world. I can hold my own but sometimes they get to me. I hate having to be at 150% every, every day when other people don't quite have to. At least that's my perception.

> OBS: *Gestures with the hands a lot as she talks. Fingers are long, graceful. Her expression is very animated, attractive and her eyes bright, light, and striking. She speaks quickly but not rushed. She's very comfortable in herself.*

I'm a person that… Discipline equals freedom to me. I'm really keyed into that. I ran track competitively in my 30's. I bowl. I've played softball for years. I like that competion. I like to push myself. That's why I like track.

No children. 2 dogs which I consider my children. I'm the only child of my parent's marriage. I have four brother and two sisters that are all half. Grew up with four brothers and one sister. One of my half-siblings died some years ago of cancer. I like family but I'm also glad that they're all in San Jose and I'm in San Francisco.

It's not been easy for me but I'm one of those who says "I'm going to make it and you can't tell me I can't."

One thing I want out of this life is that I'm a good person and that I was able to give to people, good, bad or indifferent. That I was able to share myself with people. I'm very much into good, close friends. Having a goodness around my space.

There's a few things I want to do in my life. I want to learn to play the piano. I've learned how to play every other instrument; I just haven't learned to play the piano yet.

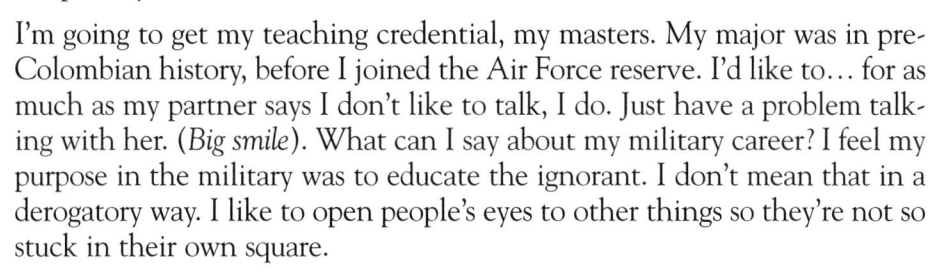

I'm going to get my teaching credential, my masters. My major was in pre-Colombian history, before I joined the Air Force reserve. I'd like to… for as much as my partner says I don't like to talk, I do. Just have a problem talking with her. (*Big smile*). What can I say about my military career? I feel my purpose in the military was to educate the ignorant. I don't mean that in a derogatory way. I like to open people's eyes to other things so they're not so stuck in their own square.

I like to cook; I love to eat. I love to be out in nature and I especially like the water. Especially the water. It's very soothing to me. One thing I love about every day is coming home and having my two dogs just love me to death. No matter what kind of a day I've had, those two puppies are happy to see me. Hopefully now that I have more time, I'll be able to get into the garden and having my back yard look decent again.

Especially since I fixed up my broken wrist which has been broken twice. Once by me and once by someone else! (*Smiles wide*).

I have an interest in psychic things. I like to… I need to get back to meditating. I really liked it when I did it but I let things kind of distract me. That's why I started yoga. To help center me again. Back to meditating and just paying attention to that little voice and that intuition. It's done me very well but sometimes I don't listen. I just get clogged up and that third eye gets just cloudy.

I don't know what else to say.

You're doing great. I have lots of questions. Too many questions! So if you keep on talking, it'll kind of just happen. You just keep on for awhile.
I'm very Catholic. But I believe in god in my own way. I don't feel like I have to do it within the confinement of a building but sometimes I go just to find some quiet and some peace.

BROWN PELICAN CASES

Cases

The one thing I'd like to get back into is running competitively because that's just me and my watch and nothing else. I like that discipline. I like to do stairs and the hills. I like that physical activity. I just crave, crave, crave that physical activity. It'll help get my couch potato body back into some sort of shape.

I don't think "couch potato" quite describes you...
Well, compared to what it used to be. I am a little self-critical.

Maybe we could take that as a point of departure. What do you mean by that exactly?
I think that I'm my own worst judge.

For 23 years, 1 month and 29 days I have been in the guard. I've done my duty. As best as I can. I've tried to mentor up and mentor down. I've done my job and I've done it very well and... I think there was always that slight...I know that I've done a good job but I don't give myself enough credit to look at the whole big picture. If, on a scale of 1-100; my whole military career is a number, I'd give myself an 80. When I retired, I had this dinner and I had people talking and awards were given and I had a lot people from all aspects of my life talking and I see that I was a 98!

When you say "down on yourself," you say what to yourself?
That I haven't been the best that I can be.

And if other people criticize you?
Oooh! Sometimes it might not even be criticism. I see it as criticism, a personal criticism or attack rather than an opinion or a thought. I turn it around to be a personal attack. I do that really well.

And the personal attack?
That my staff don't know what they're doing in their day-to-day tasks, I would take as a personal attack on me because I see it as my responsibility that my staff gets the training and everything they need to do their job.

What's an attack?
To me, an attack is; if I just would think really quickly; it would be a point that I have no control of what is going on. Not that I'm a control freak! But they

want to throw the blame. For instance, when I'm at work; I'm doing my job. It's quiet. There's no noise. And there's another man there, my equal, his department is not quiet but I get blamed. And I have nothing to do with that department.

Somehow, you're sensitive enough, that they get you.
Yes.

So tell me, the Air Force reserve… it's a state job? Not Federal?
Yes, the California International Guard.

Why did you sign up?
I was at college and since my family was poor, I was on the financial assistance program. The criteria for that was that I had to take certain classes having to do with my heritage.

> OBS: *makes the claw sign for "had to take."*

So I had to take Mexican-American studies, and pre-Colombian history and we would have counselors help guide us in our college careers. I played with the idea when I left high school of going into active duty Air Force because I loved the uniform and I wanted to see the world. When you're poor, you haven't even been outside the city you live in, that's all enticing. And in my second year of college, I was getting disenchanted with…that I didn't fit the mold back in 1976-77, of what a Mexican-American, a Latina woman, needed to fill and I started having problems with counselors. I didn't fit into their idea of what a Latina should fit in. I should be into La Raza; I should pronounce my name in Spanish rather than English. And I didn't feel that I needed to do that!

I wanted to go down my own path, the way I wanted to deal with it, without any influence and if I made a mistake somewhere down the line, well what the heck, it was my mistake.

I didn't want to do it! I'm me! And I should be ok just how I am. So my skin is brown and my last name is (common Spanish surname) but I'm still a human being and I still have feelings and wants and desires and I got disenchanted with school. And I thought oh, I can look into the military thing again. And my cousin suggested the International Guard. You can *choose* what you'd like to go into! "Bingo!" So I took this test and they said you're really good at this and this. And they said, "How would you like to go into medical equipment repair?" And

Cases

I said, "What's that?" I wanted to be in the medical field and they said your mechanical and electronic scores are high, especially for a female…

Why the medical field?
I've always had this kind of affinity for medical. I wanted to be a physician at one point. I liked the whole caregiver thing.

What do you like about the caregiver?
You can make a difference when someone's not feeling good.

What I do, it makes things better for the outcome. One thing I learned, when I started taking these classes and I volunteered at hospitals, that I'd get too emotionally involved. And that would be my downfall. Because people die. And they get sick for long periods of time and I realized early that I had a hard time separating that. So my job was just the right chemistry. I could be in an area where…

So it's intentionally abstract?
Yes. In a very emotionally engaged… I would take people's pain and hurt and stuff on and it was very difficult, almost impossible, to be in a space with someone and know that it's ok not to take that on. I would feel a need to want to help them; make them soup, wash their hair, whatever, and that makes me cry all the time.

I have an extreme affinity for the elderly. I think that comes from being raised with my grandmother.

What was your rank?
Senior master sergeant. E8.

How come not "officer?"
You're the second person in a week to ask me that! I think I was just comfortable being in there, one of the guys, rolling up my sleeves. My partner said, "You obviously went into a supervisory role, you're a manager, people love to work with you…"

You're ambitious and competitive and it's a natural…

I think that maybe somewhere, I felt that if I became an officer, I was not going to be… In the military, it's very…(makes hierarchical gesture). It would be hard-pressed to keep up this officer role and be myself.

Tell me about water?
I love water. Water is…I feel like water cleanses my soul. I love water because I feel it rejuvenating, very spiritual, very cleansing, it feeds my soul.

What do mean water? Any water, like a shower or a bath?
The ocean. It could be a lake but I prefer the ocean. Any ocean. I don't mind lakes and stuff but ocean….

Do you ever fly in your dreams?
I do. I've flown and seen the world from up high. I recall watching…like flying from now to where the pyramids were being built. Being like a butterfly watching all this happening. Being able to move and watching all the different parts of all the objects. Just watching.

So you both fly in space and in time.
Yeah, I have. When I wanted to be an Egyptologist, or an archeologist. Then I found that there are snakes out there and uh-uh.

Ever have an interest in birds?
I used to like to watch the robins when they come in springtime, with their red breasts or the blue jays. I'd sit and watch them. Pelicans scare me. Because one tried to attack me one day! I was minding my own business, in Monterey and one came after me. They said it was because I had food in my hand but…

That seems really unusual.
People around me thought it was unusual! (Laughs)

Rx: *Pelec-o 30C*

FOLLOW-UP 2 WEEKS LATER:
OBS: *Comes in dressed in patterned coat, less made up.*

BROWN PELICAN CASES

Cases

Why don't you tell me from the time I saw you last.
Well, I did the remedy and I felt pretty good. Took another 2 doses after the first one.

> OBS: *Voice sounds much younger, softer.*

That weekend, I felt pretty bad, when I called you Monday, and you said that's to be expected so then I actually started feeling better. Till this week. Then the headaches started coming back. So yesterday, still had a headache. It wasn't like a 5. I took a nice shower; had the warm water beating on my neck, using the massager and I went to bed early and I woke up feeling good, really good.

So at the beginning, you took the remedy and right away you felt something?
Later that night, a friend asked me how my headache was and I noticed that the headache was missing and I hadn't noticed it was missing but just for short periods of time.

FOLLOW UP 2 MONTHS LATER:
> OBS: *Looks completely different. Looks white skinned, wearing glasses, hair going grey. Wearing deep red turtleneck.*

So how have you been?
Good. The last couple of weeks had a slight headache but because I was under an extreme amount of stress. Because taking care of partner undergoing shoulder surgery.

Besides the headache, any other change?
I feel all around better.

I feel a little bit more balanced, if I could say that. I'm just feeling better all the way around.

I love my friends. There are people I see at work that I consider my friends and also my acquaintances. I like to cook; I like to have my friends over and cook. That's what I do. I like that. I need that. I like yoga. To me, it's like freedom where for an hour and a half, I don't have to think about anything than trying to get something right. Because I like that discipline. That's why I loved the military so much, so much as I did. That trying to get it right.

FOLLOW UP 1 YEAR:
> *OBS: Hair definitely silver grey. Wearing bright red sweater.*

I started getting headaches again. About 2 weeks ago.

Any particular reason?
I think just overly stressed. I feel like I've hit the wall. I've been very emotional. Very weepy. Very moody in the last month. I think I'm going through a little depression.

Do you think this remedy did anything?
Oh yes! I went off the remedy, when I had my knee done and had all those narcotics and blah blah. I didn't realize until I pulled back and looked at it. It controlled my allergies. I had more energy. I could be tired but…not like now, when it can be 6:30 or 7:00 and I sit down and fall asleep. I'm not sleeping as well. I might sleep for 10 hours but it's not restful sleep. I have a lot of mind chatter.

The big thing is the energy and my allergies. Because people around me would ask, "Are you on some new medication?" because there's a bunch of us and we normally all suffer together. I didn't get it till afterwards, when I realized that I hadn't been taking the remedy and my nose was dripping and I had all this nasal congestion and my eyes were wanting to fall out of my head.

Rx: Remedy was repeated in the 200C with good result.

Cases

SCARLET MACAW Ara macao

Case by Jonathan Shore.

CASE 1:

Woman returns many years after having been given *Ignatia*, which helped her chronic fatigue.

> COMMENT: *She has a certain diathesis: light and thin and sort of intense and bird-like. Long thin bones in the face. Gestures with long thin fingers, fingers spread out, long hands. Fine-boned. She is carefully made-up, dramatic; this says that it's important how she looks. She's vivacious, engaging, attractive, related. It's important for her to have communication. The sexual energy comes into the picture in some way – she's not directly seductive. But the care in her appearance is not so much about fastidiousness as it is about the way she relates to people.*

She never really fully relaxes. When she walks along she thinks, "How am I supposed to live?" She has been involved in her spiritual path for 30 years, yet she still has the question: "what is life or how does one live?" Underlying issue: **"Am I doing it right?"**

She perceives all the information from her environment and **then adjusts herself to behave according to the signals she perceives from others to 'get it right.'** This makes her sad about herself. Relationship is very important to her. Always asking if she's doing it right. "I very much want contact with another person. I want it very specifically."

> COMMENT: *She gestures with her hands like outstretched claws repeatedly.*

I want something from my husband that he doesn't give me. I've trained myself not to want that from him, so I try to spread the need around to other people.

I was wildly, passionately engaged in a virtual email relationship with a gay man in London that had to do with this part of myself that doesn't come out hardly ever. That part was where **I have my voice** and passion and I'm fully alive and free. I felt that I was interesting, flavorful. This part is important because it makes me feel like me. I'm in contact with myself. But I also love to go into meditation where I disappear.

I can experience myself as responsible, hard working. I put a lot of effort into what I do. Diligent. This other part is just free of that.

Her responsibilities don't lie in her home. She's responsible for a spiritual community. It's not to care for the material needs of this one or that one. Yet there's this trap between being herself, an exotic, expressive individual and being in a community as a figurehead, responsible leader. As a younger woman, I had none of this feeling of responsibility. When I entered her spiritual community, this all came on me.

I care about it. It's really what I want to do. But this other part doesn't get to come out: there's a freedom and wildness and a 'flagrancy' to it. It's a combination of beauty and energy and splendor.

The more I talk, the more I feel totally split…I've had this feeling from childhood. Have I gone too far? Is it too extravagant? I have to pull back. I have a fear of being too colorful. Maybe I'm taking up too much space. I'm just kind of splashing. Then I think, 'Oh, I'm too out there.' It's humiliating.

> OBS: *Humiliation has come up a number of times. Aversion to asking questions in groups. But when she gets going, she makes the leap and gets over it.*

Didn't like our big home as a child. Ran away when five. House felt cold. Mom was cold and mean. I didn't get to be colorful. It was a drudge. Felt alone, an orphan. I didn't feel comfortable in existence. It was mostly my family. When I got out I had a great time: putting on plays.

Came because had surgery on R knee some months before which hadn't healed and discomfort is now in the whole leg.

Also has insomnia.

Rx: *Ara macao 30C*

Follow-up one month:
I feel strangely calm inside for being such a tense person.
My knee seems to be recovering from surgery. The knee is definitely responding. There's more a feeling of being centered and inside myself, which is always an issue for me.
I seem to be eating less.
No more low-grade buzzing sensation. It had come as a sort of pulsating wave.

Cases

> COMMENT: *She had not complained about it, because she did not recognize it as a problem. But because it went away, it's safe to assume it was pathological.*

Feeling more relaxed. In that sense, I don't recognize myself. It's not my job to fix what's out there. I can flow with things and still let them be as they are. It's letting go of a lot of responsibility.

She recalls a painting she saw some years ago: a woman's head with two huge birds on either side of her head; they looked like firebirds, as in Russian iconography.

CASE 2:

Presented by Caroline S. Walrad, Ph.D., of Palos Verdes, California, June 14, 1999.

Main Complaint: uterine bleeding, progressing to hemorrhage/ long periods with the last being 35 days to present. She is scheduled for hysterectomy the next week. Chronic depression.

> COMMENT: *Wearing scarf and beautiful decorative pin. Birdlike redness through skin/ nose/ cheeks. Delicate features. Softly spoken. Holds hands like a claw. Laughs/ loves to laugh. Direct eye contact. Attentive listener. Sensitive to environment. She takes in stimuli. Interested and speaks of my environment. Artful. Teaches piano, which is the first thing she tells me upon sitting down.*

Had successful cervical surgery in June – cells clear of cancer
Long and heavy periods of bleeding starting in December
Crying with bleeding/fatigue and exhaustion
Surgery made the complaints worse
< Peanuts and peanut oil
Chronic fatigue and depression/ feels depleted

Emotional:
"Hopeless helpless, stopped taking steps, cut off."
Weepy daily/feels isolated from husband "I isolated myself from him."
Husband supportive of her. "He is caring and thoughtful."

"Feel at crossroads: been for a long time." Sees therapist from June 98 until Dec. Could not afford to see therapist and started to bleed when stopped going to therapist. "Felt stuck, felt like torture/ painful physically and mentally/ allow myself no rest."

Does not sleep well.
"I am angry, I want to study piano but I feel guilty that I should make a better living in the corporate setting.
"My husband makes me feel guilty. I am an artist. I don't want to give up my creative work."

She feels badly about one woman friend. Her friend became busy and does not see her any more. She cannot figure it out. They used to get together on a weekly basis. Her friend and she were "together on a heart path and deep spiritual path, but now she has her own life without me."
She loves hugs. Gave me hugs three different times in the consultation.

Growing up:
"Mom was not a nourishing person and would not do things to show love.
"I used to bite my nails. I worried about my safety and security.
"My mother was not a place for love. I must do work on my feminine side. I want to have relationships with women."

From an alcoholic family/ did not have her needs met. Feels "I must protect my boundaries. I can be brought down easily.
"I felt like soaring when I was a kid. I felt jealousy from my family be-cause of this. I needed to be honored for what I was.
"I am tired and feel like I constantly struggle. I want to learn how not to.
"I must be patient and let synchronicity happen and have faith in that process."

"In June '98 I felt the universe was not supporting events. I was in perimenopause and had felt under tremendous stress from finances for a long time and it had taken its toll. I wanted to work on issues with my husband and he did not, so now I am working on things myself. I lack courage. I do not have it when I need it.

Cases

When I was younger I felt more empowered and independent. Now I must reflect on other things to heal. I have been doing a lot of work on my ego. To be strong meant to build up ego when I was working in corporate setting. After I quit, I wanted to work on my spiritual path more" (crying).

"I am mad at the universe and stopped doing things, like no longer being able to talk to my therapist. It does not feel safe talking to my friends. **I am torn between wanting to make a change and feeling responsible for it and how to get support from people around me.** It is best to pull in and be quiet and I haven't quite figured it out. I have had losses in friendships that have been quite devastating."

"I knew of poverty. My mother reminded me often when dad was on strike. I remember the way people looked at me when pins held my skirt together. Sisters in school looked at me. There was much we did without, emotionally and physically. I am grateful for my parents because they do have a lot of goodness in them."

Bleeding:
Crying with the bleeding – fatigue and exhaustion. Menses are heavy "they burst out like a gel." Dark as a gel and very large clots.

Q: How large?

"As large as my hand." After the surgery the clots and blood are a little redder. Currently in 35th day of bleeding without stopping. Heaviest days 13-24.

OTHER PHYSICALS/ GENERALS:
Hair loss/ lots of fine hair (not in clumps)
COLD/ always hands and feet
Allergies to cats, dogs, bird feathers, horses
Dyslexia
Craves: 'carbs,' bread, pasta, loves potatoes/ good appetite/ hungry often
Drinks little/ likes iced tea/ no hot coffee or tea
> vegetables, fruit, garden burgers
< fish, chicken, turkey, peanuts (3)
Perspires all over >open window
She brought in a typed sheet of paper with all of her nutritional supplements on it. It filled an entire 11-inch page.

SLEEP:
"Not the best with the change."

DREAMS:
Recurring Dream: "I am driving and asking for directions."
She is on one side of a mountaintop and wants to get to the other side. The 'tract' between the two tops was too skinny and she couldn't cross. "I found a little boat like a Nest. There I was sitting in my husband's arms and could not get across"
"My dreams are limiting"

Q: *If homeopathy and I could give you one thing today, what would it be?*
"Have space to be creative: I do not need a lot. Friends and family come to visit me and then they would leave when I wanted them to. I want to be in nature and do things like bird watching, take nature hikes. I want the courage to be alone."

Q: *Tell me more about your 'space'.*
"When I was growing up I had no space. There was one bedroom for six kids. Everything was stuffed into drawers and I had one drawer for all things. I always was seeking to go outside of the house. If I had money, it was a negative. I am very different from my family and that was easy for them to see.

COMMENT: *articulate and uses hands to talk.*

Rx: *Ara macao 30C*, one dose

SCARLET MACAW CASES

FOLLOW UP JUNE 24, 1999, ONE WEEK LATER:
She called me and said, "Thank you." Fatigue gone; energy ++++. She canceled her surgery, and was going to the OB/GYN instead. Bleeding stopped. No more "Dark and Gloom"

FOLLOW UP JULY 19, 1999:
Still allergic to feathers. Naps every day. Sensitive skin, flaky scalp, and dandruff. Red and itchy and burning scalp. Still has allergies. Had a regular period. Hot flashes stopped (she now explains she had them every night.)

Rx: *wait*

Cases

FOLLOW UP OCTOBER 1999:
Telephone consultation: Depression starting to return.

Rx: *Ara macao 30C*, one dose

FOLLOW UP JANUARY 2000:
Office visit: depression returning and longer bleeding during menses.

> COMMENT: *Wearing a bright red sweater with a blue and red silk scarf and a pin. I found her vibrant.*

Rx: *Ara macao 30C*, 3 times (divided dose)

FOLLOW UP JUNE 2000:
I called her. She feels GREAT. She went for counseling with her husband to consider a divorce. It is mutual decision to go. She has begun teaching piano full time and has a full load of students. She felt wonderful. Felt "assured and confident." She "trusts in the universe." They are divorcing, selling their home and she is moving into a small but wonderful back part of a house where she has fruit trees and can hear the night animals. She can walk outside in her little garden.

FOLLOW UP SEPTEMBER 2000:
No need of remedy. Feels better than in June.

CASE 3:
Presented by Douglas Brown, CCH, FNP, RSHom (NA)

INITIAL CONSULT 7/14/01: 9 yr. old girl, "C."
Bullies at school. Stressed me to see bullies torturing my friends. Felt helpless, hurt. In my heart felt really down low. That my friends were being hurt. That people were being hurt.

> COMMENT: *She's a sensitive, poetically expressive soul.*

Fitting in is stressful. Finding friends.
Anger that I was kept back. Very angry (3). A little embarrassed.
Angry when people get hurt. Angry when I'm forced to do work without much help. Doing solitary work. No connection. It wore me out.

COMMENT: *The connection with the group is very important to her.*

I love to read (3). Felt anger when told to write about one of a set of topics. Stressed by having to write. I press my fingers together; feel tension, when writing. Anger (3). Writing with a clenched fist. I HATE WRITING. I LOATHE WRITING! (4)

COMMENT: *Tremendous and startling contrast between love for reading and hatred for writing.*

I love Harry Potter. It sucks me in. I can't stop reading. Imagination. Fascination. Swiss Family Robinson. How to fit into life. Figure out how to live there.

COMMENT: *Second mention of issue of "fitting in."*

I like animals (3). Dogs and horses. They're so active. I want to have a collie; they're so gentle.
I like swimming, love swimming.

COMMENT: *She's passionate about many things.*

I want to be a really good swimmer. Not really competitive. **Come up with my own way of being, my own strokes.** It gives me joy to be in the water. I feel more connected to my birthplace. I feel so joyful (3). So happy to be in the water. I learn really quickly at strokes. Really quickly.

My favorite ball sport is baseball. Don't really like to be competitive against other teams. I like giving my best at it and going for it. Running for bases.

I like to run. I'm not good at it; I don't win races. I feel joyful. I feel like I'm flying. I don't have to 'put in' exercise. I love to exercise a lot (2).

COMMENT: *She's joyful, passionate; loves to* **be in her body and feel the movement.** *She feels she's flying.*

I love riding my bike. I feel I can go so fast. Nice family time. The joy of riding my bike. It really lifts me up. I have a lot more joys than troubles.

I asked about her relationship with her brother.

SCARLET MACAW CASES

Cases

I really love him but he's really annoying. I'm mostly really happy to be with him. We call each other best friends. He hates to wake up, just like I do. Now I baby-sit him, but it's more like playing together.

Once I walked by him and he started screaming. Mom told me to go away when I wanted to be playing right there. Angry! Confused. Don't know what I did and then I'm sent away. Curious as to why he did that. It's mostly fun to be with him.

> COMMENT: *I feel she's genuine here; that she gets into a conflict and doesn't know what she did that caused the problem.*

I want to stay in childhood. Joy!

When I get angry I don't get ordinarily angry. I have **bigger** feelings. I'm scared of my feelings. It scares me when I'm angry. I feel all shriveled up, useless and helpless. My feelings are coming out and lashing at me. They scare me. I don't like to be at scared.

I can't control my anger. It's very destructive. I feel outraged. I loathe everything in the whole entire world. I didn't want to be alive. I wanted to die right then and there. More and more feelings get added to each other. Create an explosion.

> COMMENT: *Her feelings are big, full of passion, and overwhelming.*

Dream?
Joyful. Me turning into a mermaid. I love swimming as much as I love reading. There's a gate at the swimming pool. Gate opened and shark swam out. I was hurt on my leg. Struggling. Shark nudged me, but didn't bite me, and I turned into a mermaid. Shark carried me back into hole where I lived.

Your feeling?
Happiness. Swimming. I love imagining my birth, being cradled by my mother, father, and midwife.

Another dream: Big Mountain. The solstice — summer and winter solstice — the mountain changes form. The stairs come. Lots of carvings. Surrounded by water. Under the surface (of the water) there are carvings of creatures; underwater dragons, sharks, fish, piranhas, dolphins. The biggest is a carving of dragon with water coming out of his mouth.

Mount Mystery: Everyone was blinded. Couldn't see anything until the next day. I dive in. The instant I touch water I turn into a mermaid. I call the carvings alive, and the mountains change. There are levers on each side of the stairway. I motion all the sharks and piranhas out of the way. The water is perfectly clear. The villagers can't see this. A few families with children swim to the steps; went up the steps. Children who didn't have masks turn into mer-people.

A magic place. Living in mountain. A crystal/magic ball that showed us anything we wanted to see.

SCARLET MACAW CASES

> COMMENT: *Many references to seeing, vision, sight, in a fantastically creative, colorful setting full of animals, water, the tropics, magic, and exploits.*

A celebration of water, creatures of the water. We especially praised the water dragon. At the first rays of dawn we had to get down. I was stranded up there.

Dreams of water, being able to see and paradoxically breathe under water are not unusual in birds.

Like a volcano rising out of the water. The dragon was HUGE, lifted me, and I climbed down his neck. He carried me down to the land. I was shaky, scared. Didn't want to be closed up inside the mountain, fall, and die. I like to help people. Moved the dangerous animals away.

Fears?
Disney movies. Scary when people are getting hurt. Bad guys. Scared when people are getting hurt. After 101 Dalmatians felt I never wanted to see a movie again.

An enchanting sky to see how everything fits in perfectly at the end…

The teacher scolded me for doing it. I didn't notice I was doing it. My eyes roll. The left eye is the main eye. It rolls up and out to the corner. Happens when stressed, when my friends are bullied, when I'm made to write.

Cases

Significant Past Medical History: Born at home; **it was a water birth**. Shortly after birth became cyanotic, collapsed. Required intubation, CPAP. Also developed severe jaundice. Later in infancy had poor weight gain, poor feeding.

Dengue fever at 2 and a half while in Cambodia. Episodic pinworm.

ROS:

Allergic symptoms of itchy eyes, sneezing; occasionally given Claritin. Photosensitivity.

Orthodontic problems.

Constipation with large stools, anal tears.

Family history of depression, suicide, heart disease.

Generals: She's warm-blooded (not so significant at this age), has little thirst, and is worst at waking and in evening.

> *Observation: She is light, thin, refined. Intense facial expression. Scaly red rash on chin.*

MOTHER: C. has developed friends with children in school and church settings and places a high value on these relationships. Her brother L. was born after C. turned 6. C. was in her Montessori School and seemed very angry with L. She was sullen, acted out often, and sometimes said that she wanted to kill herself. C. has continued harassing behaviors towards L. through the present, with a few glimpses of very caring behavior lately.

Changing schools was very hard for her. She lost a friendship, and there are fewer potential friends. She wants to go back and recreate the fun times they had. Immersed herself in reading. Sneaks into the bathroom, where the lights are, and reads far into the night. When some children harassed her at school one day because she didn't have a clue about TV shows, she didn't know she was being harassed because she was reading and had tuned them out completely. She has a lot of compulsive type behaviors:

>Fingernail biting
>Toenail biting
>Reading compulsively. Will re-read Harry Potter several times over.
>Eye rolling
>Widen her eyes; fix her stare at something for a few seconds
>Looking out of the corner of her eye, turning head to see straight ahead
>Clicking big toes over adjacent toes

In school was sullen. Greeted and departed with other children with a handshake, no hugs. Spent hours and hours practicing cursive writing technique. **There was no spontaneous free flow of writing.**

When teacher killed a wasp C. cried, said the wasp had been murdered. Teacher ended up crying with C.

Major problems trying to get C. to do her work. She's easily overwhelmed, **much of it busywork that was very repetitive or re-writing material written by others.** She continually fell behind. C. was not allowed to write freely, and continued to work on cursive handwriting technique for the first half of the year. They said if they put her in a creative writing group before completing her cursive work, then she would write in print (horrors!). We continued to lobby for more free-writing opportunities. The only writing asked of C. was endless lists to copy. One day C. came home saying, School killed my big imagination." We went to talk to the principal, who responded, "If you would get all your work done then you would have time to do the creative stuff you like." We pulled her out of school; they said they didn't know what to do with a girl like C.

A story: C. brought home her math work at the end of her school year. 7 wks in a row was the exact same basic addition math facts, maybe 80 problems. They wanted her to be able to complete this in a specified time. Each week she didn't finish it and they would reassign it the next week. This illustrates two things about C. She doesn't want to do things at a quick, prescribed rate (she knew the math facts) and she has enough sense of self that she is not going to change the way she does something to meet someone else's expectations, that she herself doesn't see a need for. She is very angry about having been given the same paper over and over.

In new school C. wanted to please her teacher with her work. But still C. clutched her pencil with a stranglehold and struggled to write even more than a few sentences. If writing is a homework assignment there were tears and fights with parents. Any suggestion that she improve, edit, or do something herself was frequently the cause of throwing down her homework.

FATHER: On May 3rd I noticed C. rolling her eyes. Both pupils would roll up and then over to the side and stay up for a few seconds. C. was aware of this and said sometimes they would get stuck up there. At first just in the evening. Dr. said it was "behavioral." It was quickly apparent that it was involuntary. On May 7th father went to pick C. up from school. C. was still in classroom.

Cases

Teacher explained that whole class had not completed their writing assignment and that she "had gotten stern with them." C. was the only one in the classroom. She was seated with her chair turned around from its usual position and was facing toward the windows in the back of the room. She was staring straight ahead, her hands clenched to the chair. She was shaking slightly, and her eyes watered. Aside from a fierce stare, her face was expressionless. I had never seen her like that before. I took all this in while telling her it was time to go home. She didn't move. When I tugged her arm it was stiff. She hit me and screamed for me to leave her alone. She cried on the way home and would not talk about anything. That night she became very upset when during another homework assignment, typing a writing project she had completed, she hit her mother and ended up crying. Later, after calming down, I was tucking her into bed when she talked with me about what was going on. She said that at school she had not been able to write. Teacher talked to her about how important writing was. C. said, 'Since I can't write there is no place for me on earth; I'm just taking up space someone else should have.' She had turned her chair to face the window and was wondering if she should jump out.

Parents have pulled her out of this school and now C. is home-schooled.

COURSE OF TREATMENT:
    7/16/2001   *Lauroc* 1M, 12C. No effect.
    10/4/2001   *China* 1M, 12C. No effect.
    3/7/2002   *Verat-a* 200C, 20X
    3/15/2002   *Veratrum* 200C, 20X to hold. No effect.

VISIT (TELEPHONE) 3/27/02:
Still lots of eye rolling. Disappointment when all the fun of birthday party was over, friends went home. Anger. Sadness. Gets boring doing the same old thing. "It made me feel happy and glad, that it's my birthday and that something special was happening.

I really miss my friends at school. Dream about friends from church. Happy and content with friends.

I didn't understand why they wouldn't let me write my own stories (at school). I don't want to write their stories. I want to write whatever I'm thinking, whatever is in my imagination. They weren't giving me the right to write what's in my imagination. Unfair. They were crushing my imagination.

What is it like to have your imagination crushed?
It's like being a parrot that has been out in the wild, made to live in a cage. It's not thought of (for itself). Not getting any attention. Not getting to do what it wants.

Plan: *Ara-m 200C*

VISIT 8/18/02:
No more eye rolling. "It's easier to accept things as they are. Easier not to fight with L. or with my parents. Remedy has been working really well.

After I took the remedy I wasn't seeing my parents as being against me. Before they said they were on my side but it didn't feel that way. I used to fight a lot with my Mom. I used to see schoolwork as another chore. Now I see it as an opportunity to learn, for my own good. So I can be more motivated to do my work well.

I don't know if it's the reduced fighting or the remedy. But I think it was the remedy that seemed to reduce the fighting.

I started writing a book report on Ben Franklin. Did it little by little. I composed a 7-page book report (Excited and proud). The same weekend I finished I learned to drive the lawn mower! I got so much done, my parents were thrilled! Parents planned a surprise party for me. My Mom was wearing blue and purple; I was confused as to why my Mom was dressed up…My parents gave me a journal as a present…since I was writing so many things they thought I should have someplace to write things down.

How do you feel about writing?
It's not one of my favorite hobbies, but it's not one of my enemies. I accept it. Don't have anything against it. Ben Franklin my favorite historical character. He invented so many things; he was amazing. A model for me, and for future generations. He even proposed to a French lady! Did so much!"

COMMENT: *Surmise: he was a creative,* **colorful character***!*

SCARLET MACAW CASES

Cases

I saw my old teacher, and didn't feel angry with her. She was really the best teacher I could have had. She didn't always attend to me; at home my Mom gives me a lot of her time and attention, and there are no schoolmates to bother me. I would really like to have a dog.

Dreamless sleep. I think I should tell you that I wrote down the dream of the Magic Mountain. It has proved to be a pretty good story!

COMMENTS BY DOUG BROWN:

C. was brought to me by her parents. In addition to eye pain, dizziness, insomnia, and other symptoms, she developed a number of compulsive behaviors, including odd rolling movements of her eyes. Her parents were concerned about the possibility of depression, as after a difficult encounter at school she became extremely upset and said she wanted to kill herself.

An ophthalmologist had diagnosed hysteria. A conventional psychiatric evaluation may well have diagnosed depression and obsessive-compulsive disorder, and stressed a family history of suicide and depression. Each diagnosis implicitly invokes a model of what is wrong: in the former case, a somatic expression of intra-psychic conflict; in the latter, and a biological inheritance of an imbalance of neuro-transmitters in the brain.

C.'s distress was upsetting the entire family, and the parents wanted, understandably, to understand their daughter's difficulties, some way of explaining it. Yet neither promised a satisfactory cure. How could homeopathy help?

After talking with C. at length, I learned that although she loved to read, she "*loathed*" writing. Curious, I asked her to tell me more about that. It seems that even though she was at a Montessori School, which is famous for respecting the individuality of learning styles, she had felt her creativity stymied. "They were crushing my imagination." Her suicidal despair at school occurred after her teacher insisted she keep her writing to the assigned topic. Eye-rolling, saliva-swishing, and other odd, automatic type of behaviors occurred mostly when she felt forced to give up individual, creative expression for the sake of the class.

"What exactly do you feel like," I pressed C., "when you're forced to abandon your creative expression?" After thinking a little, she suddenly responded with an image: "Like a parrot in a cage!"

What a fascinating metaphor, I thought. A parrot, after all, is the embodiment of creativity denied. In spite of all its color, it cannot voice anything original, but simply "parrots" back what it is told. I researched what was known about the homeopathic remedy made from parrot feather, known as *Macaw*.

A proving of a feather of the Scarlet Macaw was carried out by Jonathan Shore in 1999, the details of which are available through Reference Works.

Themes and symptoms, which came up through the proving, which were also strong in C.'s case include:

> Tension between INDIVIDUALITY AND THE GROUP
> Tension between the sense of self and the need for expression
> Expression of what is really oneself versus being an integral part of family and society
> Individuation
> Relationship / Group
> Individuality vs. group
> Individuality, sense of
> Feeling of self
> Nervousness, sensation of
> Relax, able to, never
> Tense

In addition to the correspondence between the proving and C.'s state, other aspects of C. helped increase my confidence in this remedy. She has a tremendous attachment to animals. Also, she has a refined, spiritual sensitivity. Shore describes people who need bird remedies as having a particularly "fine vibration, light yet intense. They are sensitive in a psychological way." This is very true of C. He also noted stabbing, stitching pains in the eye, and vision disturbances in the provings of hawk, raven, and eagle. While eye symptoms did not specifically come up in the Macaw proving, it is possible that eye symptoms are common to the bird family.

After two better-known remedies that seemed indicated by repertorization of symptoms failed to act (*Laurocerasus, Veratrum album*), I prescribed a single dose of *Macaw*.

The results have been dramatic. Two weeks after the dose she announced that she was "considering giving up her aversion to writing." Three months later, her mother reported that her daughter is full of joy, and that "she now identi-

Cases

fies herself as a writer!" The eye rolling and other compulsive behaviors have completely stopped. In addition, C. no longer is oppositional and difficult about studies, or about getting along with her brother. C. reported with joy that she was given a writing journal as a present, "since I was writing so many things they thought I should have a place to write things down."

RING DOVE (WOODPIGEON) *Columba palumbus*

This is a case by Jonathan Shore.

CASE 1:

11-year-old girl, somewhat plump, longish hair, which gives her the appearance of having a short neck.

The girl has been treated homeopathically since birth. Many remedies were given with no success. A year ago the mother brought her back. This is the case from that time.

CC: Chronic cough for almost a year.

> *OBS: Looks sad – throughout the whole interview she is fiddling with her hands and fingers; she is twisting a little thing; puts it in her mouth; puts fingers into her mouth. Jacket zipped up tightly. Hair disheveled. She is holding herself to be small, contained, keeps things inside.*
>
> *COMMENT: the girl's mother is crazy. As a child, she had one of these terrible lives: molested by grandfathers, uncles and aunts. But she has a husband now, who provides her with material security, the opportunity to lead a spiritual life. Now she is connected to the lineage of her guru, has dreams of her guru's guru, and is very deeply committed to a life of service.*

The daughter has never encountered the molesting kind of people. Her family is loving. But she has inherited the mother's kind of energy around sexual stuff. One of the physical pathologies of the daughter is that her vagina closes and they must use steroid cream to keep it open.

The mother has been very sick her whole life; so the child began to worry she would be like her Mother. The girl says: "Ever since I've been sick I have had a worry. It's because I thought it was my fault I was sick." *Note: Meaning if she does not get it right, she will end up like her mom.*

She seems young for her age. Really she's quite sick.

If she has diarrhea she cries that it's because she ate the ice cream.

Q: What do you really like to do?
I like to go to Maui.

Cases

Q: *What is it about Maui that you like?*
The beach.

Q: *What's the worst thing?*
Going to the market every day.
"We have five birds, six goldfish." Have two cockatiels, etc. Mother says that the girl was a bird person in her former life. Mother: "She's one of the happiest people I've ever known. She and her brother play for hours. They carry on. The birds are the kids' home life. They love the birds. She is a bird woman."

Q: *If you could be whatever bird you'd like to be, what one would it be?* "Macaw." The mother says "No, Eagle." Note: *This is what her mother wants her to be.*
The girl likes that birds fly and are pretty. They live in trees.
Mother: "Her vagina is closing up again. When she was very young, she took on my incest trauma. It started hurting her from before she was verbal; the inside was hurting her. She would come to me and cry and say 'I have all these worries'.
"She and her brother play for hours. They play with birds and things. She does have friends from school. She'd like things to be perfect."
"The girls in my class are mean. I don't wear their clothes. They're snobby, snotty."

Q: *What do you call it when you play with the birds?*
They step up (motions a ladder-like movement with fingers) your fingers. She used to want to be a vet, now does not want that anymore. It's too hard; she does not want to be responsible, she wants to breed birds.

Analysis: This is Dove: sensitive, the world is harsh, the sexual abuse and guilt.

Rx: *Colum-p 200C*

FOLLOW UP IN THREE MONTHS:
Q: *Did the remedy have an effect?*
Yeah. I guess it had some.
Q: *Like what?*
It made me express my emotions.

Q: Like what?
It maybe made me more aware of things.

Q: Like what?
What's happening around me. (OBS: *she looks a bit more open, face is more expressive.*) I had a couple of dreams.

Q: When you came you were quite sick with the flu. How long did it take to get over that?
Her mother thought she was getting better right away. Still coughing, but the cough is less.

Q: Stomach pains?
Well I get a lot of that. Lasts a few hours. Like if I do something, I think it's my fault.

Q: If you do something like what?
Like not being nice to someone. Or if I had stomach aches. Not taking good enough care of my pets, my fish. Dreams that her fish died.
Her brother and she would play with two alligator toys. "We'd play that the alligators love each other but it sort of got out of hand so we don't play that anymore."

Q: You mean they had sex with each other? (OBS: Chin quivers, tears come.)
Vagina opened. Used old, old cream but only had to use it a few times. The mother says that when the vagina opened up, dreams as if the girl had actually been molested started to appear.

FOLLOW UP IN SIX MONTHS:
I'm OK. I just make sure I don't have too much ice cream. Mother: then she'd get diarrhea.
Used to have abdominal cramps and diarrhea and come into mother's room and then she'd say, "It's all my fault. I had too much ice cream."
Has ice cream every day, but bowels are "not too bad."
Had a stuffy nose and allergies, but is fine. Hasn't gotten a real cold since March. (Mother goes into every symptom.)
Likes to read a lot. Likes to get in the tree house and read for two hours.
Likes to go outdoors and catch bugs.

RING DOVE CASES

Cases

> COMMENT: *I used to have doves and let them go out of the cage for a while. The doves would do this; hang out in the tree. They never went anywhere.*

The mother opened the girl's vagina only 2/3 of the way. Then the mom quit fiddling with it. She looked today before appointment and it stayed open 2/3 of the way. The girl is getting more independent. She wants Mom out of the way.

FOLLOW UP ONE YEAR LATER:
Much more direct and open.
Vagina has stayed open.
Remedy has worked for the acutes as well.
Onset of menses came at age 13. Normal flow.

CASE 2:

This is a case taken by Sharon Stanley on Feb. 21, 1999. Description: Stocky. Long hair gives the appearance of short neck.

A young woman in a blue T-shirt with long brown hair. She had a dinner on Saturday with a particular couple of guests. Was worried about doing the party. She dreads having to fix food for people. This was a high-powered couple, connected to her husband's company. Brings out all her insecurities about her lack of success.

> OBS: *lots of hand movements, long fingers, all the movement starts from the wrist and she can bend her fingers backwards in a curve.*

Theme with me: I'm not one of the good people.
I used to say, I'm going to commit suicide.

Q: *Say more about that.*
Since my sister committed suicide. I became very depressed in my twenties. Can feel things are pointless. It helps if I am excited about something.

> OBS: *Her voice is quite flat.*

I was very religious then too.

I was so lonely, after my sister died.

I was sixteen before someone came along who taught me how to learn to ride a bike. Early, her Dad felt she was too young to ride a bike. When she finally got one, she hid it because she was too ashamed that she didn't know how to ride.

> OBS: *Her world is constituted of shame. It doesn't matter where she finds herself. Whatever it is, she thinks, "I didn't do it right. I'm ashamed of this." She feels unworthy. Feels different, unacceptable for how she is.*

I live with a sense of shame about how I've managed my life. Looks back and understands why she's lived her life as she has.

Still she doesn't fit. In office, doesn't like gossip, doesn't chatter. It isn't that I look down on these people.

Likes to read. More introspective. I tend to be kind of cerebral. I don't let go easily. I very rarely let my hair down.

I liked my junior year in Europe. Liked taking music classes, even though classmates were 20 years younger than her. I enjoyed it. On the other hand, was in choir with high school girls who were really mean. That was a mistake.

As a child, lonely. Even before Kathy committed suicide.

I just hated my Dad.

RING DOVE CASES

Q: *Did he molest?*
"Yeah." Father molested her older sister who committed suicide. "It's a problem, it's an issue today, that memory is unreliable."

Likes to dance – did even when she was young. There were girls who ridiculed her. "Ridicule – I really have a thing about it. I have a fear about it. It goes back to not feeling loved and this whole perfectionist thing of not feeling loved."

Q: *Tell me about your birds?*

Cases

"I really love them. I had the feeling that the birds chose us. It had a rightness about it. At night, when it's time to go to bed, they're like two little fluff balls. I feel perfectly content watching them."

> COMMENT: *The dove motif is prevalent.*

When they moved here, she did not want to. She wanted to go to the East Coast. Her husband said he couldn't move to the East Coast. He said he couldn't stand it. "I would never say that. I would never say I couldn't stand it. I know I can endure anything."

> COMMENT: *Who would say that? Only someone who must have suffered terribly and endured.*

I sometimes feel that it's my fault. Sometimes I slam cupboard doors.

Dream: pulled her nephew out of water who was drowning; I saved him. Still remembers the feeling of it. That feeling of salvation.

UTI, which she tried to treat herself. Later got a urethritis which was treated though may still not be normal.

Sex drive inactive since she got married. Has masturbated just to improve her sex drive, but she's not into it. "I don't care."

There's a hymn, "Spirit of God Descend upon my Heart." The spirit of Christ descends in the form of a dove. One line of that hymn I have always resonated with: Don't give me the big dramatic stuff, but take the dimness from my soul away. Teach me to love thee as thy angels love. One holy passion filling all my frame. The kindling of the heaven descended dove. My heart an altar, my life long flame.

> OBS: *There's a sort of heaviness about her. She's sort of earth-bound. There's something about dove and spirit that lifts her up. You can see this while she recites the hymn.*

Rx: *Colum-p 200C*

FOLLOW UP IN SIX WEEKS:
Tired for a day or two. Had returned from vacation, but it felt different than usual. Life is going on as it has.

Dream the night after remedy with a bunch of doves and delight.

Has begun to practice and play the piano again which feels very good.
Job hunting.

Spiritually, went on a retreat. "It was really an extraordinary experience. The discussion and my participation – I was really grooving. Afterwards, at least 3 or 4 people approached me and told me how much my insights meant. That's unprecedented. Normally I say things and they're met with silence.

"The priest approached me and thinks that I have that spiritual gift. Ever since we got those doves, last August, those doves have changed my life. This retreat was really something."

"Monday night at work I realized, 'I feel great' and I couldn't explain it."

Common to Dove cases 1 and 2:
- Both have a feeling of shame, bad, wrong, guilt – it's my fault. Issues around sex – with shame.
- The world is a harsh place.
- Slow development. The second case is an older, tougher, more compensated version of the other.
- The physical structures are similar: more dumpy than elongated. In both cases other girls were being mean to them. They both felt pain deeply.
- There is a quality of sweetness. The second case said her birds were sweet. The mother of the girl referred to a sweetness, like you don't see in other girls these days.
- Perfectionism, wanting things to be perfect.

CASE 3:
Case taken by Alize Timmerman, Hahnemann Instituut, Netherlands.

NOVEMBER 2001:

ALIZE'S OBSERVATIONS: Woman, 59 years old. Graying, neatly groomed. High eyebrows. Often looks away, to the outside, or up in the air. Gesturing, almost helpless with arms (as if flapping wings that don't fly). She is small; her posture has a Baryta-look. Her friends, who are also my patients, always have given me the impression about her that she is so peaceful, kind and full of warmth and attention to her friends; they are very fond of her. While she often has the desire to be on her own, she will never ever say no. She is quite confused about her life, but very easy and acceptable to the outside world. Very, very peaceful.

RING DOVE CASES

Cases

Hives, skin irritation, on her bottom, on her entire body, but not on abdomen and back. Bumps. She says: "That's it." She's angry. Does not enjoy life. Tired.

Anger, great anger. "Everyone could walk over me." Feels very vulnerable. She cannot do anything with the anger – it cannot come out. Everything is too much.

I have to be the quiet child, lie down quietly and not open my mouth. Just take it.

We have to throw it out! Crying helps.
Thought I had left my fear behind me. I don't dare to take any steps, If I step outside, they can see me and I will die. I identify with a mole; I prefer to be underground, hibernating with food and warmth.
Her birth was not wanted. Her mother wanted to commit suicide. "I was a 'present'. She poured her heart out to me, too much. But I was not well received by the others." She was blue for 1 1/2 years, a sad coldness (*Lauroc*). She was put in bed with her brothers to keep her warm. "I liked that, I got attention. My sister denies that, she denies me, which is very painful. I can understand that – she is so easily frightened. She tries to hide from life."
I was in the way. I was the smallest one, needed a lot of attention. Endless breastfeeding, I could not be without it.

Mother died, again not saying goodbye.

Ex-husband went with a much younger woman. We divorced 6 years ago. I cried on the sofa. The traitor. **He left me alone**. I could not believe it. My heart was broken."

When I listened to music I felt everything. I could be ecstatic over beauty. I used to enjoy being by myself so peacefully. Then I would cry in bed at night.

It's difficult to care for myself. It costs enormous amounts of energy to do things. I don't do anything for myself. I am blocked from doing things for myself.

Fear in dark, being made mad, she could not express herself.
As a child she saw everything (clairvoyantly), they laughed at her. She saw dead people.

She does not remember huge pieces of her past. Was **abandoned** by her father when the chips were down. Since her grandmother and aunts died she realizes that something was wrong; that **she was kept at a distance**. She is starting to feel more about it.

She feels everything in her heart. Her heart is her "pain point." Her heart pulls her into the past. It feels a bit crazy to feel so deeply but it also feels very good.

She imagined herself flying high seated on a big bird – something with Atlantis.

She is infatuated with birds. Calls herself a night owl. Sees a nest of eaglets.

Rx: *Bubo-v 30C*

7 WEEKS AFTER INITIAL VISIT:

> COMMENT: *Treatment with Owl did not have a big effect. Nothing is worse, nothing is better. Maybe a slow improvement. She does not want a BIG change.*

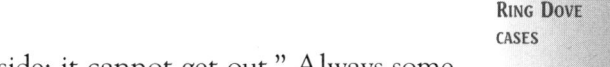

"It's crying on the inside. The grief is inside; it cannot get out." Always some homesickness; crying for what is lost and what she cannot get back.

I am a night owl. I don't take any steps to live. I want to get moving for myself. I have a hard time with regularity. I don't feel like anything. I am tired. I don't push myself. I am in my own way. I have no joy. I cannot see the light.

I am so cold. My bones actually get cold; I need to take a hot bath to be warm.

Cannot express anger. Trying to ignore that part of myself. I allow it to live in the dark underground. I withdraw, I need to withdraw."

DREAM: I could take a step down into my own consciousness, last night, half dream, half awake, I could stay there. I was not afraid. There were very dark enormous clouds, like waves, and I could just look at, and the water, I know it was very important.

I don't understand how people get the energy or awareness to undertake things; I don't have that at all. I lost a huge piece of energy after mother died.

Cases

I feel it in my heart – (holds hand on her heart) my heart is especially a very painful area.

I eat a lot of chocolate, sugar in tea; my life would not be worthwhile if I could not have tea with sugar. Maybe it would be ok if it was warm water with sugar. That is truly important. I can forego everything, but not tea with sugar.

It is very easy for me to see when someone else needs something and then to offer it. I have not been in a shop for about half a year to buy anything for myself. I would prefer it if I could just order it and things would enter my house that way. Beauty can touch me." She points to a statue in the room and says that beauty can touch her. Yesterday I had some hunch that I should be doing something again, like painting, not that I am very good, but to work things out.

Rx: *Colum-p 30C*

6 1/2 MONTHS AFTER INITIAL VISIT:
Organizing is easier.
Fear of what she may or may not find.
Fear of teaching.
Thinking much more of herself.
Working in a team is a good process; I don't withdraw as much.

I listen more to my own voice. Is it ok to make mistakes?

> OBS: *She is talking much more.*

Abuse: universal grief over some part of the world; it is changing.

This period of time was HEAVY. I have more of **a feeling for the justice of everything.** My cat just died a beautiful death. I have to get used to her not being there. I miss her. Everything is bigger in her absence. I am afraid to make mistakes. It would be like I abandoned her, it would not be worth anything.

My body is tired. **Tired and warm.**

Rx: *Colum-p 30C*

10 MONTHS AFTER INITIAL VISIT:
I am changing socially.

Her skin is worse, she has many pimples. She is planning some trips. "It's nice. A very different path. It's going very well."

Easier to do things for myself. Easier to let things go.

What do they think about me? **Am I doing it right**? I thought I looked a fool, then got angry and said: "You have to help me." I am vulnerable while things are changing.

It's ok for things to go well. Even when I don't feel like it, I try it.

I met some nice old people from my youth and said, "Let's go out to eat."

Feelings of energy. "Still don't know how to manage that. I don't know if people will think of me as strange. I don't want to participate."

Still have cold feeling in my bones, <cold.
Energy is better.

Rx: *Colum-p 30C*

RING DOVE CASES

10 MONTHS AND A FEW DAYS AFTER INITIAL VISIT:
Rx: *Carc 40C/5*

NOTE: From C4 homeopathy it is known that Carcinosen works best when made from the 5th trituration.

11 MONTHS AFTER INITIAL VISIT:
> Chaotic. Energy is better.
> I am in no man's land, neither here nor there.
> I keep my house in darkness; everything feels worse if it is not dark.
> I have a lot of questions. I cannot manage.
> There is too much organization. I don't know what I want. I am afraid I will just drop out and do nothing. I need a purpose. Things are not clear. Which direction should I take?
>
> OBS: *she seems restless and hurried*

Rx: *Colum-p 30C*

Cases

13 MONTHS AFTER INITIAL VISIT:
I had a lot of pain, could not stand it.
It was a magical period, it feels good, and I am in the flow.
My creativity is back. I feel happier.
Grief about my abortion. I really wanted the baby. Who would it have been? I allowed myself to be influenced. Now I am angry at my ex and have a lot of grief.
Things are clear. Now I have cut off relations with ex-husband.
I feel in the flow. It gives me peace. I am content, ecstatic, and open.
I used to be worse in winter, now I am better.
I am better at taking care of myself. There are clear changes. I can cook for myself and feel good about it.
I accept that I need to rest. And I take my rest.
Things are better with sister. Better with expressing myself forcefully. Better enthusiasm.

PHYSICALLY: Trouble with left shoulder is gone.
Forgets her leg, otherwise she would have been checking it. "Legs are restless still (I am so used to it)."
Acts more quickly. Always lands on her two feet.

Rx: *Colum-p 30C*

ALIZE'S ANALYSIS:

The case looked very much like a *Staphysagria* case, but had bird-themes. I only had a little information at that time, but I knew Dove is close to *Staph*. I gave the remedy (Dove) to another case which had urinary problems and abuse and never was angry about it; she kept being friendly to the one who sexually abused her. I recognized that the "energy-field" of this person was quite similar to the energy of the other person: nice, friendly, very peaceful. Everybody loves these people. They have no need to dominate and keep their problems distant from the world. They never complain, and even when they do, it is all told in a warm attractive way. This case also will sooner or later need *Alumina*, as she is missing a basic structure in her background. Everything is vague from the past; her experiences are not integrated. (C4 information from *Alumina*).

RED-TAILED HAWK *Buteo jamaicensis*

CASE 1:
This is a case by Jonathan Shore.

RM: age 64. Tall, thin, fine-boned, refined. Leans back in chair. Eyes often look out into the distance.

The title of an autobiography he wants to write is *Surviving Life*. Feels he has the abilities to heal and guide in exceptional ways. Teaches Chi Gong. Is an East-West Psychologist. Has been trained in meditation (Theravada), Aikido, Shiatsu, Traeger, and Swedish massage. Interests are all around altered states of consciousness. "My real focus is creativity. If anybody can reach their creativity, they will be well. That's how God is in us."

Had a bad flu. Hadn't cancelled work in 20 years, which he did now "This felt like I had a horrible disease that I wasn't going to get over. It was emotional as well as physical. I've never felt that way before. Then, I was getting over that and I had a car accident. That triggered all the allergies I had as a child – as a teen." He was allergic to 48 or 54 substances. "It's like I'm going back and re-visiting everything in my life."

OBS: Makes claw sign, a claw like gesture with the hand.

"I don't know where to go with it. I don't know what to do with it.

"One of the major things in my life was my brother's birth on my fourth birthday. He was hydrocephalic and was not supposed to live. He's had seven heart attacks, a kidney removed. Just recently his legs were black-blue from here to the tips of his toes. I was very carefree until I was four. Then I became very serious. I knew then that my father was not a responsible person. I was to be responsible along with my Mother. I have never had a fear of death, because I've faced it every day of my life. I have a fear of him dying or my mother. But I've had that charge. I took that on when I came here. My dad was a terrified man. He was really incapable of responsibility."

Patient lived with his mother and brother but recently he took his own apartment. He moved out when he knew he didn't have the patience to help them. "But I knew I could help them when I moved out and was healthy myself. I'm setting limits on my responsibility more and more."

Cases

Q: How does it feel to be responsible?
"It feels normal, the way to be, the way I am – to be responsible. There's a comfortableness in being responsible. If it goes too far then it's uncomfortable. It's not quite to enjoy or dislike it. When I want to do it, it feels good. When I don't want to, it makes me angry."

Q: Responsible?
"To do those things one knows and feels are one's real obligations. There's a heart element to responsibility. With my friends, I don't have to be responsible for them, but I can make suggestions. With my brother and Mother and even my Father, I love them very much and wanted, want, to see them happy. So it's an outgrowth of love I think. It's natural for me."

> OBS: *The idea of Aurum, but performance and duty doesn't really come out here in this case.*

"It's more an inherent obligation to my family, to these people around me. It's an a priori event. I'm not compensating for something, it just is. It's the fundamental moving force for me."

"I forgot something. I'm sorry. A year ago I had a dream my Mother died. And I have never felt such pain as I did then. Absolute total, complete, agony. I was running after my Mother trying to find her. There was a demon who was trying to get her. I caught the demon (usually I'm powerless in my dreams), ripped off his head and smashed it."

Q: Recent feeling of illness?
"Very deep. Very subtle. It's a feeling that I can't depend upon my body the way I used to."

Q: Now, what would you like from me?
"I'm having these headaches that go all over my head and they are not being resolved." Had them in 20's, resolved by acupuncture. Not working now. "Also this illness thing."

Rx: *Bute-j 1M*

THREE WEEKS AFTER REMEDY:

"Headache within a few hours chased itself around head, lodged in back of head, which I'd never had. Then it disappeared altogether. Then I had hives, which I have never had. Then I had welts. It started around my middle. In the last four or five days it's down to my ankles and up to my hairline. Also the first day the asthmatic tightness in my chest disappeared and I had no coughing at all. **Remember I told you I had this insidious disease for 18 months. That was the most dramatic thing. Within three days it felt like it disappeared from the core of my being and I don't have that at all any more.**"

Six weeks after remedy:
Improving. Had said in last interview that after driving away from the 3rd visit, he felt the energy of his father. He thought he had worked through all that material. Experienced the energy of his father and how it held him back and realized that his father's energy was bound up with his allergies and he could now let it go. A psycho-spiritual transformation.

CASE 2:
Case taken by Judith Reichenberg-Ullman.

JM: 44 years old. Phone consultation, April 2001.

I'm a mess
Getting better I think
My first concern is emotional
Taking Prozac, which I really thought long and hard about. I've been on it for 3 months
Before Prozac:
Lots of anxiety
Outright depression
Days that I called black-hole days
Couldn't even cope with making a grocery list much less getting to the store
Low, low energy
Lots of fatigue
I've had 5 miscarriages and had a lot of grief about that

RED-TAILED HAWK CASES

Cases

I had a real attachment to bringing a second child in, and then had to face my husband's addictions
Still thinking about adopting or foster parenting
Doing Al Anon, wonderful, spiritual
My own counselor is good

Realizing I do have capabilities to let my life be what I want
For my life not to revolve around my husband
My hope is to stop Prozac

Coming to terms with the addictions and Al Anon has been tremendous growing for me
An awesome process
Almost to the point of being grateful for husband's addictions
Forced me into a place where I had to grow or shrivel up
I've done good work re recognizing self-esteem, self-confidence, control, and care taking

Worst days would be when I'd fall into despair about being an alcoholic addicted to pot
Tremendous anger issues

I'd feel immobilized, scared to death, bordering on panic attacks
Was feeling helpless and powerless
Wanting to change things
Plan A and plan B, obsessing about it; filled with anxiety and despair
I just couldn't stop my mind
Not able to be present
Stuck in this mindset. What should I do? What should I do?
Unable to make a decision
Leaving my husband has never been my first option
Felt a lot of judgment from friends and family to move on
How could I live with this guy?
Al Anon has helped me get out of that despair, anxiety, and depression
I have a life now and much more compassion and love for him

On bad days, I just want to shake him and ask, "Why are you still doing this?"
My frustrations with him are usually remedied by working on my own stuff

Other bad days previously- **so, so tired**
Oppressed by fatigue
My son would be my first priority
I'd be so listless
Desire was there but energy wasn't
Couldn't get enough sleep
Wanted to go in a hole, wrap myself in a blanket, pull the floorboards over me
That's when I went to a doctor and asked for antidepressants
I was lying on a sunspot on kitchen floor
Could lay there all day if I could

I just felt lethargic
Would wake up in bed and feel like I could sleep the whole day
So tired that I would close my eyes at stoplights

I've had so many people check my thyroid
Super dry skin
I tend to be cold
More constipated than lose stools but only occasionally, but I have a lot of fiber in my diet
Doctor kept changing remedies for me; she even went back to herbs

Walking helped; getting out and moving. **Getting out in fresh air always helped**
Exercise
I didn't seem to have any motivation
Didn't care about cleaning the house, fixing my hair
Was hard to get motivated to do the normal things that people do

RED-TAILED HAWK CASES

Cases

I'm impatient
Patience is one of those things that has always challenged me
I pick things up quickly
My son calls me "sharp"
I pick things up quickly at lectures and want them to move on
Good at reading, writing, editing
Very shy, introverted
My energy is drained by being around people for too long
I really struggle with small talk
Shallow talk zaps, bores me
I'm not very interested in it
Social inhibitions
I freeze up
Talk too much in social situations
Nervous prattle
Want to be liked
Don't want to be the only one there not talking to other people
Nervous, embarrassed

At its worst, I get belligerent
Trips to his home have always been challenging
I feel disconnected from him when we're there
It pushes a lot of buttons of insecurity, lack of confidence
and I get mouthy
His grandmother could see through that

Another example: Had just graduated from college. Was interviewing with different companies. It was a cocktail party. I was really nervous; hadn't done it before. Remember walking around having these disjointed conversation; saying these totally moronic things.
Trying so hard that I just blurt things out
Getting better due to spiritual growth
Getting better about being okay with silence
That's allowed me to connect better with people

Still not good at a party
End up being in a corner having a deep one to one conversation with someone

Intense would describe me
I have big feelings, big desires, and big ideas
Don't stay tepid
Foul-mouthed and fairly dramatic when angry
Gesticulating

I move into the other side when I'm pushed too far
Visiting husband's home; he lied to me; was out till the wee hours. It was 3 AM.
He came in pretty toasted
I was so angry
Just crazy, crazy
He was afraid I was going to tell his parents
I was throwing my arms around
Saying I didn't deserve that
He'll applaud my performance and we'll both laugh about it

When working for insurance company. Workload was getting so out of hand
I was handed the umpteenth million file; threw the whole stack up the air
A sort of a release
Everyone laughed

? *Crazy*
Just out of control
I'm not controlling or editing it
I haven't done that in a long, long time
Journaling helps me let it out; or walking it out
Of course, meditating is really good. I've started to do Tai Chi also
When I had that building up at the time, I don't think I had
an awareness for it
This button-down, anal type person running around on a schedule

RED-TAILED HAWK CASES

Cases

Pushed by the clock
Always trying to do the right thing
Then blowing up when pushed too far usually by my husband.

I'm Type 1 in the enneagram
Self-righteous
Always trying to do the right thing
Dutiful child, student
Trying to be punctual because that's the right thing to do

I have these judgments and get pushed by that
With that comes judgment
Can be supercritical of myself and others
Really good at troubleshooting
The trouble spots leap out at me
My focus tends to go to what's wrong

I can remember being self-righteous
Pissing people off because I was trying to make something right
We should do something this way or that way

I can remember being in an airport elevator; we were commenting
on the Braille thing. Friend noticed that something was missing.
I remember going semi-ballistic about it; went on and on
and on. Getting off on it. Trying to fix every small thing in he world

At the insurance company I always wanted to fix things
Not happy when they couldn't see that my way was better
Husband talks about my having to be right
Arguing
For example: I'm deadheading petunias; husband commented.
I knew I wasn't doing it the right way; that I was taking a shortcut,
but I got defensive, said I was doing it the right way. It was such
a relief when I admitted it.
I have to be right

Maybe a fear of condemnation
That maybe he'd come down on me
A less-than feeling
Not feeling good about myself
Ties in with getting mouthy and belligerent when afraid
I'm not going to let anyone hurt me, so I'll go on the offensive
so I don't have to take a defensive role

? Being right
The strong feelings that I hold
Opinionated is word many people would used to describe me
Stubbornness
Pretty strong-willed
Sort of narrowness
Before so focused in, narrowed in, invested that this was right

Remember arguing to the death when I knew I wasn't right
Somehow protecting myself

? If not right
Belittlement, embarrassment, shame

I took a lot of teasing from older brothers when little
Their taunting. They hurt my feelings a lot
They told me, "Don't go away crying. Just go away."
So maybe the tough, outer mask was for them
The face I would present to husband's family or to him about deadheading
Inwardly afraid, trying to protect myself
Just being belittled, shamed, embarrassed, humiliated
When I say those things, my brothers come to mind so there must be a connection there

Grew up middle child of 7 in small town in Wisconsin
Older sister, 2 older brothers, 3 younger sisters

Red-tailed Hawk cases

Cases

Didn't have close relationship with my older sister
"The boys" and "the girls" so I didn't have a role
Started being mommy's helper because older sister didn't want it
I tried to put order into the chaos
I took on that care-taking role fairly early out of my own need for order and out of care taking
I was always aware of how tired, overwhelmed mother was, but I never had a domestic bone in my body
I was a tomboy
My dad wasn't emotionally present
He was more involved hunting and fishing with the boys
Father was uncomfortable touching us
My dad had a horrific, grassfire temper
I remember been sizzled by that
Torched on the spot
He stuffed a lot of things so his anger would blow
I walked around on eggshells, tippie toes

I was a good student, good reader, competitive
I lacked confidence. **Was really shy. It goes beyond shy**
A confidence or self-esteem issue
Couldn't face the audience at the Christmas concert
Another girl was making the point that no matter what was offered to me, I would say "no"

I was just too shy even to accept things that I wanted
I didn't want that attention on me
Don't focus on me, look at me, pay attention to me
Just forget that I'm here
I just wasn't comfortable with having people focus on me
I've always had a spiritual orientation
Raised Catholic
But knew it didn't fit for me early on
Spiritual experiences as child
The rapture

No one else in the family had those convictions or experiences
Those small, little boxes of religion didn't work for me

Needing to be outside absorbing sky
Favorite was at night looking up at stars
Could blow a gasket when little by trying to absorb the infinity of the sky
I would go out and try to absorb with my mind how many stars there were out there
To comprehend the enormity of infinity
It would tweak my brain
Something comforted by the indifference or sameness of the sky
It's there, always the same
But there's this peace that's not emotional

I just had a need for it
My mom called it "sucking sky"
When I was irritable, she told me to go suck sky
I love sleeping out under the stars
I think that's why I moved to Montana

> COMMENT: The nickname for Montana is "Big Sky Country"

Tend towards claustrophobia
Don't like elevators
You couldn't get me into tunnels or caves
From an early age I was absorbing the "universeness"
The bigness of space
I was looking outward to finding big, expanding, vistas
That continues to be my orientation with work
A broad brush person
Detail work is actually painful for me
I thought two semesters of accounting in college for example was actually going to kill me

? Now

RED-TAILED HAWK CASES

Cases

My emphasis is spiritual; it's great for that
I've learned to tolerate detail work
The sky is still huge
We live up on a hill
Vistas that we love
Thankful for having the space just to breathe in

This desire to soar into the sky
Really attracted to birds
Have been my whole life
The flying aspect
Love to see hawks circling
I can get into a space where the joy starts bubbling
I just want to take off with them and sore

I've had lots of dreams:
As a kid, lots of dreams about running down hill and flapping my arms
Then I would take off
The joyful, lifting feeling of taking off into the air
Sometime when looking out at a vista, I have a desire to take off and fly

Outside and air is important to me
I have a lot of trouble with those long flights like to India
Almost feel like I need oxygen
What helps is pressing my face to the glass
I need space and air
At concerts, I can't sit in the middle
When I was at church and had to sit in middle pew, I had to plan my escape so I could get out
We have a teacher in India; huge crowds
I could only do that by making a pathway in my mind to escape
Those small spaces are really hard for me

There's a connection with me with watching birds soar, expansive
It's a spiritual thing for me
I can also think of it when I'm in a joyful space
? Not interested in astronomy, physics
Have never been able to see constellations very well
I like watching the sky move
The moon changing phases and stars moving across the sky
But can't recognize constellations

Clearly a hawk
I just like them circling
The way they glide
It just seems so free
It seems like they're above it all
Noble comes to mind
They feel noble to me
Maybe I would feel that way about eagles if I saw them more
Hawks are more common and I see them more often

Irrational dreams of ending up as a street person
My material needs not getting met
I've often thought those were a result of my father not
being there

Husband's father told me if I ever needed anything, he would be there for me
My own father has never made me feel that safety net from him
Never thought anyone would take care of my security
I'd have to do it myself
So feeling safe in the world has been something I've really
had to work with and I still struggle with that sometimes
That was my anxiety pre-Prozac
Difficult child
To be a single mom
Not feeling safe in the world still raises its ugly head

RED-TAILED HAWK CASES

Cases

Even yesterday I was driving past the flophouse hotels
Feeling so sorry for the people living there
Thinking, "But for the grace of God, there go I"
We do volunteer work at the shelter so I do that on a daily basis

? Other recurrent dreams
Two and they both involve my mouth
One is my teeth are falling out
The other is having a mouthful of gum that I can't get out
Dream about losing teeth
Mouth was disintegrating
Filled with this black, sawdust like material
Never any pain with getting the teeth out
One tooth then more and more and more
They keep coming

With gum dream; trying to get this sticky gum out of my mouth; trying to pull it out. There's more and more and more

Cyst in left hand at base of middle finger
Doctor said it's the biggest one he's ever seen
I've actually scheduled surgery and cancelled it a few times

Upper neck and back
Stress in trapezius
Headaches with various diagnoses past 10 yrs; pain can be all around my head.
Intense pain focused around my left eye
Accompanied by sinus congestion; under eyes, across nose and stiffness in neck
That's my most chronic thing that bothers me
Heat helps them and Ibuprofen
Much milder the past year
Used to be migraine-level where I could hardly stand it

I've had really painful periods
Last D&C was in June
Fetus had died each time
Now I have adenomyosis
I wonder if it's because of all of the D&Cs
Had an ovarian cyst in one of my ovaries
When finally got period in November, 5 or 6 months after D and C, it only lasted one day, nearly blew my ovary
Previous cyst was gone
Uterine tissue has grown into the muscle of the uterus; on the Ultra Sound they looked like pockets of blood
I'm only having a one-day period and not a lot of pain
Was bound and determined to do the first miscarriage myself
Adenomyosis started 5 months after last miscarriage
Hormones have been normal

Skiing injury; severed my R Achilles tendon and knocked out knee
R bunionectomy
Still have trouble with that foot
My bone structure in both feet is not very good
Orthotics and a spacer

? Favorite foods
Kind of indifferent to food
Don't like broccoli
So much of my time now is spent on meals
? Sleep position
Either side, more on R

Rx: *Bute-j* 1M

PHONE CONSULTATION SEVEN WEEKS LATER:
Doing well
Cut back my Prozac
My mood has definitely improved

RED-TAILED HAWK CASES

Cases

Needing about 10 hrs of sleep
Tired by four
Incredible dream activity
Interpersonal stuff
An old boyfriend, a co-worker
Things that were never resolved

The cyst on left hand is not painful
Feels like it's reduced in size
Before painful 3 times a week
A month of no pain before remedy
That's continued
Last period only two days
Pretty amazing

Pretty upbeat, confident, positive
An overall, general sense of well-being
Not feeling like I have to control everything
Better at accepting, being in the moment
Tripping pretty lightly and it feels great

A pretty big crisis with my husband's workplace
He might get fired but I'm doing well; security buttons aren't being pushed
A trust in God, a higher power
Those are really big strides for me
Not obsessing about things
I don't feel that indecisiveness is a problem either.
Confidence has come back
Before conflict about whether to go back to work or not
It all cleared up. I'm not going back to work. End of story
A lot clearer about interacting with husband's parents
I think it's because of my clarity
Energy good till the afternoon then I'm ready to take a rest break
I try to give myself half an hour rest or meditate

Reading Thich Nhat Hahn
Doing walking Buddhist meditation; trying to be more mindful
Less pushed by duty
Not making to-do lists anymore
My new mantra is "I don't have to do anything
if I don't want to," and it's all working fine
I'm just walking lightly
Confidence is coming back in relationships, too
Not feeling isolated because I'm choosing to be alone
Not needing to engage people in conversation and
I'm learning, too, about listening
I've never been a very good listener because I've worried about
what I would say
Never realized how wonderful the power of silence is
Husband is expressing appreciation for how non-reactive, supportive,
 loving, and compassionate I am
Haven't felt the need much to get out and suck sky
Happier with my own piece of sky
Not a pushing need
I'm just more comfortable with the space that I'm in
For a day or two, I noticed a very minor letdown after cut back on the
Prozac; a little anxiety, negative thinking
No dreams of ending up as a street person
A real possibility of husband getting fired and
I haven't moved into fear
The fear of being in a place like that is gone
Not a need to manipulate, control
Walking down the path feels really good
A couple of headaches the past few days; minor compared to what
 they used to be
Seeing a chiropractor who works with cervical vertebrae.
Still pain in shoulder blades when I take a deep breath in
No more dreams about teeth falling out
I think it has to do with having a real bite to my communication

RED-TAILED
HAWK
CASES

Cases

I really feel that it's been really helpful

(NOTE: *Has apparently been taking Bute-j 1M as a daily LM!*)

Analysis: Headaches.

Rx: *Bute-j* 1M in water twice a week for one month then once a week

PHONE CALL EIGHT WEEKS LATER:
I'm struggling to maintain some sanity
Husband is quitting job; he filed a grievance against boss
and it backfired against him
Husband has addiction to marijuana and alcohol
Son is picking up on our financial problems
Marriage is in jeopardy but it isn't something I want to do
I gave up a good paying job to stay home with son

Has taken *Bute-j* 1M once a week
My mood is okay

Going to spend two weeks with husband and his parents on farm
in Michigan
I swore last year I wouldn't do that

Cyst on hand is totally pain free, doesn't bother me at all
Absolutely pain-free menstruation; periods are still 1-2 days
One new injury: I wiped out on son's scooter and hurt wrist

Some sexual dreams with husband
Memories of having sex with all kinds of people
I didn't want to have sex with
Doing work with my counselor about that
Trying to understand what I want from husband
and be able to communicate that to him
Less of a need to "suck sky"
Mostly go out for the coolness of the air; refreshing
But not this need to escape into space anymore

Exploring the possibility of moving in with another woman
I can't tell him what he wants me to say

Rx: *Bute-j* once a week while going through this, then one dose every two weeks. *Arnica* 1M to take and 30C to hold for future.

Red-tailed Hawk cases

Cases

BALD EAGLE *Haliaeetus leucocephalus*

CASE 1:
Case of Divya Chabra. 14 year-old girl. 1993 Cerebellitis.

This 1993 case predates the Jeremy Sherr Eagle proving by three years. While taking the case Divya felt so strongly about the girl needing Eagle that she made the remedy herself into a 30C from the blood of an Indian eagle. This case was presented at a LIGA conference in Amsterdam.

Can't walk; spent 3 months in bed
Unstable, unbalanced
Severe headache. Felt brain burst, eyes red, watering
Had to sit or lie.
Needed injections for headache.
About to do important exam
< **Noise.**
< **Talk. Head jarring**.
> **Quiet** music, calm, alone.
< If someone rude, won't speak back, afraid to hurt them, won't say anything back.
< Fighting, **rudeness, violence**, even in movies
Slightest thing hurts me a lot. I'm not stable with noise around me.

NOTE: Cerebellitis affects balance.

With noise my nerves pull. Hands **hurt with noise**. I close my fists to bear the noise.
I don't like human nature. **I hate human nature.** Selfish.
< Scream. **Rude.** Especially blame when I have not done anything.
< **Poverty on the road. Am I the only person who feels this?** Why?
All comes into me and stays with me.

I'm sad but can't say it. I feel better with it inside me. Don't like to show tears. If I cry I show so many others and I hurt them with my tears. I hate being blamed. **People don't understand me.** Dislike **gossip. Criticism.** They hurt me only. Why can't people be straightforward? People should understand people. They should not fight or scream. People are selfish. I hate money. This is mine/yours.

I love airplanes. Flying. Heights.
 > Looking down; tall, skyscrapers feel good.
I love music, nature. Get calm.

OBS: looks at sky, trees, birds

< **Pollution**
> Clouds, > monuments, > plants,
> Travel. Like to know about things.

I would love to fly all my life. To be a pilot. Victory in plane. High above. Feel great. High above the world. Feel light and don't feel burdened by responsibilities.

I like creation. God created nature. Love pets. Dogs, **Seals, Dolphins**. Parrots. I like to help beggars but people say don't go too close; it's dirty. **Dolphins are free;** they don't hurt people. The eagle flies so high, above the world.

Mostly I need to be silly to get attention but then I'm upset that people don't see my intelligence. If I could be any animal I would chose eagle. Dreamt of eagle.

Rx: Friend went to the zoological park and got Eagle blood and made into 30C.

Follow up:
Headache better; concentration is better.

Second Follow up:
Exams went well. Not tense. Studied well. Slept well. No dreams anymore. Mix with people more. Accept things as they are. Less depressed. Happy person.

Third follow up:
Strong, not weak. Understand people better.

Fourth Follow up:
I understand myself more. Understand people more.

Bald Eagle cases

Cases

CASE 2:
Case by Jonathan Shore.

Attractive muscular young woman with very striking clear blue eyes.

This was Jonathan Shore's first bird case. He had treated this woman for years, with *Cann-i.* and *Nat-p.* with good results. This case spans many years and is presented here in summarized form.

INITIAL INTERVIEW:
I do art. I don't know what else to say. I'm sitting here and my hands are freezing. That's all I can think about. So now I'm here. I'm starting to work on other things. I don't know what to say.

You need to ask me a question.

It's hard for me because I've got to work with people. I work with people in a gym. And people talk to me, but I can't listen. It's like I see their mouth working. I don't know where I am. It's like my mind is somewhere else. It takes me awhile to get back. It happens just sitting here. It's easy to be with that tree out there. It happens to me often. I'm driving and then…I don't know where I am or where I'm going. Then I wonder if I'm losing my mind. It's embarrassing even though I'm by myself. It doesn't get scary unless I'm driving on the freeway and I notice I'm not staying in the white lines.

When I'm home, I sort of pace around the room. And it takes me awhile before I get used to being there. I go back and forth in these sorts of patterns. I'll pick something up and set it down and forget where I set it down.

It's horrible if I have to go to the grocery store. I get absolutely overwhelmed with all the color. I forget what I came in for. It's like I'm on sensory overload. Then I get nervous and think the people will think I'm shoplifting. So I put something in the cart.

> OBS: *The element of guilt and shame are already clear. Actually no shoplifter would do that.*

Frustrating. May end up with stuff to feed her cats and nothing for her to eat.

What's new is how often she spaces out. When she was really small, mortified to go to a shopping mall. Could hardly see – would get tunnel vision. Tendency is to sit as far away from people as she can where she can see them. Then she feels safer. In a restaurant, she has to sit with her back to the wall so no one can be behind her.

Aversion to having her back somewhere where she can't have something solid behind it.

When anxious, her vision contracts.

As a child slept flat on her back surrounded by her stuffed animals limiting her field of vision but allowing her to see everything in it.

Doesn't know what she's afraid of. When she was little, was afraid of monsters. Was afraid of things she would invent in her imagination. Example: in a dark room, walk with back against wall until gets to light switch.

More aware of people's physical space. Is aware of where they begin and end and hers as well.

> COMMENT: *We see a combination of confusion and circumspection. Eagles are very private animals. It's not deviousness.* **Eagles will not land; will not alight if there is a human even within a very long distance**. *These organisms are very sensitive so sensory input can be very difficult to handle. Sometimes they want to be by themselves because the sensory input is too much and it's going over and confusing the intensity of their lives.*

LATER INTERVIEWS:
Energy up from her heels, up her back. Feels stuck. "Want to move to get away from it. It makes me kind of jumpy. My center of balance isn't quite right. What seems to fix this is getting away from people, in a confined space. Worse to be around people and around my animals that are trying to comfort me. I kept thinking, 'Leave me alone. Don't touch me.' I felt I needed to keep all of my energy in for my own healing"

Dreams (These were reported intermittently over some years):

She was in the ocean and there was this whale and the whale was covered with markings, with icons, ancient inscriptions. And the whale took her down. They went down together. And there, way down at the bottom was her sister

Cases

in law. They were trying to reach her sister in law. They could not get deep enough to bring her up. The next day she got a call that her brother and his wife were involved in an automobile accident and the wife was in a deep coma. She knew the wife was going to die. She didn't say anything. She had tried to save her but had been unable to do so.

COMMENT: *This is what is meant by the relationship between the worlds.*

Recurring feather dream where I find four feathers. I've had this dream for seven years. I'm always collecting four feathers. People try to distract me. I find these four feathers. Working on building wings in Australia. Don't ask me why.

I was in Australia. I walked into a room in a Victorian house, which I recognized as an old house of mine. On the floor was a pair of wings. One was almost finished. They were made of the all the feathers I'd collected over the years. I walked over and touched the wings and they were real. One was 3/4 finished. I get distraught when I don't have one of these dreams because I'm working on completing this.

I went into a pen and found a huge golden eagle was pinned down to the ground. Kept asking the foreman why he'd immobilized the bird and pinned him down. He wouldn't answer. Recurring dream of that situation. It's devastating to see the bird like this. I realize it's not dead, because when I walk around it, it picks up his head. I'm sort of afraid of it because of its claws. This last part, which doesn't happen very often, I'll take it to a veterinary office where there are a whole bunch of birds in different states of distress. **They reach out to take hold of me.** It's so upsetting, because I don't know what to do.

Feels things in dreams are coming into real life.

I dreamed about crow feathers and now there have been crows in the trees for three weeks leaving feathers all around and I'm collecting them and can use them.

Recently she cannot sleep. She sees things at night that are waking her up 4-5 X a night. "I see images sometimes if plants, sometimes animals, sometimes they're figures but they're not human figures at all. I wake up before I see it. I wake up and then I see it. I haven't drawn it. I've tried to grab it." Wakes every 2-3 hours.

Energy feeling is all over body. I feel like I could just explode. I got so wound up at one point, that I felt if I couldn't get it to come out in my art, which is where it should come out, I would pick a fight with somebody which is not like me. It's such an extreme amount of energy.

Aware of doing things that are a little odd for me. Usually does her artwork outside. Collages of found objects: sticks, feathers. "I have a ton of ideas but I can't get anything to come out of myself. It puts me into a kind of panicked mode. I've got a show coming up." Now has brought everything inside house and keeps everything closed. Doesn't like people looking at her stuff anyway, until it's ready. This feels like there's something more to it. It's more alchemical. Wants things to sit in a pile for 3-4 weeks until they're ready. The odd part is, it's as if I'm in this kind of a thin membrane, and if I could just poke through it. Or I'm sitting on the edge of a cliff and if I could get pushed off the edge of the cliff I would go and it would be incredible. It would come spilling out, come flying out. But it's not happening.

Rx: *Haliae-lc 30C* (which was all that was available).

BALD EAGLE CASES

THREE MONTHS AFTER REMEDY:

Art stuff is happening like crazy. Now I can do anything. Pretty soon, every day after work, would come home and work another seven hours, after working 8.5 hours at work.

Presences that were coming to her have been alleviated. It had been disturbing her.

"There's been such a shift. I feel like I'm in myself in a different way. The energy that came before, felt like a foreign thing. Now it feels like it's everywhere, where it should be."

Left store and felt someone was running behind me. Normally that would have made me tense up and nervous. But now, it was almost as if I could see behind me and I felt him running past me and his energy went right through me and it didn't disturb me.

Today I went to lunch and realize I sat in exactly the opposite place, right in the middle of the room.

I've had great flying dreams.

Cases

I've had some odd bird dreams. I'm not actually looking for feathers any more. Now, I'm aware that I have them. I'll find them and say, "I already have them." It's been taken care of and it's really exciting.

A dream I had quite a while back, that I'd forgotten about. (This was when she began to have feather dreams.) It was half-bird, half-human. It had the head of a raptor. I was being chased by a lot of people; they were pecking at me and chasing me. It ran in and scooped me up and carried me off. In the act of doing that, she lost her feathers, which was the human part. And she told me that if I kept the feathers and put them back in her, she would grow back all her feathers.

After I took the remedy I heard the ringing in my ear I used to have as a kid. It was like the ringing of the bell in a Zen temple that brings you back when you have been too far outside yourself. I had forgotten all about this sound. Now it has come back.

THREE YEARS LATER, AFTER AN ACUTE:
The remedy eliminated everything.

The dreams came back after the 30C. I slept really soundly, woke feeling really rested. It makes me feel balanced and right. More clear. All of my antennae functions and intuitive functions are back on. As opposed to what I said before, that I was half blind because my dreams were not clear.

CASE 3:

Case by Jonathan Shore. Young woman: tall, thin, long blonde hair, brown eyes, aquiline features and prominent nose. She definitely has these strong big eyes. She's nice, vivacious.

"I like your office."

> COMMENT: *She says that before she even sits down. She is immediately relating to you. Others come in, sit down and say nothing, waiting for something to happen. This gives you an impression of relationship and communication.*

Massage therapist.
Has a four and a half year old boy.

We live on an acre and son goes to school right across the street.

Just finished college. Still doesn't know what she wants to do.

Taking an acting class. Surprised since she's usually so timid and shy in a group. But in acting class, finds she likes to be in the center of attention. Has never had something come so easily.

Tension in body; so much she can't handle it, jaw, hands, headache, almost like it's too much energy. "I'll try to exercise, I get shaky, I get really hungry. Body will hurt from being too tense." After a couple of weeks of that, falls into a heap from complete exhaustion. "Then I am wasted and it's hard to even talk.

All the energy and body tension come with stomach aches, boils on skin and scalp. The scalp gets red and itchy, the scalp lasts 10 days, the skin ones last 15 days.

May have a pretty long period; 7-8 days and is really heavy 5 days. Right at the end of menses is back into the energy again. It will last a week. Two days ago could hardly move. The next week will begin PMS, moods fluctuating, more uptight one day. Feels like she constantly has her period because she doesn't have more than a week off from the constant fluctuation.

It helps to eat. Forgets to eat. Nothing sounds good. Will go through a few days of not being able to eat. Once she begins, will remember how hungry she is and eat a lot for a few days.

Is a person who needs a lot of alone space. As long as she gets it, she does a lot better with people.

"How am I doing? Is it your turn to ask questions yet?"

> COMMENT: *You don't feel there's deviousness, nor is she manipulative. But you feel there is something that is holding her back.*

"I'm very fast. I do things quickly. By the time it's time to eat, will be eating while I'm making the food. Will burn it, or turn the stove on too high. This is frustrating to my husband who is much more low key and slower paced. Have I talked enough now?"

Working with Buddhism. Likes that it's very accepting. "Upbringing was very strict. I had thrown out religion for a very long time. I didn't want to have anything to do with the dogmatic religions. I still had a strong spiritual side, but I

BALD EAGLE CASES

Cases

did not know what to do with that. I feel like I've been under so much pressure in my whole life; I'm in a jar with the lid on. I'll shake with the pressure. Now I feel like the lid's coming off. The shaking isn't so much tension as it's just energy."

Has a lot of things to make up for. Doesn't want to waste any more time or make any more wrong turns. Has had periods where she's felt lost and doesn't want to be lost any more.

A lot of pressure on herself to be a good mom. Whatever other people tell her, feels she's not doing enough or doing a good job: I am not being a good mom, or I'm guilty or whatever.

For many years, all of my high school years until 21 or 22, I had horrible nightmares all the time. For six months, when I was 18, I had to sleep with my mom because my nightmares were so bad. **My life was primarily my dream life**, I had a hard time to relate to people in the day. When I would tell people my dreams, they didn't know what I was talking about. **Almost like waking dreams, I was open to different levels.**

Experienced a lot of terror during those years. I would just hide out from the regular world. I did a lot of babysitting; took care of my nieces and nephews all the time. Got into massage as I felt like that was not overwhelming for me.

Got into therapy, which ... I would believe whatever anyone would tell me. Now it's embarrassing. In a lot of the therapies I would get a lot more lost. I would believe whatever they would tell me. It's embarrassing what I would believe.

The last few years, having a child was really good: being grounded. Being a mom and all."

Doesn't have the nightmares anymore. "I was able to turn off the dreams; the opening to other levels. I just prayed and prayed about just shutting things off.

"Would wake and see entities right there at her bed: old men and old women like archetypal old men. Some of the harder ones; you'd wake up but your body's still asleep so you can't move. There would be things flying at me, like astral projection. Some magical dreams.

I was a unicorn with another unicorn. Or I'd be in a fairy type of land. Then a few times when I'd have a magical feeling; a few times I did open my eyes and there was this big cluster of lights that would come in my room and it felt like home to me. So every time I saw it I would have this longing to be with it. The second I would reach out to it, it would go away. (Weeps) That happened for about a year.

"My dad was a judge working during the day; he was a drinker at home. Parents were really strict old-fashioned Catholic. My mom was so scared, that even to say the word 'body' was a bad word. Seven kids. There were constant fights and constant chaos every night, every morning. I stayed really close to my mom for some kind of protection. It was pretty crazy in the house. My brother was a pretty bad drug addict and alcoholic. He'd come home and then he'd leave and my parents would get crazy and a lot of it would get dumped on me. Maybe in my dreams I felt so good because I could not deal with my real life. Liked gymnastics a lot as a child. Always trying to make the world better. There's just no way a person can do that, especially for a huge family.

"The hardest part was trying to figure myself out and trying not to hurt anyone else while I was doing that. I didn't want to make any mistakes that would hurt other people. I was always so concerned with not hurting other people."

Could will herself to be in another place. Found everything looks reversed; like left is right. Colors were different. Got attached to her body; wanted to learn how to live in her body. For a while she was bird watching, which was really calming. "When nursing, would sit outside and learned how to call like they would call. I haven't done that for a while."

Q: *If you were a bird, what kind of bird would you be?*
I first thought it was an eagle. **But the thing that I draw myself as has big blue wings**. I don't know what they are. I draw myself a lot like I'm a bird person. Also the feeling of open and expanded feels really good. So I like those open, blue wings. I draw birds a lot, like I am a bird person or something.

> COMMENT: *This is similar to Eagle Case 1. Background more pathological. Pressures were more. Father and brother are alcoholics. Miasmatic roots were strong. More pathology here. This woman was lost. The other case said her dreams kept her on track and reminded her of her purpose. This woman got pushed right out there.*

Rx: *Haliae-lc 1M*

Cases

FOLLOW UP IN SIX WEEKS:
Called as still had shakes and exhaustion. You said, don't worry; it's working.

Maybe ten days later, realized that the everyday things were changing.

Used to sit in front of computer and would experience so much body tension. But now she started writing whatever came up instead of what she was supposed to do. Began writing stories and all the tension started going away. Now can't wait to get to the computer to write stories and is not having any of that tension any more.

Used to feel she had so much creativity but it had no way to come out. The remedy helped open that up, bringing out into the front.

Last month had no PMS! "Didn't know menses were coming. This month it's due any minute and it's the same, only I am tired and I have a little backache, but no PMS again.

"I've just been feeling more alive again. I feel much more even, at ease and accepting about myself. Before if I'd try something new, right away I'd think it was stupid or soft. Now I feel more like my 5-year-old son who will just keep trying something. I feel more open.

Q: Dreams?
I used to have sense in my dreams of people in my room. This one was kind of funny; it almost felt like a message that things were ok. I used to have this recurring dream that someone was holding me down in my room; it was a very physical feeling. Two weeks into remedy, it became like a wonderful lover instead of a horrible energy holding me down. It was very loving. It was between a dream and reality. I didn't want it to go away.

CASE 4:

Tina Quirk case from *The American Homeopath 2000*.

The patient is a 45-year old woman, divorced, caring for two school-aged children. She is slender, has a high forehead and long, black hair with a natural white streak. Soft-spoken, even-toned, she occasionally tears up, but never cries.

You can help me with depression and being on edge. Life is too much. I am a sounding board for everyone. I'm worn out. I grew up in a monotone,

Southern Baptist family, a conservative background. I married an Italian, non-monotone, outspoken, bangs on the table. The two backgrounds clashed. He couldn't relate to me. He wants to be obeyed (tears up slightly). Too much.

This weekend I worked late, came home to a phone message from the man upstairs from my ex-husband's apartment. He heard screaming and called the police. My daughter was wrestling with her father. Then, on Sunday, my son was dropped off six hours early at my apartment. I wasn't home and my son, who is 10 years old, stayed in the park alone. I can't deal with him. It is perpetual insanity.

BALD **E**AGLE CASES

My mental parts are going   I am ready to cry, it doesn't take much to make me cry; it's especially difficult at work

It is a perpetual daily clash with my son or my husband. It used to be with my daughter. They throw it into turmoil.

I can't deal with a husband abusive to us. Frustration for so long. No patience. I'm sick of it. I can't do it anymore. I hate myself. He is crazy and I am going crazy (tears). It feels like I have no emotions. Hopelessness.

I used to be a positive person. Sleep – all I want to do is sleep. I have dreams of sleep – it is a superior reality. A release. I keep a journal. I thought, when he goes crazy it will be a record of his insanity. (Stares off and becomes dreamy-eyed for several seconds) I wish I were dreaming right now. Just thinking about dreams feels good. I dream about being in different places – in a beautiful old home on the shore, which belongs to a gay guy. Very professional, dark, with antiques. Warm, peaceful, a beach with water, still water.

Q: Any dreams from childhood?
Stairways, rickety old ones or up a mountainside to a plateau. Up a mountain with my mother. It is a rocky and craggy path, a pleasant road. Lightly dusty. Then the road crumbles and becomes six inches wide. I look over the edge and am astonished at how high we are and then turn back.

I don't want to be so on edge. I'm on a plateau and don't know when I will get off. I've never been stuck in my life.

I can't focus – it's like static, like static. I can't think on one thing for very long.

Cases

In my daily routine, there is no happiness. I am always needed for something. I question myself. I am not sure. I've been dissected by so many professionals. Am I right, not right? I am angry, annoyed, tired, and depressed.

I have a back problem. After the divorce my **right shoulder and up the neck were tense.** My muscles were so tight that the discs were going the wrong way – pinched.

I want to say I quit, I'm not doing it anymore. I'm ready to hit, punch, belittle. The basic point is he is crazy, my son is going. I am the kids' only hope. I am going crazy. I want to level out, get armor and help, fortification.

My whole family is conservative. Their feet are on even ground. They handle everyone down the road. Even, not spiky. I am destroyed, here or there. It scares me. I am out of control.

My husband deteriorated, everything was angry. I am getting like him. Everything makes me angry.

Q: How was your childhood?
It was great. I lived in a small town. My mom worked when I was in high school, but was home the rest of the time. It was a small community, with sidewalks. Kids and dogs. Very safe, **free, easy.** Horseback riding. No worries. I could achieve anything I wanted to. I went to church every Sunday, did the religious thing. In high school I was rebellious, experimented with a few drugs, nothing big, bad or ugly. I went to art school. It was a new experience and opened me up – eye opening.

I am six years younger than my brothers and sisters. There was some tension. The accountant stole all my father's money. With my husband things were flying. We detached ourselves from craziness, but it was a nice little dream. The frustration is unending.

More and more I don't care. What's the point? It is terrible, life. Endlessly frustrating. I go to work, I can focus there, do my job well, efficiently and disappear, I don't have to think. My former self was usually happy. I am so into my own depression and guilt. I can't express it. I used to tell the kids stories. I avoid stories now, because they are all about being smashed, killed or devoured.

I am tired of being angry. I can't be rational. I absorb anger, deal out anger. I am ugly and bad, never before. I read about meditation, but can't sit there because the trash is so heavy. I can't get rid of it to get to a clean place. I want to wash my hands and walk away. I am ready to strike, my voice gets louder. I need to smooth out the rough edges.

I like music, classical. Rock and roll is violent and negative, deceiving and killing and sexually perverse. I can't stand TV. It is the downfall of the world. It is not intelligent. I like to read and get my own vision of the story. TV is like being hypnotized. The commercials are just pushing drugs, pain-killers and hemorrhoid medication.

Q: *How are you with weather?*
I love warm weather, hot is OK. I am a chilly person. I hate cold. I get chilblains – fingers and toes, they hurt when cold. I am learning to layer. I dislike gray rainy days and winter. I am looking forward to spring. I like the bay or seawater, by the water, it is peaceful. I feel penned-in in the mountains. I also like peaceful water in the woods. I hike a lot. **I like the birds and the breeze in the woods**. I definitely prefer the outdoors.

I love seafood, fats, rich sauces. I used to eat sweets and caffeine – five cups a day. I drink tea, hot in winter, cold in summer. I sip it all day long, usually cold drinks.

I was slapped in the eyes as a kid. I had bronchitis a lot. I wake with mucous in my throat. I had pleurisy a few years ago.

I have a curvature of the spine. I was in a car accident in high school. I cracked the windshield with my head. **That's why my neck is a wreck**. In college two years later, I had a lot of fainting, when going from squatting to standing up. I would black out or get very dizzy.

I have low blood pressure. I have had herpes, but no flare up in three years.

Rx: *Haliae-lc 30C*

Follow up (6 weeks later):
I am feeling better. I haven't been drinking coffee. I am not so depressed or so easily angered. About two weeks ago I started feeling calmer and not so quick to anger. I leveled out; I am more in control of my emotions.

Bald Eagle cases

Cases

I am not worn out so much. My crying is better. I feel hopeless only occasionally, not daily. I don't sleep so much anymore. I am not feeling on edge as I was before. My focus is somewhat better and the kids are better. I had a few bouts of insomnia for a few weeks after the remedy, but sleeping is better. I have had vertigo two or three times in the last week, a light-headedness, doesn't last long. I used to have this ages ago. My face is breaking out and my appetite is bigger. I am having headaches, which I haven't had since just after my divorce. I had spotting only during my period, never happened before.

Rx: Wait

FOLLOW UP (5 MONTHS AFTER THE REMEDY):
I have been feeling well until two or three weeks ago. I had a bout of insomnia, my mind clicking constantly. I am a little depressed, not to the level of before. I am not able to relax; I need to be busy or I feel worthless. I have been feeling on edge for a while. My anxiety is resurfacing.

My headaches are less frequent. I am getting more short-tempered. Tiredness is not as much an issue, but I am drinking four or five cups of tea a day. My focus is OK, not fabulous. I am not spotting at all during my period; everything is normal. My appetite is still voracious.

I had a dream about my mother. I was concerned about her and coaxing her off rooftops. She was on edge, ready to go.

Q: How would you rate your response to the first dose of remedy?
In the beginning an 8, now I am slipping big time.

Rx: Repeat *Haliae-lc 30C*

FOLLOW UP (6 MONTHS AFTER THE REMEDY):
The remedy worked really well and lasted a good long time. Now I am feeling a lethargy. I need caffeine to begin my day. I am dreaming constantly. I feel I've been on another plane all night. I had a dream about a gorgeous bird with scarlet red feathers, the size of a pony. It was in a stainless steel room, alone. There was a rectangular window. It was motionless and staring out of the window, looking out past me. I was dumbfounded by its beautiful feathers. The door on the left side opened, but I couldn't let it out. There was such sadness in its eyes because it had to go back in. It started staring again.

I am having low moods and inadequate feelings. Am losing my patience with my daughter too much. It is a perpetual, perpetual drain. I am having insomnia again. I need to be busy. I am not so anxious. My headaches are back again. I feel a loneliness most of the time.

Rx: Repeat *Haliae-lc* 30C

FOLLOW UP:
Now, eight months after the remedy, the patient has had one more repeat of *Haliae-lc* 30C and is doing well.

CASE 5:

Case taken by Eveline Franken and Alize Timmerman of the Hahnemann Instituut, the Netherlands.

Woman, 52 years old

Physical therapist with a practice in a home for the elderly. "I am running on empty there. I have given very much, now it's time for me."

In June 2002, she was pecked on the head by a jackdaw. She was walking in a forest, a young one sat on the path and the jackdaw suddenly attacked her. After that she had a fever for months, she was afraid of tetanus.

She went to hospital and examination showed an intestinal cancer, at the junction of large and small intestine, which had spread to two lymph nodes.

She had the operation on the infamous September 11 (the day of the terrorist attacks in the United States). When she came to, the world was on fire. After that she had radiation: "I was *locked up* in the hospital."

"I have a feeling that that bird pecked me awake."

When she was 3 years old, she had Bornholmse disease (Note: this is an acute infectious disease, which in the early stages resembles typhoid, so she was quarantined) and she was actually locked up in a cage in the hospital.

"I am a person with peculiar diseases."

As a child she was never taken seriously. There was a complete denial of her being; as a reaction against this she behaved completely like a 'street flower,' (someone who blossoms outside the house only). She was a tough girl who played like a boy. Often she came home full of bruises.

Cases

Animals are her healers. From the age of 13 until 27 she had a dog that was her best friend. In the meantime she has started a practice as physical therapist for animals.

As a clairvoyant, especially when it comes to animals, she locates missing pets.

She kept bees for many years.

She has a feeling of **homesickness: "I don't belong here; I belong in nature."**

Her most important goal is to **feel free and without cares**, to feel one with nature. For years she was a **fanatical motorbike rider**.

She experiences contact with the spiritual only in nature.

She is bothered by worries in her **neck, tension in her shoulders** and a feeling of worrying, a sort of 'do-or-die' situation. "A person creates all kinds of things himself, so he can also heal everything himself."

Carpal tunnel syndrome and a feeling of heaviness in the lower arms.

She dreams of all kinds of birds; kingfishers, coots, colorful crows, robins and eagles. And about whales, orcas, dolphins, snakes, lizards and frogs.

A dream of dolphins that are swimming in channels that are too narrow, and they cannot escape from them.

Dream: She was caring for a hurt coot. She held the little bird to her breast; it wanted to stay with her. Suddenly she felt an enormous talon of a 'godly eagle' on her right shoulder. She thought: "He can fly **so** high!" She was awed by the power of the eagle. Next she felt she was going to take an astral journey. Her mother who was also there saw she was about to faint and called the doctor. During the astral journey she saw the sign of an unfolding staff of Aesclepius.

Rx: *Haliae-lc 30C*

ANALYSIS:

Her enormous desire for freedom, her love of nature, and the feeling of the Godly power and touch of the eagle on her shoulder, these all pointed clearly to the use of *Haliaeetus*. I started with a 30C. She needs no directions at all, she dowses when she needs it.

The most important thing was that she found the courage and wherewithal to arrange all the earthly things that she was previously avoiding. She sold her practice, managed her finances, all her business affairs are taken care of.

She is now completely dedicated to healing herself and finds all sorts of healers. She believes they will come to her as she needs them. She has started painting with a lot of intense colors, very expressionistic.

She does still have problems finding time to enjoy herself. When she finds herself getting down, she dowses for herself and calls to say: "I now need *Haliaeetus* 400C." Then I make it for her and send it and she improves again and finds the energy again to actually use the freedom she now has since arranging her affairs.

First saw her 2 years ago. She used 30C 3 times and the 400C she took half a year ago.

BALD EAGLE CASES

CASE 6:
By Dr. Mariette Bernstein of Capetown, South Africa

14 DECEMBER, 1997:
Patient is a 27-year-old man, works with computers. He has been in psychotherapy for many years.

PRESENTING SYMPTOMS:
I have terrible pain. Neck pain. It's unbearable. It makes my work difficult. It's from childhood abuse. I repressed it all and then I started having flashbacks. I get extreme muscle tension. Pain in back of neck into trapezium. Muscle tense and knotted, especially on the left. When I remembered what had happened it clamped up. I have had ganglia removed and a 'fasciectomy.' Was on morphine and Pethidine (opiate). The nerves are now growing back. A severe cramp all the time. Difficult to go to sleep with the pain.

> COMMENT: *He has dark straight hair. He is serious, glasses, round head. He gives the case without any expression.*

Very abusive father who abused sexually and physically. It started from a few months old until 12 when they divorced. I would numb myself and distance myself. I'd leave my body and watch from the ceiling. I just shut it all out. I have a sister who is 3 years older. She was also abused after he started with me.

I was unplanned. I was not wanted. No attempt at abortion. I advanced by milestones, very fast. Hypnosis takes me to the age of 2, a lot of physical abuse

Cases

then. Being hurt with pins in the hands, left arm twisted until it shattered. I was hit a lot with anything at hand. He used to grab me at the back of my neck and head and push me into a room and 'creatively' hurt me. Sexual abuse started at 4 or 5 years, about once or twice per month. Stopped when I was 11. I was very quiet and very frightened, afraid to have friends in case something happened. At 6 he beat my dog to death in front of me, that was the most traumatic thing. I was always afraid of dying so that I could not protect my sister. Now I brought it closer (the dog event). If he took it out on me, he'd leave the others alone. I nevr expressed anything. He would beat me unconscious.

Academically always the top. I had a broad general knowledge. My memory is phenomenal. I always knew the answers so it led to trouble with peers. I was bullied a lot. They'd gang up and beat me. I never fought back, ever. I always thought that I was to blame. Relationship with mother was distant, mother Victoria. Sister shut herself off with books. I was always outside in the yard. I ran away at 5 'it was not worth my while.' Moved school frequently because I was bullied. All the teachers would become suspicious and mother would move me. After 12 he would come and watch me play sports, I could never play well enough. After schooling I asked him for financial backing for university. He made me match him drink for drink and then he said he would pay, but he did not. I felt disappointed again. I never had my hopes up. Expectation are/were zero.

Recently he asked me for money because he is now down and out and I said absolutely no. It felt awful. I want nothing from him, not even an apology because it would not be sincere. I would want an apology from my mother. Mother wants appearances, she's the 'perfect' mother. She is always involved with abuse cases at her school, she knew about it. I was treated like an animal. She divorced because he was having an affair. I have ceased contact with her too.

When I confronted her she said she did not remember. She cannot assume responsibility. She said she was powerless.

Q: About sister?
We are very close the past 6 years, but I could not support her during those years because she had become a target. It's made me very strong; there's nothing I cannot deal with. It's made me not trust the world. I am perceptive to others' suffering. I am very weary of all people, especially authority figures.

I hate injustice. I have a very keen sense of injustice. I hate suffering, wars. Very sympathetic to others suffering and lacking love.

> COMMENT: *He helps a lot of people but he does not want them to know.*

I am very good at controlling my emotions with fiancée. I am learning to let go.

Q: What would you do if you had a magic wand?
I would go back in time and take myself out of that situation. I would have myself removed.

I want to be the rock in my children's lives. The person they can turn to. I fear that my 'good' life now will be taken away. Every time it's good, I fall to the depths of a trough. I have tried to live a flat-line life, not to have peaks. (*His voice all through is also a flat monotone*). I have never ever lost my temper, ever. I never wanted to.

Food is a necessity. If there was a way not to eat, I would go for it. **Averse to chocolate.**

Q: Pets?
An African Grey (Parrot).

Q: Caged?
With horror he said **NO!** (*That's the first time he shows any emotion*).

Q: Sports?
Never liked water. I love air sports. I would be a soaring bird, a vulture or an eagle. I love being in the sky alone. It's very good for the soul.

> COMMENT: *Now he's finally showing a bit of emotion.*

I like the mountains best. I want to be high up. I have always wanted to be as high as possible. The higher the safer I feel. I find myself laughing because I am so happy (*and now he looks happy*). I fly gliders.

When the neck is particularly bad, then one or other of my ears will go bright red and hot and the other ear will be icy cold. I have blacked out with the pain. I could never sleep because I never knew when he would come. After the tapes

BALD EAGLE CASES

Cases

I would have diarrhea. I was given a lot of chloroform for 'stressed' tummy. Enuresis till 9 years old, every night. I felt like I had betrayed myself. I should have been able to control it. Mother would be upset and angry and he'd administer 'discipline.'

Q: Recurrent dreams as a child?
Of being scared, frightened, hurt. Of being staked to the ground face down through hands and feet and having skin peeled of my back by a group of men, till about 10 or 11 years old. Since then I don't remember dreams.

Feel uncomfortable in crowds or parties. I don't like people near me.

> COMMENT: *He said to my secretary while he was waiting for me, he must hear the birds sing. Will not be caged in burglar bars, so he moved from his apartment to a place called 'Lone Hill.' He hates electric storms.*

Rx: *Haliae-lc 200C*, single dose, and 15 placebos.

8 January 1999:
Felt a lot better the first week, not so well the second week. Neck pain was better but is now back. Emotionally felt a lot better the first week. Been feeling anxious off the remedy and cannot think why. Did a lot of regression. Slept like a baby twelve hours a day the first week and had very nice dreams. Dreaming is a milestone. I had so much energy. Now I am back to getting to sleep at 3:30 a.m.

His fiancée says he is not as distant nor as serious. He changed his job because he was in a rut.

Been having diarrhea and skin has been terrible.

Rx: 15 Placebos

22 January 1999:
Better for 2 weeks. Still a lot of neck pain the first week. Pain is from 10 out of 10 to 7 out of 10 in severity. It's made a vast difference. Not taking pain killers at all. I have been feeling nice, not feeling miserable. A nice flat, steady life. I love gliding with the eagles in the mountains. Sleeping not well, I wake tired. I don't recall dreams. I battle to shut down after the day. In Johannesburg I am a caged bird. His job is ok. Skin and diarrhea is gone. As soon as I go to bed

my neck cramps very badly over the scalp and down the arm. I feel like something lurking in a dark pond. I lie awake till 3 or 4 a.m. until I am exhausted. Pains at night are the worst. Hardly aware of the pain during the day. As soon as I am in a happy conscious zone, my unconscious flares up and it's terrible. After the remedy I took complete stock of my whole life, I could remember everything. I could not do that before homeopathic treatment. It was all good stuff. I recounted 6 to 700 happy recurrences. My memory is back. Dreams allude me. I have become a little more distant again. In the mountains pain is negligible. I put this yoke around my neck again at night.

Rx: *Haliae-lc 200C* and 15 doses of placebo.

8 FEBRUARY 1999:
Pain is totally gone. Had another regression and 'talked to the muscles.' Been in a very good mood. I am a happy little pumpkin. I am remarkably at peace. Fiancée is happy that I am back to what I should be. **I am more affectionate.** No more unpleasant memories to deal with. Gastric problems are all better.

ANALYSIS BY MARIETTE BERNSTEIN:
About 6 months after this he brought his new born baby for a consultation. He said he was fine and he had never had pain again after the last remedy. **He said he had written to his father and forgiven him.**

This case was more a matter of recognition of Eagle after seeing a Divya Chabra case at an international congress where Divya prescribed Eagle and made the remedy up for her patient. The language of this patient matched the language in the Chabra case and reading the provings and finding that Eagle is one of a few remedies with an aversion to chocolate, made me dare to prescribe the remedy. His love of gliding, aversion to being caged, strong emotions regarding injustice, his desire to be up high in the mountains, all matched the Chabra case.

Cases

RAVEN *Corvus corax principalis*

Case taken by Jessica Jackson, LAc.

40+year-old woman, short, feathery black hair, plain blue shirt, prominent nose, strong bones in face. Sharp features. Dark, arching eyebrows. Runs fingers through hair often. Places fingertips over mouth. Has intense look, of desperation at times; eyes are bright.

CC: spinal injuries.

Prone to crying easily. Burst into tears easily. Looking at my depression now as maybe an issue through my whole life but more pronounced now. What brought the current thing on was house painting and had a ladder injury resulting in my spinal injuries. Psychologically attached to being able to use my hands and my body. Have lost the ability to earn money that way. I was uninsured at the time. All the people I was connected with stopped talking to me. Was involved in a lawsuit.

Past four years after accident … you know, sometimes there's an opportunity…all the issues I'd been ignoring have come to the forefront. **Sexually molested** by both parents. Work issues. (Starts to cry). Interactions with people. Earning a living. Major issues. Although I'm working these issues, I'm sinking into a depression. Only leave house to check mail and buy groceries. Interact personally with no one. **Feel threatened by people**. Doing therapy for past 2 years, good, and past 3 years before, that was a terrible experience.

Working on healing old wounds. Think I'm being helped by someone and they do exactly what I don't want. Suicidal thoughts. Started planning it this time; started getting rid of some stuff. Getting rid of stuff that doesn't matter. Don't want to leave a mess behind. Then switched to needing to move from Mendocino to where I could be anonymous.

Years of meditation and yoga practice. **Can maintain an observer stance** to the worst of life's problems.

> OBS: *Moves very little.*

Trying to find out what happened to me in my family on my own. Mom seems to be very depressed, psychotic depression. What was really going on?

Doing it all on my own without any help from anyone in my family saying, "this is what the reality was."

Can't seem to shake depression no matter what I'm doing. Can't seem to get myself out of it.

OBS: *Trying to hold back tears.*

Reliving childhood experience of hiding. If I don't talk to anyone, an old pattern, how I could hide and be safe. Acting out these older patterns without any ability to control myself. When I was dealing with my things the other day, realized it was a bit over the edge.

? *What happened with the first therapist?*
On a psychic level, after the injury, **felt I was reliving my entire childhood**. Even going to bed and not being able to move; like being reborn on psychic level. The therapist; I had never gone to therapy because of yoga background and therapy was of the mind so why bother? But I was in a bad way. No friends; lawsuit attacking me. Her approach was – now I see it as very bad boundaries – the hug and kiss and I related a memory of a bad experience at a sink and she brought me to the sink and gave me a kiss; giving me a good experience, which I thought was sweet at the time but I got very attached to her. So I said, ok, now I'm attached, so what now? And she said if you saw me at the side of the road and my car was disabled, you could call for help but that would be the extent of our relationship.

? *What did that mean to you?*
That I had no value. I wouldn't even stop for a stranger. I might call for help if I was a mile down the road. In my assessment, she started getting close to me and had to deny me. But she also acted out my mother. Even the incest was reenacted. The examples are coming in a negative way.

? *How was she like your mother?*
Felt a lot of deprivation around physical contact. She was volatile, out of control. Both parents sexually molested me when I was younger and stopped when I could speak and complain about it.

? *What was that like for you? When it was happening?*

RAVEN CASES

Cases

I'd come out of therapy more confused then when I went in and more worried about what she did and why did she act that way and I still don't know. One time, her physical appearance was entirely different. Her hair was white and pulled back. Told me to close her eyes; she didn't want me to see her. Entangled. Having bad boundaries. Where my mom saw no difference between herself and her children.

I had no resources, no friends, and no work and was quite desperate. My friends, in retrospect, I was with the wrong group of people. The person whose house I was working on was an integral part of this group I was in. Took me to this hospital by ambulance and was told nothing was wrong with me, because I had no insurance. Told I'd be ok in 3 days. 8 weeks later, could not get out of bed. Was using a bedpan. This friend who was a chiropractor and now is no longer my friend, said I need to get an attorney because the doctors won't see you without money or insurance. And the community turned against me, even those that had been treated very badly by the homeowner.

Moved 5-6 times so I could heal my wounds and have a nervous breakdown. Got to be questioning, "**What's real?**" I was told it would be 3 days to be walking around and that was not real. I was even uncertain about my ability to drive here today because I've been so closeted.

? Tell me more about that feeling.
Feel safer to stay in my house, and not exchange with anyone. I've had bad experiences. And part of me thinks that I need to see that I'm not responsible for other people's bad behavior, like I still think I'm responsible for my mother's insanity. But there's still part of me that reacts. Job at art center for 7 months. Put in charge of whole set of accounts, creating it from scratch. This was complicated and I tended to work overtime and **thrived on working hard**, conscientiously, thinking all this trauma on my back is over now. Then someone in the office, and I don't completely understand what happened, she and I had a difficult thing. **I set my boundaries with her for interfering in something personal of mine** and she went into. . . she stopped working, stopped making deposits, would leave the office without telling anyone. So I wasn't getting supported. Went to the boss several times and said, "She's got to do her job." And the boss said she has emotional problems and he was going to help her with her emotional problems. But after 8 weeks of no one doing anything, I lost my temper. I called the woman a bitch; she threatened to sue the art cen-

ter and I lost my job. Later I found out that because she wasn't doing her job, they had to cancel $60,000 worth of classes and some of the money was missing which she was in control of. But because I lost my temper, I was out of a job. Had just gotten a raise 2 days before.

? In the moment you lost your temper, what happened?
I had gone upstairs to the boss and told him I was going to bring the matter up at the staff meeting because I need a resolution. I was furious. And this person who had completely shut down around me gave me a look. And I went over to tell her I'd tried to work things out with her and now did she want to say anything? She said no, so I said, "you bitch." But there were other things. And I'd just gotten this raise, begrudgingly. I was furious because I was working so hard to make the place organized. And the Board was putting pressure on me. They're still my friends, and **there was this sick other person who had all this control over things.** Just like my mother. Who everybody walks on eggshells around and no one addresses the issue.

So got another bookkeeping job and there was another dynamic there of an old guy, the controller, who tripped over the owner's dog and got a detached retina and went completely blind. The dynamics of the work situation that regardless of his nasty behavior, they were going to keep him there because of the accident. And he stopped me every time I tried to do something that was a normal bookkeeping procedure. He wasn't paying bills. Told the boss about this negativity in the office; don't want to hear from people who he's promising to pay and isn't paying them. So boss promised a meeting the next day and they said, this isn't working, here's your paycheck. So one of the Board members from the art center hires me immediately to do his books. And he's losing his eyesight. **This is the second person losing their sight coming to me for a job.** But he didn't want a bookkeeper; he wanted a caretaker. Couldn't admit that to himself. Had me running all over the place doing things for him. So I set my boundaries and I changed jobs with another bookkeeper, to another job with another older man who was losing his sight! Three men in a row. I always go right to, "What is the cosmic thing here? **Am I being blind to something?**" And he wanted me to do his grocery shopping, etc. And if that had been in the job description, I wouldn't have had an issue with it.

Ran into a dear friend, or who was a dear friend, and he's suffering from depression and a recluse like myself. We had a very uneventful meeting. Said, "We

RAVEN CASES

Cases

can't help each other, I'm sorry." Next day I got a phone call from him and he knew my sexual history, and he said "It takes me 3-4 days after I see you to get my head back on straight; you are the most fucked up sick person I've ever met and someone else told me to stay away from you and I could help you with your problem if you weren't so fucked up and sick." And I said, "Yes, I'm having a hard time here, no doubt," and then it dawned on me that he meant sexually. So I said, "Are you saying you could help me out sexually?" And he said, "Yeah, if you weren't so fucked up and sick." So I told him, "What makes you think I'd be inclined to do that with you?" He said a couple of other derogatory things and hung up. And I wondered, what had I done to have this happen?

Part of the lesson is to see that I didn't do anything. Don't want to put myself out there again. Don't think I'm seeing the truth here that I have no responsibility for how things happen at all. Like for my crazy parents.

My mother's an only child. She had 4 children. I was third of four. She was always very erotic and erratic. Uncontrolled. Hot tempered. Sadistic. **Almost like being tortured on a daily basis**. My father was… I remember his sexual abuse more. I think he justified it by my being a child. What I think happened; I can remember my father coming into the bedroom, putting his hands under the covers, squatting down next to the bed, telling me not to look and masturbating me. Think my mother caught my father doing it and he explained it as a way to put the baby to sleep. **What I remember is "leaving."** Couldn't handle the experience. Remember later being in embarrassing situations, once with a lover and when I came to, they were waiting for me to come back. Would leave because I couldn't go anywhere; no escape from that manipulation. People play games and I'm the victim. I remember catching my mother doing this to my infant brother; I was 10 and he was in the crib screaming his head off. I yelled at her, "You're doing the same thing to him that you did to me." She smacked me across the face. **So I knew but I didn't know. I didn't know what it was then**. My older brother… none of us have any relationship with each other. No trust with each other. No trust that our mother will keep out of our lives. Once with my brother I brought up the subject of sexual abuse and he said, "oh yeah, I remember that all the time. But you're still alive; stop complaining and move on with your life. She didn't kill us." And my sister will not talk about anything. She's completely shut down. Can't make a decision for herself. But she says our childhood was completely fine and I don't know what you're talking about.

I often got hit for no reason. For things I don't know how they were wrong.

I cry all the time. I can't get out of it. I stay in the house. Feel I'm making psychological progress but… I could move. I could pack up. But if it's not better here, then I'm making things worse. I'm in a place now with low rent. A beautiful setting. You can have a nervous breakdown and nobody…you couldn't do it in the city. I'm hoping that a change of scenery will help but I don't know if that's true.

If I'm not doing anything, my body doesn't hurt me. If I do, I get reminded I have a back injury. Should I go back to school? Then I get caught up in I'm not a good student, school is terrible, how can I do this? I am quite a pot smoker these days. I've always smoked pot; but before this I would not smoke socially. It was not a form of entertainment. It was around meditation and evening retreat. I wouldn't answer the phone, meditate and go to sleep. Now I wake up and smoke a joint because I don't know what I'm going to do with my day. Anxiety of not having anything to do. So smoking helps. My other therapist played quite a trick on me about pot smoking. I'm now seeing it as not something which causes depression but a symptom of depression.

? Why smoke now?
Well I can get up and shower and eat and then what? Do I have anything to do? That I can create? I can't think of anything. I can't do anything. So soon I'm having an anxiety attack. And what a worthless, terrible person I am. Rather than deal with that, I'll smoke a joint and then I don't care. I'll shift into something else and then I don't care.

? What's the discomfort talking to people?
Because I'm feeling too vulnerable. And I take everything very personally. I don't want to do vulnerable in front of anyone. This therapist I had; that trust was betrayed and she even gives workshops on trust and betrayal. So she has some lesson to learn.

I think people I've chosen as friends conform to an old pattern and they are people who are judgmental, critical, and narcissistic. I somehow attract these

RAVEN CASES

Cases

people because of my psychology. But it only reinforces for me that I'm of no value to anybody.

? Describe one of these friends to me in detail.
A friend who's a pretty popular chiropractor, a high-energy person. I went from living in spiritual communities for 10 years. Went in at 21 and came out at 31. Hadn't even had a checkbook till then. That was a trauma for me; I thought I was getting too involved in the world. A checkbook is a worldly thing to have. Then dropped into a lesbian community. Had relationships with women before but never been in the political community of lesbianism before and most of the people, the group of women who rejected me were all gay women, the woman who's house I was working in was a gay woman. Part of me is still trying to figure this all out. Anyway, my chiropractor friend is a powerful person who thinks very highly of herself. I moved out of the ashram and living by myself for 10 years and living near another ashram and really doubting whether my interactions with people were healthy or not. Invited me to rent a room in her house; she had financial issues and her roommate moved out and I'd been becoming too withdrawn so I did. Took two flights of stairs to get to the door and I'm following her and she goes into the house and locks it. And I'm outside thinking this is ludicrous. I knock and she takes her time and I say, "Why did you do that? Why did you lock me out?" And she says, "Oh, it was just habit." So my whole exchange with her was this sadistic power trip. I would always scratch my head and wonder what is going on here? I don't know what it was. It's a behavior I would never think of. She had a friend who was dying of and people were all taking turns taking care of this woman. A very noble thing, I thought. In the spiritual community, you get sick and you just go off into your room and figure out your karma. And you don't get help in that way. So I'd be painting, and she'd work late and I'd cook a nice meal, doing things generously because I wanted to. And she thought I was stupid for doing those things. Why would I do anything for free? Voluntarily? So when this friend got sick, it was easier for me to cook a meal for this person and someone would bring it over. And I did this for a year. One night, these people came over to our house for dinner and I cooked this big meal and these were not my friends; these were her friends and they said, "We can't believe how you could do this, cooking all these meals week after week, when you're at the office and practicing." And I said, "What's going on?" I

couldn't believe it but **she hadn't told them it was me doing all the cooking. She was taking credit for it**. And I thought, ok, this is her ego; this doesn't matter to me. Then she came to my house, brought her bicycle into my living room and oiled the chain on my living room floor. Got oil all over my carpet. **And didn't even think; didn't even apologize**. The last straw for me...

At that point, I started to withdraw. I didn't call her; I waited for her to call me. She started teaching a workshop on how to be an effective listener and a good communicator. She called me; 45 minutes we were on the phone and she started to say what a good response she'd gotten. She started to articulate on the phone [speaks very precisely] speaking in this way so I could get the gist of how good a communicator and good listener she was. She did this whole number on the phone and I could hear her girlfriend's son in the background and eventually she asked, "So how are you?" And I replied, "Oh well, you know, and...hello? Hello?" and I could hear the voices in the background. She'd put the phone down and walked away. Which I've seen her do to other people. So I hung up the phone. And she called up hours later and said, "I don't know what happened. We must have gotten disconnected." And I said, "I heard you put the phone down. How could you do such a thing? After telling me what a good communicator and listener you are?" That was the last straw.

? What was the feeling? When she's oiling her chain...
I just get shocked. Why would anybody do such a thing? So I get into a little self-doubt. Was that real, what I just saw?

More recently, I have this friend who has a birthday near mine. And I bought her a present; she has a back injury and she's talking about getting her woodshop together to make little things and I bought her this little tool. I bought myself a chainsaw. And that was it. She stopped talking to me. Months and months later, she finally said, "That present was too expensive. You spent too much money on it. You made me feel indebted." And I thought, "Well, you could have brought the present back." She said, "Well, I just didn't open it." So now this person is out of my life because I bought her a birthday present.

? What did you think about that?
  I don't know! And so...

RAVEN CASES

Cases

? No! You must think something. It's upset you.
Well, I think here I'm relating to somebody. I think this person really understands me. We've had deep conversations. Why can she not talk to me about this? Why did she have to just not talk to me? When I asked her, "Well, you just made me feel indebted." So why couldn't you come and talk to me about it? Take this stupid present back; I don't mind.

See I go right to a place in my head that I'm not worth…if someone can't come and talk to me about this then I'm not worth the exchange. If somebody can't explain himself or herself to me, then I must not be worth it. If I think I'm connected to someone, some deep conversation, some sharing of emotion, some intimacy on some level, then…was I really saying that? I don't know? There's always speculation about people's response. I'm left to speculate, just like in my family. Was my mother depressed, was she mentally ill, or was she just a nasty woman who hated her kids?

? What do you dream about at night?
I'll be honest to say that when I smoke pot, my dreams go right out the window. If I'm not smoking, my dreams are very visual. And I wake up and wonder, **what is the reality**? Was the dream the reality or the waking state? I have a hard time figuring it out. I dream in really good color. I have dreams that are I'm the observer; lucid dreams where I watch what happens. Very aware of being a watcher. They stay with me for a while. If smoking, I have no memory. **Lots of dreams of water; of the waves, and oceans**. In one, I was with a friend who I thought was an evolved guy. A peaceful dream. I could see fish. Could see ocean with massive waves that would come and break before they got to me. I turned around because I heard somebody and I was face to face with myself and so scared it woke me up. Frightening to look and see myself. Terrified to see myself; to turn around and be nose to nose with me. But I think in the dream I was looking for myself, in some old, dusty forgotten place.

Think I was terrified when I was a kid all the time. When I get in a bad emotional state, I think of crawling under a table, going into a closet. **Hiding. Duck and cover.** One thing that kept coming up was a closet in my house where I used to hide. Something about this closet. So I built a reproduction of this closet in my house. Mortified and terrified because I never knew what my mother was going to say or do to hurt me. She said to me one time that she would lie awake at night and think about ways to kill me. Lie awake all night and fantasize about ways I can kill you. And I was in grammar school. But now if I think of her as being a depressed mother, that makes perfect sense to me. But it's just coming to me now that maybe she was just depressed and my own depression is allowing me to see this. That maybe she wasn't just crazy and out of control, maybe she was really mentally ill. She'd get upset and grab a butcher knife and chase me around the house with a butcher knife. Like psychotic. So you ask if I was terrified in my life, and yes, I was terrified.

? What did you think would happen?
I thought she'd kill me. Her reactions were out of control; beyond anything rational. Picking up a pot of spaghetti sauce—my Italian mother—and throwing it over her head, all over the kitchen because we didn't do something right while we were cleaning the kitchen. Pasta dripping all over the kitchen. Or turning the table upside down. Or saying something really disgusting while we were sitting down to eat so we'd all lose our appetites and not eat. This instance at the kitchen sink, my sister washing dishes and me drying dishes, every night, the same routine, and every night my mother would pass by numerous times and she would reach inside our thigh and pinch us with her fingernails and we had to stand there. It was like torture. "Mom, please don't do this; we hate it." And every night we'd go through the same thing, **because we were her property and she could do whatever she wanted** with us. When I was in therapy, I had a phone conversation with my mother; I lost my kid brother from a cocaine overdose. I lost my train of thought. I got a call from my mother. And she said, "You know I'd really like to get a monkey and I could put a diaper on it and I could feed it like I used to do with you kids and it could be my plaything like you kids used to be." I couldn't believe my ears. That she thought of her kids as playthings. Makes perfect sense if she was an only kid and didn't know about sexuality or didn't know any of those things to think that an infant can't talk, has no value, has no anything; I can do whatever I want to this and who's going to know it? Just a little monkey I can play with.

Rx: *Corv-c 200C*

Cases

FOLLOW-UP AT ONE MONTH:
So do I have light in my eyes?
Oh, yes, there is light.

    OBS: *seems more settled in her seat*

Now there is. I'm completely off coffee. I slept a lot for the first few days. My sleeping schedule is completely different. It's not a complaint. I'm sleeping later in the morning. Instead of going to bed at 8 and getting up at 4, I'm going to bed at 10 and sleeping till 7 or 8 which is a different cycle after years and years. And I've had some very good days where I almost feel like a normal human being again. Been taking the remedy about twice the amount, taking the remedy as soon as I get up then I can function.

That's fabulous.
Yes it is fabulous. A couple of days where I didn't take the remedy first thing in the morning and I slumped right into a depression. So I feel I'm going through this adjustment; of stabilizing. Days have not been perfect but I've had very very nice days and this is all I have left (gives remedy bottle). Had some days where the remedy made me feel really really good and times when I'd have an anxiety attack that I had nothing to do so then I'd go into smoking a joint; just a hit before going to bed. **But pot consumption is way down.** I'm dreaming a lot more but I can't quite grab them; but I knew I had a dream. My therapy appointment this last time was just giggling and laughing.

So I think your expertise and intuition is right on so thank you.

Fighting a little lethargy. Can't quite get motivated to take the next step.

? Is there any rush?
I haven't worked since July so a part of me thinks I should snap to and get back to work but I understand I'm coming out of this. I really am and I'm kind of preparing for something to happen. I don't know what it is but I definitely realized I'm in a wrong place but I don't know where it is. So I'm tossing stuff; organizing stuff. Been cleaning my carpentry tools with a bit more enthusiasm. Packing them away. So I **can almost feel an optimism** that I wasn't able to feel before. Bet you love me saying this.

Sure do!
I think it's a funny thing, I don't know if I can explain, but these issues I've been dealing with on a psychological level, somehow got healed a long time ago but that there was some other covering over me that didn't allow me to see that those issues were healed [holds one hand in front of her like a claw, relaxed]. And now I'm thinking that all these things, some of these things, are unfinished business. I'm not involved in it the way I was.

? How's your back?
I stopped my treatment. Acupuncturist was going to Baja for a month and I was having one more treatment before he left and I decided to cancel because I hadn't been pushing myself and my back wasn't hurting and there's a psychology that was holding me about being disabled that I wanted to get out of. Should've had a treatment today; been close to a month now that I haven't had a treatment. A little achy but nothing that's really bothering me.

? How's your heart been?
It's opening up a little. I'm letting light into it, too. So now it's opening; it's opening.

RAVEN CASES

? How's the social scene? Any strange encounters? Feeling uncomfortable in that community? Have you been into to town?
I have gone into town; to do my business and there are a couple of people; I've given your name to as a result who I have very nice connections with. And I'm also seeing I'm being vindicated; my behavior has been vindicated in several regards.

? How are your animals?
Good. Actually saw 2 phenomena on the way down. There must have been 30-40 ravens flying around at this bridge on the way. They were hovering over the bridge. So I thought maybe there was something dead. And I also saw a hawk fly right in front of my windshield and it was just like it was frozen there. Beautiful.

Cases

PEREGRINE FALCON *Falco peregrinus*

CASE 1:
Case by Bruno Galeazzi taken in March 1999:

Patient is a 38-year-old woman. She married when she was 20 and divorced one year later. Works in an animal beauty center (cleaning, taking care, selling food for pets).

Presenting symptoms: she suffers from gastritis and colitis; stitching pains, bending double, with fainting sensation. In '97 gastric ulcer and erosive gastritis; in '99 antrum gastritis (diagnosed via gastroscopy).

Past History
Her family: much fighting between her parents: dad very closed and yielding, suffered his wife's aggressiveness. P. developed the idea that she had not to "disturb" too much in her family.
Polio vaccine side effects in the first months of her life, she slightly limps.
In 1983 had a son born before term; he died soon after birth. Voluntary abortion in Dec. '97.

Generals
Chilly; perspires under axillae if excited.
Always had little hunger and if under stress doesn't eat at all.

Sleep
She tells nothing about sleep and dreams in the first visit.

Mentals
Tends to amplify everything.
Likes flying with the modern version of the parachute (hang gliding), likes art and spiritual matters.
Not able to watch the TV news because suffers when looking at world troubles.
Cries, and if she cries her pain in stomach gets better.
Gets angry if she sees lack of humanity.
Feels extremely her emotions (sad or happy, whatever).

Always dedicated herself to the needs of other people.
Doesn't stand compromise.
Optimistic, likes life.
Love for animals.
Likes having friends, very sympathetic.
She's trying to feel that she exists.
Feels she has a volcano inside herself that desires to explode, needs to share. energy, giving and receiving with the world.
Feels much love and desire to give inside herself.
Feels she wants to get out from the egg.
Always thinks she has many physical defects, sees others as better than she.
Sensation of being fragile, like glass.

> COMMENT: *At this point of the visit I told her I was planning to give her Hawk. She smiled, she was surprised: she likes eagles and hawks a lot. Moreover, she is not able to paint, but when she feels sad she draws hawks on the walls of her house and feels better. The third visit she showed me some photos with her drawing of the hawks on the walls: they looked like perfect images of true hawks, also she gave me a present of a hawk painted on a river stone: I have it on my desk, it's perfect!*

She feels well when flying.
In everyday life she feels like a chicken.
When she attended a speleology (spelunking) seminar she felt she was neglecting the ethereal part of herself. Speleology is a sport for masochists.
Always when she writes her thoughts she says she would like to start to fly but she feels like in a cage; she feels she already has the wings but she's still impeded.
When she flies (hang glides) she likes to fly with the hawks following the ascending warm air.

Rx: *Falco-p* 30C, 10 drops night, morning, night (10 succussions).

FALCON CASES

Cases

FOLLOW UP AFTER 3 WEEKS:
After the remedy: many symptoms for several days.
After the first dose (night): violent pains in her stomach, stitching pains from the stomach extending to the back (so violent that she wanted to go to the hospital, but didn't).
After the second dose: all the pains are gone.
The following days: pain in abdomen < after eating, that continued for about 10 days; the pains shifted then to the arm following the Large Intestine (acupuncture) Meridian.
A dark scotoma (blind spot), already present in the last 2 years, seemed enlarged after the remedy, then back to normal dimensions, like a spot.
After 10 days: whistling in ears.

> COMMENT: She started having pain in stomach (and ulcer) after a strong emotional trauma with her boyfriend. She left him, but she was pregnant and, because of the therapy against ulcer, decided for abortion.

Much desire for colors like **yellow and blue.**
Much influenced by the weather: < before thunderstorm.
< North wind.
Now she is able to express anger (never had been able to before). She compares herself to a hawk in vertical dive.
After 10 days: telephone:
Gastric pains back again.

Rx: *Falco-p 30C,* 10 drops night, morning, night (10 succussions)

FOLLOW UP AFTER ONE MONTH:
After the remedy: strange dreams for two nights.
Gastric pains up and down.
Hunger (in the past she had little hunger and could go to sleep without dinner).
She clearly perceives that all the times that she expresses anger her stomach is safe (much more able to express anger than in the past).
Now she is able to feel (positive feeling) that she exists in others' eyes.

Sensation of blocked energies in her hands that are waiting to be pushed out.

Now able to say all that she feels and thinks.

After the first dose of the remedy: sensation of a ball of fire in the stomach that gets rid of a mass of seaweed that enveloped it.

Much desire to love people.

Much idealistic: suffers a lot when a person shows a mask.

She has broken a relationship that had ups and downs.

Dreams: around the theme of fertility, pregnancy, giving life (I can send you the details).

Has been thinking of her first baby that died in 1983.

A dream: she was in the hospital and saw a dead baby in an aquarium.

A dream: her sister with her child; the patient was playing with a doll and was experiencing much love like she could have experienced for her real child.

Much fear about having another child but she desires this a lot.

There's another friend that now is calling her: she is still waiting, but feels much protected by him and she likes this feeling.

After abortion in 1997 she thought to commit suicide, she felt she had "touched the bottom" in her life. For several months she flew a lot.

Some summary:

Mid '97 she drew her first hawk.

September '97 beginning of gastric pains.

December '97 abortion.

Now she would like to draw a hawk diving on a dove: but she's scared by this image. Then she thought that she would prefer to be able to draw a hawk that protects a dove, but she doesn't know how to draw it. She can't stand the idea of the hawk killing the dove. She is in pain for the dove.

She has been sweet, proper, sensitive to other sufferings for such a long time (she compares herself to a dove).

She remembers that when at primary school she won a prize for her goodness. She felt this as a spite they did to her. She was just timid; in herself she was feel-

FALCON CASES

Cases

ing much more aggressive, an "earthquake." That time she realized that judgments can be so wrong.

Since her childhood, her family and at school, everybody wanted her to have a proper and good behavior. She behaved in this way because she saw that others liked this, she did so to please others.

Now she remembers that after the first dose of Falcon the whistling in her ear and pain in her leg came back: same symptoms that she had in her childhood (leg with poliomyelitis).

Rx: *Falco-p 200C*; 10 drops night, morning, night

FOLLOW-UP:
She is doing wonderfully about stomach and abdominal pains and, most of all, she feels great on the psychological level.

COMMENTS BY BRUNO GALEAZZI:

I have used *Falco peregrinus* in several other cases. I prescribed *Falco-p* after searching the following symptoms in MacRep, that seem to be strong in the remedy:

> Mind; DELUSIONS, imaginations; worthless, he is
> Mind; DELUSIONS, imaginations; trapped, he is
> Mind; DELUSIONS, imaginations; body, body parts; brittle, is
> Mind; DELUSIONS, imaginations; ugly, is
> Mind; DELUSIONS, imaginations; prisoner, she is a
> Mind; DELUSIONS, imaginations; glass, she is made of
> ("fragile" in my understanding)

In some cases the first thought was going to *Thuja* and this brought me to *Falco-p* that better matched the case. The patient usually improves dramatically in her sensation of existing as a person, the Ego becomes stronger, the Self has more strength to express its deeper identity; usually the patient says that she feels strong enough to take her own place in the world. Most of my *Falco-p* cases are young females, age from 20 to 45.

CASE 2:
Case by William Shevin

> COMMENT: *The patients in the following two cases were students, and both had the sensation of being trapped in adverse circumstances. They both responded well to the prescription of* Falco peregrinus disciplinatus.

10 YEAR-OLD BOY: JUNE 2001

CC: school problems, possible learning disability, possible ADD

The history is given by the mother: Years of boredom at school, leading to discouragement, diarrhea, lethargy, and difficulty getting up in the morning. The greatest problems are in getting ready for the school bus in the morning – he just doesn't want to go. He is tired in the morning, sick. He eats breakfast and then has an urge to use the bathroom, but he doesn't really have a stool. He is somewhat better from eating. This only happens on school days, so mother is clear that he is trying to avoid going to school. This aversion is getting progressively worse. He pleads to stay home, saying he wants to stay with his mother. When she doesn't allow it, he is angry and resentful.

He is looking for some change. He says school is "pointless." He says "why can't we move on, why do I need to write down the answers if I already know them? I'm done and I still have to wait for people. I only have 2 friends in my class."

He has lost hope (for change), feels, discouraged, and can't see how he is useful, or that school is useful to him. He learns very quickly. "The teacher explains everything and I don't need it." When he is bored, acts as if he is trapped, lashes out, throws arms around, can't speak his words fast enough, may bang his head in frustration ("Don't you get it?") He may also feel powerless, and weeps in anger.

He can have a hard time falling asleep, then in the morning he can't wake up. He likes to play computer games, soccer, and run around in the lawn sprinkler. He is best with one friend at a time; they act weird. One on one, he is respectful and honest, and shares his feelings without hurting the other person.
He likes pizza, pepperoni, taco sauce, and salsa.

Weather: dehydrates easily, at soccer camp in the summer. He is a "bullet" on the soccer field.

Cases

Lately, he is more restless. He shies away from compliments, can be very quiet and be overlooked. When he "taps into something of interest," he is running over with ideas, articulate, clear speech, and doesn't stop until it is finished.

He is compassionate and willing to make peace at his own expense.

He is sensitive to noise, especially to yelling.

For a while, he was home schooled, but he became anxious to "not know what they were talking about (the kids at school)." He worried that he was behind. He doesn't want to be the last one done. He is stimulated by the attention of one person, but feels left out in a group.

He has dreams of loud noises, or of being chased by evil men. He fears thunderstorms.

The family is socially intact, without unusual stresses.

Physical examination was unremarkable, as was a complete blood count and urinalysis.

Rx: *Falco-p 200C* (Helios), single dose.

Follow up one month later:

He is "good," according to his mother. All symptoms were worse for 3 days. "Caged and rage." They took a long car ride the very next day after the initial dose. He wanted to get out of the car, asking, "When are we getting there?" in a very dramatic and angrily toned manner. His mother described him as "restless, let's go here, there", and also aggressive.

Before, if angry, he held it in. Now he is expressing himself verbally, and with hand gestures. Mother states that he is "facing his anger, the source of it, rather than hiding, or going to her.

He began to warm up, noticed especially at night. Formerly he piled blankets on, now very much less. His mother noted that he became more playful, "angry like a bear." She "saw more colors in him."

He is not as tolerant as he formerly had been. He was getting up earlier in the morning, waking up "conscious" (instead of "lifeless and not together.")

He reads a lot, staying up late to do so. He has always concentrated better in the evening.

Appetite is good. Mother notes that he tends to "dehydrate" easily.

A thunderstorm passed unnoticed.

OBS: *he was brighter, more alert, and active.*

FOLLOW UP THREE MONTHS AFTER REMEDY:
Appointment cancelled, as he was well. I called to inquire and his mother reported the following. " He is finding his freedom in his own choices. Not needing to be reminded to do his homework. He is interested in what he is reading, as well as in his writing. His writing is more thoughtful and neat. He has stopped having temper tantrums, which formerly would have occurred particularly if he had to go somewhere against his wishes. There is no anxiety or other problem in getting onto the school bus in the morning. He enjoys coming home on the school bus this year, instead of needing to be picked up by his parents. He is enjoying his 5th grade classroom.

He has continued to be well.

He wrote a poem sometime in September 2001. According to his mother, he wrote it "in just a few minutes" and somewhat illegibly ("scratchy, as if he 'clawed' it and wrote it at the same time):

FALCON FREEDOM

I'm a bird locked away,
I'm a bird who wants to play,
I want to speed among the air,
I want to be freed among the land,

Can I be free?
Can I once again soar through the air?
Can I stray again please?
Can I divide the air again?

I want to soar through the land,
I want the air to hit my face again,
I want to dive down and strike prey,
I want freedom!

FALCON CASES

Cases

CASE 3:
Case by William Shevin.
18-year-old male, April 2002.

The problem is suicidal ideation, which began 4 years earlier. He doesn't recall the initial circumstances, but was "down a lot, unhappy." The feelings come on suddenly ("I'm fine and then within 5 minutes I'm ready to do something bad.") He feels irritable, doesn't want to be around, and that everything is wrong. He notices "all the stuff that isn't perfect," and just wants to end it all. This happens if he fails a test, has a conflict with a friend, or if he is in trouble with his parents (as in when he punched a hole in the wall in a rage while experiencing built-up frustration).

He is angry with, and blames himself. If he forgets to do his homework, he becomes very annoyed, and thinks of all the little things that bother him, all the things he has to do but doesn't want to do. He is a perfectionist, and has been since childhood. Even as a toddler, he analyzed and figured things out. He wants to figure out what people's motives are, why they do the things they do. He is curious, always interested in what is going on.

I ask what are the things that he decides to take on. He is a drummer, and likes all music, especially jazz and jam bands like the Allman brothers. He likes to improvise, and **feels free when playing music,** that there is "no me saying do this, that what I'm playing comes from me." He also likes to hang out with friends, skateboard and snowboard. With these activities, he experiences "**complete freedom in the flow, the turning,**" and he likes to go "**really fast**." He was the fastest player on his team, and played defense. **In this position, he could "hang out and react, wait until the other player had committed himself."**

The worst situation is school, in which he is "bored all the time, learning stuff you'll never need; you can't do anything about it, just have to sit in the chair." In this circumstance, he is "bored out of his mind, and feels that he can get along without listening."

He is respectful, good for his word, and likes to help people (though this is not a big theme in his life.) He doesn't lose his temper unless provoked, in which case he becomes really angry, edgy, intense, explosive.

He has a **fear of snakes, and he also dreams of snakes**. His appetite is poor in the morning for the past year, but otherwise "good – I'm a growing boy."

He has mild pollen allergies, in which he feels stuffed up, and lazy.

> OBS: He sat directly across me, with his mother directly to his right. He leaned into the corner of the chair next to her, and so faced me more than her. There was no animosity or other disturbance in their interaction. He spoke quite readily, but also accepted his mother's contribution when she made it, or when I questioned her directly. He had a plastic bottle of water with him, and twisted the neck of the bottle, screwed and unscrewed the cap, and at one point in the interview appears somewhat aggressive in the twisting. He was alert, and somewhat tense. He could be engaged in the interview, described himself readily, and made good contact, and maintained physical distance. If pressed on point, he was quite willing to cooperate. He appeared to enjoy the process of the interview. It had a somewhat upbeat and abrupt cadence to it.

Socially, he was adept, had a good circle of friends. His family was intact and without significant disturbing issues.

Rx: *Falco-p 1M* (Helios), single dose

ONE MONTH FOLLOW-UP:

"I don't want to kill myself every day, only 2-3 times since (the first visit). Those feelings were of brief duration, however. "

He started feeling better within a week of the dose. He wanted to play drums more, and played in a more excited manner. He said he didn't know if the feeling, at that time, was "good." Mother felt him to be more open, noting that he went on a fishing trip with his father (which he denied was "meaningful").

He "confronted" his father about the father's "non-communicative" manner.

> OBS: he seemed somewhat more relaxed.

Rx: Wait.

SIX WEEKS AFTER THE REMEDY:

Telephone: according to his mother, he is "down in the dumps." He had been doing "really well, but just had a car accident." He totaled his car (no one was hurt seriously). He has had some suicidal thinking but "not as often."

Rx: repeat *Falco-p 1M*, one dose.

FALCON CASES

Cases

OBS: He improved quickly following the dose.

FOUR MONTHS AFTER THE REMEDY:
He is now well out-of-school, and excited to be going to college. Asked about his suicidal thoughts, he replies that he "has things to live for now." There are no "bad thoughts, since at least 2 weeks before school ended.

At his usual allergy time, he had only a "little cold" in the last two weeks. No other symptoms of allergy. He was staying up late at night.

Rx: Doing well, no medicine.

I did not see him again until mid-July of 2003, but had contact with his mother. He used the remedy on a few occasions in the following year, once when the anger seemed strong and there was any hint of suicidal thinking. This happened after he was robbed on the street, losing all his book money at the beginning of the year. He bounced back very quickly after the remedy. He had an acute epidemic flu-like illness that winter, and recovered very quickly after *Falco-p 1M*.

In mid-July 2003 he was again feeling symptoms (albeit milder) similar to the original presentation. The primary external stress seemed to be inactivity and boredom, this time primarily relating to his work situation. He had used the remedy in the 1M potency a few weeks before without much response. He responded quickly and well to *Falco-p 10M*.

COMMENTS BY BILL SHEVIN:
Neither of the boys in Cases 2 and 3, nor the other patients for whom I've prescribed *Falco-p* successfully, have been violent towards others. I have the impression that patients needing this remedy are usually restrained, with internalized anger, although they may still be intense. Outbursts of frank violence could presumably occur.

In the two cases presented here, the trapped sensation was accompanied by anger but also with lethargy (in case 2), and suicidal ideation, tension, and anger (in case 3). The feeling of being trapped, and of being powerlessness came up often in the proving, as well as feelings of humiliation and shame.

They both objected to doing schoolwork, which they found boring. In both cases their academic abilities were excellent, and their assessment of the work as "boring" can be easily understood.

In both cases, I initially saw them soon before the end of the school year. Case 2 had a very intense emotional reaction in the first 3 days after the remedy, following which his behavior changed dramatically and the following fall he adapted very well to school, even enjoying it. Case 3 went away to college and so it is more difficult to assess the changes during that time. He certainly tolerated the 2 months left of his high school career better after the treatment, and clearly responded well to re-administration of the medicine on several occasions, including physical illness.

Neither of these two patients presented with significant physical pathology. In another patient in whom *Falco peregrinus* produced dramatic benefit, one with **severe dental phobia** (as part of a Post Traumatic Stress Disorder), there is a strong and rather accurate clairvoyance, especially to the needs of others, especially her family, and a strong sense of guilt if she is unable to help. This stress can trigger gallbladder inflammations, as well as clenching of the teeth and polyarthritis, all of which have been greatly helped with *Falco peregrinus*. In addition, she is more tolerant of cold, has increased vital heat, and notes less intolerance of touch and constriction. I have the impression, at least in two adults whom I have seen benefit from this remedy, that there is a very strong sense of obligation.

Jonathan Shore M.D. described falcons as being the most acrobatic of the raptors, capable of very high speeds and abrupt changes in direction. This was true of both these patients, who were **agile and had quick reaction** times as soccer players. Case 3's jazz drumming style was described as pyrotechnic. I have also seen similar ideas in other cases of people responding well to Falcon – exertion accompanied by a kind of joy in motion and activity. **Activities like skiing, skate or snowboarding, flying, fast driving, etc., are likely outlets for these patients.**

Other cases: I have a few other patients doing well with this remedy.

The first is a 66-year-old woman whom I treated with *Natrum phosphoricum* in January 1998.

Eagle Case 2 had also responded well to *Natrum phosphoricum*. This remedy should be considered in a differentiation with bird remedies.

FALCON CASES

Cases

The primary issues were anxiety, digestive problems, and hypertension. Grief was a strong factor in the history. She did very well, with relief of the anxiety, normalization of the blood pressure, as well as the digestive problems. She did not return for follow-up after the third month of treatment, as she felt quite well, had normal blood pressure even after having stopped her antihypertensive medications. She returned 5 years later with recurrence of the anxiety and a dermatitis beginning around the eyes, spreading onto the face and then to the hands. Both problems had developed at the end of the prior year. The only external stress had to do with a social obligation she had been involved with for several years. She was "irritated and bored," and didn't really want to be involved any longer. She was unable, however, to express this and to extricate herself from the planning and execution of the event. She experienced a return of two fears that began at the age of 17, one of looking into the closet, and one of being stabbed in the back. She recently had dreams of her granddaughter being kidnapped. She worried about the welfare of others (primarily family members). She is extremely sympathetic, and somewhat clairvoyant. *Falco peregrinus 200C*, single dose was given. Her hands started to clear within the first week. In the second week, she felt emotionally better, more able to hear her co-worker's stories (primarily their problems) without "depression." The irritability diminished markedly. The rash continued to clear. The two fears also cleared.

The second patient is a 20-year-old female that I first treated in 1998. She has **moderate cerebral palsy, with a noticeable impairment of gait** (very tight heel cords, especially the left side), seizure disorder (moderately controlled on Depakote), and recurrent febrile upper respiratory tract illness with frequent absence from school. I gave a number of remedies, which did not have any appreciable effect. In March 2002 I gave *Falco peregrinus 1M* (Helios). This was based on her reactions of anger when not allowed to do as she pleased, mostly having to do with social situations (in which, because of her disability, she was unable to participate fully), **dreams of snakes**, an expressed angry wish to be "out of this handicapped body," a strong sense of conscientiousness towards her responsibilities at home, and a strongly sympathetic nature. Admittedly, this is not much to prescribe upon. The remedy had, however, a very dramatic effect. I convinced the parents not to use anti-pyretics the next time there was a febrile episode, and she got through it without much difficulty. By the third month she had become more vocal about her unhappiness with her disability, became "more aware of who she is" (according to her parents), and also became more flexible in her musculoskeletal system. The improvement in mood and activity continued, but relapsed after a couple of seizures in the fall. The dose of Depakote was increased, but she became more "babyish, afraid to move forward (an image from the original case, consistent with her reluctance to ambulate). *Falco peregrinus 10M*, in a single dose, was administered. Following this, ambulation again improved, to the extent that she was able to run. As of this writing, July 2003, there have been no febrile illnesses for 5 months, and in general she is quite well. There were premonitory signs of a seizure in January, which did not, however, develop. She has continued to take Depakote.

DIFFERENTIAL MATERIA MEDICA:

Anacardium orientalis: Poor self-image, internalized anger, feeling trapped or restricted, and outbursts of anger can be strong elements in Anacardium orientalis (and many other medicines).

Aurum metallicum (and salts): The strong sense of duty and intolerance of failure are common for both remedies. The suicidal feeling in Falcon, at least as seen in the case of M. presented here, comes not from failure to succeed at one's responsibility, but rather the feeling of being trapped in something that is meaningless, without redeeming value. Vithoulkas (*Materia Medica Viva* vol. 1) reports a case of *Aurum metallicum* in which dreams of flying occurred, but otherwise this theme (of restriction) does not seem important in the Aurum cases I have seen.

Sepia: The (probably overdone) image of Sepia as an overworked caretaker, worn out, irritable, averse to company could be confused with Falcon. Exertion ameliorates Sepia patients, but their instinct is to remove themselves and to be still. Exertion rouses them from "depression." In Falcon, the instinct is to break out and move, to be free.

There are many other possible comparisons. The repertory (Synthesis, v8) lists Falcon in the rubrics related to aversion to domestic duty, and the delusion of having neglected one's duty. These and related rubrics in homeopathic repertories should be looked at carefully in this regard. *Cuprum metal-*

Cases

licum (and salts) could easily be thought of, considering the tendency of Cuprum patients to be tense and controlled, yet eager and even demanding to move forward.

CASE 4:
Case by Alize Timmerman of the Hahnemann Instituut, the Netherlands.

MAY 2001:
48-Year-old man. Sleeplesslessness. Lethargy. Negative nervousness. Dwelling on things – turning things over and over in my mind. The more tired I am from not sleeping the more I do that.

What things?
I am just coming out of a project. I am looking for a new job. I stayed too long on the last job, a dot.com project in Australia, which was not funded. This is the time of life for changes. I want to change lots of things in my life.

I have had a career that has been **extremely international**. I have been very **successful**. I have **achieved** a lot. I have paid the price. Too much **travel crossing time zones**. This has really affected my sleep. It **affects my family**.

Physical problems?
Injured shoulder, bone spur, left shoulder, << working on computers, **nerves pinched.**

I had a football injury and a bad bicycle accident. Sitting in airplanes for 14 hours does not help. Being cramped makes it worse. Working on a computer makes it worse and I have to work on computers a lot.

I have allergies.
My **ears were itching** all my life. A doctor told me the itching comes from the ear pushing the wax out. In my left ear the Eustachian tube is too small and the ear gets blocked from time to time. When the ear is blocked the **shoulder gets cramped** or vice versa, I don't know what comes first.

I have lots of little things that together make a larger problem.

What happens when you don't sleep?
I tend to be a very positive person with a lot of **willpower** and both of those seem to be not as good lately. Now I tend to dwell on things negatively. It

came slowly over many years. I had a very good career, many successful company re-structurings, making change happen. I did a lot of physical travel, was away from home a lot. I **feel a bit TRAPPED** because what I do really well does involve extending myself in that way. If the problem is in India I have to physically be there. Most companies hire me because I am willing to do that. Now I don't want to do that anymore but I don't have a lot of alternatives. It's a matter of finding a new groove using the same skills. It's a challenge. I have this maybe from my grandfather, this ability to see solutions.

In business, **when I see a problem, I see a solution** right away; then I just want to get on with it. I just want to put things in place. In business you have to include people in the solution, you put them in place and then they carry on. **I don't have the patience for the nonsense of people**. I don't particularly like the games of politics. I don't have the patience for that. The corporation itself is more interested in politics; I have left 2 corporations over those issues – these breaks are difficult.

Once things are fixed, then I get bored; when I am bored I notice the politics more. I am more a leader than a manager. I have opened new markets, new countries, new regions; I have done a lot of groundbreaking work. I don't have the skills for management, but it sometimes happens that I do need to do some managing, and then it's stretching for me.

It's been extraordinarily difficult sometimes. More difficult than for others.

A lot of the things that made me good were not really me; they were more like what I thought I should be.

I have the role model of two extremely interesting grandfathers. I spent a lot of time with them. They never pushed me. But I admired them too much; I tried to follow in their footsteps. They had huge successes and achievements and they made it look easy. I did it, but it was difficult.

Now I want change, but I gravitate to the same patterns, extensive travel, hard work, and jetlag. Jetlag is very difficult; I used to **overcome it by willpower**. Now I am looking for work within the same time zone, still the same kind of work because it's what I do, but without the excessive travel and time changes.

Sleeping – I sleep in 4 hour cycles. It's as if I sleep until I am not exhausted anymore and then I wake up and I am wide-awake. I would love to sleep for 8 hours straight through. I wake up at almost 4 o'clock precisely, no matter where I am.

FALCON CASES

Cases

Do you know what kind of work you want?
No, not exactly. A start-up is more stable than a restructuring. If I go somewhere to do a project, I will keep my family here and **keep my family stable**. It might be healthier for me to like a stable job. My self-image has historically been as someone who can go anywhere do anything with essentially nothing.

I don't know how to deal with stability really. When you travel a lot, the little mundane things just don't happen – and even then you can always delegate the little things. I am not a detail person, I have **a helicopter view, I see the big picture**. I see the 5 or 6 key details and force the people on the ground to deal with the detail work

I don't really even have any knowledge about the small details of life, what the football team is doing etc., I would only know about the politics in China or something.

OBS: *Clawed hand in gesturing.*

I only have friends who have similar kinds of experiences – who travel a lot also.

One grandfather was a very successful businessman. He had a big overview. He was a world-class archaeologist, world-class hunter, a world-class photographer; he was a big influence on me. He was one of these people who made everything look easy. He had a photographic memory. My other grandfather was a US council with a big overview as well. He gave me **ove of travel** – and had me meet lots of interesting people. Both were big people in all ways.

I am used to reconstructing things for myself, now I am looking for help to try and construct something new for myself. I never figured out what I wanted for myself. I know only what I think I want or what I should want.

I wear myself out.

I can actually manage lots of details, I have a **tremendous willpower**, a kind of drive; just getting things done was important – but it was very stressful – I paid a very big price.

I dehydrate very easily

I like salt and sour.

CRAVE protein. I can eat a whole can of tuna, or chicken, **any kind of fish**.

Thoughts while awake?
I think about work situations at night when I am awake; the negative story builds – sometimes you almost indulge in it like a game. Dwelling on – **thinking in circles**, more when I am tired, even sometimes during the day, it wastes time, it's negative, and it keeps you from doing other things.

That's more why I am here really, cause it's not really my nature, but maybe it's kind of my nature, because in my job I think about things, but now it's negative, it's not productive – **in the past I could bring tremendous focus, more than most people – sometimes I would go so sleep and wake up with the solution** – but when it goes in the wrong direction, the negative – now it just goes around – if you cannot activate it, it cannot become a solution. Now I procrastinate a lot. Before I would come up to a difficult situation and I would find a way to get past it; now I just pull back.

I have had a rough time sleeping for maybe 15-20 years.

It started maybe in 1989. I lived in Indonesia then. I was doing a re-structuring project that required **tremendous focus** – lots of brainstorming sessions in the night. I got a promotion to Cambodia because I did such a good job. I left my wife in Indonesia, we had an actual separation for a while then, and that was very stressful for me. My marriage is very important to me, my parents divorced four times. In Indonesia I got a flu, I got very sick, I was alone, the maid found me on Monday. I was dehydrated, went to an Indonesian hospital where they overdosed me with antibiotics.

Now I tend to pull back instead of **driving through** –I feel like a rubber band without stretch. Almost as if I am afraid to be that sick again. It was terrible, all alone and sick in that way.

My wife and I then had a separation – now we are back together and we have a wonderful daughter.

My mother died when I was 4, dad married, divorced, married, divorced. Maybe I have some insecurity from that – it's possible that I don't believe at all in continuity – I don't see it existing for myself. It's difficult to make a com-

FALCON CASES

Cases

mitment when you don't believe commitments lead to continuity. My stepmother remarried and her family restored Victorian houses – I inherited great grandparents from all the remarriages. They introduced me to many different things. I tried many different things in university; I tried architecture and design for a while.

Rx: *Falco-p 30C daily for 3 days*

Follow-up 3 weeks after initial visit:

It's confusing because it seems to have worked so well. Slowly I began to feel more confident. The funniest thing was that I suddenly found myself spontaneously positive about things that I would have been negative about 3 weeks ago. If I wanted to do something, I would just say 'get on with it' and do it. I did not realize I had fallen in to such a hole. Things seem possible again.

Still some challenges with sleep. One person thought I have sleep apnea; I will get tested for it.

Why?
I have all the symptoms. I have cramps in legs at night and I wake up because I cannot breathe.

My hay fever is still there but less.

In general I do put problems/challenges in the back of my head and then I think about these things at night. I can concentrate well at night, but not if it makes me too tired. In the day I can concentrate well if I am not tired.

Looking for work seems more positive. Before I was self-sabotaging, really. Now it seems possible to find something different. I am looking at different possibilities now.

I have a lot of unresolved issues from my youth.

I have been a change manager. **I don't accept authority**. I am ok while I am changing things, but when they are done then I am not ok. I am constantly looking for things to improve. The problem with that is that I look at being happy in the future only. Maybe I should try to be happy in the present and look for a different kind of work, rather than always needing to change things.

I would like to spend more time with nicer people.

I used to teach **handicapped and blind** people to swim. I have never figured out how to make a living doing that at a level I am used to. Now I am looking at working for a non-profit, doing some work to give something back.

I have done a lot of things wrong in the last 20 years in terms of pushing and using my physical body to do it. Now I am not willing to do those difficult things. The challenge is to find something to do now.

In the last year I got **blocked**. I looked at lots of jobs but did not apply.

Generally, most jobs I have gotten, I have **sensed** the job and the companies have created a job around me**. I don't fit in a little box**.

I really came to you because I was **blocked**. Because I need to resolve these things from the past.

My values have spun out of control a bit. I want maybe to learn to be happier with less. To find healthier things to do maybe. When I was younger, **wherever the top was, that's where I was going.**

I am very intuitive. I cannot do accounting, but I can look at a balance sheet and just know that it is not ok.

I need to be working within a month. My best chances are in these high-pressured positions. I am considering a position in Germany – even though I would hate it. I would do it because of the money. I would keep my family here to keep them stable.

I don't know even if I could do a local job. One of the things with my work, with traveling, **is that you never get involved with the local stuff**. People don't get to know you and you don't get so stuck in local stuff. I could start my own company, but I don't do it. It's almost as if I **don't want to make that kind of commitment**.

The remedy has made me more confident that I can make that commitment. I need to re-structure myself and to stay healthy.

My parents were not wealthy growing up, but we always had enough. We always had high-class values. Part of that is that you do things; you are not allowed to do nothing. The people I look up to and try to be like are my 2 grandfathers – these were not ordinary people, they were exceptional, I am not at the same level as them. I tried to be like them even though I knew I was not at the same level.

FALCON CASES

Cases

I studied sociology for a while and I wanted to be a juvenile delinquent judge – but then I went in to business. I could see myself being a reasonably good teacher and enjoying that. I don't know what I should be looking for. I stopped thinking that there is one correct thing in life, you just do some things well and then good things come your way; I stopped even doing just some things well.

I have always **lacked a little bit of discipline**. I am a **strong anti-authority figure**. I was not happy at home before the divorce. I was swimming, but that's a very structured life, getting up at 5, swimming 2 hours before school, then school, more swimming and homework; and at the end of my tired day I would hear my parents fighting. Then I started getting into trouble at school. I never did really bad stuff, but **I would NOT do things**, not write papers, etc. If I think something is stupid, I just won't do that. You pay the price for being right.

What I lack right now is something to shoot for – a target. I cannot see that target for myself. I am wandering around. If I see a job and know that it won't make me happen I say 'why bother.'

Rx: *Falco-p* 30C in water, 4 drops 3 x daily

NINE WEEKS AFTER INITIAL VISIT:
Things continue to seem a little bit better.

My willpower has increased a lot. I have become more positive. My attitude is better. I wish I could up the dosage. I still procrastinate and that always hurts me. That is improving a little bit also. I have to see if I can find more time. I feel more stable.

Still waking up and thinking at night. Thinking about possibilities. But positive. I must find some stability.

But I have always been like Indiana Jones. I always want **to climb and get to the top**. Go anywhere, do anything, with nothing. But it's not for me now.

I need to be strong and stable and yet I always steer towards difficulties because I love solving problems. Now I am thinking I must find the right kind of job, be stable and then do the next step. It seems a bit like a weak approach. It does not work for me. **I always move upwards**.

I feel like I have gotten into some bad habits. The habits are still overpowering. I have held back some and maybe self-sabotaged some jobs, but that is slowly shifting. I feel like I can do more things. A new job is always a stretch for me.

I sense that I need a lot of stability. But if I see a stable job I think I would probably go crazy in that position. I am in trouble if I am bored. I am so used to flying somewhere and if I am not doing that it feels wrong. My wife teases me if I am home for a while; she says: "Isn't it time you took a trip?"

Concentration still not so good, but it's partly avoiding things.

My **neck is still stiff** but only if I don't sleep enough.

My allergies are quite a lot better.

Sleep has been generally much better. Maybe have some bad nights and when I have a bad night, usually I have 2 or 3 of them. When I have bad night it has a worse effect on me than for most other people.

I still tell myself too many negative things about things that cannot happen. This has helped me in my problem solving jobs, but in my personal life it does not help. I cannot just walk past a problem; I always notice it. Now I feel there are many possibilities, but I say 'there's no point doing anything about that.' I have 80% a feeling of success and only 20% a feeling of failure. Sometimes I really exaggerate those 20%. And it should be better. Little problems become bigger and medium problems become huge. Then I work them in my mind over and over again. Almost like building a story around them. The problems become huge and then they keep you from doing other things.

I can always find solutions to everyone else's problems. I am very empathic, but often way too much. I allow myself to be influenced.

Rx: *Falco-p 30C* in water

Two and a half months after initial visit:
Family is good. I **am a visionary**. **Highly developed**. I have even more of an overview. I am easily influenced. But I am 100 % focused on the customer.

Sleep has gotten a bit worse. Then I lose some willpower again. I want to be a superman, able to do everything, but I cannot do that. I lose some identity.

Rx: *Falco-p 200C*

Cases

FIVE AND A HALF MONTHS AFTER INITIAL VISIT:
More self-confidence even though he is financially at rock bottom.
Energy is increasing.
Cramps in legs better.
Allergies better.

Rx: *Falco-p 1M*

EIGHT MONTHS AFTER INITIAL VISIT:
Some problems with stiff neck.
Still looking for a job, but it's difficult.
Feels positive.
Had a blocked nose for some time.
Still in the 4-hour sleep cycle, but sleep is good.
It is much better with the 1M.
A feeling he no longer looks negatively at himself.
Good energy and good sleep, now between 4 – 6 hours.
No allergies.

Rx: *Falco-p 1M* in water

NINETEEN MONTHS AFTER INITIAL VISIT:
He has a new job and wants the support of a homeopathic remedy.
He had a quarrel and felt bad after that. After this quarrel he feels not quite good enough, with a somewhat negative look at himself. As a whole he does not look at himself so negatively. He has to read a lot of instructional material. He likes the new job.

Rx: *Falco-p 200C*

ALIZE'S ANALYSIS:

Some important things with *Falco-p*:

A long period of being dominated by someone.
Negative look upon themselves: understand that the positive energy, which is usually used for the work, becomes internalized when the person is not working. In these cases the psychic talents become the saboteur of the self.
Care of family.

Fear of chaos. Anxiety about his life being chaotic. Notice his talk of stability for his family.

Strong feeling of conscience.

This patient has an enormous need for communication. He talks so much that sometimes the patient is no longer able to communicate at all.

In this patient we see a strong expression of self-confidence but at the same time there is a strong shyness.

Often in younger days, because of a lack of ability to identify with a parent, there is an inability to become a self, to self-identify. This is often due to a change in the family situation, divorce etc. Then you grow up not knowing who you are or what you want. This often gives a feeling of having been abandoned.

Because of his frequent travels and all the different countries this continues for him the sense of lack of self-identity. He even says he likes the short-term component of the job because it keeps him from having to deal with the nitty-gritty of relationship.

Learning to deal with many different people and cultures develops a high sense of intuition. Because there is a lack of identity and there is a not really knowing of the self, he never really develops friendships with other people.

Also because they don't have a strong sense of self there is often abuse.

On his case, with the travel and business there is an over-identification with money and spending as a compensation for not having any real bonds.

There is a strong sense of insecurity and desire to care for the family because of the insecurity about knowing whether they are really a part of the family or not.

In him the developmental phase of identification does not occur properly in childhood and it is what he is still looking for as an adult. He expresses this in so many ways. In college by not really selecting a major, studying this and then that. Later by not being able to commit to any one company, country, project.

It's possible that he really wants to become the authority himself but when he gets close he is confronted with his own shyness.

He is discouraged and afraid. He has in some ways a very low opinion of himself. He has tried very hard to get jobs without success and that is also discouraging. He feels stuck and as if he is left outside society, abandoned all over again.

FALCON CASES

Cases

✓ In his project work he likes to come up against the boundaries of what he can reach. He likes to stretch beyond himself.

Feeling of injustice or unfairness.

He is both afraid of authority and a bit defiant of authority. He does not want to be criticized or receive the bad opinion of others.

✓ He puts things off until the next day and then is angry about that.

RUBRICS:

Ailments from domination
Anger from contradiction
Anxiety about his family
Anxiety about the future
— Intuitive, clairvoyant
Concentration difficult while reading
— Confidence, self in, alternating with timidity
— Confusion about his identity
Fear of danger
— Delusion, division between himself and others
— Delusion, neglected his duty
— Delusion, trapped
— Discontented with himself
— Discouraged
Escape from his family, desire to
Estranged from his family
Fear of poverty
— Forsaken feeling
— Isolation, sensation of
— Injustice, cannot support
— Nature, love of
— Sensitive, certain persons to
— Thought persistent
— Will, loss of

- Back, pain, general, cervical region
- EARS, stopped sensation
- Extremities pain, Cramping, Night, Lower limbs, calves
- Respiration, difficult
- Sleep, sleeplessness, general, thoughts from
- Waking too early
- Waking, persistent thoughts about work, with

This patient also has a number of larger themes from the bird family:
- Desire to travel (fly)
- Overview
- Intuition
    Issues with hearing.

FALCON CASES

Cases

TURKEY VULTURE *Cathartes aura*

Case taken by Nancy Tichenor.

Woman in her mid-30's. Spanish appearance. Dark black hair; wearing a black shirt. Prominent cheekbones, nose and upper teeth. Shrugs a lot through the interview. Very contained, not much facial expression.

CC: Skin. Looks rough like acne scarring.

Been treating it topically. On face since 1994; very prevalent. "If I treat it topically, it'll just come out someplace else."

Started on the pill for 3 years; 1988-1991. Skin trouble went away then; it prevented outbreaks. Stopped pill and had self sterilized in 1994, then skin got bad again. Been constant since then. Considers herself relaxed and not stressed out.

>OBS: *Hardly moves.*

"Don't realize stress directly. Little things at work (shrugs); don't get upset at work at all. I like my work. Just don't like the interview process, talking about myself. **A pilot for a major airline**. Selling yourself is not my thing at all. Would rather show what I can do, if they like it, great. Not a matter of confidence; I'm confident I can do the job. That's why I'm here. A lot of things I take for granted, or are not important to me, are important for other people in this job. That you can perform under stress; that you don't panic. That's a given for me. If I couldn't do that, I wouldn't want the job. I'd be putting myself into a situation I wouldn't want to be in.'

"I'm married. We live separately because of the job. He's a pilot too; works on the East coast. That's a little stress. I'd like to live together and keep the job but that's not possible right now. It's easier for him. At times it's hard; at times it's a relief—sometimes it's good being on your own. Don't have a lot of other friends. Colleagues. Nobody I can say, c'mon let's get together."

Sterilized?
"It just feels right; it's part of me. Private. Didn't want to have kids. Knew at the time, I was working towards being a pilot."

"Had no idea what I was into after school. Didn't like school; the pressure to perform or show interest in things I had absolutely no interest in."

"Had an arts class. Had a teacher who let us do what we wanted. I enjoyed that. I enjoyed the reading in English and German but not being tested on it or being asked questions in depth about it."

"Having to show that you knew something. Always been told I **don't participate enough in class**. If I know it, I know that I know it. The whole school thing, where you have to show that you know it, or you have to prove that you know something, I found unnecessary. No anxiety about performance. In some ways, I went into those places a little too relaxed. 'Oooh, you're a pilot!' everybody says, like it's a big deal. I like my job; I know I worked hard for it, but anybody can do it. You can get the training and just do it. It's a possible job; it's not brain surgery. If you really want to do it, you can do it. So I always thought, being a woman, I wouldn't get special treatment. I shouldn't be playing it down, because it's an important position; you have to react; you're responsible. But just like a bus driver, you're responsible for the bus but no one says 'Oooh you're a bus driver!'

"I like the view! It's also a power thing. It's a powerful machine and you're in charge of it. I like it and it's fun; that's why I do it."

Dreams?
"A recurring dream **that I couldn't see properly**. I could just see the ground in front of me; **I didn't have the whole view**. I remember being very disturbed the first time. The last few times, I remember thinking, 'oh, this again; it's just a dream; it'll go away.'

"**I always had animals** while I was growing up my mom thought I should work in a zoo but that never interested me.

"We had a parrot. He was like another kid. Slept during the day and when we got home, he was ready to have action. Wanted all the attention of a four year old. I wanted to go out at night and be with friends but always knew this parrot was home alone and lonely. Felt **guilty** not being able to be with the bird. He wasn't in a cage, he was running around the apartment but had his wings clipped so he couldn't fly. It was a stupid thing, to have a bird in the house. I would never do that. But I like parrots. When I was in Colorado, there was a big parrot in the lobby and I sat with him. They don't talk much. They just roll

TURKEY VULTURE CASES

Cases

over and cuddle. They're so funny. When I was there, he was allowed out of his cage. They can cause a ruckus, they can scream and they can make a nuisance."

Rx: *Cathartes aura, 200C*

FOLLOW UP 7 WEEKS LATER:
Comes in wearing a light blue shirt.

"Still got the **inflammations** but not as bad; not as many at a time. The **tooth thing** is still there. I felt really good for awhile; happy; felt like I'd taken the right thing."

    OBS: *Smiles more.*

"I've been working out a lot. Using the fitness room now at hotels more. Used to be bored on exercise bikes. Enjoys mornings more now, because with working out, I take a hot shower and then can go to sleep. It's helped me sleep. I still don't enjoy getting up at 4am but ok now that I get enough sleep. The **constipation doesn't last a week now**; it's over sooner, like that day or when I get a break."

"With husband, it's really good. I don't have that feeling of 'why can't we be together? Why can't we live together?' Being separated. It's ok if only 4-5 days but when it turns into weeks I don't like it. I used to be preoccupied with what he was doing. I wondered what he's doing and why we can't be together. But that's definitely improved. I'm no longer thinking about him that much. Now it's turned around and he's flying out here more! His schedule hasn't changed, he hasn't said anything; but he probably has noticed that I'm not nagging him to come out here so much. Before I always wanted to be together. Now it's, whatever, it'll happen."

    COMMENT: *The practitioner had just completed the Turkey Vulture proving when this client came to see her. The practitioner recognized the various bird family issues in the case and knew to give Turkey Vulture because the patient had terrible suppurating skin eruptions.*

ANDEAN CONDOR *Vultur gryphus*

Clinic Case from The Hahnemann College of Homeopathy. Case taken by Tanya Baldwin, student homeopath with Jonathan Shore supervising.

I'm a female.... That's a joke.

> OBS: *She says this very straight-faced; she is very stern.*

The reason I'm here is twofold. One I have an interest in homeopathy. My main points; I think the biggest consideration I have is that right now **I'm probably more than halfway through my life and I don't feel I've accomplished what I want to accomplish**. I have a sense of not being able to accomplish what I want to do. This manifests as fatigue, depression, and a general sense of ***it's not right***. That's my phrase to myself. I live in a spiritual community. I live in a household with seven people. I have lived in a community for 30 years. **I teach courses to people about death and dying**. I lecture around the world. I'm a bookkeeper. I have three children. I'm about to be a grandmother. I have a relationship with a partner that's 13+ years. I have some jealousy issues around that. He's 12 years older than I am. **I work 14-16 hours *every* day and have done so for 20 years**.

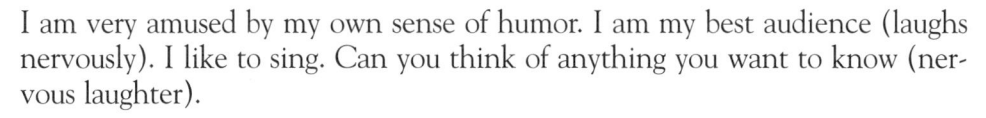

I am very amused by my own sense of humor. I am my best audience (laughs nervously). I like to sing. Can you think of anything you want to know (nervous laughter).

What else?
I'm a middle child. My mother was very fortunate to live in Minneapolis, MN when I was born... She had natural childbirth. I was born with no anesthetics, an easy birth. My younger brother and I still don't have the best of relationships. My mother was divorced from my father when I was maybe four or five. My mother has been married three times. I have been married once. I have three children.

> OBS: *All her statements are strong and emphatic. Her jaw juts out.*

I'm at a loss for the moment.

If I could have the optimum ... I would like to see myself with a great sense of enthusiasm and hopefulness. I would like to have greater focus. That would be very nice.

ANDEAN CONDOR CASES

Cases

Let's get in with physical symptoms because they're nice and very easy to deal with, **pain on the side of my temple here** (right side). I have had periods of time when it's been consistent. Generally the pain is dull and throbbing, and always present. Infrequently **it gets sharp**. I've had my eyes checked. I've tried the medication you take for migraines; I've taken a couple of things like that. Not particularly effective. That's a pretty ongoing symptom; I've had it for about two and a half years, more in the past year.

I have a **lump that I've had for years, right on top of my chest bone**. Right near the sternum. It will get sore, tender, kind of achy, especially to the touch. Over the course of 20 years what I've used for that, with great success, is *Chelidonium* 12X. I've taken that effectively.

I've had poison oak systemically. About 11 years ago I got poison oak so bad that it went into my system. Three years ago I had that virus flu that was going around, and I got poison oak. The remedy that I take for that is *Rhus-tox* LM23.

You take this daily?
No. Oh no. When it happens, I take a drop and then maybe another one 24 hours later, and then it's gone. Clears it up.

I tend not to take Arnica very frequently, either Arnica or Rescue Remedy, for emergency stuff. Those are the only remedies that I use on a regular basis.

I have plantar fasciitis, very much improved now. That's the swelling of the tendons and the fascia around the arches in the feet. It was recommended to me that I take an ibuprofen to decrease the swelling and it gave me nosebleeds. I put my feet in ice water two or three times a day and I wear support hose. I always wear support hose.

I've had charley horses all my life. What I do for that is eat bananas. I have problems with my gut, but I think everybody does.

From what you've said so far, do you expect I'd get a good sense of who you are?
Probably not.

Would you be willing to tell me more?
Well, let's see. (Very long pause.)

This is probably going to be a difficult task for you, but I can tell you a couple of stories that might help. I don't think that you're going to be able to get a better understanding of me by what I say about me. You might be able to get a better understanding of my organism. To get a better understanding of me, we're just going to have to be present together for longer.

I think it would be helpful…
My situation and who I am – two different things. My situation is that things are less than optimum. Who I am? I'm just a being on the planet, like the rest of us.

To find the best remedy for you, we need to know what makes you different from the rest of us.
(Nervously) I've never thought about that question.

You can start, if you're willing.
Nothing that I'm aware of. **All beings are the same on the planet**. It's just the way they manifest that's different. What's different about me from anybody else? I don't know.

What is it that you would like to get from homeopathy and what would you like from us. I described that at the beginning, the capacity to have hope, renewed enthusiasm, and hopefulness.

If you can tell us more about…
Let's see, lack of enthusiasm. You know, when you wake up as a kid and you're really happy to meet the day. That's a really positive framework. I don't have that any more. **Lack of focus**. I have like **sixteen things that I have to get done all the time**. I'm not able to put one aside. I have **all of them at one time in my view**. I need to be able to pinpoint on one to get it done. That's what I mean by focus. That's the kind of focus that I need. This isn't necessarily something that's remedied. Maybe it's something that's learned. When I look at my capacity to do, my capacity to do is less, and that's not acceptable to me.

Why?
Because there's that much to do.

ANDEAN CONDOR CASES

Cases

What do you do?
I'm in the middle of writing a book. **I have five languages that I have to have a book translated into before I die.** I need to have centers set up in 20 countries and I only have it set up in three.

Why?
Because it's my job.

I think I don't quite still understand. Why is it your job?
I'm trying to think of a good analogy so I can make it clear. I'm at a loss for a good analogy here... I'm able to get it done, I believe in having it get done, I'm capable of getting it done, and I see the need for it.

Can you tell me about this book?
Oh yes, **The Book of the Dead**. You know, Elizabeth Kubler Ross.

I work with people who are dead or dying. I work with their deaths. I teach people to work with the dying, when they are at the point of their death. I'm what's called **a terminal midwife**.

Why do you do this type of work?
Why do I do this kind of work? Why do you do homeopathy?

What brought you to this work?
I don't know. **It's just the way things line up. I've been doing this for almost 35 years**. It's the same as singing. Why would I not sing? I mean, I have a voice, I sing.

What is the meaning of this work to you?
What is the meaning? Do you know what natural childbirth is? You know it is taught. You can prepare for natural childbirth. In that dynamic, you know there's certain techniques that you learn, breathing, massage, **so that you're prepared to have a good birth, I mean death**. I used to do natural childbirth and then I read Kubler-Ross' materials and that work is directly translatable into dying.

The reason I teach courses on death and dying is so people have the option.

The hopelessness, the lack of enthusiasm, is that connected to this work?
Uh-huh. Not being able to finish it. I'm getting older.

When you do this work, how does it make you feel?
Well, sometimes I feel like there's a lot of energy connected with it because people get excited about having an option for their death. Sometimes I get tired and really lonely because nobody's helping me. Sometimes I get a lot of gratitude because it's pretty amazing stuff that I do. Sometimes I get really desperate because I don't know how I'm going to manage it. I don't like that feeling.

Most of the time I'm having a problem with my focus. All the preparation time, the organization time, the thinking about, I'm not happy about that because I'm not doing well at that. So that's pretty discouraging. That's not so much fun.

ANDEAN CONDOR CASES

What else?
I can sit and reminisce about giving a workshop to 200 people in El Salvador, and that felt pretty good. And then I haven't finished the book. So there are parts that are alive and parts that are not.

Anything more that you think is important?
Anything that I think is important. I would say – let's see a diplomatic method of putting this. I have considerations that my partner does not need me and that doesn't make me feel too good. I've brought the subject up a couple of times and it hasn't been resolved. I'm one of these people that's not going to rock the boat too much, but every once in a while I get a little bit distraught. And then I think of leaving the situation, or moving away; basically running off. So it's probably a pretty important factor.

Can you tell me more?
I've been pretty reliant on this relationship for support for a long time now. So, considering that it might be over is disturbing. It's difficult. That could also all be my own imagination, my own internal trip. That's a big part of my own considerations. I can't think of anything in specific in order to describe…

You mentioned the feeling that he doesn't need me. What does it feel like that he doesn't need me?

Cases

Well, for along time I was in his awareness range and then I'm not. You're either in the radar screen or you're not. And now I'm not.

What does that feel like?
It's devastating to me. I think some of it is like a reliance, always connecting with… It's a vacancy. It's like a big hole.

Can you tell me a little bit more about that? That vacancy, that big hole.
I guess I'm a person that has considered, maybe incorrectly, that I've been not in the **position of control** over my life. **My position of control over my life gets disturbed by people leaving, people being sick, or like what I've just described, people being vacant,** not letting me in; in such a state that I don't want to deal with anything any more. It's a very all-encompassing feeling. It makes me dysfunctional. It's not something I would recommend for the picture. I would like it not to be part of the picture. But, of course, you don't have a choice on those things.

Can you tell us some more about that?
Which? The sensation of vacancy, or the hole, or people leaving?

All of the above.
Well, my daughter left. I have twins, and one of the twins left when she was 16. My son left also, but that was mutual. We decided it was fine for him to go live with his dad when he was 12. The son and she stopped communication. Those are the two main instances really. There are areas I do not dwell on. Let's put it like that. If it overtakes me and I end up weeping and carrying on, then I have to remove myself from the scene. Anything that interferes with my functioning doesn't meet with my approval. **A driven individual**, you may have noticed. I don't like to be dysfunctional. Anything to make it a mistake I consider an area of dysfunction – moods, states, all that stuff.

You mention that you work for 14 to16 hours a day for how long?
32 years.

So that's a lot of work, raising three kids.
Only 13 years (in her current relationship)….

How much time do you have for a relationship?
No, no time for a relationship. Relationship is within the community. What I do doesn't overlap with what he does, so we don't have any time together.

What's the problem for you that there's a shift in the relationship now?
(OBS: Looking up and to her right). The difficulty for me is I always felt that his heart was engaged in knowing about me or wanting to know about me or making sure I was OK, or like that. It doesn't feel like it any more. And I think I could be OK with that if that was the case, but if I ask him he says that he doesn't know if that's true or not and I don't want to pressure it. **So I'm kind of in limbo**. It's the being in limbo that's the problem.

Because?
Because if it's a decision that needs to be made to not live together anymore, let's make the decision and live with the consequences. I don't like the wondering what's going to be happening. It kind of bothers me.

Is that true for other things in your life?
Uncertainty. Yes. Uncertainty bothers me.

Tell me about that.
I think it's **that control thing**… that's my method of dealing with things, being in control… **I don't like uncertainty**…. It's the same thing as lack of focus. I don't like any of them. I think of that as an impediment to getting things done. Getting things done is one of my main operating modes, finishing things. You know, a bookkeeper is a great job. I love being a bookkeeper. I'm always certain in my bookkeeping world. It's either reconciled or it's not. **The books either balance or they don't. Nothing else is quite so clear**. Music.

What sort of music?
I was trained in classical music. I was trained with a coach who was a Toronto Opera coach. Now I sing with a choir. I sing with my mother. My mother is also classically trained. She and I make music together. Singing is a good thing for me. Singing alone, singing with a group, doesn't matter. I like to perform. I like preparing things. I don't do it much. I did a recital when I was 40 and another when I was 45. I like listening to music. My daughter and I have the

Cases

same voice, so we have some duets. Sometimes we have a trio: my mother plays piano and my daughter and I sing.

What is it about singing?
Well, there are all kinds of things. You can get into **real good discipline** with singing. You can be optimistic with singing. Singing is a means of sharing with other people. **It's a communion**. That's always good. Again, we're looking at an **area where I have a lot of certainty**. Singing is a good tool for icebreakers and being happy at parties. You can sing along with a guitar.

When you sing, how do feel?
If I am singing something that's a difficult piece that I've prepared and worked hard for, then how I feel is, depending on my preparation level, either confident or disastrous. I try to never sing when I feel disastrous. Confident, yes. I have a lot of confidence in my singing and my voice. It hasn't failed me yet. You know, it's a gift. It's a gift.

Is it pleasurable?
You can get into a state of bliss if you know how to do it right. The instrument, the voice, the physical machine, if you get it all lined up right; you can get into that state. I enjoy singing. It's as good or better than bookkeeping.

So, getting your work done is very important to you, getting your task accomplished. What would it feel like if that didn't happen? What would it feel like to know that you might not finish?
It will feel like it feels now. Very hopeless.

Tell me some more.
No, **hopeless** is the best word. **Hopeless and devastated**. It's not like a marriage. This, no, there's no way to evaluate this. If I don't get it done I'm going to feel bad. I feel bad about this already. I'm already too old to get it done.

If you don't get this work finished before you die, then what happens?
If I don't get this done before I die, that will be my problem for me. If I don't get it done before I die and don't teach anybody else about it, that'll be worse.

Yes, maybe somebody else will pick up on. You know it took 40 years in this country after they published the Evans-Wentz book for it to get into common culture…. Yes, maybe somebody else will do it. That'll be good. If I don't do it then I don't have a way to make sure that it'll get done the way I want it to get done. **I won't have control over it**. I guess it's mostly that I don't see anybody else who could actually do the job, to give the feeling that it could be handled by anyone else.

So there's nobody else to take over?
Not that I know of.

So the feeling there is of being alone?
It's not just being alone. You know, **there are all sorts of crafts in the world that die because nobody's kept them going**. I'm not in that situation. I know exactly the truth. There is material that can be made available to people in other languages. That's not the way I want to leave it. I want it in at least five different languages. And I don't speak those languages. I have to go find people to do it, and get them published. It's a long process. But I won't have a very good life if that's the case.

I need to understand why it's so important to you that this gets done.
Has anybody in your family died? Were you at their death? And were you able to do (what was necessary). So, you're a person who has some sensitivities and interests and understandings that allow you to be with a loved one with they die. In our culture and in most cultures, we don't have that any more. … In our culture, all that got lost. (She goes on talking about natural childbirth movement and its parallel to death and dying movement.)

What is the meaning of this to you personally?
What is the meaning to me of having a conscious death? It's an option. It's an option.

To have a life without options is what?
A life without options? Life is all options. Life is all choice.

What would it be like for you to not have the option of choice?

ANDEAN CONDOR CASES

Cases

For me, to not have the option of choice... I don't know. Maybe it's more like resignation or something.... The only thing that comes to mind is it's not fair. That's not fair! .

If you don't have options, then you don't have control, so what is it like to not have control?
It's not fair. That's my response. It's just a kid's response... Just like a little kid, nine-year-olds especially. They're very much into **fairness and justice.**

What is it about justice and fairness?
Oh, **when things aren't fair, they're not right**, there's nothing you can do about it. You have to just resign yourself to the consequences.

Is that what you do?
No, unfortunately, I'm unwilling to resign myself to the consequences. That's why I have so much trouble... I am unwilling to do without choice, even if it's imaginary.

So if something is unfair or unjust, how do you react?
> OBS: *Patient looks absolutely dejected and stares at practitioner for a while. Shakes her head no.*

Unsuccessfully.

What do you mean?
I'm not able to make it change. That's an area outside of my control. It's a nonfunctioning area. There's not anything that can be done about that kind of thing.

It might help me to consider what you think to be unfair.
Oh. Um, I don't think I can give you any good examples. That's not an area where I'm successful. I don't see justice or fairness.

You don't see justice and fairness at all?
Not in areas that I have anything to do with.

Give me an example from your own experience.

No, I can't think of any areas that there are.

Is there anything else you can tell me about control. That's come up a lot for you, this idea of control.
    OBS: Patient has lots of long pauses when asked questions – looking off into space and thinking, staring dull.

Perhaps we're not getting a complete picture here because we're describing the things I do with myself, not the work I do with others. Almost all of the work I do is with others…

Are there other aspects of yourself that you'd like to talk about?
I live in a house with seven people, in a community; I'm a core bookkeeper. All of those are team things. I don't want to have the impression that all the things I do are being in control all the time.

I don't think control has to imply that you're not a team player also. I also have a lot of areas in which I'm a team player.

And those are important to you?
Yes. They have to do with how I earn my living and where I live. Yes, they're very important.

I'm not sure what you need to know. I don't live my life alone. I live my life with a number of people. I live every aspect of my life with a number of people.

Do you have any connection or do you have anything to do with birds?
Birds? There's a bird that lives in my house. Somebody once called me tree. My partner's daughter and his son are birders. His brother is a birder. I don't know the names of birds. That's probably all about birds.

When we had started, way back, and you were talking about your relationship and you had said that there were some issues about jealousy?
Yes. I'm jealous. Jealous of interactions, or supposed interactions, or supposed interests, or caring, or concern for other people besides me.

Can you give me an example?
About a year ago, we hosted a talk. I was doing tickets. My partner walked in and was flirting with this other person. It was blatant. That's an example.

ANDEAN CONDOR CASES

Cases

Any other examples?
Nah. Just that.

Is jealousy something that you've ever experienced?
Nope. Luckily for me, I've never had to deal with it before now.

What about dreams. Can you tell me about a strong dream you've ever had?
I've had a lot of dreams. I guess it doesn't matter which one I tell you. … This dream takes place in Falls Church, Virginia, which is where I lived when my mother was working in Washington, D.C. I'm at a church picnic (this church, in real life, sent me to a lay ministry program in Washington, D.C. for summer). In the dream, there's a picnic going on. I find myself exposing my right breast and touching everybody at the table with my breast. It was completely natural, part of a blessing.

What's the feeling in that dream?
Very positive. Wonderful feeling, very hopeful.

Can you tell me the feeling? Very positive is, what's the feeling that comes with that?
Connectedness. It's very sunny. It's very on the earth. It's very wholesome an nourishing. Blessing, feeling of grace. Connectedness, I think that's the strongest sensation.

So the emotion?
Warm and sunny and together. It's probably a feeling of acceptance.

Do you have any other strong dreams that come to mind?
Sure. From the opposite end of the spectrum. This dream is from about November of 2001, after the terrorist attacks. We live about 40 minutes from an air force base. In the dream, I'm looking at the sky from the direction of the air force base. It's gray, and the planes that are coming. They were the regular airliner places. In the dream the letters on the plane change to El Al and a couple of Arabic letters. The next thing in the dream is a tower, like a guardhouse or a watchtower. In the dream, the planes are shooting the guard in the tower, and then I wake up.

What's the feeling in that second dream?
That's what I refer to as a prophetic dream, a lucid dream, because I knew I was dreaming at the time I was having it. My overwhelming sense during the time of the dream was to wake up and communicate the dream to others so that they would know the situation. I wasn't surprised. It wasn't unexpected.

ANALYSIS BY JONATHAN SHORE:

Her big thing is not enough time. But you didn't have the feeling that when she accomplished it she was ever going to be able to rest. She never said, "I feel trapped or I feel stuck."

She does say, "I'm not going to get it done. There's not enough time. I feel alone, it's hopeless, and a deep sense of despair." It's hard to argue with that in the case.

It was hard to bring her alive.
There's haughtiness. A lot of irritability.
Like *Nux vomica*, but not a Typhoid miasm patient.
What about Cancer miasm? Could she be *Ignatia*?
Thinking of trying Condor (*Vulture gryphus*) **to see the reaction, as they're so involved with death.**

Rx: *Vult-g* 1M, plus 6x daily; FU 1 month
Note: Patient was mistakenly sent *Vult-g* 200C, plus 6x daily

First follow-up February 2003:

How are you?
Improved. Improved energy, improved focus. I'm **having a bowel movement every day**, which is something I've never had in my life, even urgency. That's a BIG change. ... There's some stress in the job situation just because the time of year it is. We had a disagreement. I found myself recalling, the **feeling of being locked in and not able to get out and sort of succumbing to it**. I used to paint a room and not come out until I finished painting it. I feel a sort of stubbornness and being locked in. It's got to be 32 or 33 years ago since that image came up. ... I painted the bathroom this wild color. That locked-in feeling was similar to the experience I had this morning.

Andean Condor cases

Cases

Three days ago I had a strong feeling like I had **a sore throat**, but it's not in the throat, it's down in the glands. I had sore throats a lot more when I was a teenager. There's a sensation, a tender spot over her left upper chest.

I had **the experience of rage**. It was controlled rage. Something wasn't fair, or hadn't been done correctly, in my opinion, and I listened to the explanation from the customer about the situation. By the time I finished listening to the customer I was ready to congratulate myself that I hadn't gotten angry, and then I exploded with my boss. This was the wrong thing; it shouldn't have happened. It was rage.

Last Saturday, I made dinner and I gave myself extra time. I had **nothing pressing with time**, which is unusual. I baked, which I haven't done for years. And I sang… that's a little bit unusual. I don't usually have time to bake and sing while I cook.

That is unusual because our last visit you mentioned there was no time. Time was running out. So it shifted for you.
Yes.

Could you give me some examples of that?
I've been trying to finish a book for five years. I teach classes… I decided I'm going to take the time I usually have for the classes and use it for my book. I got offered another client and I decided I'm not going to take that client; I'm going to work on my book.

What's that like?
Oh (sighs), that's a deep pleasure. It's a relief.

You asked for enthusiasm and hope. Has that shifted for you?
Yes. I was thinking about that the other day. I don't know that I'm going to be able to give you a specific example, but I would say that, in general, my sense is of more hope, not worldwide… Here's a good example. I've had the first chapter of my book done for over a year, a year and a half, and I haven't sent it to anyone to look at. I haven't shown it to anyone before.

You haven't shown it to anybody?
I had shown it to another person, but not for review.

Why is that?
It doesn't feel like it's finished. I didn't want to show it.

The fact that you sent it off now?
It's an unusual situation. One of my students in Spain asked how my book is going, and I said, "I haven't worked on it for a year because I haven't had time." They wanted to see it.

Anything else about enthusiasm and hope?
Well, I'm trying to learn about enthusiasm. I don't believe that it's necessarily something that pops up. I'm trying to discover things about it. I'm sort of experimenting with enthusiasm, allowing myself to experience something enthusiastically.

ANDEAN CONDOR CASES

Can you give me an example?
I love to sing. By the time my choir rehearsal arrives, it's 8 o'clock and I've been **up since 4 (in the morning)**, so I'm a little tired. By the time it's over I feel great. I'm trying to think of these things as a doorway.

So you feel you have more energy?
Oh, absolutely. Energy, I would say on a scale of 1 to 12, I was about a 3, and I'm a 9-1/2 or 10. I don't wear out. I don't have to take a nap. Now if I get up, I have enough energy to do prayers for a while and go to my morning meeting, and feel I have enough energy for the day.

You also had improved focus. Can you tell me about that?
It may not be a good definition of focus… If I can keep the focus on what I have to do and also be able to do something else, that's very good. … I have some photographs of my daughter's wedding that I want to scan and send off two remedies at the same time.

When you were talking about focus without penetration, what do you mean by penetration?
To get down to the bottom of all of it. In bookkeeping, there's always the need to make sure that things are balanced. In bank reconciliations, either it reconciles or not. That's pretty cut and dried in bookkeeping; it's not so cut and

Cases

dried in the rest of life. I haven't yet figured out how to get it to completion. But I don't feel like it's impossible, or I'll never be able to do it, or like it's hopeless, which was my experience when I was here before. ... It's not out of the realm of success.

We had spoken about your remedy and that it was Condor, right?
Being light and being able to fly, and having strong arms and being able to fly. That Robert Redford movie, *Days of the Condor*, it's probably before your time, about espionage. The Condor was a code that was within the books that they were producing for camouflage and within three days their organization was completely penetrated. In that story, the idea of the condor is something that is strong and able to survive without actually knowing what the game is.

Can you identify with that?
Oh definitely. Of course. Well, somebody who goes around the planet and talks about death, and helps people learn about their death is not exactly mainstream. If you want to do something like that you have to find out how people are thinking about their death, and their loved one's death. You have to be not necessarily disguised, but not blatant.

Do you know about the symbolism of the condor?
No. It's a bird. I'm sure there is some.

We had mentioned that it's the intermediary between this world and the next.
Oh, that's right.

Has anything come up concerning relationships?
    OBS: *She sighs deeply, and seems to hold back tears.*

I would say that no event has come up, but for myself I'm just a little bit more relaxed about the relationships that I do or don't have. Maybe, to a certain degree, a little bit less needy about someone too. I have a household member that seems to find some way to know that whatever way I'm doing it in the kitchen is not right. Rather than blowing up at a housemate who wasn't able to be pleased, I said, "You know, I'm not going to be able to please you."

Are there any areas in which it's touched you?
Probably weight loss. I haven't had any withdrawal symptoms from going off coffee. Probably I have lost weight. Energy is better. I don't feel as needy in relationships.

We're really thrilled with the results. Is this what you'd expect?
Yes. I think it's very good.

We're happy that we've been able to help you with the book.
It feels good.

The work that you're doing is really important, and it's an honor to be able to help you get that done.
Believe me, I'm honored to be put in the place to get that done. I had premature twins, you know. You don't expect that. Then the question is, "Can I handle that?" I'm feeling now that probably I'll be making some changes in my work schedule so I can get it done.

ANDEAN CONDOR CASES

JONATHAN'S ANALYSIS:
This bird is a different sort of energy. It's very smart. This bird (condor) doesn't attack. It doesn't need to attack anything. It's not a raptor really. It's a scavenger; it's a vulture. In this case, the center of the case was very clear – the absolute obsession with the issues of life and death. Not in terms of anxiety about life and death, but of the necessity to assist that transition, to bring the message of the transition between life and death.

Rx: *Vult-g* 6x daily

Follow-Up June 15, 2003:
There are a variety of things to cover. I'll cover the most prominent in my mind first. It seems like every two weeks I'm sick. I was in bed all day yesterday and the day before. I do not have sustained energy. I have low energy. I have just getting by energy. I did well on my trip. I did teach 13 workshops in 8 days. I was back East. I'm continuing. I do have my book in my first draft. I do have my energy. My long view is gone. My immediate view is with me. Somehow I don't have breath; I don't have energy for a long view. I just have energy for what's in front of me now.

Cases

My main physical problem is with my legs. My legs and feet are a wreck. They either ache or swell. I have good shoes, I put my feet up, and I'm doing the normal stuff.

The last time I talked with you was that I was having a bowel movement every day and I have never had that my whole life. That's changed but I will say I'm having more regular bowel movement, more frequent than I can recall. It seems like I lost weight when I first go the remedy, but whatever I had lost during that time, that's come back. I don't have any changes in my diet. Diet is the same.

It's not just my feet. It's the legs. This area right before the knee. There's swelling in the calves, and this section right before the knee. Let's see, bruised, so that it aches. Not walking on it is good. Walking on it is painful. Walking now is not fun. Walking is endured rather than pleasurable.

When did that start?
It's got to be at least two months. We had the tax return cycle. That would have been April 15, sometime after that. Because I went pretty well through the tax season without too much problems.

What else can you tell me?
I've been having a lot of charley horses. I'm prone to them. I've had them all my life. I had one on one leg for 12 hours. The next day I woke up, in the middle of the night, it was the other leg. And I was sure if I grew another leg I was going to have three. That was two weeks ago. And I took a lot of calcium, yogurt. Now I try to get in the pool every couple of days now, exercise the legs a little bit, strengthen them. I usually get it in the right leg first, and then I get it in the left.

Still taking a daily dose?
Yes.

Did anything happen when you slipped back? On the mental level?
What happened?
Two months ago was the end of the tax season, April 15. On the mental level, what was going on? There's a new additional stress in the life. I got made a

board member. That means I'm now legally responsible for a lot more than I was voluntarily responsible. That means I have to attend board meetings twice a week. There's now a lot of financial stress in the organization. I'm now putting in 10 hours a week on this. It's got seven divisions. The overall corporation has seven divisions.

Why did you take it on?
Well, I'm one of these driven people. You know, they need the help. My skills fit some of the need. I can help with my skills.

How do you feel about this extra work?
Well, let us say it's a burden. It is a burden. That's probably the biggest change. I got a sponsor for my book, so now I can publish. The first draft is out. So that's been good. My timing on it hasn't been as consistent as I like. I have set myself a schedule and I haven't been able to stick to it. I think that board thing is the biggest thing. It's not the most pleasant. ... You have to cut things and disappoint people, and things like that. That's part of it.

Is that the hardest things, making the decisions?
Making the decisions isn't hard. It's trying to make other people deal with the consequences of it.

Will these decisions impact your book?
Not in terms of having in published, but it will in terms of writing it.

How are you doing?
It's not at as high a level, but it's definitely not down where it was. My physical form just seems to have lost some boost. So that's a regression, but not at all to the extent that it was before. Certainly being sick or feeling sick every two weeks is not good. I don't have the sense of desperation or despair that was before?

Is this something you had before (getting sick frequently)?
Yes. I did have this in college. It's like a healing crisis – you go through something you had before. My last year in high school, I went to work and got sick. I went to college and about every month I had swollen glands and a sore throat. Came home, went back to work (summer break after first year of col-

ANDEAN
CONDOR
CASES

Cases

lege), and had mononucleosis. Last week, when my glands were swollen out to her, I was thinking, I wonder if this is a healing crisis?

How far back do the legs issues go?
Charley horses, cramps in the legs, I remember having those as a teenager. I remember having them all the time. I've always had them. I don't recall having them this strong, this frequently, for maybe 10 years, maybe 8 or 9 years. But it's something I've been prone to, charley horses. That's why I eat bananas.

What was the story in that high school/college what was going on?
That's a pretty common thing. After high school, go to work in the summer and then go to college. That's pretty much the norm. I wasn't the only person doing it.

Was there any particular reason you wanted to do it that way?
Well, I never thought about not doing it.

But the fact that you were getting sick so often. Do you have any sense of why that was?
When I went away to college and I got sick, I just figured it was because there was so much going on. And I've never thought about why that was. I had been sick before that. Not really sick. I got pneumonia really bad one time. No, I haven't thought about it. My mom made a joke about it. When we graduated from high school, we got luggage, meaning when you are out of high school you should be able to look after yourself – that means, enough job skills to be able to support yourself.

Why this time's particularly interesting to us is it's seems like the remedy's regressed you back to that time.
Well, let's see. Historically it was a cataclysmic time. My mother worked under JFK. He was shot. I was living in Washington, D.C. I graduated when most of my friends were going to school or going to Vietnam… I was going to live at the YWCA and learn how to be a **cross-country bus driver**.

What was the appeal of that?
You know, you're in control of the situation yourself. You're on the road. This is a big element in my life. You're on the road. Something about traveling. I

was 16. it was a romantic notion, having an adult life without having to pay too many dues for it.

What do you mean by dues?
You don't get to be an adult. You have to earn adult status... somehow you'll magically be living someplace and having this job that'll pay your way... It's that kind of naïve picture. You go from one situation to another without having to make all the metasteps.

What about singing at that time?
Yes, that was what I was doing. I went to college as a musician. I went to school in the music department. That's where I went.

ANDEAN CONDOR CASES

Are you still singing spontaneously?
Actually, I will share one tiny little song with you, not because it's related to my voice, but how it came up the other day. Do you know Bert and Ernie? There's a song: You've got to put down the ducky if you want to play the saxophone. This is what I'm going to have played when I die because it's leaving one thing behind and moving to the other.

Rx: *Vult-g 12C* daily

FOLLOW-UP SEPTEMBER 2003:
She called to say that the 12C has worked really well and she feels great.

Cases

HUMBOLDT PENGUIN *Spheniscus humboldti*

Case by Jonathan Shore.

It is questionable whether to report a case with such a short follow up period. The rationale for doing so is his long history of unsuccessful homeopathic treatment and the dramatic ameliorating effect of the remedy which indicates that if it is not the true simillimum it is at least close enough to give a feel for the sort of case which can be expected to respond to Penguin. There are two additional factors of interest. The first is that although I had not thought of Penguin since the time I participated in the proving some 2 years before, shortly into the interview the idea of this remedy came clearly to my mind. The second is that when I came home from the office that same day and opened my e-mail the first one on the list read "Do you have penguin?"

This patient has been under homeopathic treatment for 10 years and received at least 25 different remedies from various practitioners that at best have had only a nominal and transitory effect.

Here is the initial interview from my practice. Only key words and phrases were recorded.

JUNE 1995:
Relationships
Dwelling. Obsessed. Hopeless. Hurt. Loathing of life
As a teenager was afraid, jealous, painfully shy. **Never believed anyone liked him**.
Stupid.
Has an **arrogant attitude**. No respect for superiors. Personality conflicts. **Litigious**, has been involved in 3 lawsuits.
Resentful and sarcastic. Hateful. Angry at the world.
Angry at injustice, **cannot let go**.
Doesn't like to give; enough has been taken from me. My soul, my heart. No rights. **Pushed aside**.
Survival and revenge.
Never cuddled as a child. Scared. Not safe. Mother was creepy. Could not stand her smell.

Dream: Recurrent dream of a big piece of shit on top of a stick. It falls on me. 100 people, even casual passers by, watch me training for a job.
Feet get hot. Must uncover. Even put in cold water. Associated with sleepiness.
Sensitive to noise. Even the slightest noise will wake him from sleep. It invades him. It is malicious.
Much better from exercise.
High sexual fantasy. Romantic love. Obsessed with unattainable women.
Violent sexual fantasy. Torture, kill. The terror they feel excites him.
Lives in very hot dry place. Hates dry weather. **Desires cool moist. Loves water, to swim in the lake.**
Desires **meat, fat, rich food**, bread and butter.
Disconnected from life. **Excluded.**
Feeling I'm going to do something wrong.
Wants to be special. I'm going to do this special thing but **I will still be left out**.
Desperate, madly in love. Thought about her for years. Daydreams about love.
Desperate longing but **I can never have what it is that I want**.
Laughed at. Humiliated.
People see I'm not really an adult and there is no hope for me.
Trapped. No freedom. Can't move. Life is being taken away.

5/22/2003:
Last visit was 4 years ago. Since then has been using nutritional supplements on the basis of hair analysis. Energy is better. More sane.
Not part of the world. I don't know how to do it.
Does well with animals. At a loss with people. **Inappropriate relationships**. Scared if someone likes him
Not doing it right. Feels responsible all the time.
Doesn't belong here – something wrong with me. Not approved of. **No right to be here**. I don't deserve to be here, I'm here on a work visa.
Dream: Man under wraps. He and his father found the casket. An old man has been living in there 100 years.
I can't live like this. My whole life is being wasted.
Loves dogs. They don't grab at you, make demands of you.

HUMBOLDT PENGUIN CASES

Cases

Suffers from romantic infatuations that can last for years.
Desires cool moist air. Getting in water feels so good.

Rx: *Sphen-h 200C*

Follow ups:
*He lives across country and has not been seen in the office again.
Here are his e-mail reports.*

6/3/03:
I took the remedy the day after I saw you and have been in a fairly good mood since. And, I think, less critical of myself and others and maybe less concerned about whether I do anything with my life. One possible proving symptom — I spent several days in San Diego and I have **a craving to live near the ocean**. I'll just let it work for several months. I'm pretty sure it is doing something.

6/8/03:
A very interesting thing has happened. All my life I have had these severe infatuations (love addiction) that simply would not go away, and were so intense that they made it practically impossible to talk to the girl I was interested or at least to talk comfortably. These have really interfered with relationships.

Well, lately I've had an infatuation that has gone on for two years, but it seems to have stopped. After I took the remedy it actually got worse for about 10 days and then it went away. Of course I'm doing other things as well, but I've never had a romantic obsession lift this easily except when I took *Alumina* years ago. This might turn out to be a really good remedy. I still don't think of myself as penguin, but when I tell friends about it they say it fits. One thought about penguin. It seems right they'd be leprous; they live all the way down in Antarctica while the rest of us live up here.

7/19/03:
The Penguin remedy is clearly working, but I have some problems with it, and I wonder if it is suppressing rather than curing. All my life I have suffered from intense romantic obsessions with girls who are not interested in me. One such obsession was going on when I took the 200C on 5-22-03. The obsession gradually decreased over the next two weeks, to only about 20-30% of its intensity.

However, it was still there and it felt like the remedy was keeping me from feeling it rather than uprooting it. I've seen this happen before with people—a remedy works beautifully for an emotional symptom, but when it wears off they are right back where they started and eventually the remedy quits working altogether. I don't know if that is what will happen here, but that's what I mean by suppression rather than cure.

The remedy also caused a feeling of not being connected to my own emotions. And it gave me insomnia. It got to where I was sleeping 4-5 hours and then waking up. Also, the love addiction was really unchanged—I was still fantasizing about her romantically, it just wasn't as painful.

I should have called or e-mailed you, but ten days ago the insomnia got so bad that I antidoted with a sip of coffee. I felt better, like my mind had been released from a vise.

For several days the romantic obsession stayed relatively under control. Then someone told me this girl has a new boyfriend and it all came back. I was just plain miserable and kept thinking about her all the time. Mind you, this is someone I've never been more than slightly friends with.

After two days of this misery, I decided to repeat the remedy. I don't have any more of the 200C, so last night I took the 1M. **Within two minutes that miserable sick feeling and obsession were gone.** I could care less what she did with her life.

Of course, that doesn't last. Today I'm back to being just as obsessed with her but it's not painful or miserable. That addictive part that insists a relationship with her is going to make my life whole is still there, but it's only about a quarter of the intensity it was yesterday. Maybe even less.

As far as what to do, it seems I have no choice but to let the *Penguin 1M* work. The hell of the romantic obsession was much worse than the unpleasantness of insomnia. But I am also afraid that this remedy is not curing the romantic obsession, just suppressing it for a period of time, which is still a whole lot better than how I felt yesterday.

Also, I don't really identify with the penguin as an animal—and usually people who get an animal remedy feel some connection with it. If there is any bird I really like it is the common loon that lives in the lakes of central Canada, my favorite part of the world.

HUMBOLDT
PENGUIN
CASES

Cases

So anyway, I'm on the *Penguin* 1M and even if feels suppressive and like nothing is progressing, I'm going to stay on it out of fear of how miserable I felt off it.

8/7/03:

I took the *Penguin* 1M three weeks ago and it is working remarkably well — far better than I ever expected a remedy to work for me. What's happening is that big issues that have really troubled me: **feeling excluded, love addiction, having a closed heart** are coming to a head very painfully and then I seem to be able to let go of them and their intensity decreases dramatically.

It's like all those years of being in psychotherapy are suddenly taking effect, but I know it's not the therapy.

When you interviewed me on May 22, while looking for a confirmatory, you asked if I liked the ocean, and my response was something like: I like lakes better but I do love the ocean, or rather I'm mixed about it. **I love the water, especially if it's a bit cool. I can stay in the water all day. The trouble with the ocean is the beach. You get out of the water and there are 10,000 people with their beach towels practically on top of each other all blasting their radios and drinking beer. It's not exactly what I'd call an idyllic outdoor experience.**

I have a history of **being thrown out of organizations**—boy scouts, youth group, and postgraduate school. I had terribly alienated the people in my field that I had to leave.

I have actually been seeing homeopaths on and off for 20 years, starting in the early 80s. During that time the one remedy I seemed to respond to was *Alumina* 1M which you gave me in March 1996. My love addiction did get better with that remedy. But what is happening on the Penguin that is different is that issues come up, are acutely painful for a few days and then resolve.

The other interesting thing with Penguin is how much more powerful the 1M is than the 200C. The 200C brought up the issues and moved them around.

On the 1M, for the first month I felt like I'd been shot out of a cannon. Day after day, the guy who went to bed at night wasn't the same person who got up in the morning. One of the things that happened in those first few weeks after taking the 1M was that I got really angry with a religious group I'm involved with because, on short notice, they planned an event I'd really wanted to attend on a day I had to work. I was as angry as I've ever been in my life and didn't keep it to myself, either. After three days the anger died down and I realized I'd **been angry about feeling excluded**, which for the most part I created. I **never really saw myself as part of the group** and was cynical and critical of a lot of their practices. After this episode I realized that I'd been missing out on the feeling of love and grace that is such a part of this group. Now I'm less cynical, less prickly and less resistant, and feel more a part of the group.

In the dream of the man under wraps, after we find the man my father wants to wrap him back up and close the casket again. The man under wraps says that is fine with him, he doesn't mind, but I know he's in denial and I can't stand the idea of his going back in there.

Another lifelong problem that seems better is **fear of doing it wrong**. I used to have terrible shame attacks if I felt I'd been obnoxious or offended someone — especially someone I really liked. I was **so afraid of doing something wrong** and so hard on myself for it. That seems to be lessening, and the flip side is I'm no longer so angry with others for doing things wrong. I used to find myself feeling really angry at people who didn't understand me. Now I'm a bit more tolerant.

8-17-03:
For a month things were pretty wild but now they've calmed down. I'm still changing every day and a new issue comes up every day. Today I talked by phone to the girl who I was obsessed with. I still like her, but the obsession is mostly gone. Before the remedy I was constantly thinking about her and my mind kept planning out how we'd get together and things we'd do, all totally unrelated to reality. And I simply couldn't let go or stop it for more than a few minutes. I'm not doing any of that anymore, and even talking to her didn't set it off. She has her own life and doesn't seem interested in me, and that's not ruining my day, needless to say my life.

HUMBOLDT PENGUIN CASES

Cases

WHOOPER SWAN *Cygnus cygnus*

Two elegant cases of Swan (*Cygnus cygnus*) appeared in *The Homeopath*, Oct. 2002 No. 87 by Camilla Sherr. The remedy was prepared from a swan's feather at Helios Pharmacy.

CASE 1:

Dec. 16, 2001. 45-year-old woman. Previously been prescribed *Puls, Ign* and *Sepia,* which acted only briefly.

"My memory is awful, I live like an animal, and I can't think or plan forward. I feel tired and weak. I can just sleep and sleep. For ages I have had returning spells of tiredness, which leave me flat on my back, like an anesthetic. You cannot stop the sleep. Some days I sleep from 7 pm until 6 a.m. I am falling asleep a lot at work. The tiredness is accompanied by shortness of breath. Have no interest in life. I can't find joy. I love my kids but have no energy for pleasure. I have no sense of humor left.

"I had a terrible depression a few years ago, crying all the time. When I was 13, my little brother died very suddenly. I never cried and went back to school the next day. Then my parents got divorced. Their marriage was awful; **they hated each other.** I would not take sides. **Mom took it out on me.** She did not want me, but did not want father to have me either. Then I was **totally suppressed by my parents.** I always had to be good and I used to get punished for the things my brothers did. My mother had 5 miscarriages and then me. **I wasn't wanted.**

"At age 17, **I got raped. I couldn't tell anyone at** the time; they would have said it was my fault.

"My marriage split when my kids were 2 and 3 years old. **My ex-husband did not find me sexually attractive.** He wanted a wife and kids, but not us. I developed **cancer of the cervix and womb** the year after we were divorced. The local anesthetics shocked me. I had a **hysterectomy** in 1990. Since then I have never been strong again. A recent shock happened when **my ex-husband attacked me** out of the blue. My muscles were torn; it was a huge shock. I don't stand up for myself.

"I feel very **unappreciated and unloved**. I feel hopeless; I just want to get to the end of my life. I'll never have friends who will like me. I hate social things. I've got nothing to say.

"The **grief is there all the time. It's like it all happened 5 minutes ago.** It is always there; I can't escape it. For me, childbirth feels like it just happened, whereas other people say you forget about it. I haven't forgotten a thing. I feel extreme hopelessness; what's the point? **Since my brother died, there is no hope, no purpose. I will never have love again or feel happy.**

"I have recurring **dreams of not being able to protect my children.**"

> Falcon also has issues with protecting children,

"I used to **dream of flying and floating** like a helicopter.

"I like potatoes. They are somehow satisfying. I can't eat fish; it makes me unhappy. I get very tearful and unhappy from alcohol.

"I have awful **neck and shoulder pains.**"

> This symptom is characteristic of the birds in general.

"My **neck feels always swollen, as if a pea is stuck in it.**"

> Characteristic of long-necked birds that swallow their prey whole: Swan, Heron, and Pelican.

"I have an **under active thyroid gland**. I could stop eating for a week but lose no weight. I get spinning vertigo and my whole body veers to the left.

"My **vision is sometimes unclear,** like looking through dirty, murky water."

OBS: *She breathes very shallowly*.

Rx: *Cygnus cygnus* 30C (Whooper Swan)

FOLLOW UP FEB. 15, 2002:
"I feel much, much better. I can think! For so long I could not hold information, but now I can plan ahead and my memory is much better. I feel happier and stronger and I'm speaking up when I should do. **I feel warmer.** I sleep better. I am much **calmer**; I don't get startled or frightened anymore.

SWAN CASES

Cases

"My neck changed from feeling hard and lumpy, to feeling swollen, like a bullfrog; it went through phases; it is much better now. My **neck and shoulders are 80-90% better, and the headaches, which were dull and always there, have gone.**

"My **vision is clear**; I can see things clearly now. Dreams of not being able to protect my children are gone. **The past griefs and pains—the emotional weight of them—are gone**. It's as if they didn't happen to me. I can think about it or not; I have a choice. The **hopeless feeling is gone completely.... I always used to say to my yoga students to be like the swan: work like mad under water but look completely serene and composed.**"

Rx: Wait. At this point no remedy was given due to the excellent progress made after the prescription of *Cygnus cygnus*.

The patient returned in early September. Over the previous nine months she had continued to improve, but a few symptoms had recently started to creep back.

Rx: *Cygnus cygnus* 30C

CASE 2:
Taken by Sarah Smith.

Woman age 31. Successful remedies in the past had included *Veratrum album*, for a total physical and emotional collapse following the termination and a split-up of a relationship. *Ignatia* had also been successfully prescribed for grief, with concomitant throat and stomach symptoms, caused by a separation from her son.

She phoned up after a **second relationship termination**. Her boyfriend of many years didn't want to take on the responsibility of being a father, and she was now in the process of **leaving him and finding somewhere to live**.

"I really thought he was my soul mate until I realized he didn't want a child. My **chest is restricted. I can't breathe deeply. Everything is caught in my throat**; difficulty in swallowing. **I have nowhere to rest my head**; my **neck is totally stiff**, with a sensation like a metal rod going through it. If I move side to side, or forward or backward, I can hear it creaking."

Rx: *Cygnus cygnus* 200C

Follow up:
After receiving the remedy, her stiff neck disappeared. Also a sore rash at the top of her neck, an old symptom, came and went within a week. Her energy changed dramatically, enabling her to quickly find a new flat. Immediately after taking the remedy, she felt as if she could sleep all day. After that, she felt very positive saying: "I decided that since nobody could help my boyfriend, instead of agonizing when I think of him, I shall visualize him with a protective light and wish him peace. Then I will visualize a decent council house, in a decent council estate, with a big happy son and a big happy me in it. Then I will visualize myself as a hugely successful producer with a mobile phone and doing lunch."

"Very soon after the remedy I was sitting in the garden, and I clearly realized I have to make contact with my mother."

It turned out that she had had a difficult childhood. Her mother, who had been married 5 times, left her when she was a teenager. She was sexually abused by her stepfather and her mother had been aware of this. Because of this she had not had much dialogue with her mother over the years. After the remedy, however, she felt driven to bring all of this out into the open with her mother, a process that coincided with a series of television programs about child abuse.

"I phoned the NSPCC (Child Protective Services). I didn't want to hand down any more of the lineage of abuse to my son, because of having kept it all in. The reasons weren't vindictive or wanting to prove a point, I just knew it had to be uncovered so it wouldn't carry down another generation and be on my son's shoulders. I feel this has very much to do with the remedy."

The NSPCC said she could take the stepfather to court, which is what she is in the process of doing now. Through this, she feels she has healed a rift with her mother, which had been there all her adult life.

"As a child, to any outsider, I looked really happy but my own feeling was of being very dark, always putting on a really happy, 'pretty girl' exterior, nobody

Cases

knows who I am. But the massive shift I wanted to make all my life but couldn't, has now happened."

DISCUSSION BY CAMILLA SHERR:

The wonderful progress made by the patient after the prescription of swan confirms what we gleaned from the first case, i.e., that *Cygnus cygnus* can be an amazing remedy for unresolved grief and disappointment, especially in cases where there is a sense of constriction in the chest or throat. Although it has only existed as a homeopathic remedy for a year, *Cygnus cygnus* has already shown itself to be deeply curative in those patients suffering from, to quote the proving, 'lost hopes, broken hearts, and tearful farewells.'

MUTE SWAN *Cygnus olor*
Case taken by Elisabeth Schulz in Hamburg, Germany

> *We were allowed to dive deeply into the world of the swan, Cygnus olor, during a trituration proving a short while before this case presented.*

In February 1997, a 44-year-old female patient came to me with bronchitis during a bout of influenza. For two weeks she suffered from a very unpleasant cough and for two days her temperature had risen to 39 degrees Celsius (101 degrees Fahrenheit). She seemed very sad and was dressed completely in black. She told me about a dream:

"I walk into a room. Everything in this room is radiating white. In the middle of the room there is a white sewing machine. Everything just seems to wait until I finally begin my creative work."

My patient's problem was that her life partner had refused sexual contact for ten years. She suffered tremendously from that. *Natrum muriaticum*, *Sepia*, and *Medorrhinum* had worked very well for her in the past but they didn't seem appropriate for this influenza. I prescribed *Cygnus olor* 30C. After an initial aggravation with temperatures around 40 degrees Celsius (102 degrees Fahrenheit) the patient recovered within a few days. Ten months after taking the remedy the patient told me that there is again a sexual relationship with her partner.

ANALYSIS:
Oscillococcinum and *Anas barbariae* (Mallard duck) are proven influenza remedies. A comparison with our swan could be interesting.

Cases

WANDERING ALBATROSS *Diomedea exulans*
Case by Pieter Kuiper (Holland).

Consultation in August 2000. Woman, 36 years old.

She comes because her brother advised her to do so for 'small annoying things'.

These are her allergy or sensitivity to the sun and skin problems in general. Also she has frequent coryza. Important is her being rather tired. This is somewhat better when she does some sports. Moreover she has intermittent bleeding between her menses, regularly.

"In spring I had some controversies on my work in the library. I'm a manager there of different departments in our town. Sometimes it's quite a struggle to deal with all the clerks within the municipal structures. Moreover it's a female organization, with all the forthcoming emotions.

"The intermittent bleedings are very annoying. I stopped with the birth control pill 4 years ago, because then my relationship which I had for 7 years stopped. 2 years ago the bleedings started, it may last for a few days and then it may stop for some days. It's troublesome; you have to think of it all the time. And menstruation as such is troublesome in the first place; you have to make all sorts of arrangements.

Since I have this job I have more headaches connected to more responsibility."

Her skin is < in the face, < with the products for care of the skin.

Has hay fever since 15 years, < in May/June. She suffers from sneezing with coryza then. < Inside the house. Often has coryza, also with sneezing and headache and obstructed sinuses.

Metrorrhagia now is brownish dirty blood. Had it already as a teenager, before and after menses, but more profuse, not dribbling like today. Then it was more part of her periods.

Now it is mainly metrorrhagia from the cervix.

"I come from an energetic family, but nevertheless I don't like sports. I have one brother and sister who both are very sporty, but I like to read and go out for dinner. I'm different from them. **I'm like a foundling.** My puberty was not nice. I felt insecure, very conscious what others thought about me, especially my appearance. Secondary school and High school were a kind of 'learning factory' and my periods weren't a party either. I was anxious not to be able to reach the bathroom in time.

"During this period I had a kind of **'flying behavior'**. I didn't want to belong to groups. The worst could be when you were considered a 'mouse'. It signified you were nothing. I started my studies in English. It was a kind of **wandering period** in 3 different studies. It was also a kind of escape.

"I let myself carry along with the winds, to have the freedom to do something in an impulse. That's who I am, not being captured in whatever.

"I want to be free and do things when I want to and not being laid down. Therefore I do not easily start another relationship."

Desires: cheese, savory things, wine.
Aversion: pasta salads.
Thirst and stools are normal.
Generally she is a little chilly, wears socks in bed during wintertime.
Her sensitivity to the sun may give some vesicles on the skin of her hands and of the external throat. Never had herpes.
Nails and teeth are normal.

Rx: *Diomedea exulans 200K* (Albatross)

DISCUSSION BY PIETER KUIPER:

After this remedy she felt generally > and also her energy improved. She did not have any metrorrhagia, but her frequent coryza did not improve much. She only had a second consultation 2 months later and not a longer follow-up.

I had the impression that this remedy fit fairly well, considering the fact that the general symptoms as well as the main complaint improved. The choice of words she uses to describe her own character is striking and was the largest reason for my selecting this remedy.

WANDERING ALBATROSS CASES

Cases

CHICKEN TUBERCULOSIS *Tuberculinum aviaire*

Tuberculinum itself needs no introduction, but *Tuberculinum aviaire*, made from the diseased lung of a chicken, much more so than *Tuberculinum bovinum*, has many more symptoms pointing to bird rather than to general tubercular symptoms.

Here we present a very interesting case from Alize Timmerman of the Hahnemann Instituut of the Netherlands. This case clearly shows the strong general bird characteristics of this well-known remedy.

First consult July 2001:

20-year-old girl. She was abandoned by her parents in China, placed in a children's home there and adopted by Dutch parents at age 3. She has an adopted sister, also Chinese, not a blood relative.

Just returned from a trip to South America, where she worked as diving companion. Since she is back in Holland she is completely uneasy.

Her back is hurting.

Four years prior (at age 16) she had an accident. Two broken legs; they still bother her. She has thick hardened scars (cicatrices). Had a pin in upper leg break and broke the other knee, and was in casts for two months. She still cannot do a lot. It's much worse for running. The knee joint is too weak. The muscles are too weak.

At age 14 she broke a wrist.

She was always into sports. Her physical therapists told her 'everything is hard as stone.'

She always wanted to make a journey after finishing high school. She chose Middle America because of the **beautiful nature.** She stopped also in the US. It was very beautiful, but everything was too expensive. She still has to pay back her debts now.

She had **complete freedom**. Now she is restricted in everything again. Now she has nothing for herself, no room, and no time. Always pressure to do things together with others.

She always has to make compromises. Cannot decide anything for herself. She does not want well-intended advice; it feels like busybodies. She cannot **stand** it!

Just leave me alone!

"I always had that. People used to call me self-centered. I always thought they could help me if I could not do something, but I always wanted to experience it for myself first. I like my impulsivity.

Now I have no place to **retreat to**. I have **no privacy at all**. All kinds of nice people want to have all kinds of nice chats. I am constantly visible. It is all so 'too much.' I am too tired.

She has a feeling that this is a transition period. She longs for a room in the town where she will study. She has a feeling of not having a home anywhere. Her parents moved, her room there is gone. WHERE IS MY HOME?

She has a feeling of being completely **stuck**.

As if she is living on the very edge of the end – does not know whether to laugh or cry. She wants to hold onto everything. Has gained some weight since returning to Holland.

As a child she had a terrific **fear of being abandoned**. She would get sudden high fevers and had fits of rage. She has lived through a lot already; constantly running from here to there.

She wants **freedom – freedom to be herself.**

Her strongest desire is **to step into an airplane tomorrow.**

She gets **flushes of heat**, very sudden. She says "when it becomes too much, I throw it OUT."

ANALYSIS AFTER THIS CONSULT:
Issues with HEAT – closed energy – holding on
  Anger – frustration, tension

DOUBLE sensation
  Wild – independent
  Wanting to attract people and also wanting to repel them
  Private/Social
  Easy; fun chatting – LEAVE ME ALONE
  Don't put your nose in my business

CHICKEN TUBURCULOSIS CASES

Cases

Travel

FREEDOM

Where is my home? I don't have one.

Attraction to nature.

Rx: *Medorrhinum 1M*, single dose (This was a prescription by her mother)

No reaction to the remedy at all.

MARCH 2002:

I returned a year ago from traveling and since then I cannot find myself.

I have a feeling like I have no place here in Holland. I cannot find my niche here.

I have problems with stool. In India I had either constipation or diarrhea.

I am **STUCK** in everything. Stuck and loose.

I am just sort of **roaming around**.

I am studying accounting there. Don't like accounting.

I am housesitting, going back and forth.

I am neither here nor there.

I **want to travel.**

I am so concerned with traveling; I want to travel much more.

I miss my freedom, the **freedom I had while traveling**.

I have a BF of 20 months – **I need FREEDOM** to be myself.

Now I am studying – and this relationship wants the next step – I am not ready for that. I want to study something different – I will finish this year out.

I think I want to study international relations.

I **want to TRAVEL** also in my work.

I **want to be around different people**, to live with, to get to know, the TRAVEL.

Holland is a good country as a base – but I want **more variation**, I want more different things.

In the past I **wanted to do something in human rights** in other countries.

But from my travels I think it is not so simple – you cannot just go into a country and think you know what those people need. Decisions are made by middle class white Europeans who have no actual knowledge of the people they want to help.

I am very **drawn to nature**.

I **cannot find my place here** anymore.

My study room is not really my room. My parents moved so my room there is gone. Weekends I am with my boyfriend; that is also not my home. I have no home.

I don't spend much money on fun stuff; I'd rather save it for an extra trip. The student life does not interest me at all. I like diving and travel photography and the students are not interested in that yet. But accounting does not attract me at all. And the town is very different from what I thought; much more right wing than I expected.

I have **always had trouble with the discipline** of studying. I always liked everything about school, but not the studying. I have always had jobs; it is difficult to find a job now. I am an outsider there really.

Adopted at age 3. Came to Holland then. Went back at age 13 with a cousin, because I insisted on going back. That was very intense, crying, calling my mom in Holland wanting to come back. I always had thought I would go back and find my parents. I always wondered why they abandoned me. I did hypnotherapy and realized I also had a lot of anger about that, not just grief.

Maybe my desire to travel has something to do with that. I am always looking for something. I think eventually I might end up in China again, but not yet, not now.

I have the names and the ages of my real parents, but I have no idea of their reasons for abandoning me. I do wonder if I have real sisters or brothers. The restlessness and the seeking have something to do with all that.

I broke off the relationship with my boyfriend. It was always a struggle. He has his own business. I could not be myself with him. I don't feel good when I am with him.

With traveling I feel good. You are always going somewhere and looking for something else that's fun. I can be traveling and then all of a sudden I have a feeling, this trip is done, and then I come home. It was also difficult to be alone while traveling. You are always a tourist, always an **outsider**. Somewhere else you can be yourself more easily.

I always have the feeling like I am alone and just have my backpack. I always **feel like an outsider** no matter where I am. I always have a feeling that I am different from others.

CHICKEN TUBURCULOSIS CASES

Cases

To find your own path, you really have to do it alone. That is the difficult part also.
Always a down time between 3 and 5 p.m. I am so tired I even to take a rest sometimes.
I am always cold.
I am allergic to alcohol; to beer and carbonated beverages.
I do want to have children. Sometimes **dream that I am pregnant**.
My dreams are vivid, but I don't remember them so well.

Rx: *Tuberculinum aviare 200C*.

ONE YEAR LATER:
Started training to become a stewardess.
Her urge for travel is stronger. The training is difficult. Not much fun.
She has a bladder infection >> with *Tub-a*.
Her intestines are much better.
Flying is a lot of fun. She wants to work now and leave her studies behind.

Analysis: Obstinate, freedom, alone, no feeling of responsibility

Rx: *Tuberculinum aviare 200C*.

ONE AND A HALF YEARS AFTER INITIAL VISIT:
My life has changed. At peace.
Enjoyed some travel. Works 25 hours per week.
Dreamt of being very angry and furious.
Everything is going well. Concentrating on one thing at a time.
My father can be quite intense. He makes it a point to mention his anti-Americanism, finds them much too 'crude.' "My father is a terribly arrogant piece of work. He can be very hurtful, very mean."

20 MONTHS AFTER INITIAL VISIT:
I was quite ill from my boyfriend's death. My knee was bad, my back was crooked. VERY TIRED. Slept a lot, needed lots of sleep.

> NOTE: *strange and peculiar: sleeping from grief.*

I can easily sleep 12 hours.
Constipation is better.

Has stopped smoking.
I read something and it does not go into my head. I am just not into it. Work is a diversion.
I do miss him after all. I see him differently now.

Does not want to be alone.
My studies are not going well. **I want to travel**. I am **always occupied with going away again**. I don't know if I can do it. I failed four subjects. I have to finish this.
I make plans all the time – what do I have to do next. I don't want to feel like I have to do it, then I won't.
I don't like this. I want to come into a good rhythm.

Rx: *Tuberculinum aviare 200C.*

21 MONTHS AFTER INITIAL VISIT:

She is studying since a week and a half – "I decided to start again after all. In a different program, business organization."
I got more clarity for myself, so I decided to study again.
I have my own room now – it's peaceful.
My studies are good, practical, business, organization; it gives me lots of options that allow me to go in all directions.

I am very busy but I feel good.
I have a job in an English pub.

I feel more peaceful inside.
My intestines are also more peaceful.

Now I want to stop smoking, that's my next thing.

I am doing more sports; I want to do a team sport instead of before, when I always did solitary exercise

Now I realize that I want to have my own life in order before being in a relationship – I am not so concerned with it – it seems like it's over. I feel free now to see others, but I have no need, I live for myself now, I do a lot of fun things, I am enjoying myself, I have my life in my own hands. I really have my own life here.

CHICKEN TUBURCULOSIS CASES

Cases

What about the need for flying?
I have a feeling that it will come. The strong need to travel is not there anymore. I like to have some regularity now.

I arranged everything myself for this course of study. I chose it and arranged my job. I feel more free having done it myself. Not with the involvement of my parents.

Intestines are more OK. Quite good now.

Rx: *Tuberculinum aviare* 200C – to take if stressed.

ANALYSIS BY ALIZE TIMMERMAN:

Why *Tuberculinum aviaire*? The feeling of no home, discontent, wants to move, injustice, wants to help the poor, wants to bring peace, wants to travel, problems with her abdomen and stools.

To want to be in the air because you have no need for a nest here on the ground. This patient never had the feeling of having a nest, does not know what a nest is.

The feeling of restlessness, wanting to be on the move all the time. She always feels better when she can move. Her spirit is better. She does get constipated often when she travels.

Her problems as expressed in the constipation while traveling indicates that she is not truly free and indicates her need for this remedy. It is interesting that she absolutely will not return to China ever to connect with her birth parents – her constipation might be a reflection of this. Now her adoptive parents are her parents and that's how it is. And when she experiences this stuckness, this is what she needs to fly away from.

With her studies, every time she commits to something, she must move away from it. It is almost as if she driven towards movement.

This case brings out very beautifully that ***Tuberculinum aviaire* is a nosode for bird remedies**.

B·I·R·D·S 473

About the Authors

JONATHAN SHORE MD, DH-T

Jonathan Shore graduated from University of Cape Town Medical school in 1968. After 4 years of hospital practice which included surgery, pulmonary medicine and psychiatry, he embarked on a search for a system of healing based on a deeper understanding of the meaning of health. Determined to establish an opinion based upon experience, not just hearsay, of the claims of the numerous methods of alternative healing, he spent a decade in intensive study of many disciplines, including Acupuncture (Taiwan, Hong Kong, and four years as senior student to Andrew KT Ming in Los Angeles), Tai-Chi Chuan, Shiatsu and Swedish massage, Integration-Breathing Therapy and Corrective Exercises (certified practitioner), Human Potential Movement (about 1000 hours of group therapy both as participant and leader), Jungian psychology (personal analysis), Gestalt therapy, Bioenergetics, Rolfing, Radiesthesia (Psionic Technique, England 1975), Iridology, Herbal Medicine, Psychic Diagnosis (Jack Schwartz), Bach Flower remedies, and Color Therapy. Towards the end of this time period, he was appointed to the post of Clinical and Executive Director of the Wholistic Health and Nutrition Institute in Mill Valley, California. This institute, founded in the mid-1970's, was the first of its kind in the United States. The result of all this investigation was the selection of Homeopathic Medicine as the superior therapy in the treatment of chronic illness, be it physical or emotional. Since 1982 he has been in the full time practice of homeopathy in the San Francisco area, both in private practice and at the Hahnemann Clinic, of which he was one of the initiating planners. Intensively involved in teaching since 1983, Dr. Shore is recognized as a significant influence on a worldwide scale . In addition to a position as core faculty at the Hahnemann College of Homeopathy, he has lectured in Australia, Austria, England, Finland, France, Germany, Holland, Norway, New Zealand, Scotland, Spain, South Africa and Switzerland. In 1992 he was awarded Membership of the Faculty of Homeopathy, England.

JUDY SCHRIEBMAN, CCH, RSHOM(NA), CHT

Judy Schriebman became interested in homeopathy in 1983, when it cured her young son's chronic asthma. Ten years later, she graduated from the Hahnemann College of Homeopathy, where she had the privilege of experiencing Jonathan Shore as one of her core teachers. She continues to study under many homeopathic teachers from around the world. She also trained as a master clinical hypnotherapist, and practices both homeopathy and hypnotherapy in her group office, E Street Alternatives, in San Rafael, California. Along the way, she has raised two children, lived four years in Tokyo, Japan, has been a political and community activist, a soccer coach, the editor of numerous newsletters, a chicken farmer, and has recently completed writing a fantasy trilogy.

ANNEKE C.H. HOGELAND, MS, MFT

Anneke Hogeland is a licensed psychotherapist practicing in Berkeley, California, and an approved consultant of the American Society for Clinical Hypnosis. She studied homeopathy at the Pacific Academy of Homeopathy in San Francisco. A Dutch citizen, she first came to the U.S. in the late sixties for college, but soon after her arrival became completely enchanted with hot air ballooning. She has traveled the world for many years as one of the first female commercial balloon pilots and set a world altitude record at 28,036 feet in 1977. As the founder of HomeopathyWest, she organizes homeopathic seminars in the San Francisco Bay Area. Her personal experience during the bird trituration provings inspired her to make the bird remedy information available to the greater homeopathic community.

Bibliography

Black, George. *Viscum Album, the Common Mistletoe*. 1899, ReferenceWorks

Cambridge Encyclopedia of Ornithology. Tim Birkhead and Michael Brooke, editors. Cambridge University Press, Nov. 1, 1991.

Lindsey, T.R. *The Seabirds of Australia*. Angus and Robertson/National Photographic Index of Australian Wildlife, Sydney, 1986.

Marchant, S. and Higgins, P.J., editors. *Handbook of Australian, New Zealand and Antarctic Birds*. Vol 2. Oxford University Press, Sydney, 1993.

Nerburn, Kent. *Neither Wolf nor Dog: On Forgotten Roads with an Indian Elder*. New World Library, Novato, CA, 1994

Orr, Robert T. *Vertebrate Biology*, Third Edition. W.B.Saunders Co., Philadelphia, 1971

Parmelee, D.F. *Bird Island in Antarctic Waters*. University of Minnesota Press, Minneapolis, 1980.

Peterson, Roger Tory. *A Field Guide to Western Birds*, Second Edition. Houghton Mifflin Co., Boston, 1961.

Peterson, Roger Tory. *A Field Guide to the Birds East of the Rockies*, Fourth Edition. Houghton Mifflin Co., Boston, 1980.

Scholten, Jan, a.o. "WAD Stories: Homeopathic lectures from a sailing trip on the Wad in the Netherlands." *Stichting Alonnissos*, The Netherlands, Feb. 2001.

Schulz, Elisabeth. "Instinct Power: A remedy trituration of Falco cherug (Saker falcon)." (First published in *Homöopathische Einblicke* No. 28, December 1996)

Schulz, Elisabeth. "Ringeltaube (Columba palumbus)." *Homoeopathische Einblicke*, Dezember 1996, No. 28. Hans-Juergen Achtzehn, Verlag Medizinisches Forum, Berlin

Schulz, E. "Schulz's Ringdove Proving." ReferenceWorks Pro 3.0.

Shore, Jonathan. "Shore's Dove," ReferenceWorks Pro 3.0.

Stokes, Donald and Lillian. *Stokes Field Guide to the Birds: Western Region.* Little, Brown and Co., Boston, 1996.

Sullivan, William. *The Secret of the Incas: Myth, Astronomy and the War Against Time.* Three Rivers Press, New York, 1966.

ReferenceWorks Homeopathic Software, KHA Associates

These websites were very helpful and informative:

http://www.blueray.com/wordsworth/mythology/mayan.html

http://www.belizezoo.org/zoo/zoo/birds/mac/mac1.html

http://www.enchantedlearning.com/subjects/birds/printouts/Scarletmacaw.html

http://www.scz.org/animals/m/scarlet.html

http://www.thewildones.org/Animals/aramacao.html

http://ww2.netnitco.net/users/legend01/hawk.htm

http://www.krislon.net/Kids/Mythology/Emperor_Shibi.htm

http://www.desertusa.com/mag00/jan/papr/ghowl.html

http://www.owlpages.com/mythology/

http://www.chaffeezoo.org/animals/peregrinFalcon.html

http://sites.state.pa.us/PA_Exec/PGC/falcon

http://www.ravenfamily.org/nascakiyetl/obs/rav1.html

http://www.siec.k12.in.us/~west/proj/penguins/main.html

http://www.auburnweb.com/paradise/birds/mute_swan.html

http://animaldiversity.ummz.umich.edu/accounts/cygnus/c._olor$narrative.html

http://www.birdguides.com/html/vidlib/species/Cygnus_cygnus.htm

http://www.wfu.edu/albatross/diomed.htm

Appendix

Note: This is a compilation of all the rubrics which we have used in the book. Neither the rubrics themselves, nor the remedies they contain are intended to give a comprehensive overview. The idea is to bring into focus once again the important aspects of both birds as a whole, as well as to give a feeling for the central features of the individual remedies.

Mind
    absorbed; buried in thought, general (Heron)
    absorbed; in her own closed world (Raven)
    accept, things as they are (Macaw)
    accepted, group, by the (Macaw)
    accepting, outside issues don't affect much (Pelican)
    ailments from
        domination (Falcon)
        domination; others, by, a long history of (Falcon)
        humiliation (Falcon)
        scorn (Falcon)
    alone; sensation of being (Heron)
    anger; cold, detached (Falcon)
    anger, general, kill, with impulse to (Hawk)
    anxiety
        compelled, when, to do something (Falcon)
        family; about him (Falcon)
    anxiety; anger; during (Raven)
    artistic; aptitude (Vulture, Falcon)
    athletic, prowess, increased (Hawk)
    audacity (Falcon)
    biting; impulse to bite (Falcon)
    biting; nails (Condor, Vulture)
    carefree, desires to be (Hawk)
    children; desire to be with (Falcon)
    colors
        charmed by (Falcon)
        blue, green, red (Macaw)
        blue, desires (Macaw)
        green, desire for (Heron)
        red, desires (Macaw)
        yellow, desire for (Falcon)

communicative, expansive (Macaw)
company; aversion to, aggr.; alternating with; desire for company (Falcon)
company; aversion to, aggr.; solitude, fond of (Heron, Owl)
company; aversion to, aggr.; walk alone, wants to (Owl)
company; aversion to, aggr.; wandering from place to place (Albatross)
concentration difficult
    conversation, during (Falcon)
    fixing attention impossible (Falcon)
concentration; impossible; irritable when he tries (Pelican)
confidence
    increased (Falcon)
    self, in (Falcon)
    want of self-confidence (Falcon)
        talking amel. (Falcon)
confident, alternating with timidity (Falcon)
confrontation, avoids, no longer (Macaw)
confusion
    driving while (Falcon)
    identity, as to his own, as if it were not his (Falcon)
    loses his way in well-known streets (Falcon, Albatross)
connection, sense of, to the group (Macaw)
conscientious about trifles (Condor, Vulture)
consciousness expanding above him (Falcon)
contemptuous (Falcon)
control, desires to (Hawk)
conversation; meaningless prattle; averse to (Owl)

courageous; danger, in spite of (Falcon)
cursing; contradiction from (Falcon)
danger; no sense of, has (Falcon)
death; talks about (Condor)
delusions
    animals, of; bedbugs (Vulture)
    animals, of; insects; creeping on face (Vulture)
    animals, of; insects; head, on back of, has (Vulture)
    animals, of; unicorn (Albatross)
    blind, he is (Owl, Pelican)
    body, body parts; enlarged (Heron)
    body; body parts; enlarged; in chest area, as if ribs bowed out (Raven)
    body, body parts; expanded is (Heron)
    body, body parts; sensation as if two sides of the body do not fit; as if there is a torsion (Albatross)
    bubbles, blood in, as if (Macaw)
    burning, everything is burning (Condor)
    dark; things looked, as if less light in the world (Raven)
    dead; persons, sees (Condor)
    defenseless, feels she is, with panic and anxiety (Raven)
    drug, taken a love drug (Macaw)
    duty; he has neglected his (Falcon)
    elongated, neck is (Pelican)
    head open, top of is (Pelican, Falcon)
    horse, horses; she is, desires to be free (Falcon)
    horses, reined in wild stallion that desires to be free, she is a (Falcon)
    injured, is being (Hawk)
    injury; receive, will (Hawk)
    invisible (Vulture)
    neck fused to head (Owl)
    neglected; he is (Hawk)
    oblique lines, like a reed swaying in the wind (Albatross)
    paralyzed; he is (Falcon)
    parasites (Condor)
    prison, is in a (Falcon)
    prostitute, is (Falcon)
    protection, defense, has no (Raven)
    queen, she is (Raven)
    queen, she is; ice-queen (Falcon)
    repudiated; relatives, he is repudiated by (Falcon)
    secure, feels, even with chaos (Falcon)
    separated; world, from the, that he is (Falcon)
    separated; world, from the; in the present and simultaneously detached (Falcon)
    shield around him, has an iron (Falcon)
    space; empty space, between brain and skull, that there is (Raven)
    spirals (Falcon)
    suffocated, she will be (Heron)
    voices, hears, name, his own (Owl)
    watched, that she is being (Heron)
desires; beautiful things, finery (Vulture)
despair; of the beauty and life destroyed by humans (Raven)
despair; others, about; poverty and ugliness is (Falcon)
detached (Owl)
dictatorial (Falcon)
dictatorial; command, talking with air of (Falcon)
dictatorial, domineering, dogmatic, despotic; control others, wants to (Hawk)
discontented, displeased, dissatisfied, frustrated; efforts with, sadness and agitation (Raven)
disgust; deceit of others, at the (Falcon)
distractions; upsetting (Condor)
    dreams
    affectionate (Heron)
    anger, family, towards (Raven)
    animals, dogs (Owl, Raven)
    animals, dogs jumping (Owl)

Appendix

animals; phoenix, of (Vulture)
animals; pooping and peeing on things (Vulture)
animals; snakes, bugs cats (Vulture)
buildings; big and beautiful (Vulture)
buildings; hospitals and clinics (Vulture)
buildings (Vulture)
caretaking; family member, legs paralyzed, with (Hawk)
clairvoyant; solving important questions of the day (Vulture)
communication (Vulture)
conspiracies (Raven)
crimes; committing (Raven)
dark and dirty, feels she is (Raven)
dirty, she is (Raven)
divorced, of getting, because husband abusive (Hawk)
excelling of (Hawk)
extravagant, feels too (Macaw)
falling, confidence with (Vulture)
falling; high places from (Vulture)
family, own (Hawk)
fly on the fall, as if (Macaw)
flying (Owl)
furniture (Vulture)
good and evil (Macaw)
group, not fitting in with (Hawk)
indecent behavior of men and women (Heron)
journeys; difficulties with (Vulture)
killing (Raven)
killing, black parrot, a (Raven)
leash, connected by, gloved hand to (Hawk)
lewd, lascivious, voluptuous (Heron, Vulture)
lying, not telling the truth (Raven)
magic (Raven)
magician's apprentice, she is a (Raven)
money (Vulture)
nature, of pristine, ruined by man (Raven)
observe; ability to, involved without being (Macaw)
observer, an (Macaw)
passive, change, unable to the situation (Macaw)
people, handicapped (Hawk)
people, of, in mobs, furious and looting (Raven)
Phoenix rising from rashes (Vulture)
poisonous smoke, an oil refinery belching out clouds of (Raven)
pollution, of, environmental (Raven)
possessions, must run back and retrieve them (Vulture)
prisoner; being taken of (Raven)
rape (Raven)
scolding (Hawk)
scolding someone for not being a good citizen (Hawk)
stealing, of (Raven)
trips, journeys; by car and bus (Vulture)
water; waves; high, of
driving
    fast; with recklessness and indifference to consequences (Falcon)
    speed, desire for (Falcon)
duty
    aversion to; domestic duty (Falcon)
escape, attempts to; family and children, from her (Falcon)
estranged
    family, from her (Falcon)
    partner, from (Falcon)
    wife, from his (Falcon)
expectation, sensation of (Heron)
exploited being, feels as if (Hawk)
extravagance (Macaw)
fastidious; appearance, to personal (Falcon)
fear
    cancer of (Pelican)
    mistakes, to make (Pelican)
    opinion of others, of (Heron)
    poisoned, of being (Raven)

suffocation, of (Heron)
flashbacks (Vulture)
focus intense (Pelican)
forgetfulness; purchases of, goes off and
    leaves them (Vulture)
give, feeling, but does not get (Macaw)
handle things anymore, cannot,
    overwhelmed by stress (Heron)
hatred; revenge, and (Falcon)
hold back, feels he must (Macaw)
ideas; abundant; ability to communicate
    them, and (Falcon)
indifference, apathy
    conscience, to the dictates of (Falcon)
    danger, to (Falcon)
    joy, to (Falcon)
    opinion of others, to (Falcon)
indignation; rage, with (Falcon)
individuality, sense of (Macaw)
industrious; alternating with lassitude
    (Falcon)
industrious, mania for work (Heron)
injustice; cannot support (Falcon, Owl)
injustice; cannot support, cool in the face
    of anger (Falcon)
intellectual (Owl)
intelligent (Owl)
interesting, desires to be (Macaw)
interference, aversion to (Hawk)
interruption, aversion to (Hawk)
introspection (Heron)
irritability (Hawk, Heron)
    concentrate, when attempting to
        (Pelican)
    driving a car, while (Heron)
leadership (fears taking) (Pelican)
longing for; good opinion of others
    (Falcon)
love
    falling in love easily (Macaw)
    people in the group, for (Macaw)
mask, absence of (Macaw)
nature; love of, and the outdoors (Owl)
observe, ability to, involved without being
    (Macaw)

observing; life, own (Owl)
passionate (Macaw)
    desires to be wildly (Macaw)
patience (Heron)
pleasing
    desire to please others (Falcon)
    desire to please others, puts on make
        up (Falcon)
power
    feeling of (Hawk)
    love of (Hawk)
quiet
    disposition (Owl)
    wants to be (Owl)
rage, fury (Heron)
    biting, with (Falcon)
    cursing, with (Falcon, Raven)
    paroxysmal (Heron)
    uncontrollable, can scarcely be
        restrained (Heron)
relax, unable to (Macaw)
rest; cannot, when things are not in
    proper place (Vulture)
restlessness; eyes, ameliorated by closing
    (Albatross)
rhymes and rhythm, drumming (Pelican)
sensitive, oversensitive; general; certain
    persons, to (Heron)
sensitive, oversensitive; general, odors to
    menses during; blood, of
    menstrual (Raven)
separate, feels (Heron)
separate, myself, ability to (Macaw)
shrieking, screaming, shouting
    anger during (Raven)
    rage, with; at injustices, ugliness and
        death (Raven)
somnambulism (Vulture)
speak
    feels comfortable to, in a group
        (Macaw)
    unacceptable to, one's truth (Macaw)
speed; desires (Falcon)
suicidal disposition (Heron)
talk, talking, talks; indisposed to, desire to

B·I·R·D·S

Appendix

    be silent, taciturn (Heron)
teacher; feels like a (Owl)
touched, pleasure in being (Macaw)
tranquility, general (Owl)
truth; desire for (Owl)
truth, speak one's own (Macaw)
understanding, desire for
    family from (Hawk)
    mate from (Hawk)
wander; desires to; home, from, and
    ranges in woods (Owl)
wilderness, desires (Owl)
will
    clearness of purpose (Falcon)
    loss of will power (Falcon)
    strong will power (Falcon)
wisdom (Owl)
    inner; guided by (Owl)
wrong; doing things (Pelican)

Vertigo
    light feeling in the head; swaying sensation (Albatross)

Head
    heat (Heron)
    lifting up of the skull, sensation of (Pelican)
    pain
        general, forehead, middle (Hawk)
        in third eye, nail, like a (Hawk)
    removed, as if calvarium is (Pelican)
    sensation of lid on vertex lifting off (Pelican)

Eyes
    dryness (Pelican)
    heat, general (Heron)
    inflammation; lids, blepharitis (Heron)
    lachrymation; constant (Heron)
    open lids, as if closed lids are wide open (Pelican)
    pain
        burning, smarting, biting (Heron)
        stinging (Heron)
    tears
        acrid (Heron)
        salty (Heron)

Vision
    accommodation; defective (Owl)
    acute (Owl)
        see even in darkness, seems to (Owl)
    blindness; sensation of (Owl)
    blurred (Owl)
    depth perception; impaired (Owl)
    distorted; eyes function independently (Owl)
    field of vision; sees objects beside (Heron, Owl)
    focal; distance changes; reading while (Owl)
    impaired, intermittent (Owl)
    impaired, intermittent, blindness with (Owl)
    large; field of vision (Heron)
    stereoscopic, hyper-acute (Owl)

Ears
    discharges; general; glutinous, sticky (Owl)
    foreign body sensation; internal (Owl)
    stopped sensation; alternating with clearing (Owl)

Hearing
    acute
        noises to, slight (Owl)
        noises to, ticking of watch (Owl)
        voices and talking (Owl)
    illusions; voices (Owl)

Nose
    epistaxis (Pelican)

Face
    drawn; jaw, lower, drawn backward, as if (Pelican)
    eruptions; acne (Vulture)
    eruptions; pustules; cheeks (Vulture)
    jaw; tightness (Owl)

loose feeling in lower jaw (Pelican)
pain, general
    eyebrows, between (Hawk)
    forehead (Hawk)
pain; general; jaws
    articulation (Owl)
    muscles, masseter (Owl)
swelling, general, lips (Macaw)
trembling; jaw (Pelican)

Mouth
    gums; tender (Vulture)
    pulsating; gums (Pelican)

Taste
    bitter (Heron)
        putrid (Heron)

Teeth
    displaced, as if (Heron)
    distended, sensation (Owl)
    folded in, on themselves, sensation of (Heron)
    large and swollen, sensation (Owl)
    location of teeth has changed, as if (Heron)
    pain; bottom, left (Vulture)
    pain; front (Vulture)
    pain; pulsating (Pelican)
        lower (Pelican)
    rubbery, sensation of (Heron)
    soft, feel (Pelican)
    soft, sensation (Owl)
    spongy, sensation (Owl)
    weakness in (Pelican)

Throat
    choking, constricting (Heron, Raven)
    constriction
        throat-pit (Heron)
        tonsils (Heron)
        uvula (Heron)
    inflammation (Hawk)
    inflammation; sore throat; septic (Vulture)
    inflammation; sore throat; tonsils (Vulture)
    inflammation; sore throat; tonsils, pus in pockets (Vulture)
    lump, sensation of (Albatross)
    pain; general (Vulture)
    pain; sore, bruised (Heron)
    suppuration; general; tonsils (Vulture)
    swelling; breathing difficult at night (Vulture)
    swelling; tonsils (Vulture)

Stomach
    appetite; ravenous; canine, excessive (Owl, Raven)
    apprehension (Albatross)
        primal fear of life, a (Albatross)
    fear felt in (Albatross)
    nausea; beer; amel. (Raven)
    nausea; vomiting, sensation of, without feeling bad (Albatross)
    tension; feeling of anticipation (Albatross)
    thirst
        extreme (Owl)
        large quantities for (Owl)
        unquenchable, constant (Owl)

Abdomen
    constriction (Heron)
    liver and region of, ailments of (Heron)
    pain, general
        hypogastrium (Hawk)
        hypogastrium, extending to, upward (Hawk)

Rectum
    constipation; general (Heron)
    constipation; urging absent (Vulture)
Stool
    loose (Vulture)

Bladder
    urination
        dysuria, erection with (Heron)

Appendix

   incomplete; obliged to urinate five or six times before the bladder is empty (Heron)

Male
   erections, troublesome; strong, morning (Heron)
   sexual; desire
      excitement of, easy (Heron)
      increased (Heron)

Female
   energy, uterus in, sensation of (Heron)
   pain, cramping
      menses, before (Hawk)
      menses, during (Hawk)
      uterus (Hawk)
   pain, general, menses (Hawk)

Speech and voice
   hoarseness (Vulture)

Respiration
   difficult; throat swelling, from (Vulture)

Cough
   echo, like an; over and over (Raven)

Chest
   constriction; tension, tightness; sternum (Heron)
   enlarged; sensation as if (Raven)
   lungs; sponge, as if lungs were a, water would run out (Raven)
   open, feeling of openness and burning love for life in chest (Albatross)
   pain; burning; sternum (Vulture)
   pain; piercing; sternum (Vulture)
   pain shooting, sharp, lancinating; sternum, in between breasts, left side (Pelican)
   swelling; lymphatic tissue; axillary (Vulture)

Back
   contractions
      general; cervical region; muscles of (Owl)
      sensation of; cervical tendons feel too short (Owl)
   eruptions; pustules (Vulture)
   neck; sensation of disappearing (Owl)
   pain
      cervical region (Owl)
      dorsal region, right (Owl)
      dorsal region, scapulae between (Owl)
   spine, complaints of (Heron)
   stiffness; cervical region (Heron)

Extremities
   awkwardness
      hands, drops things (Macaw, Albatross)
      lower extremities, knocks against things (Macaw)
      lower extremities, stumbling when walking (Macaw)
   constriction; lower limbs; thighs (Heron)
   eruptions; papular; upper limbs, wrist (Albatross)
   heaviness, tired limbs; lower limbs; legs (Albatross)
   lower limbs
      tension, lower limbs
         tendons (Hawk)
         thighs, tendons, hamstrings (Hawk)
   pain, pulling sensation, lower limbs, legs, thigh (Hawk)
   pain; upper limbs, wrists (ulna side) (Albatross)
   perspiration; general; upper limbs
      arms (Owl)
      hands (Owl)
   thigh, tendons of, pulling (Hawk)
   tingling, prickling, upper limbs (Owl)

Sleep
    heavy (Albatross)
    short; general, catnaps in (Heron)
    sleeplessness (Albatross)
    sleeplessness; thought, from, revenge (Raven)
    somnambulism (Vulture)
    waking; frequent (Heron)

Chill
    shaking, shivering, rigors (Albatross)

Skin
    desquamating; fingers (Vulture)
    eruptions; discharging, moist; honey, like (Albatross)
    eruptions; papular (Albatross)
    eruptions; pustules (Vulture)
    itching (Condor)
        bedbugs, as if (Vulture)
        crawling sensation (Vulture)
        distressing (Condor)
        formicating and crawling (Condor)
        intolerable (Condor)
        parasites, as from (Condor)
        scratch, must (Condor)
    peeling (Vulture)
    rash (Vulture)

Generalities
    clumsiness (Macaw)
    clumsiness, unwieldiness (Heron)
    coldness (Albatross)
    coldness; fear, from (Albatross)
    coordinated, very (Macaw)
    coordination affected, disturbed (Macaw)
    food and drinks
        fish; desires (Heron)
        fruit desires (Macaw)
        green foods, desire for (Raven)
        meat, desires (Owl)
        meat, desires, chicken and (Owl)
        nuts; desires (Heron, Macaw)
        olives, olive oil; desires (Heron)
        salty, desires (Vulture)
        spices, condiments, piquant, highly season food; desires (Heron)
        sunflower seeds, desires (Macaw)
        vegetables; aversion (Heron)
        water, desires (Owl)
    heat; extending; upward (Heron)
    shaking; fear, from; cold sensation, with (Albatross)

B•I•R•D•S 485

Index

Note: This index does not include the "Provings" or "Cases" sections of this book. It is indexed only on prominent features in the "Introduction" and "Key Features" sections.

A

Abandonment, in Hawk, 19, 57
Abdomen. *See also* Stomach
   in bird remedies, 23
   cramping in, severe menstrual, 65
      Falcon for, 122
   pain in
      stabbing, cutting, 23
      stabbing, stitching, 21
Abuse
   of child
      in Falcon, 113
      Heron for, 86
   sexual
      in Dove, 51
      Swan for, 152
   suffering of, in Dove, 51
Acceptance
   vs. freedom, in Falcon, 113
   in Macaw, 44
Accipitridae, 30, 56, 88
Acne, 125
   Vulture on, 132
Activity
   below the surface, in Heron, 79
   peak, at noon, 129
Addiction
   in Falcon, 113
   opiate, Raven for, 108
Aello, 132
Aggression
   in Raven, 48
   in Swan, 147
Aggressor, consolation and love of, in Dove, 51
Air, open, desire for, 21
Air sacs
   in bird, 27

   in Pelican, 40
Air spaces, bird, 27
Allergies, Heron for, 86
Alone
   in Condor, 135
   desire to be, 19
   in Hawk, 57
Anacardium orientale, *vs.* falcon, 122
Anatidae, 30, 146
Andean Condor. *See* Condor, Andean
Androgyny, in Wandering Albatross, 156
Anger
   in Falcon, 112
   in Hawk, 59
   smoldering, at being left out/excluded, 142
   suppression of, in Dove, 51
Anger (external), in Raven, 99
Anhalonium, *vs.* Owl, 74
Animal kingdom, 29
Animal mind, 18
Ankles. *See* Extremities; Limbs, lower
Anseriformes, 30, 146
Anthrax, Turkey Vultures on, 132
Anxiety
   in Pelican, 36–37
   in Raven, 103
Apart, set, in Wandering Albatross, 155
Aphrodisiacs, Dove meat and eggs as, 54
Aphrodite, 54, 151
Apollo, 151
Appetite
   disturbance of, 21
   of Raven, 107, 108
Ara-m. *See* Macaw, Scarlet
Ara macao. *See* Macaw, Scarlet
Ard-h. *See* Heron, Great Blue
Ardea herodias. *See* Heron, Great Blue

Ardeidae, 30, 76
Arms. *See* Limbs, upper
Artemis, 151
Athena, 73–74
Attention, inability in focusing of, 18
Authors, about, 474–475
Autism, Heron for, 86
Aversion to company, in Hawk, 57–58
Away from home, Wandering Albatross for, 159
Awkwardness
   in extremities, 23
   in Macaw, 44

B

Back, 21, 23
   in Owl, 69
Baker, Kim, Raven proving of, 109, 253–276. *See also* Raven, proving of
Baker, Virginia, Red-tailed Hawk proving of, 65, 202–208
Balance, in Heron, 83
Bald Eagle, 88, 88–97, 97. *See also* Eagle, Bald
Baldwin, Tanya, Andean Condor case of, 431–451
Baryta, *vs.* Dove, 51, 55
Beak, 27
   of Heron, 83
Beautiful, in Raven, 103
Bedayn, Greg, Raven proving of, 109, 253–276. *See also* Raven, proving of
Being in the moment, in Pelican, 36
Belladonna, 108
Belonging, not, in water birds, 26
Below the surface activity, in Heron, 79
Bernstein, Mariette, Bald Eagle case of, 385–389
Bible, Dove in, 51
Binomial nomenclature, 28–29
Bird groups, DNA studies on relationships between, 31
Bird symptoms, common. *See* Characteristics, bird

Birds of prey. *See* specific birds
Black and white, in Raven, 102–103
Black and white issues, in Penguin, 141
Blindness, fear of, 22
Blocked, 133
Blue, in Scarlet Macaw, 47
Body temperature, bird, 27
Bone structure, light, in birds, 20
Bones, hollow, 27
Borderline personality disorders, Raven for, 108
Boundaries, affirming being as individual, no respect for, 99
Breaking things, in Vulture, 126
Breathe deeply, desire to, 23
Breathing constriction, in Swan, 147
Brown, Douglas, Scarlet Macaw case of, 326–336
Brown Pelican. *See* Pelican, Brown
Bubo-v. *See* Owl, Great Horned
Bubo virginianus. *See* Owl, Great Horned
Bumps, itching, 38
Bursitis, of right shoulder, in Owl, 69
Bute-j. *See* Hawk, Red-tailed
Buteo jamaicensis. *See* Hawk, Red-tailed

C

C4 homeopathy, 169
C4 trituration, 169–170
   in Brown Pelican proving, 172
Calls, bird. *See* Vocal sounds
Calm
   in Heron, 78–79
   in Pelican, 36–37
Cannabis indica, *vs.* Bald Eagle, 96
Carcinosin
   vs. Dove, 54
   vs. Pelican, 41
Care of others, restrictions in, Hawk and, 64
Carrion feeders, 131, 136, 137
Cases, 309
   of Albatross, Wandering, 464–465
   of chicken tuberculosis (Timmerman), 466–472

Index

of Condor, Andean, 431–451
of Dove, Ring, 337–348
   case 1 (Shore), 337–340
   case 2 (Stanley), 340–343
   case 3 (Timmerman), 343–348
of Eagle, Bald, 368–389
   case 1 (Chabra), 368–369
   case 2 (Shore), 370–374
   case 3 (Shore), 374–378
   case 4 (Quirk), 378–383
   case 5 (Franken and Timmerman), 383–385
   case 6 (Bernstein), 385–389
of Falcon, Peregrine, 402–427
   case 1 (Galeazzi), 402–406
   case 2 (Shevin), 407–409
   case 3 (Shevin), 410–416
   case 4 (Timmerman), 416–427
of Hawk, Red-tailed, 349–367
   case 1 (Shore), 349–350
   case 2 (Reichenberg-Ullman), 351–367
of Macaw, Scarlet, 320–336
   case 1 (Shore), 320–322
   case 2 (Walrad), 322–326
   case 3 (Brown), 326–336
of Pelican, Brown, 310–319
   case 1 (Hogeland), 310–311
   case 2 (Shore), 312–319
of Penguin, Humboldt (Shore), 452–457
of Raven (Jackson), 390–401
of Swan, Mute (Schulz), 463
of Swan, Whooper, 458–462
   case 1 (C. Sherr), 458–460
   case 2 (S. Smith and C. Sherr), 460–462
of Vulture, Turkey (Tichenor), 428–430
Cath-a. *See* Vulture, Turkey
Catharsis, in Vulture, 125
Cathartes, 128
Cathartes aura. *See* Vulture, Turkey
Cathartidae, 30, 124, 134
Cervical vertebra, bird, 27
Chabra, Divya
   Bald Eagle cases of, 368–369

Bald Eagle proving of, 251–252
Characteristics, bird, 13, 17–26
   conceptual organization, 17–18
   disorientation in time and space, 18
   dogs, 25
   dreams of water, 25
   drugged sensation, 18
   empathy, 19
   freedom and travel, 19–20
   impartial detachment, 18
   intuition or natural knowing, 18
   music, 26
   perfectionism, 20
   relationship, 19
   rising above, 24–25
   spiritual awareness, 19
Chest
   in bird remedies, 23
   constriction of, in Swan, 147
   sharp, stabbing pains in, 23
   stabbing, stitching pain in, 21
Chicken tuberculosis, 466
   case of, 466–472
Child abuse
   in Falcon, 113
   Heron for, 86
Children, protection of, in Falcon, 111
Choice, in Condor, 135
Ciconiiformes, 30, 76, 124, 134
Circe, 62
Clarity, emotional, in Pelican, 37
Classical provings, 167–168
   modern, 168
   modified, 168–169
Classification
   of birds, 29
   in mineral remedies, 17–18
Claustrophobia, Falcon for, 122
Claw sign, 20
Claws, of Hawk, 62
Clay, Macaw eating of, 45
Clean, in Penguin, 142
Clean and dirty, in Raven, 102–103
Cliques, in Penguin, 141
Cloaca, 27

Clumsiness, in extremities, 23
Cob, 148
Coldness, in Falcon, 112
Color vision, bird, 28
Color(s)
    in Eagle, Bald
        colors before the right eye; rainbow, all colors of the, 92
        desires white, 90
    in Falcon, 113
        charmed by, 114
        yellow, desire for, 114
    in Heron, Great Blue, desire for green, 80
    in Macaw, bright, 44
    in Macaw, Scarlet
        charmed by blue, green, red, 47
        desires blue, 47
        desires red, 47
    in Swan, white, 147, 151–152
Colum-p. See Dove, Ring
Columba palumbus. See Dove, Ring
Columbidae, 30
Columbiformes, 30
Common bird symptoms. See Characteristics, bird
Communication. See Vocal sounds and communication
Community role
    in Dove, strong feeling of, 51
    in Macaw and Pelican, 19
Company, aversion to, in Hawk, 57–58
Concentration, difficulty with, 18
Conceptual organization, 17–18
Condor, *vs.* Turkey Vulture, 32
Condor, Andean, *134*, 134–139, *139*
    case of (Shore and Baldwin), 431–451
    core idea of: world of living and world of dead, 135
Condor, California, Turkey Vulture and, 130
Confidence, falling fast with, in Condor, 135
Confusion, mental, in Pelican, 36
Connection
    in Heron, 77–78
    in Pelican, 35–36
    in Wandering Albatross, 155

Connection/separation, in Macaw and Pelican, 19
Conscientiousness over details, in Pelican, 36
Consciousness expanding above him, 24
Consolation, great ability for, in Dove, 51
Constriction
    in breathing, in Swan, 147
    in chest, 23
        in Swan, 147
    in throat, 22, 26
        in Swan, 147
Control, in Condor, 135
Corv-c. See Raven
Corvidae, 30, 99
Corvus corax principalis. See Raven
Coryza, 22
Courtship. See Reproduction and mating
Coyote, Raven and, 107
Cramping
    in back and extremities, 21, 23
    severe abdominal, menstrual, 65
Creativity, in Raven, 107
Criticism, in Dove, 51
Cunning ways, in Raven, 48
Cutting pain
    abdominal, 23
    extremity, 93
    uterine, 23
Cygn-cy. See Swan
Cygn-o. See Swan
Cygnet, 148–149
Cygnus-co, 147
Cygnus columbianus, 147
Cygnus (constellation), 151
Cygnus cygnus. See Swan; Swan, Whooper
Cygnus olor. See Swan; Swan, Mute
Cysts, itching, discharging, 125

D

Daily life world, in Bald Eagle, 89
Damage, in Raven, 101
Dark and light, in Raven, 102–103
DDT
    on Bald Eagle, 94

Index

on Pelican, 39
Dead, world of, and world of living, 135
Death
    of the old, 137
    preoccupation with, Andean Condor for, 139
    in Raven, 101
    transition to, 132
    in Wandering Albatross, 156
Deception, in Raven, 100–101
Defensiveness
    in Hawk, 57
    in Mute Swan, of nest, 149
Delicate vibration, 20
Delicateness, 20
Delusions
    head open, top of is, 24
    separated; world, from the; in the present and simultaneously detached (Falcon), 25
    in teeth
        of softening, 22
        of weakness, 22
Depression, in Hawk, 59
Destination, impossible, searching for, in Wandering Albatross, 155
Destruction, in Raven, 101
Detachment
    in Heron, 77–78
    impartial, 18
Details, conscientiousness over, in Pelican, 36
Detoxification, in Vulture, 125
Diamond, purity in, 37
Diet and feeding habits
    of Albatross, Wandering, 158
    of Condor, Andean, 136–137
    of Dove, 53
    of Eagle, Bald, 94
    of Falcon, Saker, 118
    of Hawk, 61–62
        providing food for young in, 57
    of Heron, 83
    of Macaw, 45
    of Pelican, 40

of Raven, 100, 105, 107
of Swans, 148
of Vulture, Turkey, 130, 131
Difficulties, rising above, in Bald Eagle, 90
Dio-e. *See* Albatross, Wandering
Diomedea epomophora. *See* Albatross, Wandering
Diomedeidae, 30, 154
Diomedes, 158–159
Dirty, in Penguin, 142
Dirty and clean, in Raven, 102–103
Discharges, on physical and emotional levels, in Vulture, 125
Disinfection, 132
Disorientation, in time and space, 18
DNA studies, of bird group relationships, 31
Do things right, in Pelican, 36
Dogs, in bird remedies, 25
Doing it right/wrong, in Penguin, 141
Domination, in Falcon, 111
Door, magic, Bald Eagle opening of, 95–96
Doubt about what is real, in Raven, 99
Dove, Ring, 50, 50–55
    cases of, 337–348
        case 1 (Shore), 337–340
        case 2 (Stanley), 340–343
        case 3 (Timmerman), 343–348
    guilt and shame in, 20
Drawing, in back and extremities, 23
Dream life, of Bald Eagle, 89–90
Dream proving, 170
Dream world, in Bald Eagle, 89
Dreams
    of dogs, 25
    of water, in bird remedies, 25
Drinking, by Doves, 53
Drugged sensation, 18
Dryness, in eyes, 22
Duality, in Bald Eagle, 90
Dutch homeopathic group, Wandering Albatross proving of, 159, 303–307
Dying, in Raven, 101
Dysmenorrhea, severe, 23

E

Eagle
    eyes of, 20
    rising above in, 24
    Sherr proving of, 12
        shoulder and limb pain in, 13
Eagle, Bald, 88, 88–97, *97*
    cases of, 368–389
        case 1 (Chabra), 368–369
        case 2 (Shore), 370–374
        case 3 (Shore), 374–378
        case 4 (Quirk), 378–383
        case 5 (Franken and Timmerman), 383–385
        case 6 (Bernstein), 385–389
Ears
    in bird remedies, 22
    of Owl, 72–73
Electra, 132
Emotional clarity, in Pelican, 37
Emotional discharges, in Vulture, 125
Emotional overwhelm, in Heron, 78–79
Emotional residue, letting go of, in Vulture, 125
Empathy, 19
Endless, in Wandering Albatross, 155
Energy, in Hawk, 58
Energy, life, descent of matter from, 15
Epistaxis, 22
Equality, in Wandering Albatross, 156
Escape, in Raven, 101–102, 107
Essence, 15–16
    of Vithoulkas, 15
Euphoria, in Heron, 78–79
Excluded
    smoldering anger about, 142
    from society, in Penguin, 141
Exotic, in Macaw, 44
Exploited, feeling, especially by family, in Hawk, 57
Expression, in words, difficulty with, 18
Extension, in Herons, 84
Extremities. *See also* Limbs, lower; Limbs, upper; specific extremity parts, e.g.,
    Shoulder
    in bird remedies, 23
    clumsiness and awkwardness in, 23
    heaviness, weakness, numbness and tingling in, 23
    lightness in, 23
    in Owl, 69
    stiffness, tension and cramping in, 21
    strength and mobility in, increased, 23
    tension, stiffness, drawing and cramping in, 23
Extremity pain
    as bird theme, 13
    in Eagle proving, 13
    in Macaw proving, 13
    severe, 23
Eyes
    in bird remedies, 22
    dryness in, 22
    of Eagle, 20
    fixed, in Owl, 72
    of Heron, 83
    irritation in, 22
    of Owl, 72
    sharp, stabbing pains in, 22
    stabbing, stitching pain in, 21
    as bird theme, 12, 13
Eyesight, of Herons, 84

F

Face
    in bird remedies, 22
    itching of, Vulture on, 133
Facts, bird, 27–28
Fairness, in Owl, 67
Falco-c. *See* Falcon, Saker
Falco cherug. See Falcon, Saker
Falco-p. *See* Falcon, Peregrine
Falco peregrinus. See Falcon, Peregrine
Falcon, *110*, 110–123, *123*
    family in, 64
Falcon, Peregrine, *110*, 110–123. *See also* Falcon
    cases of, 402–427

Index

case 1 (Galeazzi), 402–406
case 2 (Shevin), 407–409
case 3 (Shevin), 410–416
case 4 (Timmerman), 416–427
nostrils of, 117
Falcon, Saker, *110*, 110–123. *See also* Falcon
vs. Hawk, 64
natural history of, 118–121
proving of, 281–283
Falconidae, 30, 110
Falconiformes, 30, 56, 88, 110, 128
Falconry, 116, 118, 119–120
Falling fast, with confidence and pleasure, in Condor, 135
Family
in Falcon, 64, 111–112
in Hawk, 64, 111
feeling exploited by, 57
struggles in, 64
in Pelican, protection of, 35
Family groupings, value of, 13, 16
Father, in Wandering Albatross, 155
Fear
of blindness, 22
in Pelican, 36–37
in Raven, 103
Feathers, 27. *See also* Wings
of Dove, 53
of Herons, 84
of Owl, 71, 73
of Penguin, 142
of Raven, 105, 108
of Vulture, 129
Feeding habits. *See* Diet and feeding habits
Feeling, lack of, in Falcon, 112
Feet. *See also* Extremities; Limbs, lower
bird, 28
Female organs, in bird remedies, 23
Figure it out, need to, in Pelican, 35
Fine features, 20
Finger, in corner of mouth, 121
Fire, in Wandering Albatross, 156
Flashbacks, in Vulture, 125
Flight
of Albatross, Wandering, 157–158

of Condor, Andean, 137
of Eagle, Bald, 94
of Falcon, Peregrine, 117
of Herons, 83–84
high
in Hawk, 62
spirituality with, 51
of Pelicans, 40
of Raven, 99, 105
of Vulture, 129
Floating, vertigo as if, 21
Flock birds, relationships in, 19
Flocks
of Doves, 53
of Pelicans, 40
Fluid balance, in bird, 20
Focus
goal-oriented, in Heron, 78
inability to, 18
intensity of, in Pelican, 36
Food. *See* Diet
Franken, Eveline, Bald Eagle case of, 383–385
Freedom, 19–20
to be, 35
in Falcon, 111
in Hawk, 57, 58, 64
from judgment, 35
Frustration, in Vulture, 126
Fullness, in head, 21
Fungi, 29

G

Galeazzi, Bruno, Peregrine Falcon case of, 402–406
Gaze, hypnotic, piercing, in Heron, 83
Generalities, in bird remedies, 20–21
Gentleness, in Dove, 51
Genus (genera), 28
Getting it right
in birds, 35
in Pelican, 35
Giving
feeling of, but not getting anything back, in Macaw, 44

more than they want to, in Hawk, 57
Gizzard, 27
Gloved hand
    in Falcon, 113, 120
    in Hawk, 120
    in hawking, 57
Goal-oriented focus, in Heron, 78
God(s). *See also* Spirituality and spiritual awareness
    Hawk and, 62
    messengers of
        Dove as, 51
        Hawk as, 62–63
        Macaws as, 46
        Peregrine Falcon as, 121
        Raven as, 100
Great Blue Heron, 76, 76–87, 87. *See also* Heron, Great Blue
Green
    in Heron, 80
    in Macaw, 47
Grief
    in Dove, 51
        suppression of, 51
    in Swan
        living, 147
        long-standing, 152
    in water birds, 26
Groaning, by Vulture, 131
Group. *See also* Flocks
    in Macaw
        vs. individuality, 43
        relationship with, 44
Groupings, family, value of, 13, 16
Guilt, in Dove, 20
Gums
    in Owl, 68, 70
    pain in, 38
    pulsation in, 22
    soft and spongy sensations in, in Owl, 70

H

Habitat
    of Albatross, Wandering, 158
    of Condor, Andean, 136
    of Dove, Ring, 53
    of Eagle, Bald, 94
    of Falcon, Peregrine, 117
    of Hawk, Red-tailed, 61
    of Heron, Great Blue, 83
    of Macaw, Scarlet, 45
    of Owl, Great Horned, 71
    of Pelican, Brown, 39–40
    of Penguin, Humboldt, 142
    of Raven, 105
    of Swan, 148
    of Swan, Mute, 149
    of Vulture, Turkey, 129
Hack, 120
Hahnemann, on provings, 163
Hahnemannian provings, 167–168
Haliae-lc. *See* Eagle, Bald
Haliaeetus, 94
Haliaeetus leucocephalus. *See* Eagle; Eagle, Bald
Hand. *See* Extremities; Limbs, upper
Hand, gloved
    in Falcon, 113, 120
    in Hawk, 120
    in hawking, 57
Handicapped children, Heron for, 86
Harmony, perfect, in Heron, 83
Harpies, 132
Hawk
    abandonment in, 19
    desire for understanding from family members in, 19
    desire to be alone in, 19
    epistaxis in, 22
    family in, 64, 111
Hawk, Red-tailed, 56, 56–65, 64
    vs. Bald Eagle, 96
    cases of, 349–367
        case 1 (Shore), 349–350

Index

case 2 (Reichenberg-Ullman), 351–367
vs. Falcon, 122
Hawking, 57, 119
Hay fever, Heron for, 86
Head
    bald, 129, 136
    in bird remedies, 21
    fullness, pressure and heaviness in, 21
    in Heron, 79
    itching of, Vulture on, 133
    lid on vertex lifting off, sensation of, 24
    open, top of is, 24
    in Owl, 68
    right-sided symptoms in, 38
    rotation of, in Owl, 72
Headaches, 21
Healing professions, involvement in, 19
Hearing
    of Herons, 84
    in Owl, 67–68, 72
Heart, bird, 27
Heaviness
    in extremities, 23
    in head, 21
Hector, 158
Helios, 150, 151
Helium, *vs.* Bald Eagle, 96
Hercules, 96
Heron, Great Blue, *76*, 76–87, *87*
    eyes in, 22
Herrick, Nancy, provings of
    Lotus, 169
    modified classical, 168–169
Hidden things, in Heron, 79
Hip pain
    as bird theme, 13
    in Macaw, 13
    sciatica, 23
Hissing, by Turkey Vulture, 125, 131
Hogeland, Anneke
    biography of, 475
    Brown Pelican case of, 310–311
Home, feel away from, Wandering Albatross for, 159

Homing pigeons, 51, 54. *See also* Dove, Ring
Hood, 120–121
Horus, 119, 121, 122
Humboldt Penguin. *See* Penguin, Humboldt
Humiliation, in Falcon, 111, 112
Hypersensitivity
    Heron for, 86
    in Pelican, 38
    in Vulture, 126
Hypnotic, piercing gaze, in Heron, 83

I

Identity, loss of, in Raven, 99–100
Ignatia, *vs.* Swan, 152
Impartial detachment, 18
Impartial observation, in Macaw, 44
Independence, in Heron, 78
Indifference, in Falcon, 112
Individual, boundaries affirming being as individual, no respect for, 99
Individual force, expression of, in falcon, 64
Individuality
    in Heron, 78
    in Macaw, *vs.* group, 43
    in Raven, protection of, 48, 99
Individuation, in Macaw, 43
Injured feeling, in Hawk, 57, 60
Injury
    in Raven, 101
    repetitive stress, Wandering Albatross for, 159
    strain, Wandering Albatross for, 159
Inner life, violation of, in Raven, 48
Instinct, in Pelican, 36
Intent, in provings, 167
Interruption, sudden, in Wandering Albatross, 155
Intrusion, in Wandering Albatross, 155
Intuition, 18
Invasion, in Raven, 100–101
    protection of inner life from, 48
Irritability, 21
    in Hawk, 59

Isolation
　in Pelican, 35–36
　in Wandering Albatross, 155
　in water birds, 26
Itching
　in Condor, 135
　of face and head, Vulture on, 133
Itching bumps, 38

J
Jackson, Jessica
　Raven case of, 390–401
　Raven proving of, 109, 253–276 (See also Raven, proving of)
Jaw
　in bird remedies, 22
　in Owl, 68
　in Pelican, 39
　sharp pains in, 22
Jesses, 120
Jet airplanes, engineerings of, 117
Joy, in Pelican, 37
Judgment
　in Dove, 51
　freedom from, 35
　in Macaw, 35

K
Kali salts, as common prescription, 14
Killing, in Raven, 101
Kingdom, 29
Knee pain, sciatica, 23
Knowing, natural, 18
　in Pelican, 35
Knowledge, in Owl, 67
Kuiper, Pieter, Wandering Albatross case of, 464–465
Kygnus, 150

L
Lac caninum, vs. Dove, 55
Lac equinum proving, of Jonathan Shore, 165–166
Lancinating pains, 21

Leadership, in Pelican, 37
Leda, 151
Left out, smoldering anger about, 142
Legs. See Extremities; Limbs, lower
Leprosy miasm, Penguin in, 26, 144
Letting go of old relationships/emotional residue, in Vulture, 125
Levels of materiality, 166, 167
Life energy, descent of matter from, 15
Light and dark, in Raven, 102–103
Lightheadedness, 24
Lightness, in extremities, 23
Limbs, lower, 23
　clumsiness and awkwardness in, 23
　heaviness, weakness, numbness and tingling in, 23
Limbs, upper, 23. See also Shoulder
　clumsiness and awkwardness in, 23
　heaviness, weakness, numbness and tingling in, 23
　in Owl, 69
Linguistic ability, of Macaw, 46
Living, world of, and world of dead, 135
Loneliness, in Wandering Albatross, 155
Loquacity, in Macaw, 44
Loss of identity, in Raven, 99–100
Lotus proving, 169
Love, great ability for, in Dove, 51
Lump, in throat, 22, 26
Lure, 120, 121

M
Macaw, Scarlet, 42, 42–49
　cases of, 320–336
　　case 1 (Shore), 320–322
　　case 2 (Walrad), 322–326
　　case 3 (Brown), 326–336
　connection/separation in, 19
　individuation in, 43
　judgment in, 35
　linguistics of, 46
　remedies to consider vs., 48
　role in community in, 19
Magic door, opening of, by Bald Eagle, 95–96

Index

Martyr, Dove as, 51, 54
Mating. *See* Reproduction and mating
Matter, descent of life energy into, 15
Meat-eating birds, gums and teeth sensations in, 70
Meditation provings, 170
Medorrhinum, *vs.* Raven, 108
Menaced, in Falcon, 112
Menstrual cramping
    Falcon for, 122
    severe abdominal, 65
Menstrual pain, 21
Mental confusion, in Pelican, 36
Messages, in Vulture, 125
Messenger pigeons, 51. *See also* Dove, Ring
Messengers of God
    Dove as, 51
    Falcon as, 121
    Hawk as, 62–63
    Macaw as, 46
    Raven as, 100
Metabolic rate, bird, 20
Methodology of provings, 163–164, 167–170
    Hahnemannian (classical), 167–168
    meditation, 170
    modern classical, 168
    modified classical, 168–169
    seminar, 170
    trituration, 169–170
Migration, of Herons, 84
Mimic, Raven as, 100
Mind
    consciousness expanding above him, 24
    in provings, 163
Mind, animal, 18
Mind, bird, 17–20
    conceptual organization in, 17–18
    disorientation in time and space in, 18
    drugged sensation in, 18
    empathy in, 19
    freedom and travel in, 19–20
    impartial detachment in, 18
    intuition or natural knowing in, 18
    perfectionism in, 20
    relationship in, 19

    spiritual awareness in, 19
Mind, delusions. *See* Delusions
Mineral kingdom, 29
    mind in, 17–18
Missed, something being, 79
Mistrust, in Penguin, 142
Mobility, increased, in extremities, 23
Modern classical provings, 168
Modified classical provings, 168–169
Mohr, Peter, Humboldt Penguin proving of, 141, 144
Molt, 28
Moment, being in the, in Pelican, 36
Monera, 29
Morphology, bird, 27
Mouth, finger in corner of, 121
Muscular system, bird, 27
Music, 26
Mystery
    of homeopathy, 163
    of provings, 164–166
Mythology and symbolism
    of Albatross, Wandering, 158–159
    of Condor, Andean, 137–139
    of Dove, Ring, 54
    of Eagle, Bald, 95–96
    of Falcon, 121–122
    of Hawk, 62–64
    of Heron, 85
    of Macaw, 45–47
    of Owl, 73–74
    of Pelican, Brown, 41
    of Raven, 106–108
    of Swan, 150–152
    of Vulture, Turkey, 132

N

Nasal obstruction, 22
Natrum muriaticum, *vs.* Swan, 152
Natural history
    of Albatross, Wandering, 157–158
    of Condor, Andean, 136–137
    of Dove, Ring, 53–54
    of Eagle, Bald, 94–95

of Falcon, 116–121
of Hawk, Red-tailed, 61–62
of Heron, Great Blue, 82–85
of Macaw, Scarlet, 45
of Owl, Great Horned, 71–73
of Pelican, Brown, 39–40
of Penguin, Humboldt, 142–144
of Raven, 105–106
of remedies, 16
of Swan, 148–150
of Vulture, Turkey, 128–132
Nature, 15–16
Nauman, Eileen, on Great Blue Heron, 85
Nechbet, 137
Neck
    in Heron, 79
    in Owl, 68
        vertebrae of, 72
    tension and stiffness in, 23
Neck pain, in Owl, 68
Needlelike pains, 38
Negativity, in Penguin, 141
Neglected, feeling, in Hawk, 57
Nervous restlessness, 20–21
Nervous system, degenerative disorders of, in Falcon, 122
Nervousness, sensation of, in Macaw, 44
Nest(ing)
    in Dove, 53
    in Eagle, Bald, 95
    in Falcon, Peregrine, 116, 118
    in Falcon, Saker, 118
    in Hawk, 62
    in Herons, 85
    in Macaw, 45
    in Owl, 72
    in Pelican, 40
    in Penguin, Humboldt, 143
    in Raven, 105
    in Swan, Mute, 149
    in Vulture, Turkey, 129, 131
Nestor, 158
Neuropathy, peripheral
    Falcon for, 122
    Macaw for, 48

Nomenclature, scientific, 28–29
Noon, peak activity at, 129
Norland, Misha, Peregrine Falcon proving of, 111, 123, 277–283. *See also* Falcon, Peregrine, proving of
Nose (nostrils)
    in bird remedies, 22
    of Falcons, 117
Not being seen, in Heron, 79
Nuclear family birds, relationships in, 19
Numbness, in extremities, 23
Nux vomica, *vs.* Falcon, 122

O

Obligation, in Hawk, 57, 64
Observation, impartial, in Macaw, 44
Obsessiveness, 144
Ocypete, 132
Odysseus, 159
Old, death of, 137
Open air, desire for, 21
Opiate addiction, Raven for, 108
Opinion of others
    desire for good, in Falcon, 113
    suffering from, on how should be in world, 35
Opium, *vs.* Raven, 108
Opposites, unification of, in Wandering Albatross, 156
Optic lobes, bird, 28
Order, putting things in, in Condor, 135
Orders, bird, 30
Organization, conceptual, 17–18
Outcast, in water birds, 26
Outrage, in Raven, 99, 102
Ovary and oviduct, bird, 28
Overwhelmed, emotionally, in Heron, 78–79
Owl
    ears in, 22
    eyes in, 22
Owl, Great Horned, 66, 66–75, *75*

B•I•R•D•S   497

Index

P

Pain. *See also* specific locations, e.g., Extremity pain
   cutting
      abdominal, 23
      extremity, 93
      uterine, 23
   lancinating, 21
   needlelike, 38
   piercing, 38
   in Raven, 103
   sharp
      in chest, 23
      in zygomatic bones, 22
   sharp, stabbing, in eyes, 22
   stabbing, 12, 13, 21
      abdominal, 23
      in chest, 23
      in ears, 21
      in eyes, 12, 13, 22
      uterine, 23
   stabbing, stitching, 21
      in eye, 12, 13
   stitching, 12, 13, 21
Pairing, in Turkey Vulture, 126
Panic, in Raven, 103
Paralysis, in Falcon, 112–113, 122
Paranoia, in Penguin, 141
Parasites, Vulture on, 132
Parrots. *See also* Macaw
   groups of, 43
Participants, in provings, 168
Passeres, 30, 99
Passeriformes, 30, 99
Patience, in Heron, 78
Pelec-o. *See* Pelican, Brown
Pelecanidae, 30, 34
Pelecaniformes, 30, 34
Pelecanus occidentalis. *See* Pelican, Brown
Pelican, Brown, *34*, 34–41
   C4 trituration in, 172
   cases of, 310–319
      case 1 (Hogeland), 310–311
      case 2 (Shore), 312–319

community role in, 19
connection/separation in, 19
eyes in, 22
general thoughts on, 189
nose in, epistaxis in, 22
Pen, 148
Penguin, Humboldt, *140*, 140–144
   case of (Shore), 452–457
   hopelessness and self-hatred in, 26
People, not wanting to deal with, 57
Perception, depth, 22
Perching and staring, in Bald Eagle, 95
Peregrine Falcon. *See* Falcon, Peregrine
Perfectionism, 20
   in birds, 35
   in Pelican, 35
Periodicity, in Hawk, 59
Peripheral neuropathy
   Falcon for, 122
   Macaw for, 48
Phaeton, 150
Phineus, 132
Physiognomy and physiology, bird, 20–23
   back and extremities, 23
   chest, 23
   eyes and ears, 22
   face, jaws and teeth, 22
   female organs, 23
   generalities, 20–21
   head, 21
   nose, 22
   stomach and abdomen, 23
   throat, 22
Piercing gaze, in Heron, 83
Piercing pains, 38
Pigeon. *See also* Dove
   vs. dove, 53
Plant kingdom, 29
Pleasure, falling fast with, in Condor, 135
Plug, 22
Podarge, 132
Poem, on Falcon, 7
Power
   in Falcon, 111
   in Hawk, 58

Powerful, in Raven, 103
Precision, in Penguin, 141
Pressure
  in head, 21
  in zygomatic bones, 22
Prey, birds of. *See* specific birds
Pride, 20
  in Falcon, 111
Prison, in Raven, 101–102
Procellariiformes, 30, 154
Prometheus, 96
Protection
  of children, in Falcon, 111
  of family, in Pelican, 35
  of individuality, in Raven, 48, 99
  in Raven, 101–102
Protista, 29
Proud, in Raven, 103
Proving(s), 161–308. *See also* specific
      remedies
  admissible symptoms in, 164–165
  of Baker, Kim, Raven, 109, 253–276
      (*See also* Proving(s), of Raven)
  of Baker, Virginia, Red-tailed Hawk, 65,
      202–208
  of Bedayn, Greg, Raven, 109, 253–276
      (*See also* Proving(s), of Raven)
  beginning of, 164
      experiments on, 164–166
  best, 166
  conditions and levels of materiality in,
      166, 167
  dose in, 169
  dream, 170
  of Dutch homeopathic group, Wandering
      Albatross, 159, 303–307
  Hahnemann on, 163
  of Herrick, Nancy, 168–169
      Lotus, 169
  intent in, 167
  of Jackson, Jessica, Raven, 109, 253–276
      (*See also* Proving(s), of Raven)
  methodology of, 163–164, 167–170
      Hahnemannian (classical), 167–168

  meditation, 170
  modern classical, 168
  modified classical, 168–169
  seminar, 170
  trituration, 169–170
mind in, 163
of Mohr, Peter, Humboldt Penguin, 141,
    144
mystery in, 163
    experiments on, 164–166
of Norland, Misha and School of
        Homeopathy, Peregrine Falcon,
        111, 123, 277–283 (*See also*
        Proving(s), of Falcon)
rationale for, 163
of Rimmler, E., Andean Condor, 135
of Rowe, Todd, Turkey Vulture, 133,
    284–290
of Schulz, Elisabeth
    Andean Condor, 139, 291–295
    Mute Swan, 147, 152, 301–302
    Ring Dove, 55, 199–201 (*See also*
        Proving(s), of Dove)
    Saker Falcon, 111, 123, 281–283 (*See
        also* Proving(s), of Falcon)
of Sherr, Camilla, Whooper Swan, 147,
    152, 298–300
of Sherr, Jeremy, 168
    Bald Eagle, 97, 251
    Whooper Swan, 147, 152, 298–300
of Shore, Jonathan
    Brown Pelican, 41, 172–190 (*See also*
        Proving(s), of Pelican)
    Great Blue Heron, 86, 227–250 (*See
        also* Proving(s), of Heron)
    Great Horned Owl, 75, 223–226
    Humboldt Penguin, 141, 296–297
    Lac equinum, 165–166
    Radium bromatum, 164–166
    Red-tailed Hawk, 65, 202, 208–222
        (*See also* Proving(s), of
        Hawk)
    Scarlet Macaw, 48, 191–198 (*See also*
        Proving(s), of Macaw)

Index

history of, 12
themes of, proving master role in, 166
in this book, 170–171
Proving master, 168
in themes of proving, 166
Psittacidae, 30, 42
Psittaciformes, 30, 42
Purification, in Vulture, 125, 132
Purity
in Diamond, 37
in Pelican, 37
Pus, 125
draining of, in Vulture, 125
Pushed aside feeling, in Penguin, 141
Putting things in order, in Condor, 135

Q

Queen-like, in Raven, 103
Quetzal, 45–46
Quirk, Tina, Bald Eagle case of, 378–383

R

Radium bromatum, Shore proving of, 164–166
Rape. *See also* Sexual abuse
Swan for, 152
Raven, 99, 99–109
in British folklore, 107
case of (Jackson), 390–401
Coyote and, 107
vs. Macaw, 48
rising above in, 24–25
Reality, in Raven
doubt about, 99
lack of, 100
Reason, in Pelican, 36
Rebirth, in Condor, 135
Red, in Scarlet Macaw, 47
Red-tailed Hawk, 56, 56–65. *See also* Hawk, Red-tailed
Reichenberg-Ullman, Judyth, Red-tailed Hawk case of, 351–367
Relating, difficulty with, 57
Relationship(s), 19

with group, in Macaw, 44
with individuals, in Hawk, 57
letting go of, in Vulture, 125
Religion, in Dove, 51
Remedies, new, need for, 14–15
Remedy image, 163
levels of materiality in, 166, 167
Renewal, in Condor, 135
Repetitive stress injury, Wandering Albatross for, 159
Reproduction and mating
in Albatross, Wandering, 158
in bird, 27
in Condor, Andean, 137
in Dove, 53
in Eagle, Bald, 95
in Falcon, Peregrine, 117
in Hawk, 62
in Heron, 84
in Macaw, 45
in Owl, 72
in Pelican, 27
in Penguin, Humboldt, 143
in Raven, 99, 105
in Swan, 148
in Swan, Mute, 148–149
in Vulture, Turkey, 131
Resignation, in Falcon, 112–113
Respiratory system, bird, 27
Responsibility
in Condor, 135
to family, in Hawk, 57
Restlessness
aimless, 21
nervous, 20–21
Restraint, anger at, in Falcon, 112
Restrictions, in care of others, Hawk and, 64
Retarded children, Heron for, 86
Returning, in Vulture
to retrieve possessions, 125
to things forgotten, 125
Right
doing it, in Penguin, 141
doing things, in Pelican, 36
getting it

in birds, 35
in Pelican, 35
urge to get it, 20
Right-sidedness, in Pelican, 38
Rimmler, E., Andean Condor proving of, 135
Ring Dove, 50–55. *See also* Dove, Ring
Rising above
    in bird remedies, 24–25
    in Eagle, 24
    in Falcon, 24
    in Raven, 24–25
Rising above difficulties, in Bald Eagle, 90
Role, in community
    in Dove, strong feeling of, 51
    in Macaw and Pelican, 19
Rookeries, of Herons, 85
Roosts
    of Falcon, Peregrine, 118
    of Raven, 105
    of Vulture, Turkey, 129–131
Rowe, Todd, Turkey Vulture proving of, 133, 284–290

S

Sadness
    in Dove, 51
    in Hawk, 59
        from being alone, 57
    in Raven, 103
Saker Falcon. *See* Falcon, Saker
Salmon, as Bald Eagle food, 94
Scarlet Macaw. *See* Macaw, Scarlet
School of Homeopathy, Peregrine Falcon proving of, 111, 123, 277–283. *See also* Falcon, Peregrine, proving of
Schriebman, Judy, 475
Schulz, Elisabeth
    cases of, Mute Swan, 463
    provings of
        Andean Condor, 139, 291–295
        Mute Swan, 147, 152, 301–302
        Ring Dove, 55, 199–201 (*See also* Proving(s), of Dove)
        Saker Falcon, 111, 123, 281–283 (*See also* Proving(s), of Falcon)
    on Red-tailed Hawk, her experiences as prover of, 214–216
Sciatica pain, in hip and knee, 23
Scientific nomenclature, 28–29
Scorned, in Falcon, 112
Scotoma, central, 22
Screaming, in Raven, 102
Sea birds. *See also* specific birds
    companions transformed into, 158
Searching for impossible destination, in Wandering Albatross, 155
Secrecy, in Vulture, 126
Seed predators, Macaws as, 45
Seeing, in Heron, 79
Seen, not being, in Heron, 79
Self-doubt, in Raven, 99
Self-reproach, 26
Seminar provings, 170
Sensitivity, in Vulture, 126
Sensitivity (emotional), in Dove, 51
Sensitivity (sensory)
    heightened, in Pelican, 38
    Heron for, 86
    of Owl, 72–73
Sensory awareness, heightened
    in bird, 21
    in Pelican, 38
Separation (from world)
    in bird, 25
    in Pelican, 35–36
September 11, 2001, Pelican proving after, 36–37, 41, 172
Septic inflammations, in Vulture, 125
Service, in Dove, 51–52
Set apart, in Wandering Albatross, 155
Settle down, cannot, Wandering Albatross for, 159
Sex, in Dove, 51
Sexual abuse
    in Dove, 51
    Swan for, 152
Sexual aggression, in Swan, 147

Index

Shame
   in Dove, 20
   in Raven, 99
Sharp, stabbing pains
   in chest, 23
   in eyes, 22
Sharp pains
   in chest, 23
   in eyes, 22
   in zygomatic bones, 22
Sherr, Camilla
   Whooper Swan cases of, 458–462
   Whooper Swan proving of, 147, 152, 298–300
Sherr, Jeremy, provings of
   Bald Eagle, 12, 13, 97, 251
   modern, 168
   Whooper Swan, 147, 152, 298–300
Shevin, William, Peregrine Falcon cases of, 407–416
Shore, Jonathan
   biography of, 474
   cases of
      Andean Condor, 431–451
      Bald Eagle, 370–378
      Brown Pelican, 312–319
      Humboldt Penguin, 452–457
      Red-tailed Hawk, 349–350
      Ring Dove, 337–340
      Scarlet Macaw, 320–322
   provings of, 65, 202, 208–222
      Brown Pelican, 41, 172–190 (*See also* Proving(s), of Pelican)
      Great Blue Heron, 86, 227–250
      Great Horned Owl, 75, 223–226
      Humboldt Penguin, 141, 296–297
      Lac equinum, 165–166
      Radium bromatum, 164–166
      Scarlet Macaw, 48 (*See also* Proving(s), of Macaw)
   Radium bromatum proving of, 164–166
   remedy prescribing statistics of, 14
Shoulder. *See* Extremities; Limbs, upper
Shoulder pain
   as bird theme, 13
   in Macaw, 13
   right, in Owl, 69
   severe, 23
Signs, claw, 20
Skin, in Vulture, 125
Smith, Sarah, Whooper Swan case of, 460–462
Smoldering anger, at being left out/excluded, 142
Sneezing, 22
Society, excluded from, in Penguin, 141
Society and socialization
   fitting in with, in Macaw, 43
   of Raven, 100
   of Vulture, Turkey, 130–131
Solemnity, in Pelican, 37
Songbirds, 26
Sore throat, in Vulture, 125
Sounds
   bird (*See* Vocal sounds and communication)
   sensitivity to, 22
   vocal (*See* Vocal sounds and communication)
Space, disorientation in, 18
Speaking one's truth, in Macaw, 44
Special needs children, Heron for, 86
Species
   bird, 27
   Hawk, 61
Speed, in Falcon, 112
Speniscidae, 30
Spenisciformes, 30
Sphen-h. *See* Penguin, Humboldt
Spheniscidae, 140
Sphenisciformes, 140
Spheniscus humboldti. *See* Penguin, Humboldt
Spider remedies, *vs.* Raven, 108
Spirituality and spiritual awareness, 19. *See also* God(s)
   in Pelican, 35
Stabbing, cutting pain, abdominal, 23
Stabbing, stitching pain, as bird theme, 21
   in eye, 12, 13
Stabbing pain, 21

in abdomen, 23
in chest, 23
in ears, 21
in eyes, 12, 13, 22
in uterus, 23
Stanley, Sharon, Ring Dove case of, 340–343
Staphysagria, vs. Dove, 54
Statistics, on remedy prescribing, 14
Stiffness
  in back and extremities, 21, 23
  in neck, 23
Stillness, in Wandering Albatross, 155
Stitching pains, 21
  in eye, 12, 13
Stomach. See also Abdomen
  in bird remedies, 23
Stoop, 117, 119
Stork, 151
Strain injury, Wandering Albatross for, 159
Stramonium, vs. Raven, 108
Strangeness, visual, in Owl, 68
Strength, increased, in extremities, 23
Stress injury, repetitive, Wandering Albatross for, 159
Stretching, in Herons, 84
Strigidae, 30, 66
Strigiformes, 30, 66
Struggles, family, in Hawk, 64
Stuck
  in throat, 22
  Vulture for, 133
Suffering
  of abuse, in Dove, 51
  from opinion of others on how should be in world, 35
Suicide, in Raven, 101
Sulphur, as most common prescription, 14
Supervisor, in provings, 168
Suppression
  of anger, in Dove, 51
  of grief, in Dove, 51
Surface, activity below, in Heron, 79
Swallowing, difficulty with, 22, 26
Swan, *146*, 146–153, *153*
  aggressive posture of, 150

swimming posture of, 150
Swan, Mute, 146. See also Swan
  aggressive posture of, 150
  case of (Schulz), 463
  natural history of, 148–150
  proving of, 147, 152, 301–302
  swimming posture of, 150
Swan, Tundra, 147
Swan, Whooper, 146. See also Swan
  cases of, 458–462
    case 1 (C. Sherr), 458–460
    case 2 (S. Smith and C. Sherr), 460–462
Swan-song, 151
Symbolism. See Mythology and symbolism
Symptoms
  common bird (See Characteristics, bird)
  totality of, 163

T

Taste, bird sense of, 28
Teaching, in Owl, 67
Teeth
  in bird remedies, 22
  of Falcon, Peregrine, 116
  lack of, 27
  in Owl, 68
  pain in, 38
  in Pelican, 38
  soft and spongy sensations in, in Owl, 70
  softening of, delusions of, 22, 26
  weakness in, delusions of, 22
Temperature, body, bird, 27
Tension
  in back and extremities, 21, 23
  between individuality and group, in Macaw, 43
  in neck, 23
  in throat, 22
Theft, in Raven, 100–101
Themes
  extremity pain, 13
  eye, stabbing, stitching pain in, 12, 13
Thirst, great, 21

Index

Throat
    in bird remedies, 22
    constriction in, 22, 26
    lump in, 22, 26
    sore, inflammatory, 22
    in Vulture, 125
    in water birds, 22, 26
Throat constriction, in Swan, 147
Thrusting upward, in Wandering Albatross, 156
Tichenor, Nancy, Turkey Vulture case of, 428–430
Tightness, in chest, 23
Time, disorientation in, 18
Timeless, in Wandering Albatross, 155
Timmerman, Alize
    C4 homeopathy of, 169
    cases of
        Bald Eagle, 383–385
        chicken tuberculosis, 466–472
        Peregrine Falcon, 410–416
        Ring Dove, 343–348
Tingling, in extremities, 23
Tomial tooth, 116
Toothaches, 22
Torture, in Raven, 101–102
Totality of symptoms, 163
    levels of materiality in, 166, 167
Tower of London, Ravens in, 107
Toxicological information, in provings, 167
Toxicology, 167
Transition, from life to death, 132
Trapped in one world, in Bald Eagle, 89
Travel, 19–20
Trembling, 21
Trespassing, in Raven, 100–101
Trickery, in Raven, 100, 102, 107
Trillium pendulum, vs. Owl, 74
Trituration, C4, 169–170
Trituration proving, 169–170
    stories arising in, 178
Truth, speaking one's, in Macaw, 44
Tuberculinum aviaire, 466
    case of (Timmerman), 466–472
Tuberculosis, chicken, 466
    case of, 466–472
Tundra Swan, 147
Turkey Vulture. *See* Vulture, Turkey
Two worlds, in Bald Eagle, 89

U

Udjat, 122
Understanding, in Hawk
    desire for, from family members, 19
    desire for, from mate or family, 57
Undervalued, in Falcon, 112
Unification of opposites, in Wandering Albatross, 156
Unreality, in Raven, 100
Unruffled feeling, in Owl, 67
Upward thrusting, in Wandering Albatross, 156
Urinary problems, in Dove, 51
Urination, frequent, copious, 21
Uterus, stabbing, cutting pain in, 23

V

Venus, 54
Vermeulen, Franz, on Hahnemannian provings, 167–168
Vertebra, cervical, bird, 27
Vertigo, as if floating, 21
Vibration, delicate, 20
Violation, of inner life, in Raven, 48
Violence, in Raven, 99
Vision
    color, bird, 28
    of Condor, Andean, 137
    distortion of, 22
    hazy blurred, 22
    keen, in Vulture, 131
    misalignment of left and right sides of, in Bald Eagle, 94
    of Owl, 68, 72
    of Pelican, 35
    peripheral, loss of, 22
Visual acuity, 22
Visual strangeness, in Owl, 68
Vital force

nature, essence and, 15–16
of Vithoulkas, 15
Vithoulkas, George, essence and vital force of, 15
Vocal sounds and communication, 26
of Dove, 53
of Eagle, Bald, 95
of Herons, 84
of Macaw, 46
musical, 26
of Owl, 72
of Pelicans, 40
of Penguin, Humboldt, 143
of Raven, 100
of Swan, Mute, 149
of Vulture, Turkey, 125, 130, 131
Voice, lack of, in Turkey Vulture, 125, 131
Vult-g. *See* Condor, Andean
Vultur gryphus. *See* Condor, Andean
Vulture, 22
Vulture, Turkey, *124*, 124–133
Condor, California and, 130
vs. Condor, Andean, 139

W

Wading birds. *See* Heron, Great Blue
Waiting, in Heron, 78
Walking, slow, in Heron, 83
Walrad, Caroline S., Scarlet Macaw case of, 322–326
Wandering, in Wandering Albatross, 155
Wandering Albatross. *See* Albatross, Wandering
Wariness, of Herons, 84
Warm blooded, 21
Water, dreams of, in bird remedies, 25
Water birds (waterfowl), 26. *See also* specific birds
teeth in, delusions of softening in, 22, 26
throat in, 22, 26
Weakness, in extremities, 23
Websites, useful, 478
Wens, 125
Whistle, 121

White
and black, in Raven, 102–103
in Eagle, Bald, 90
in Swan, 147, 151–152
Will
in Falcon, 64, 111
in Hawk, 58
Wings, 27. *See also* Feathers
of Albatross, Wandering, 157
of Dove, 53
of Falcon, Peregrine, 116
of Herons, 84
of Macaw, 45
of Owl, 71
of Pelican, 39
of Penguin, Humboldt, 142
of Raven, 107
of Vulture, Turkey, 129
Wisdom, in Owl, 67
Witness, beyond good and bad, 18
Woodpigeon, 50–55. *See also* Dove, Ring
Words, difficult expression of, 18
Worlds, two, in Bald Eagle, 89
Worthlessness, in Raven, 99
Wrists. *See* Limbs, upper
Wrong, doing it, in Penguin, 141

Y

Yelling, in Raven, 102
Yellow, in Falcon, 114
desire for, 113

Z

Zeus, 96, 132, 151
Zygomatic bones, pressure in, 22

B•I•R•D•S

B•I•R•D•S

B•I•R•D•S